second edition

Cognitive Development

JOHN H. FLAVELL

Stanford University

Prentice-Hall International, Inc.

ISBN 0-13-139981-0

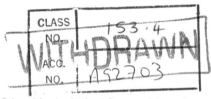

Printed in the United States of America

10 9 8 7 6 5

ISBN 0-13-139981-0

Prentice-Hall International (UK) Limited, *London*
Prentice-Hall of Australia Pty. Limited, *Sydney*
Prentice-Hall Canada Inc., *Toronto*
Prentice-Hall Hispanoamericana, S.A., *Mexico*
Prentice-Hall of India Private Limited, *New Delhi*
Prentice-Hall of Japan, Inc., *Tokyo*
Simon & Schuster Asia Pte. Ltd., *Singapore*
Editora Prentice-Hall do Brasil, Ltda., *Rio de Janeiro*
Prentice-Hall, Inc., *Englewood Cliffs, New Jersey*

To Ellie, Beth, Jim, Ralph, and Ben

Contents

Preface

The intended audience for this book is anyone who has reason to read about human cognitive development. I hope and expect that it will be comprehensible and interesting to readers with a very wide range of backgrounds: people interested in the topic but with little or no background in psychology; undergraduate and graduate students in general, developmental, cognitive, educational, and perhaps social psychology, various fields of education, and possibly other social sciences; perhaps even postdoctoral professionals in these areas. It certainly should be suitable as a text for either an undergraduate or a graduate course.

Several things were done in hopes of making the book useful to a wide variety of readers. Many references are cited in the text, especially secondary sources that would provide quick access to much of the primary research literature in an area. Some readers will find these quite useful; others obviously will not. On the other side, I have explained the meaning of most technical terms used, even those that people with only a little background in psychology might know. I have also tried to make the exposition straightforward and readable, and also perhaps a little lighter and less formal than textbooks sometimes are. I personally do not enjoy reading most textbooks and therefore would like this one to be, if not actually enjoyable, at least not wholly unenjoyable.

This edition of the book differs from the first edition in a number of ways. It contains nine chaptes rather than seven. It includes wholly new or thoroughly revised and updated chapters on developmental changes during early childhood (Chapter 3), during middle childhood and adolescence (Chapter 4), and in social cognition (Chapter 5), perception (Chapter 6), memory (Chapter 7), and language (Chapter 8). This edition covers more of the field than the first edition did and also treats what it covers more thoroughly. In keeping with recent trends in the field, there is less emphasis on Piaget and his developmental-stages conception of cognitive growth, and more emphasis on Gibsonian, information-processing, and growth-of-knowledge approaches. Emphasis is also given to the surprisingly precocious cognitive competencies of infants and young children that recent research has documented.

I wish to express my deepest thanks to Deanna Kuhn, Columbia University Teachers College; Katherine Nelson, The Graduate School and University Center of the City University of New York; Robert S. Siegler, Carnegie-Mellon University; and Henry M. Wellman, University of Michigan for their helpful advice in the initial planning of this edition; to Rochel Gelman, Michael Maratsos, and Steven Pinker for their useful suggestions concerning the treatment of language development (Chapter 8); and to Eleanor Flavell for her critical reading of the manuscript. Sincerest thanks are also due to Ruth Prehn for typing the manuscript; to Barbara Preece for her assistance with the references; to Linda Benson, Louisa Hellegers, and John Isley of Prentice-Hall, Inc., for their expert help in turning plans and manuscript into a book; and to Stanford University's Department of Psychology for numerous forms of support. Finally, I am especially grateful to Ellie Flavell for her patience, encouragement, and help throughout the writing process.

ACKNOWLEDGMENTS

The author would like to thank the following for permission to reproduce material in this book:

CAMBRIDGE UNIVERSITY PRESS. For the excerpts from *Social cognitive development: Frontiers and possible futures* by J. H. Flavell & L. Ross (Eds.). Copyright © 1981. Reprinted with permission of Cambridge University Press.

LAWRENCE ERLBAUM ASSOCIATES, INC. For the excerpts from *Perspectives on the development of memory and cognition* by R. V. Kail & J. W. Hagen (Eds). Copyright © 1977. Reprinted with permission of Lawrence Erlbaum Associates, Inc.

JOHN WILEY AND SONS, INC. For the excerpts from *Handbook of child psychology* (Vol. 3) by J. H. Flavell & E. M. Markman (Eds.). (P. H. Mussen, general editor.) Copyright © 1983 by John Wiley & Sons, Inc. Reprinted by permission of John Wiley & Sons, Inc.

ACADEMIC PRESS, INC. For Figure 6-1 from R. N. Aslin, Experiential influences and sensitive periods in perceptual development: A unified model,

Introduction

COGNITION

The really interesting concepts of this world have the nasty habit of avoiding our most determined attempts to pin them down, to make them say something definite and make them stick to it. Their meanings perversely remain multiple, ambiguous, imprecise, and above all unstable and open—open to argument and disagreement, to sometimes drastic reformulation and redefinition, and to the introduction of new and often unsettling concept instances and examples. It is perhaps not a bad thing that our prize concepts have this kind of complexity and instability (some might call it richness and creativity). In any event, they do seem to have these properties, and therefore we would be wise not to expend too much of our time and energy trying to fix them in formal definition.

Problems in Defining and Limiting the Concept of Cognition

So it is with that concept called *cognition*, the development of which is the subject of this book. Obviously, it is important here to communicate some ideas and images about the nature of cognition, but it is neither possible nor desirable to define it and limit its meaning in any precise or inflexible fashion.

The traditional image of cognition tends to restrict it to the fancier, more unequivocally "intelligent" processes and products of the human mind. This image includes such higher-mental-processes types of psychological entities as knowledge, consciousness, intelligence, thinking, imagining, creating, generating plans and strategies, reasoning, inferring, problem solving, conceptualizing, classifying and relating, symbolizing, and perhaps fantasizing and dreaming. Although some of these activities would surely be credited to the psychological repertoires of other animals, they nonetheless have a decidedly human-mind ring to them.

While no contemporary psychologists would want to exclude any of these traditional components from the cognitive domain, they would feel it necessary to add some others. Certain components would have a somewhat humble, less purely cerebral-intellectual cast to them. Organized motor movements (especially in infants), perception, imagery, memory, attention, and learning are possible cases in point. Others might look more social-psychological than the word *cognition* usually connotes. Instances here would include all varieties of social cognition (that is, cognition directed at the world of human versus nonhuman objects) and the social-communicative versus private-cognitive uses of language. Once embarked on this course of broadening and restructuring the domain beyond the classical *higher mental processes*, it is very difficult to decide where to stop. One is finally led to ask, what psychological processes can*not* be described as "cognitive" in some nontrivial sense, or do *not* implicate "cognition" to a significant degree? The answer is that mental processes habitually intrude themselves into virtually *all* human psychological processes and activities, and consequently there is no really principled, nonarbitrary place to stop. To be sure, this book says little about such noncognitive-sounding things as emotions, personality, aggression, and so on. There are many *practical* reasons for slighting these and other topics, such as space limitations, lack of an adequate data base in some cases, consideration for teachers' and readers' expectations about what a book with this title should contain, and sheer personal preferences. The point to be underscored, however, is that there is no *principled* justification for excluding them. What you know and think (cognition) obviously interacts in a very substantial and significant way with how you feel (emotions), to take but one example. Depending only upon the state of existing theory and empirical evidence, a longer or shorter cognitive story could be told about virtually any phenomenon mentioned in an introductory psychology textbook. We only have a single head, after all, and it is firmly attached to the rest of the body.

The Need for a Broad and Complex Conception of Cognition

If there is no nonarbitrary place to stop once we go beyond a narrow, purely higher-mental-process image of cognition, why go beyond it at all? The answer is that we simply cannot talk coherently and realistically about the nature and development of cognition without enlarging and complicating that image. There is a deep and a not so deep reason why this is so.

The not so deep reason is that processes like perceiving, remembering, evaluating other people, exchanging information with them, and so on, are routine functions of the brain and mind; they simply are as genuinely "cognitive" by any reasonable definition as syllogistic reasoning is. Moreover, as described in Chapter 2, children exhibit intelligent-looking patterns of motor and perceptual behavior well before they can operate with symbols at all, let alone engage in syllogistic reasoning. It would seem arbitrary in the extreme to christen children "cognitive" only after they had achieved the ability to engage in the more exalted forms of cerebration.

The deep reason is that the psychological events and processes that go into making up what we call "thinking," "perceiving," "remembering," and the rest are in fact complexly interwoven with one another in the tapestry of actual, real-time cognitive functioning. Each process is believed to play a vital role in the operation and development of each other process, affecting it and being affected by it. This idea of mutual, two-way interactions among cognitive processes is an exceedingly important one. A paper by Frijda (1972) on theoretical models of long-term memory illustrates this point. Since memory is the topic, readers of Frijda's article are hardly surprised to encounter words like "recognition," "recall," "storage," and "retrieval." However, the idea that human memory simply cannot be meaningfully discussed without reference to all manner of other, very cognitive-sounding processes is forcibly brought home as the readers also encounter expressions like these: "idea," "meanings," "logical consistency," "inference," "knowledge," "strategies," "problem solving," and "intelligence." Lest they still be tempted to regard "memory" as a distinct and autonomous cognitive component, they are assured that "the distinction between remembering and problem solving is a gradual and imprecise one" and that "inference processes in particular play an important part in recall" (Frijda, 1972, p. 26).

Frijda's disposition to implicate a veritable host of plain and fancy cognitive processes in his account of how memory operates—all of the mind, practically—is not unusual in present-day theorizing about memory. Nor is memory in any way a special case in this respect. Single out for analysis any other process or category of processes you wish—perception, imagery, reasoning, classification, and so on—and it could readily be argued that all the others affect it and are affected by it in one way or another. What you know affects and is affected by how you perceive; how you conceptualize or classify things influences the way you reason about them, and vice versa; and so on and on. If we pretend for purposes of psychological analysis that the human mind is a machine or device that carries out a variety of mental operations to achieve a variety of mental products, the present argument would be that it is a very highly organized device, one whose numerous "parts" are richly interconnected to one another. It is not a collection or aggregate of unrelated cognitive components, but rather a complexly organized *system* of interacting components. It would be tedious to keep pointing out these interactions throughout the book, but it would be well to bear in mind that they are ubiquitous in cognitive functioning.

THE NATURE AND DEVELOPMENT
OF THE HUMAN COGNITIVE SYSTEM: PIAGET'S VIEW

At present there are two dominant views of the nature and development of the system, the *information-processing* view and that of the great Swiss psychologist Jean Piaget. These two views are by no means incompatible and many contemporary developmental psychologists favor some blend of the two. Piaget's conception is the better one with which to begin, especially because Chapters 2 to 4 heavily emphasize Piaget's work. The information-processing approach is discussed in Chapter 4. Before Piaget's view is described, however, a few cautionary remarks are necessary about the relationship between Piaget and this book.

Piaget's contributions to our knowledge of cognitive development have been nothing short of stupendous, both quantitatively and qualitatively. Moreover, his ideas about cognitive growth are often very complex and difficult to grasp, even when presented as an integrated whole, at length and in full detail. Piaget's ideas are particularly prone to distortion, oversimplification, and general misunderstanding when one tries to integrate brief summaries of them within a more general narrative about the field, such as this book aims to be. That is, the danger of misunderstanding is very great when they are presented briefly and discontinuously, one set of ideas at one point in the narrative and another set at a later point. A reasonable conclusion from these facts is that, unless they do some supplementary reading (e.g., Flavell, 1963; Furth, 1981; Ginsburg & Opper, 1979; Piaget, 1970a), readers may be destined to mislearn at least some aspects of Piaget's theory in the course of (I hope) learning something interesting and substantive about cognitive development in general.

ASSIMILATION-ACCOMMODATION AS A MODEL OF COGNITIVE FUNCTIONING. Piaget viewed human cognition as a specific form of biological adaptation of a complex organism to a complex environment. The cognitive system he envisaged is, however, an extremely active one. That is, it actively selects and interprets environmental information in the construction of its own knowledge rather than passively copying the information just as it is presented to the senses. While of course paying attention to and taking account of the structure of the environment during knowledge seeking, the Piagetian mind always reconstrues and reinterprets that environment to make it fit in with its own existing mental framework. Thus, the mind neither copies the world, passively accepting it as a ready-made given, nor does it ignore the world, autistically creating a private mental conception of it out of whole cloth. Rather, the mind builds its knowledge structures by taking external data and interpreting them, transforming them, and reorganizing them. It therefore does indeed meet with the environment in the process of constructing its knowledge, and consequently that knowledge is to a degree "realistic" or adaptive for the organism. However, Piaget made much of the idea that the mind meets the environment in an extremely active, self-directed way— meets it more than half way, as it were.

Piaget's conception of how the cognitive system interacts with the outside world may become clearer if we examine his concept of *adaptation* more closely. Cognition, like other forms of biological adaptation, always exhibits two simultaneous and complementary aspects, which Piaget called *assimilation* and *accommodation*. While it is convenient to talk about them as if they were distinct and separate cognitive activities, it must be kept in mind that Piaget conceived of them as but two indissociable aspects of the same basic adaptational process—two sides of the same cognitive coin. Assimilation essentially means interpreting or construing external objects and events in terms of one's own presently available and favored ways of thinking about things. The young child who pretends that a chip of wood is a boat is, in Piaget's terms, "assimilating" the wood chip to his mental concept of boat, incorporating the object within the whole structure of his knowledge of boats. Accommodation roughly means noticing and taking cognitive account of the various real properties and relationships among properties that external objects and events possess; it means the mental apprehension of the structural attributes of environmental data. The young child who painstakingly imitates her father's gestures is "accommodating" her mental apparatus (and thence, her motor gestures) to the fine detail of her father's behavior. Assimilation, therefore, refers to the process of adapting external stimuli to one's own internal mental structures whereas accommodation refers to the converse or complementary process of adapting these mental structures to the structure of these same stimuli. In the more obviously biological adaptation of ingestion-digestion of food, organisms simultaneously accommodate to the particular structure of the food (chew hard or easy, digest with the help of this enzyme or that, depending upon what the food is) and assimilate the food to their own physical structures (transform its appearance, convert it into energy, etc.). In cognitive adaptations, we can say that individuals simultaneously accommodate to the particular structures of the objects of their cognitions and assimilate those objects to their own cognitive structures.

Another example may serve to point up the extreme interdependence or indissociability of assimilation and accommodation, the sense in which they really are but two aspects of the same cognitive process. Suppose I show you a symmetrical blot of ink on a piece of paper, ask you what it reminds you of, and hear you say that it resembles a bat. Piaget's theory would say that you had cognitively accommodated to certain physical features of the blot and had used these as the basis for assimilating the blot to your internal concept of a bat. It is important to recognize that you did not merely accommodate to an external stimulus; that is, you did not just passively and mindlessly scan the blot and "discover" a bat "that was really there." Without a preexisting, well-elaborated conception of bat in your cognitive repertoire you would certainly not have been able to detect and integrate into a whole perceptual structure the particular constellation of blot features that you did. In other words, your accommodatory possibilities were just as surely limited and constrained by your assimilatory ones as your assimilatory possibilities were by your accommodatory ones. Obviously, if there were no bat-compatible physical properties in the blot to be accommodated to, there would be no assimilation of the blot to "bat"—that is, no perception of the blot as resembling that animal. If the ink blot took the form of a thin, straight line, for instance, there would naturally be no temptation to construe it as a bat. Not quite so obviously, perhaps, but just as surely, if you had no cognitive bat concept to which to assimilate the blot, your accommodation to the blot's various physical features would be entirely different. If the perceiver were a 1-year-old baby, with a belfry as yet devoid of bats, the perceiver would not process the structural information contained in the blot as you did and would not see it in the same way that you did because, in a manner of speaking, the perceiver's mind's eye would differ from yours.

In Piaget's view, therefore, in any cognitive encounter with the environment, assimilation and accommodation are of equal importance and must always occur together in a mutually dependent way. His model of the human cognitive system stresses the constant interaction or collaboration of the internal-cognitive with the external-environmental in the construction and deployment of knowledge, with both factors making a vital contribution to this construction and deployment. What you know already will greatly shape and constrain what environmental information you can detect and process, just as what you can detect and process will provide essential grist for the activation of present knowledge and the generation of new knowledge. To return to our first two examples, the wood chip likely would never metamorphize into a boat if it could not float and were not vaguely boat shaped, and the father's gestures could not be mimicked if the child could not assimilate them to motor action patterns she already possessed.

ASSIMILATION-ACCOMMODATION AS A MODEL OF COGNITIVE DEVELOPMENT. Thus Piaget's assimilation-accommodation model provides a valuable general conception of how people's cognitive systems might interact with their external environments. However, it is also a particularly useful vehicle for thinking about cognitive development—that is, about how the child's cognitive system might gradually evolve with maturation and experience. As we have seen, the model is well set up to give an essentially non-developmental, atemporal description of the mind-environment interaction, a description that holds true of any mind interacting with any environment at any given moment of time. The present point, however, is that it is equally well set up to describe how a mind might gradually develop and change its structure and content through repeated interactions with the milieu, and is therefore a particularly useful model to communicate in a text on cognitive development. Let us reconsider the wood-chip example to illustrate how the model might help us think about cognitive growth as well as about cognitive functioning.

In the situation we are imagining, a young child is playing with his toy boats in the bathtub and suddenly notices in the corner of the soap dish a tiny fragment of wood from a broken pencil. He picks it up, and after some deliberation (he has sailed many a boat, but nary a wood chip), gingerly places it in the water. Upon discovering that it floats, he adds it to his armada and emerges from his bath some time later a wiser as well as a cleaner child. The question is, in what way wiser, and through what sorts of wisdom-building (cognitive-developmental) processes?

Let us credit him, at the beginning of the bath, with a certain organized body of knowledge and certain abilities concerning the concrete, functional properties of the main entities in the situation (toy boats, small, nondescript objects, and water). He knows much about their characteristic look and feel and also something of their characteristic reactions to his actions upon them. We could say that he has already achieved a certain level of cognitive development with respect to this microdomain of his everyday world and consequently, in Piaget's terms, he assimilates it and accommodates to it in specific ways that faithfully reflect this cognitive-developmental level. As a result of the new things he did and observed during this particular bath, however, that level will have changed ever so slightly, and consequently his future assimilations and accomodations within that microdomain will also have changed ever so slightly.

Let us suppose he has discovered (accommodation) some things he did not know before about what little pieces of wood can and cannot do (float rather than sink, make only a tiny splash when dropped in water, fail to move a big toy boat when they bump into it) and about what one can and cannot do with them (sail them, make them bob to the surface by holding them under water and then letting go, give them rides on top of other toy boats). Additionally, during this process of "minidevelopment," the content and structure of his mind and its capacity to construe and interpret this microdomain (assimilation) has also altered slightly. For example, his functional class of boat-like entities has now generalized to include at least certain small lightweight objects that do not closely resemble the more typical and familiar instances of this class (e.g., his toy boats). Subsequently, this small change in conceptual structure may permit him to construe (assimilate) still other kinds of objects as novel candidates for boat play. Moreover, the category of boat-like things may now be functionally subclassified for him into big, strong ones and small, weak ones, whereas it may previously have been a more or less homogeneous, undifferentiated class.

Thus, in the course of trying to accommodate to some hitherto unknown functional properties of a relatively unfamiliar sort of object, and of trying to assimilate the object and its properties to existing concepts and skills (trying to interpret them, make sense out of them, test out his repertoire of actions upon them) the child's mind has stretched just a little, and this stretching in turn

FIGURE 1-1. An assimilation-accommodation model of cognitive growth. Mind₁ (i.e., of some given developmental level) is very gradually transformed into Mind₂ (i.e., of some arbitrarily higher level) as a consequence of correspondingly gradual changes in assimilatory and accommodatory possibilities. These changes in turn result from the continuous exercise of these mental functions in the course of adapting to the environment.

broadens slightly his future assimilatory and accommodatory possibilities. By repeated assimilation of and accommodation to a given milieu, the cognitive system evolves slightly, which makes possible somewhat novel and different assimilations and accommodations, with these latter changes producing further small increments of mental growth. Thus, the dialectical process of development continues in this gradual, leg-over-leg fashion. $Mind_1$ (i.e., at some arbitrary point in its development) makes possible $Assimilations_1$ and $Accommodations_1$ (i.e., assimilations and accommodations of a particular, characteristically $Mind_1$ type), the informational products or feedback from which help to generate $Mind_2$, which then makes possible $Assimilations_2$ and $Accommodations_2$, which again yield new information to provide some of the developmental raw material for $Mind_3$, and so on. Figure 1-1 illustrates the developmental process just described.

It is clear why such a development would be slow and gradual. Each Mind represents but a small, imperceptible departure from its immediate predecessor; it is rooted in, constrained by, and free to deviate but slightly from that predecessor. It is also clear, however, that a very, very substantial modification in the human cognitive system could eventuate from year after year of daily, virtually continuous assimilation of milieu to mind and accommodation of mind to milieu. Thus Piaget's assimilation-accommodation model seems to have the right properties to characterize the childhood evolution of our cognitive system, as well as to characterize the functioning of that system during a particular interchange with the environment. The model makes childhood cognitive growth a logical outcome of repeated cognitive functioning, suggests that it should be slow and gradual, and allows for a considerable amount of total developmental change, given a whole childhood in which to accumulate. These are the very properties we think human cognitive development does in fact possess.

It becomes apparent in Chapters 4 and 9 that Piaget's model can be criticized and that the question of how the process of cognitive growth is best described and explained is still unsettled. However, a plausible working conception of how the child makes cognitive advances is useful to have at the outset, before examining the nature of those advances (Chapters 2 to 8). Piaget's assimilation-accommodation model is just such a conception.

AN OVERVIEW OF THE BOOK

The major landmarks of general mental growth from birth to adulthood are chronicled in Chapters 2 to 5. The principal emphasis in Chapters 2 to 4 is on

Piaget's work, although the ideas and research findings of others are also included in those chapters. The development of social cognition is described in Chapter 5. Chapters 2 to 5 may therefore be considered the core of the book, since they describe children's growing intellectual mastery of their social and nonsocial environments. Chapters 6 to 8 deal with the ontogenesis of perception, memory, and language. These three topics, together with the growth of social cognition, are currently receiving a good deal of research attention by developmental psychologists. Their inclusion reflects the book's emphasis on a broader rather than a narrower view of cognition. Finally, some major questions and problems concerning cognitive development are discussed in Chapter 9.

This book has some idiosyncracies of which the reader is entitled to be aware. It is probably a more "personal" book than most texts. First, I did not feel as constrained as many textbook writers might to cover all the topics in the field. In general, a topic was likelier to get included to the extent that I: (1) found it interesting to read, think, and write about; (2) already had a fairly deep, "insider's" acquaintance with it, perhaps because I had previously written or done research in that area; (3) felt I could write a coherent account of it, in the space available, that a reader unfamiliar with the field of cognitive development could comprehend and remember.

Second, the topics finally selected by these idiosyncratic criteria were also approached in an idiosyncratic fashion. My approach tends to be somewhat more description oriented and less explanation oriented than that of many developmental psychologists. There is, therefore, considerable emphasis on describing *what* cognitive abilities and knowledge children develop and, if known, the sequential steps involved in their formation. This contrasts with an emphasis on trying to show what factors or variables (e.g., in children's cognitive experiences and environments) generate, facilitate, or impede these developments. Although it is true that there are problems in deciding what constitutes an explanation or a cause of cognitive growth (Chapter 9), this book's emphasis on description would undoubtedly appear excessive to some developmentalists.

Finally, the book contains a fair amount of informed opinion and educated guess where (most everywhere, it sometimes seems) the facts are not solid. Those opinions and guesses are mostly my own, and others in the field would undoubtedly disagree with some of them.

In sum, this book was meant to be, and I hope is, an adequate introductory textbook on cognitive development. It is also, however, very clearly an expression of my personal views and biases as to what can and ought to be said about the field at this time.

SUMMARY

The concept of cognition favored in this book is a broad and inclusive one, covering more than such traditional, more narrowly "intellectual" processes as reasoning and problem solving. The human mind is conceptualized as a complex *system* of interacting processes which generate, code, transform, and otherwise manipulate information of diverse sorts.

Piaget's *assimilation-accommodation* model describes how this cognitive system interacts with its environment, and, by means of many such interactions, undergoes developmental change. According to this model, the cognitive system plays a very active role in its cognitive interchanges with the environment. It creates a mental construction of reality in the course of numerous experiences with its milieu, rather than simply making a mental copy of what is experienced. Each cognitive encounter with the world always has two aspects, *assimilation* and *accommodation*. Assimilation essentially means interpreting or construing external data in terms of the individual's existing cognitive system. What is encountered is cognitively transformed to fit what the system knows and how it thinks. Accommodation means taking account of the structure of the external data. According to Piaget's model, therefore, the cognitive system simultaneously adapts reality to its own structure (assimilation) and adapts itself to the structure of the environment (accommodation). By repeatedly attempting to accommodate to and assimilate novel, previously unassimilated environmental elements, the system itself gradually changes its internal structure—that is, cognitive development takes place (see Figure 1-1).

The plan of the book is as follows: Chapters 2 to 4 contain an account of general conceptual development during infancy (Chapter 2), early childhood (Chapter 3), and middle childhood and adolescence (Chapter 4). Chapter 5 takes up the development of social cognition. Then Chapter 6 describes developmental aspects of perception, Chapter 7, memory, and Chapter 8, language. The concluding discussion (Chapter 9) deals with outstanding questions and problems in the field. Even though the book obviously is intended to be an introductory text, it probably reflects the author's own personal views about the field more than is true of many introductory texts.

Infancy

One hardly needs to read a textbook to recognize that there must be staggering differences between the cognitive system of the very young infant and that of the very young child (0 to 1 versus 18 to 30 months of age, let us say). These two organisms scarcely seem to belong to the same species, so great are the cognitive as well as the physical differences between them. The very young infant is an intellectual zero to the casual observer; he or she appears to have no "mind" at all. Though there is now a great deal of research evidence to show that such a judgment does not in fact do justice to the baby's capabilities, the intellectual gap between the neonate (newborn) and the 2-year-old child nonetheless remains enormous. It is clear to casual observer and researcher that unlike the very young infant, the late-infancy and early postinfancy child can represent and communicate information by means of symbols (in speech, gesture, drawing, play, etc.), can solve a number of concrete, practical problems by the intelligent, planful use of simple tools and other means, possesses a considerable amount of practical knowledge concerning his or her everyday world of people, objects, and events, and much else besides.

This marked contrast between newborn and early-childhood cognitive systems can perhaps be brought home more forcefully by considering the following "oddity problem," as the specialist in learning would call it. We are presented with a newborn infant, a 2-year-old child, and an adult. After watching each of these three "stimuli" behave for a while, our task is to pick the one who seems most different from or unlike the other two as a thinking and knowing creature—that is, as a cognitive organism. I would definitely select the neonate as the odd one out in this comparison and suspect you might do the same. Despite the obvious and undeniable intellectual differences between the two older members of the trio, they both strike us as being endowed with "minds," and with decidedly human ones at that. The young infant just does not give such an impression to most people (the infant's parents are, of course, mercifully excused from this oddity problem), notwithstanding what is really a rather trifling gap in chronological age between it and the 2 year old.

The objective of this chapter is to convey some of the highlights of the truly momentous cognitive transformation that takes place during the brief interval between early infancy and early childhood. The first two sections of the chapter describe the major landmarks of infant cognitive growth, using Piaget's six-stage model of the development of sensory-motor intelligence as the basic framework. Special attention is paid to the eventual attainment of the capacity to use and comprehend symbols, possibly the most significant and far-reaching outcome of the sensory-motor period.

The third section concentrates on a very special acquisition that takes place within this general process of sensory-motor development—namely, the acquisition of the all-important object concept or concept of object permanence. The pioneering ideas and observations of Piaget dominate both of these sections. However, important work has also been done subsequently by other psychologists on these same topics. The fourth and final section reviews recent thinking and research, especially concerning the development of the object concept.

SENSORY-MOTOR INTELLIGENCE

Infant Cognition as Sensory-Motor Intelligence

If the 5-month-old infant can be said to "think" and "know" at all, she certainly does not appear to do so in the usual sense of these terms. In what sense, then? What *does* the infant have or do that permits us to talk meaningfully about the nature and development of "infant cognition"?

What she demonstrates, in an increasingly clear and unambiguous manner as she grows older, is the capacity for organized, "intelligent-looking" sensory and motor *actions*. That is, she exhibits a wholly practical, perceiving-and-doing, action-bound kind of intellectual functioning; she does not exhibit the more contemplative, reflective, symbol-manipulating kind we usually think of in connection with cognition. The infant "knows" in the sense of recognizing or anticipating familiar, recurring objects and happenings, and "thinks" in the sense of behaving towards them with mouth, hand, eye, and other sensory-motor instruments in predictable, organized, and often adaptive ways. Hers is an entirely unconscious and self-unaware, nonsymbolic and nonsymbolizable (by the infant) type of cognition. It is the kind of noncontemplative intelligence that your dog relies on to make its way in the world. It is also the kind that you yourself exhibit when performing many actions which are characteristically nonsymbolic and unthinking by virtue of being so overlearned and automatized—for example, brushing your teeth, starting the car, mowing the lawn, visually monitoring the grass in front of you for obstacles while doing so, and so on. It is, to repeat, intelligence as inherent and manifest in organized patterns of sensory and motor action, and hence Piaget's description of infant cognition as presymbolic, prerepresentational, and prereflective "sensory-motor intelligence."

Sensory-Motor Schemes

In the previous chapter, I spoke of the child's assimilating external data to   and accommodating   to external data, with the blanks variously filled in with "mental framework," "favored ways of thinking about things," "cognitive structure," "conception," "concept," and similar expressions. All of these terms refer to some sort of enduring cognitive organization or knowledge structure within a child's head that does the assimilating and accommodating. When talking specifically about infantile, sensory-motor assimilating and accommodating, as contrasted with developmentally more advanced, symbolic-representational forms, Piaget would fill in the blank with the word *scheme*.[1]

---

[1] In many secondary sources, the very same Piagetian concept goes by the name *schema* (occasional plural: *schemata*). *Schema* is a mistranslation of the Piagetian French original, *schème*, perpetrated by writers (the present writer prominently among them) insufficiently versed in French, Piaget, or both.

The meaning of *scheme* is easier to convey by example than by formal definition. A scheme generally has to do with a specific, readily labelable class of sensory-motor action sequences that the infant repeatedly and habitually carries out, normally in response to particular classes of objects or situations. The scheme itself is generally thought of as referring to the inner, mental-structural basis for these overt action sequences; it is, in other words, the cognitive capacity that underlies and makes possible such organized behavior patterns. Thus, the young infant who automatically sucks anything that finds its way into her mouth would be said to possess a "sucking scheme"—that is, she possesses an enduring ability and disposition to carry out a specific class of action sequences (organized sucking movements) in response to a particular class of happenings (the insertion of suckable objects). Similarly, one can talk about sensory-motor schemes of looking, listening, grasping, hitting, pushing, kicking, and so on. A scheme is a kind of sensory-motor level counterpart of a symbolic-representational level concept. An older person *represents* (thinks of, verbally characterizes) a given object as an instance of the class, "nipple"; analogously, the baby *acts* or *behaves* towards the same object as though it belonged to the (functional) class, "something to suck."

A very important property of schemes is that they may be combined or coordinated to form larger wholes or units of sensory-motor intelligence. For instance, once she has achieved a certain level of cognitive development, the infant is capable of pushing aside ("pushing" being one motor scheme) an obstacle in order to seize (another motor scheme) a desired object. We see a similar integration of sucking and manual prehension schemes once the infant acquires the systematic tendency to bring to her mouth anything her hand chances to grasp. As elementary schemes gradually become generalized, differentiated, and above all, intercoordinated and integrated with one another in diverse and complex ways, the infant's behavior begins to look more and more unambiguously "intelligent" and "cognitive."

This discussion of Piaget's concepts of sensory-motor intelligence and schemes might mislead you into thinking that all infant knowledge is knowledge of procedures—of how and when to perform this or that action or sequence of actions. However, as we see in this and subsequent chapters (Chapters 5 to 8), infants also learn and know things that seem more like information about the world than like ways of acting on it. As examples, they can recognize familiar objects and events and can even form concepts or categories (e.g., Cohen & Strauss, 1979; Ross, 1980; Strauss, 1981).

Adapted Intelligence, Imitation, and Play

We can now say that the infant's cognitive activity consists of *assimilating* external data to internal cognitive-structural units called sensory-motor *schemes*, and of simultaneously *accommodating* these schemes to the structure of the external data. For instance, the baby assimilates a rattle to his grasping scheme; he "interprets" it, behaviorally speaking, as something that can be grasped. In the course of doing so, he simultaneously accommodates his grasping scheme to the specific physical properties of that object. That is, he adjusts his hand actions to the particular size and shape of the rattle, thereby grasping it quite differently than he would a sugar cube, for example.

In most such interactions between sensory-motor schemes and external data, assimilation and accommodation contribute about equally, with neither aspect seeming to be more salient or important than the other. Piaget uses the term *adapted intelligence* to refer to this, the prototypical situation in which assimilation and accommodation are roughly in balance.

They need not be in balance, however; one or the other may dominate. If the emphasis should be on accommodation rather than on assimilation, the cognitive behavior will take the form of imitation (modeling, copying). If I imitate or copy your behavior as precisely and faithfully as I can, I am obviously putting all my cognitive effort into adapting or accommodating my behavior to you and your idea, rather than freely reconstructing or assimilating your behavior in accord with my own ideas. If, in contrast, the accent is heavily assimilative rather than accommodative, the outcome will be play or other self-expressive, less literal and "realistic" cognitive activities (fantasy, creative thinking, or even autistic or delusional thinking). If, instead of slavishly parroting your behavior, I decide to execute a modern dance routine that expresses and symbolizes how your behavior makes me feel, the balance has obviously shifted towards a predominance of assimilatory activity. A photograph of a landscape is heavily accommodative; a Salvador Dali landscape is heavily assimilative.

Let us return now to the sensory-motor infant. If he explored the properties of a stick to find out what he could do with it (trying to "understand" the stick, in the sensory-motor meaning of the term), assimilation and accommodation would be in approximate balance and the infant's exploration would constitute an act of adapted intelligence. If he tried to mimic the appearance or behavior of the stick with his own body (e.g., banging first stick, then finger on the table), the accent would be on painstaking accommodation and we would label his behavior as imitation. Finally, if he pretended the stick were his doll, blithely ignoring blatant physical differences between stick and doll in order to do so, the accent would be on free assimilation (i.e., of the stick to his doll scheme or "concept"), and we would say he was playing. All three forms of cognitive functioning—adapted intelligence, imitation, and play—are included in the description of sensory-motor development later in this chapter.

Cognitive Motivation

Up to this point I have described a cognitive system that is sensory-motor rather than symbolic-representational in type, and one that functions and gradually transforms itself developmentally by simultaneously assimilating data to schemes and accommodating schemes to data. The nature or qualitative character of this scheme-data interaction was also said to vary from play through adapted intelligence to imitation, depending upon the relative preponderance of assimilation versus accommodation. I have said nothing, however, about why the sensory-motor or any subsequent cognitive system should ever operate in the first place, nor about the circumstances under which it would be most likely to operate with maximum intensity and persistence. What needs to be added is an account of cognitive motivation—that is, of the factors and forces that activate or intensify human cognitive processing. Once we have some idea about the mind's power source and favored fuels, we will finally be ready to describe its developmental itinerary during infancy.

Human beings obviously exercise their knowledge and cognitive skills for a wide variety of reasons, in order to attain a wide variety of goals. Some of these reasons and goals are basically noncognitive in character; they are *extrinsic* rather than *intrinsic* to the cognitive system itself. The infant who grasps and sucks his bottle simply to satisfy his hunger rather than to learn about the graspable and suckable potentialities of bottles is clearly activating his sensory-motor skills in the service of an extrinsic, noncognitive need or goal. The same is true of the 3 year old who makes intelligent use of a pair of footstools to obtain an out-of-reach cookie, and of the high school student who studies hard solely for parental approval.

More interesting, however, is the fact that a very great deal of human mentation, at all developmental levels, is intrinsically rather than extrinsically motivated. That is, the cognitive system is often turned on and kept running by purely cognitive factors, rather than by bodily needs or other motivational sources. The following behavioral episode, brief though it is, illustrates most of the factors of this sort that psychologists have identified:

> Standing by the side of a low table the 12 month-old girl bangs on a pegboard with a block she has been holding; at the far end of the table the lid of an improperly closed coffee pot produces a loud rattle. The little girl freezes; her eyes explore the table top. She hits the pegboard again, and the small movements of the lid attract her attention. She moves over, picks up the lid, and rattles it against the pot; then back to her pegboard and block. She bangs: the lid rattles. The little girl gurgles, a wide smile appears on her face. A glance at her mother—still with that enormous smile—and on with her banging and the pot's rattling, to an accompaniment of gurgles, babblings, and small bounces of delight (Bronson, 1971, p. 269).

Why does the little girl bang on the pegboard in the first place? While it may sound like circular reasoning to say this, the best answer is that banging things to see, hear, and feel the results represents a common, probably universally acquired sensory-motor scheme, and it is simply in the nature of schemes to exercise themselves repeatedly, especially when first acquired. To ask why the child bangs when provided with a banging scheme and a compliant object to bang with is, for Piaget and many other psychologists, much like asking why she breathes when provided with lungs and air. There exists, in Hunt's words (1969, p. 37), "a system of motivation *inherent in* information processing and action" (italics added). Consistent with this idea is research evidence proving that babies can be operantly conditioned using interesting sights and sounds as the only rewards. That is, babies will "work" (make repeated motor responses) for the sole privilege of viewing pictures, listening to voices, and so on, just as they would "work" for traditional reinforcers such as food. The idea that cognitive activity is often intrinsically motivated does not mean that the disposition to engage in it could not be heightened or diminished by environmental factors. There is every reason to believe, for example, that sustained exposure to intellectually barren life circumstances can indeed substantially reduce this disposition. What it does mean is that there is a "natural bent," so to speak, to make use of the cognitive instruments that the species' evolution and individual's development have provided, and that the various noncognitive factors modulate this bent rather than actually create it *ex nihilo*.

When the coffee-pot lid makes a loud rattle, the little girl freezes, visually explores the table top, and hits the pegboard again. This illustrates that certain classes of inputs to the cognitive system tend to turn its operating volume way up. When these kinds of inputs are received, ongoing activities get temporarily suspended, the child becomes somewhat tense and aroused, and a variety of attentional, curiosity, exploratory, and other information-seeking behaviors are likely to ensue. The inputs that have this remarkable property may vary somewhat with the child's age, but at least from early-middle infancy on they will surely include: (1) stimulus events that are novel or not recently encountered; (2) events that are, considered in relation to the child's cognitive level, relatively complex rather than simple in structure; (3) events that are unanticipated and surprising—that is, those that conspicuously violate her expectations as to what should happen in the present situation; (4) events that are puzzling and confusing, that lead to conflict or uncertainty in the child's mind. Notice that all of these events have the capacity to elicit the child's cognitive interest and activity only by virtue of their *relation* to her cognitive system. An input is never "puzzling," "surprising," and so on, in and of itself; it is so described only if it proves surprising or puzzling *to* someone. Precisely because of differences in the makeup of the infants' cognitive systems, the very same stimulus event may have the capacity to elicit surprise and its cognitive *sequelae* in an older infant but not in a younger one, or vice versa.

In early infancy, before the child has built up through experience many expectancies about how things should be, certain absolute, inherent-in-the-physical-stimulus types of input properties are the dominant elicitors of cognitive interest and action. In particular:

> The infant is predisposed to attend to events that possess a high rate of change in their physical characteristics. Stimuli that move or possess light-dark contrast are most likely to attract and hold a newborn's attention (Kagan, 1970, p. 298).

Other attentional predispositions are more species-specific. For example, it now seems very likely that young infants are innately predisposed to attend preferentially to human speech versus other sounds (Gibson & Spelke, 1983; see also Chapters 5, 6, and 8).

Such absolute properties do not lose their eliciting power in the months and years following early infancy (a moving object is likely to attract anyone's attention), but the more relative, child-times-stimulus ones like surprise and uncertainty become much more significant in these later periods.

A number of psychologists have put forward, in one form or another, a more specific hypothesis concerning these relative properties (McCall & McGhee, 1977). According to this hypothesis, the child is particularly intrigued by inputs that are somewhat or *moderately discrepant* from her current knowledge and expectations—that is, by events that are partly but not fully assimilable to her existing cognitive schemes. For an infant who has recently acquired a set of implicit expectations as to what human faces look like, for example, the hypothesis asserts that a picture of a distorted face (one eye placed in the chin region, etc.) should elicit a lot of cognitive interest and exploration. Such a stimulus is a seductive blend of the familiar and unfamiliar, of the expected and unexpected, and therefore should provoke a great deal of assimilative and accommodative effort. In contrast, a normal face should be less interesting to such an infant because it is wholly familiar (thus representing low versus moderate discrepancy), and a picture of a space craft should also be less interesting because it is wholly unfamiliar and incomprehensible (high versus moderate discrepancy). A variation on this same hypothesis has it that *moderately complex* (again, relative to the child's cognitive level) stimuli are more likely to elicit interest than either very complex or very simple ones.

This hypothesis has a lot of surface plausibility and one feels that there simply has to be some truth in it. Nonetheless, efforts to verify it experimentally have so far met with mixed success (Cohen, DeLoache, & Strauss, 1979). It has been difficult, for example, to determine just how "discrepant" a particular stimulus is for a specific, individual child, inasmuch as such a determination must depend upon a very accurate diagnosis of that specific child's cognitive level in relation to that particular kind of stimulus. Moreover, the particular kind or dimension of discrepancy involved may make a difference. Another problem, I suspect, is that at certain times and in certain psychological states, infants and older people alike may actually prefer to process comfortingly familiar, readily assimilable, low-discrepancy objects instead of tackling the more challenging and problematic, moderate-discrepancy ones. Our little girl's *initial* bang on the pegboard and her tacit anticipation of the kind of noise it would make might be a case in point (her *subsequent* bangings are something else again). As we are about to see, cognitive activity may also be recruited in enterprises that entail little if any uncertainty, surprise, unexpectedness, borderline incomprehensibility, moderate discrepancy from existing schemes, or the like.

The remaining highlights of the vignette also illustrate some important points about cognitive motivation. The little girl explores and experiments until she discovers the cause of the unexpected rattling noise, shows signs of extreme pleasure and satisfaction when she does discover it, and then repeats her banging again and again with great gusto. As indicated earlier, the states of cognitive uncertainty, surprise, puzzlement, interest, and so on, engendered by the occurrence of novel, unexpected, or otherwise not readily assimilable events, usually lead to cognitive activities designed to rectify the situation. Depending upon her level of cognitive development, the child may thereupon search and explore systematically or unsystematically, grope blindly or experiment intelligently. If she succeeds in mastering the problem, in finally comprehending that which initially was incomprehensible, a characteristic outcome is the sort of tension release and sense of pleasure shown by the little girl. Comprehension and understanding, especially following sustained cognitive effort, are likely to constitute a very positively reinforcing state of affairs for human beings of all ages. There is some research evidence, for example, that infants as young as 3 to 4 months of age may be capable of cognitive as well as social smiles and vocalizations. That is, in addition to smiling and gurgling at people, they also seem to smile and gurgle when they succeed in recognizing (assimilating, "comprehending") nonsocial stimuli.

Implicit in what has just been said is the notion that part of the motivation intrinsic to cognitive functioning is the motivation to master problematic situations, to be effective with respect to one's environment, to be competent. It is widely believed that this aspiration towards mastery, effectiveness, and competence is an important part of the cognitive system's power source. The little girl joyfully repeats her rattle-producing activity at least partly to savor and exercise her new-found competence to cause such an interesting phenomenon. Indeed, the whole behavior episode was the preamble to a paper whose title began, "The growth of competence . . . ." There is reason to think that infants, and perhaps older children and adults as well, are particularly motivated to reproduce actions of their own that they perceive as causes or instigators of interesting environmental events. Our 12 month old would no doubt be cognitively titillated by the bang-rattle sequence even if someone else did the banging. It could still puzzle and surprise, still give sensory pleasure, and so on. But the fact that *she* produced the rattle, and also *knew* that she produced it, added enormously to its interest. Any seasoned baby watcher would predict that, had someone else first executed the sequence, the child would have immediately hastened to try it herself. There is even a hint in the research literature that babies may become emotionally attached to objects whose behavior is often contingent in this way on their own behavior (Watson, 1972). Such a process might even conceivably contribute to the baby's attachment to the mother and other "responsive" human beings (Yarrow & Pederson, 1972).

The foregoing has been a rather long story about the intrinsic aspects of cognitive motivation, and it would be nice if there were some kind of memory aid or mnemonic device for remembering it. The ideal mnemonic device would virtually prevent people from forgetting the item to be retained even if they tried. My favorite is a mnemonic I heard once for remembering the (approximate) height of Japan's Mount Fujiyama. Just recall that there are 12 months and 365 days in the year and you automatically get your answer, 12,365 feet. It happens that there does exist a fairly good mnemonic for reconstructing much of what has been said in this section. Simply ask yourself with what a human cognitive system ought reasonably to be endowed if it is to have a good chance of learning the enormous number and variety of things that members of our species do, in fact, routinely learn. If you, as evolution's architect, wanted to build an efficient, human-type knowledge-acquisition device, what sort of design would you adopt?

It would seem sensible, first of all, to design it so that it did a lot of spontaneous, noninstrumental, intrinsically rather than extrinsically motivated cognitive functioning. The system should be disposed to notice and do and remember things even when no noncognitive needs (e.g., for food) are served thereby; it should exercise its schemes for the heck of it as well as for practical ends, for fun as well as for profit. There is so very much to learn that the system should not be permitted to lie around idle except when some tangible gain is in view.

The cognitive system should also be biased to attend to those situations or features of situations that present it with the most information, and especially, information that is new and therefore worth learning. Thus, its attention ought to be captured more by the contours of objects (contours are effectively zones of light-dark contrast) than by their interiors, and more by moving objects than by still ones. Moving objects are obviously apt to be important ones to pay attention to (human beings being prime examples), and contour, of course, provides information about an object's shape and hence its identity. Learning would also be facilitated if the cognitive system were innately pretuned to members of its own species and their behavior—for example, their speech. Even more adaptive in this respect, perhaps, is the system's marked responsiveness to those relative, child-times-stimulus type properties mentioned earlier. Novel, surprising, puzzling, discrepant, uncertainty- and curiosity-provoking, or put most generally, non–readily-assimilable happenings—these are precisely the ones a learning, developing organism *ought* to be designed to notice, explore, and seek to understand, for they constitute the essential nutriments for its cognitive progress.

Needless to say, the cognitive system should be amply rewarded for its successful efforts at understanding such happenings—that is, for the bit of learning and cognitive development it has achieved—and so we provide it with a purely cognitive kind of pleasure and sense of satisfaction whenever understanding dawns. We shall also want to make the system take pleasure in rehearsing its newly developed competence again and again, by itself and on its own. Such rehearsal for mastery's sake will tend to solidify and stabilize this competence through the overlearning it provides.

In sum, we have designed an organism that idly learns when there is no practical need to do so, that tries to learn what it most needs to learn, and that finds it rewarding both to learn these things initially and also to solidify and perfect its learning through subsequent practice. The human child appears to be just such an organism.

PIAGET'S SIX STAGES OF SENSORY-MOTOR DEVELOPMENT

The age range designated for each of Piaget's six stages is meant to be only a very rough average. Individual infants might therefore pass through any of the stages more rapidly or more slowly than these crude age norms would suggest. The *sequence* of stages, however, is believed to be absolutely constant or invariant for children the world over. Thus, Piaget claimed that no earlier stage is ever skipped en route to any later one and no stages are ever navigated in a developmental order other than the one given. Finally, the accomplishments of each stage are said to cumulate—that is, skills achieved in earlier stages are not lost with the advent of later stages.

As you know, most research studies in psychology make use of dozens or even hundreds of subjects. The developmental sequence about to be described, on the contrary, was based solely upon Piaget's very detailed, day-by-day observations of his own three children, observations made some fifty years ago. How seriously, then, should we take his story about sensory-motor development? As I suggest in the final section of this chapter, subsequent research with large samples of infants has largely confirmed many of Piaget's observations, although aspects of his developmental account warrant revision or reinterpretation.

Stage 1 (Roughly 0 to 1 Month)

The infant comes into the world equipped with a variety of reflexes. Some of them are of no cognitive-developmental interest because they are destined either to remain unchanged with age and never become cognitively relevant (e.g., the sneeze) or to actually disappear entirely (e.g., the Moro response, a specifically infantile type of startle pattern). Others, like sucking, eye movements, and movements of the hand and arm, are destined to undergo significant developmental changes as a function of constant exercise and repeated application to external objects and events. Piaget attributed a great deal of importance to these latter reflexes because he regarded them as the initial, innately provided building blocks of human cognitive growth. He conceived of them, in other words, as the infant's first sensory-motor schemes.

During the initial month of postnatal life, Piaget observed what appeared to be very small but possibly significant alterations in sucking behavior. Although cautious on this point, he felt that these alterations might reflect minimal, beginning changes (consolidation, stabilization, generalization, and differentiation) in the structure of the infant's sucking scheme. Moreover, he believed the changes to be at least partly due to repeated practice and experience with "suckables" of different types—for instance, a soft and milk-producing nipple versus a harder and more arid thumb. Such experience-based changes in the sucking scheme would certainly comprise a humble but genuine instance of that gradual, "leg-over-leg" type of Piagetian developmental process described in Chapter 1 (pp. 6 to 8). Subsequent research by others has amply verified the occurrence of very early developmental changes in the sucking response:

> With lips tightly closed, the newborn's initial sucking pattern consists of an indissociable, almost unitary mass movement for creating negative pressure in the whole buccal cavity. A first successful execution sets the whole action going, but from there on there is change . . . ." What is striking by the fourth week is that these earlier, undifferentiated patterns have been differentiated into a series of integrated components (Bruner, 1967, pp. 7–8).

It need only be added that the behavior and development ascribed to Stage 1 is largely of the "adapted-intelligence" variety. That is, Piaget believed that nothing clearly identifiable as either "play" or "imitation" occurs this early.

Stage 2 (Roughly 1 to 4 Months)

This stage is marked first by the continued evolution of individual sensory-motor schemes, and second by the gradual coordination or integration of one scheme with another. On the first point, individual schemes associated with such processes as sucking, looking, listening, vocalizing, and prehension (grasping objects) receive an enormous amount of spontaneous daily practice—recall our earlier discussion of intrinsic cognitive motivation. As a consequence, each of these schemes undergoes considerable developmental elaboration and refinement during these months. To continue with the Stage 1 example, sucking continues to be perfected as a motor skill. Toward the end of Stage 2 it may even occur anticipatively in response to associated visual or kinesthetic cues—in response, for instance, to the mere sight of the approaching nipple or the mere sensation of being held in the accustomed feeding position.

More interesting than this perfecting of individual, isolated schemes is the progressive coordination or coming-into-relation of one scheme with another. For example, vision and audition begin to become functionally related. Hearing a sound leads the infant to turn his head and eyes in the direction of the sound source (McGurk & Lewis, 1974). The activation of his listening-hearing schemes with their auditory assimilation-accommodation processes induces a corresponding activation of his looking-seeing schemes with their visual assimilation-accommodation processes.

Two other important scheme-scheme coordinations that get well established in Stage 2 are those of sucking-prehension and vision-prehension. In the case of sucking-prehension, the infant develops the ability (and very strong inclination) to bring to his mouth, and suck, his hand and anything the hand may have grasped, and also to grasp whatever may have found its way into his mouth. The coordination of vision with prehension permits the infant to locate and grasp objects under visual guidance and, reciprocally, to bring before his eyes for visual inspection anything an out-of-sight hand may have touched and grasped. The evolution of vision-prehension coordination is the more noteworthy development of the two, because an ability to coordinate hand and eye will prove to be an extraordinarily important means or instrument for exploring and learning about the child's environment. Recent research indicates that the beginnings of coordination and integration of sensory systems (vision with audition, vision with touch, etc.) are more precocious than Piaget suspected and that, contrary to his belief, some degree of intersensory coordination may even be present from birth (Gibson & Spelke, 1983; Mendelson, 1979; see also Chapter 6).

Piaget also reports some initial, quasiimitative or preimitative behavior during Stage 2. The infant may be a bit more likely to repeat one of his own habitual responses if someone else mimics that response immediately after he has made it. In other words, he may "imitate" (?) someone's imitation of his own action. A Stage 2 infant may also show what could be the dim beginnings of play behavior. For instance, he may "playfully" (?) repeat and repeat an already well-mastered, highly overlearned response routine—out of sheer assimilatory pleasure, in Piaget's opinion. It may be unwise, however, to try to read too much into these rather ambiguous, would-be forerunners of imitation and play.

Stage 3 (Roughly 4 to 8 Months)

The Stage 2 acquisition of visually guided manual activity helps make possible a new behavior pattern that constitutes the major achievement of Stage 3. The pattern begins when the infant chances to carry out some motor action, often a manual one, that happens to produce some unanticipated but perceptually interesting outcome in the environment. The pattern ends with the child delightedly repeating the action again and again, apparently for the sheer pleasure of reproducing and reexperiencing the environmental outcome. The child might grasp and shake a new toy, for instance, and that new toy might unexpectedly respond with a rattling sound. Whereupon, the child of this stage is likely to pause in wonderment, hesitatingly shake it again, hear the sound once again, more quickly and confidently shake it a third time, and then continue to repeat the action again and again for a considerable period of time.

There are several things to be said about this behavior pattern. First, students of learning will quickly recognize it as a variety of operant conditioning: A response occurs more or less spontaneously (shaking the toy), is immediately followed by positive reinforcement (the interesting sound), and the response thereby becomes more likely to recur. There is now definite evidence (not available to Piaget when he made his infant observations) that babies younger than 4 to 8 months can be operantly conditioned using sensory reinforcers of this sort. Consequently, it is a fair bet that some version of Piaget's prototypical Stage 3 behavior pattern may actually appear spontaneously prior to this stage.

Second, the behavior pattern is reminiscent of our 12-month-old girl's banging-and-lid-rattling sequence (pp. 16 to 18). In contrast to the 1 year old, however, the infant of 4 to 8 months is probably still too immature to have even an implicit, sensory-motor level sense of cause-effect relations, and will accordingly show none of the older child's efforts to explore the cause of the enjoyable perceptual experience. There is reason to doubt if the younger infant even distinguishes clearly between his motor action and its environmental result, whereas it is certain that the older infant makes this basic distinction.

Third, for the very reason that the action and its environmental result are likely not clearly separated in the Stage 3 infant's experience, Piaget is loath to credit him with a clear and unambiguous capacity for intentional, deliberate, goal-directed action. It just does not quite seem justified to say of him, as it will of the Stage 4 infant, that he kept shaking the toy *in order to* produce the sound—that is, as an intentional, deliberately selected means to a clearly separate, anticipated end.

Finally, despite these limitations, the Stage 3 pattern represents genuine cognitive progress because it possesses one crucial feature. The infant of the two previous stages has been, in a manner of speaking, more preoccupied with his own actions than with the environmental effects these actions might produce. There is a kind of empty, "objectless" quality about the way the younger infant exercises his sensory-motor schemes. He seems to suck for the sake of sucking and grasp for the sake of grasping, evincing relatively little interest in the specific physical and functional properties of the objects sucked and grasped. From Stage 3 on, however, the baby shows an increasing interest in the effects of his actions on objects and events in the outside world and in learning about the real properties of these objects and events by carefully attending to those effects. The baby thus becomes more cognitively as well as more socially "extroverted" in the course of sensory-motor development.

He gradually becomes an object explorer rather than a mere scheme exerciser, and the first small signs of this change are manifest in Stage 3.

The beginnings of genuine imitation are unmistakably present in Stage 3. However, it appears that the infant of this age is usually capable of imitating only: (1) those behaviors of the model (person imitated) that he himself already produces spontaneously (thus, he is unlikely to imitate novel responses); and (2) those behaviors of the model that he can see or hear himself produce (thus, he can imitate vocalizations and manual gestures but not, say, facial expressions). The distinction between serious and playful exercise of schemes likewise becomes a bit easier to make in this stage than in Stage 2, but clear and unequivocal instances of play are still hard to diagnose.

Stage 4 (Roughly 8 to 12 Months)

The major novelty of this stage is the appearance of unmistakably intentional, means-ends behavior. The child's actions are now unquestionably purposeful and goal directed, and for this reason look more "intelligent," more "cognitive," than those of previous stages. As in Stage 2, individual sensory-motor schemes become coordinated and integrated. However, the schemes in question are now primarily those outer-directed, environmental-effect-oriented, Stage 3 ones just mentioned, and their integration is more clearly an integration into a means-end action pattern. In Stage 4, the child intentionally exercises one scheme, as means, in order to make possible the exercise of another scheme, as end or goal. He may push your hand (means) in order to get you to continue to produce some interesting sensory effect (end) you had been producing for his benefit. Similarly, he may push aside (one motor scheme) an object in order to grasp (second motor scheme) another object.

There is also a parallel between Stage 2 and Stage 4 regarding the use of signs to anticipate events. It was said of the Stage 2 infant that he sometimes could respond anticipatively to a sign of an impending stimulus rather than having to wait until the stimulation actually occurred; he might occasionally commence sucking movements at the mere sight of the looming nipple, for instance. The Stage 4 infant also does the same thing, of course, and does it much better. In addition, however, the older child can read signs of impending events that are not directly connected, in stimulus-response fashion, with his own behavior. His mother starts to turn towards the door and the Stage 4 child may cry in anticipation of her departure. We might say that the younger infant anticipates the incipient exercise of one of his schemes whereas the older infant anticipates the occurrence of some event in the outside world. This change in how signs are read, in what they are taken to be signs *of*, is obviously in keeping with the aforementioned developmental trend towards cognitive extroversion, towards a heightened concern with the outside world in contrast to one's own purely egocentric, "objectless" actions.

The two limitations on imitative skill noted in connection with Stage 3 are now largely overcome. First, the infant now shows the ability to imitate behaviors which are in some degree different from those he customarily performs. This is an enormously significant developmental advance, because it means that he henceforth has the possibility of *learning* by imitation, or more generally, through observation of the behavior of others. As Bandura and numerous other psychologists have stressed (Stevenson, 1972, Chapter 20), this sort of observational learning can be a very potent source of cognitive-developmental advance at all ages. Second, the infant can now imitate actions that he cannot actually see or hear himself perform, such as opening and closing his eyes after watching someone else do it. That is a remarkable cognitive feat, when you think about it, and how the infant does it is presently a total mystery. Sometimes his imitation of such actions is analogous rather than exact: He might, for instance, open and close his mouth instead of his eyes when the model does the latter.

Meltzoff and Moore (1977, 1983a, 1983b) and other investigators have recently claimed that infants younger than 1 month (i.e., in Piaget's Stage 1) can do the latter type of imitation. As examples, it is reported that newborns will stick out their tongues or open their mouths in direct response to seeing an adult model perform those actions. If these startling claims prove to be true they will add further support to the view mentioned earlier (p. 22)—namely, that contrary to Piaget's belief, information from different senses is to some degree coordinated or integrated innately, prior to postnatal experience. However, other investigators have recently challenged these claims. They either have failed to replicate these findings of neonatal imitation or have argued that the behaviors observed by Meltzoff and Moore (1977) were not really imitation (Uzgiris, 1981). What the final verdict on neonatal imitation will be is difficult to predict; however, it probably cannot be accepted as a proven fact on present evidence (see Chapter 6).

Play becomes much more clearly playful at this age. For instance, after "seriously" practicing a new means-end integration for a while (an instance of adapted intelligence), an infant may ignore the end and pleasurefully exercise the means (play). As a case in point, one of Piaget's children began by practicing the feat of pushing an obstacle aside to obtain a toy and ended up by ignoring the toy in favor of pushing the obstacle aside again and again for fun. Play, like imitation, is beginning to become differentiated from adapted intelligence to become a distinctive instrument of cognitive growth. Whatever other functions play might serve in the child's life (and there are probably quite a few), no one has ever doubted that it is a major vehicle for learning and mental development.

Stage 5 (Roughly 12 to 18 Months)

Since, according to Piaget, symbolic-representational as distinguished from sensory-motor ways of knowing begin to manifest themselves during Stage 6, Stage 5 could be regarded as the last "pure" sensory-motor stage. Its essence is a very active, purposeful, trial-and-error exploration of the real properties and potentialities of objects, largely through the relentless search for new and different ways to act upon them. Infantile cognitive extroversion is now at its height; the child has a resolutely experimental, exploration-and-discovery oriented approach to the outside world. Present him with a novel object and he will actively try to lay bare its structural and functional properties by trying this, and that, and yet another action pattern on it, often making up new variations on old action patterns in the course of doing so. Similarly, whereas the Stage 4 infant would be apt to carry out a means-end behavior sequence in a more or less fixed, stereotyped way, the Stage 5 child would be likely to vary the means scheme in a deliberate, let's-see-what-would-happen-if sort of attitude; he might, to refer back to a Stage 4 example, remove the offending obstacle this way, then that way, then still another way.

With his strongly accommodative, exploratory bent, the Stage 5 child often discovers wholly new means to familiar ends. For instance, Piaget describes his discovering that an out-of-reach object can be secured by pulling a string attached to it, or a small rug on which it rests. These particular examples are intriguing because they might be early precursors of tool use, a type of intelligent behavior which is currently of great interest to primatologists and other students of hominid evolution as well as to developmental psychologists. Unpublished studies by Dr. William Charlesworth at the University of Minnesota suggest that the ability to use a variety of simple tools undergoes considerable development between 18 and 24 months of age—that is, just after the completion of Stage 5.

Given his active attempts at accommodation to the fine details of his environment, it is not surprising that the Stage 5 child proves to be a more painstaking and accurate imitator than his Stage 4 counterpart. His superiority is especially noticeable, predictably, when a successful imitation requires some trial-and-error experimentation on his part. The distinction between serious cognitive adaptation and lighthearted play becomes yet easier to see in Stage 5. For example, the child will sometimes elaborately complicate and ritualize some simple response, not because doing so teaches him anything useful or accomplishes any practical purpose, but for the sheer fun of it.

Stage 6 (Roughly 18 to 24 Months)

"Roughly 18 months on" would be just as accurate a dating for this stage, because its most important achievement remains an essential attribute of cognitive functioning for the rest of the individual's life. That achievement is the ability to represent the objects of one's cognition by means of symbols and to act intelligently with respect to this inner, symbolized reality rather than simply, in sensory-motor fashion, with respect to the outer, unsymbolized reality. The Stage 6 child shows a beginning capacity to produce and comprehend one thing (e.g., a word) as standing for or symbolically representing some other thing (e.g., a class of objects). Moreover, the child becomes capable of mentally differentiating between the symbol and its referent—that is, the thing the symbol stands for. As an example of this differentiation, the symbol could be physically quite different from its referent object and still be treated as a representation of that object. Similarly, the child might spontaneously produce the symbol and think about it even when the referent is not physically present. For the child to name a present object that he *sees* is quite possibly a symbolic act; for the child to name an absent object that he has just *thought of* is unquestionably a symbolic act. Responding to internal, self-generated objects of cognition is decidedly *not* a sensory-motor activity. Piaget refers to this newly developed, Stage 6 capacity for representation as the *semiotic* (or *symbolic*) function. The emergence of this supremely important function is worth a few pages of discussion. Let us begin with Piaget's account of adapted intelligence, imitation, and play à la Stage 6, in order to maintain continuity with our stage-by-stage narrative of the sensory-motor period, and then let us explore some additional comments about the semiotic function and related matters.

The Stage 5 child discovers new means to attain his behavioral objectives by overt, trial-and-error experimentation; he studiously varies his external behavior and, by doing so, may hit upon an effective procedure for achieving his goal. In contrast, the Stage 6, symbolic child may try out alternative means internally, by imagining them or representing them to himself instead of actualizing them in overt behavior. If an effective procedure is found in this fashion, by taking thought rather than by taking overt action, we might think of it more as invention or insight than as trial-and-error discovery. Accordingly, Piaget refers to this aspect of Stage 5 adapted intelligence as "the discovery of new means through active experimentation," whereas its Stage 6 counterpart is called "the invention of new means through mental combinations."

A celebrated example of the latter among Piaget readers was conveniently provided by his daughter Lucienne at the tender age of 16 months. Lucienne wanted to extract a small chain from one of those old-fashioned, sliding-drawer type matchboxes, but the drawer opening was too small for her to reach in and get it. After some unsuccessful, Stage 5 type fumblings she paused, studied the box, slowly opened and closed her mouth a few times, then quickly widened the drawer opening and triumphantly retrieved the chain. It seems reasonable to interpret her mouth movements as a primitive nonverbal, symbolic representation of a possible but as yet untried behavioral means to the desired end. To be sure, her representational response was very similar to its referent physically and was also produced in the same immediate situation. Nonetheless, it would take unusually tough-minded and skeptical observers, I think, to find nothing of the genuinely symbolic and representational in this behavior. It could even be argued that the Stage 4 infant's analogical imitation (e.g., opening his mouth when the model opens her eyes), which is rather similar to Lucienne's action, is a primitive form of representation (Mandler, 1983). There are certainly areas of gray between clear-cut sensory-motor cognition and clear-cut symbolic-representational cognition.

Stage 6 imitation and play also bear the clear imprint of a developing semiotic function. The child is now capable of *deferred imitation*, in which actions witnessed but not imitated on a given occasion are spontaneously reproduced in full detail at a later time. One of Piaget's children, for example, watched in mute fascination while another child threw a three-star temper tantrum. She then produced an excellent imitation of it the next day. As with Lucienne's mouth movements, the symbol (imitation of tantrum) physically resembled the referent (original tantrum). Unlike the mouth movements, however, the symbol was produced at considerable temporal remove from the referent, and therein lies the clearly symbolic character of deferred versus immediate imitation. The child presumably generated some sort of internal representation (possibly a visual image) of the tantrum as a guide or model for her imitative action; it was not a simple, more clearly sensory-motor case of precisely accommodating to an external, physically present, immediately perceptible model. McCall, Parke, and Kavanaugh (1977) also observed deferred imitation in 26 month olds and further showed that imitative skill continues to develop after infancy.

Pretend or *symbolic play* makes its first appearance in Stage 6 and, like imitation, continues to develop during the preschool years. At 18 months, Piaget's daughter Jacqueline said "soap" while pretending to wash her hands by rubbing them together; at 20 months, she pretended to eat bits of paper and other inedibles, saying "Very nice." The representational, purely symbolic quality of this kind of play is obvious.

It may be wise to take stock of what has been said so far in this section before delving further into the nature and development of the semiotic or symbolic function. In my experience, Piaget's six-stage account of general sensory-motor development tends to be difficult for most people to learn, and especially to retain or remember. It tends to be hard for students, and it also tends to be hard for card-carrying developmental psychologists (myself included). There probably is no really good mnemonic for keeping it all straight, but Figure 2-1 may be of some help. It is easier to remember any sequence of items if each item bears some logical or otherwise meaningful relationship to its predecessor and successor. Would that one's telephone number were 123-4567, for instance. Figure 2-1 tries to play up whatever relationships of that kind can be found in Piaget's sequence, in hopes that it will seem more rational, and thereby prove more memorable.

More on the Semiotic Function

It may be worthwhile to recommence by pointing up the momentous differences between symbolic-representational thought and sensory-motor intelligence. Sensory-motor actions must proceed slowly, step by step, one action at a time. Symbolic-representational thought can be much faster and more freely mobile in its operation; it can range over a whole series of past, present, and future events in one quick sweep of the mind. The former is by its very nature more oriented towards actions and concrete, practical results, whereas the latter can be more preoccupied with knowledge per se; one focuses more on acts and outcomes, the other more on information and truth. The former is ineluctably concrete and earthbound. The latter is potentially abstract and free to soar, and, in fact, becomes increasingly so as the child matures. Indeed, it can eventually even take itself as its own cognitive object; that is, a relatively mature mind can think about its own thoughts. Finally, the former is necessarily private, idiosyncratic, and uncommunicable to others; each baby is imprisoned in her own separate cognitive world. The latter comes to make fluent use of a socially shared symbolic system (natural language) and can thereby communicate with, and gradually become socialized by, other human beings.

We have already seen that the semiotic function can make use of a variety of symbolic media; it is not synonymous with the ability to speak and understand language, for instance. Piaget cited several expressions of the semiotic function that first appear in late infancy or early childhood: deferred imitation, symbolic play, drawing, mental images, and, of course, language itself. The development of imitative ability is thought to play a very important role in the genesis of all of these processes. As indicated earlier, infants gradually become quite good at imitating objects and actions that are imme-

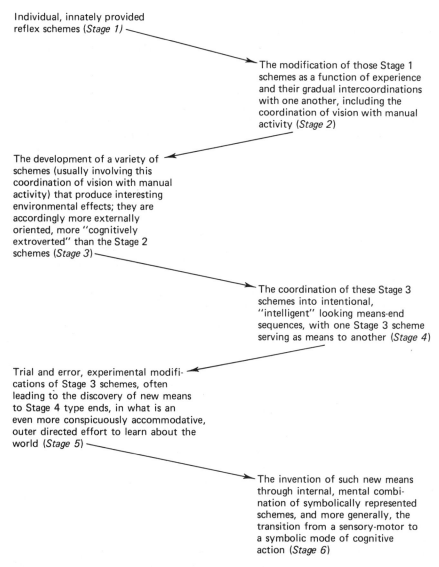

Individual, innately provided reflex schemes *(Stage 1)*

The modification of those Stage 1 schemes as a function of experience and their gradual intercoordinations with one another, including the coordination of vision with manual activity *(Stage 2)*

The development of a variety of schemes (usually involving this coordination of vision with manual activity) that produce interesting environmental effects; they are accordingly more externally oriented, more "cognitively extroverted" than the Stage 2 schemes *(Stage 3)*

The coordination of these Stage 3 schemes into intentional, "intelligent" looking means-end sequences, with one Stage 3 scheme serving as means to another *(Stage 4)*

Trial and error, experimental modifications of Stage 3 schemes, often leading to the discovery of new means to Stage 4 type ends, in what is an even more conspicuously accommodative, outer directed effort to learn about the world *(Stage 5)*

The invention of such new means through internal, mental combination of symbolically represented schemes, and more generally, the transition from a sensory-motor to a symbolic mode of cognitive action *(Stage 6)*

FIGURE 2-1. A mnemonic for recalling the highlights of Piaget's sensory-motor stages regarding adapted intelligence (developmental changes in imitation and play are not included). Each earlier stage can be construed as a reasonable foundation or prerequisite for the one immediately following, and each later stage can be thought of as a plausible next developmental step, once its immediate predecessor is achieved.

diately present. From this base, they develop the ability to generate symbolic surrogates, and overt and covert copies of absent, purely remembered objects and actions. Symbolic play uses both surrogates (e.g., bits of paper in place of food) and overt copies (pretending to eat the paper) of absent referents; deferred imitation obviously generates an overt copy of the original event;

and a mental image of something can be regarded as a kind of covert, internal imitation or copy of that thing.

It is language, however, -that eventually assumes preeminence among these various expressions of the semiotic function. Piaget's view of the relation of language to thought is probably the dominant one in contemporary psychology, but was once controversial (e.g., Furth, 1970; Macnamara, 1972; Nelson, 1973). In the past, some scholars viewed the language-thought relation as essentially one of "*LANGUAGE* (thought)"—that is, thought was regarded as either virtually identical to natural language or else as utterly dependent on it for its functioning. Correlatively, the development of cognition was seen as either synonymous with the acquisition of language capability or else as completely parasitic on, and derivative of, that acquisition. In marked contrast, Piaget took what might be depicted as a "*THOUGHT* (*Language*, mental image, drawing, etc.)" position. In the first place, he pointed out that thought, in the form of sensory-motor intelligence, begins its development well before language does. In addition, postinfancy thinking skills can mature to a surprising degree without benefit of language skills: Deaf children who have not yet acquired much if any ordinary language or sign-language skills can unquestionably think. Moreover, just as with normal children, their thinking skills also improve as they grow older (Furth, 1971). At the same time, Piaget willingly conceded that language does become by far the most important of a human being's symbolic vehicles. Furthermore, it does undoubtedly serve thinking and knowledge in various direct and indirect ways from early childhood on, and it may even be indispensable for certain higher forms of cognitive endeavor (see Chapter 8). Unlike mental images and other symbolic media, therefore, it is depicted here as "*Language*" rather than "language."

According to this line of thinking, not only does intelligence begin its development before language does, but it also provides the cognitive wherewithal that makes the very development and use of language possible (see Chapter 8). It is the development of the semiotic function (i.e., of a general, cognitive capacity for symbol use) that makes it possible for children to use words symbolically in the first place, just as it makes it possible for them to evoke covert mental images and overt deferred imitations as representations of nonpresent realities. Moreover, there is reason to think that semantic development is, in good part, a matter of learning how *what you already know* is expressed in your native language (Chapter 8). For example, 12 to 24 month olds can intelligently group (categorize) and order objects manually on the basis of various functional and physical relationships that hold among the objects, even though they may not yet be able to name most of these categories and relationships (Nelson, 1973; Ricciuti, 1965). The young child's months of sensory-motor activity have provided him with a great deal of this kind of preverbal knowledge about how objects can be related to one another, and it now remains to map all this knowledge into a linguistic system, so that he can tell himself and others what he knows implicitly.

Ross (1980) has recently provided a particularly convincing demonstration of prelinguistic knowledge of conceptual categories. Children of 12, 18, and 24 months of age were first shown, one at a time, a series of ten toy objects belonging to the same conceptual category, such as furniture. Then they were shown a pair of objects consisting of another member of that category (a round green chair) and a member of a different category (a round green apple). Even the 12 month olds paid more attention to the apple, the member of the novel category, suggesting that they must have been mentally representing the ten pieces of furniture as similar or related in some way. This implicit categorization could not have been grounded in the children's knowledge of the names of the category or category members; 12 month olds have not yet learned words like "bookcase," "stool," and "furniture" (see Ross, 1977). Nor could it have been based on perceptual as contrasted with conceptual similarities among the category members; bookcases just do not look like stools. The developmental study of categorization abilities in infancy is currently emerging as a lively area of research (Strauss, 1981).

Piaget and many other psychologists take the position, then, that language development largely follows on the heels of general cognitive development, not the other way around. Macnamara puts it this way:

> I have continually insisted on the child's possessing nonlinguistic cognitive processes before he learns their linguistic signal. By this I do not intend to endow the infant at birth with a complete ready-made set of cognitive structures. I accept Piaget's thesis that children gradually develop many of the cognitive structures, which they employ in association with language. Neither do I suggest that the child has a complete set of cognitive structures at the moment when he begins to learn language. All that is needed for my position is that the development of those basic cognitive structures to which I referred should precede the development of the corresponding linguistic structures. Since the acquisition of linguistic structures is spread over a long period, there is no reason that the acquisition of the corresponding nonlinguistic ones should not also extend well into the period of language learning (Macnamara, 1972, p. 11).

WERNER AND KAPLAN'S ACCOUNT OF EARLY SYMBOLIC DEVELOPMENT. Even the briefest summary of the genesis of symbolic thinking would be remiss if it did not include something of Werner and Kaplan's (1963) interesting analysis of the topic. As with Piagetian theory, it is unavoidable that I oversimplify Werner and Kaplan's ideas in the following synopsis. In their analysis, the major entities in any symbolic act are the *symbol* itself, the *person* producing or comprehending it, and the symbol's *referent*. Initially, these three entities are largely fused together, or psychologically undifferentiated from one another, and a very important aspect of the development of symbolization is their mutual breaking apart, differentiation, or "distancing." The present summary deals only with the progressive distancing of first, person from referent, and second, symbol from referent.

Early in the sensory-motor period, the person's actions and the environmental objects these actions bear upon (the referents of her future symbols) are not clearly distinguished or dissociated from one another. As is explained more fully in the next section on the object concept, objects are not yet seen as separate entities located "out there" in space, wholly distinct and independent of the self and the self's actions towards them. Therefore, a subsequent developmental process of differentiation or distancing of person from referent must exist. Werner and Kaplan aptly refer to this process as a movement from a psychological world populated only with "ego-bound things-of-action" to one containing "ego-distant objects-of-contemplation." Schaffer, Greenwood, and Parry (1972) have reported a developmental change that might reflect this movement towards a more objective, detached, and contemplative view of external objects. Infants of 6 to 8 months immediately grasp and manipulate both familiar and unfamiliar objects placed within their reach, whereas older infants are more apt to hesitate and visually inspect (ponder? "contemplate?") unfamiliar objects before touching them. Werner and Kaplan also cite a study that obtained rather similar results (1963, pp. 69–70). Until externals attain the conceptual status of independent entities "out there," to be pondered and contemplated rather than automatically assimilated to ("devoured by" one almost wants to say) some customary scheme of action, they cannot become true objects of symbolic reference.

Werner and Kaplan make some plausible suggestions about the early development of referential behavior (cf. Chapter 8). They suppose, for example, that manual *pointing* might have, as its sensory-motor precursors, actions such as turning to look at an object, reaching towards it, or touching it. The conscious and deliberate act of calling someone's attention to something by pointing at it is a symbolic act. It is a fair guess that a being capable of this sort of behavior has acquired a reasonably clear self-object differentiation—that is, a clear idea that she is one object "over here" and that the thing she is pointing to is another, wholly separate and independent object "over there." Similarly, Werner and Kaplan argue, those strainful, "call sound" vocalizations that usually accompany the baby's motor strivings to see or touch an object may be the developmental forerunners of demonstrative *naming*. Thus, once the child has attained the necessary contemplative conception of objects and a basic capacity for symbolization, there are—lying around in her repertoire, so to speak—these various reaching and calling behaviors, all ready to be converted into symbolic acts of manual and verbal reference. In short, Werner and Kaplan have identified, within the sensory-motor period, some rather interesting analogues and possible ancestors of the symbolic-referential act of pointing with finger or voice.

Also developing at this stage is a differentiation between symbol and referent as well as between person and referent. This particular differentiation is already somewhat familiar to us from Piaget's account of early symbolic development. Werner and Kaplan again distinguish between motor-gestural and vocal symbols while showing parallels in their developments. In both cases, the age trend toward symbol-referent differentiation or distancing takes two forms.

First, symbol and referent become more physically different from one another. In the motor-gestural case, the imitation (symbol) may become less literally and precisely a duplication of what is imitated (referent). Werner and Kaplan cite, for example, a 3 year old who represented the water stirred up by a passing boat by simply trembling her hands; the referent is not the action of another human being, and the imitation of it is suggestive rather than exact. In the same way, early vocal symbols sometimes resemble what they represent (e.g., a child imitating thunder by making a rumbling noise) but eventually become wholly unlike their referents (e.g., the spoken word "dog" bears no physical similarity to the creature for which it stands). This developmental trend can be seen even more clearly in the case of symbolic or pretend play (Chapter 3).

Also, in both instances the child becomes increasingly capable of distancing symbol from referent in time and space—a point that Piaget also emphasized, you remember. In the case of motor-gestural symbolization, deferred imitation is a stellar example of how the model (referent) and the imitation of the model (symbol) can occur at different times and in different settings. In the same manner, vocal names first may be meaningful to the child only in the immediate presence of the objects they denote, and only subsequently may be produced and comprehended in the absence of their referents. For other interesting discussions of the nature and early development of symbolic-representational capacities, see Harris (1983), Huttenlocher and Higgins (1978), and Mandler (1983).

THE OBJECT CONCEPT

Piaget's *object concept*, or *concept of object permanence*, refers to a set of implicit, common-sensical beliefs we all share about the basic nature and behavior of objects, including ourselves. We tacitly believe, first of all, that we and all other objects coexist as physically distinct and independent entities within a common, all-enveloping space. I am an object in that space, so are you, and so is this book; we are all more or less equal-status "co-objects" together, each of us with our own individual quantum of space-filling bulk and our own individual potential for movement or displacement within our common spatial habitat.

We also implicitly understand that the existence of our fellow objects, animate and inanimate alike, is fundamentally independent of our own interaction or noninteraction with these other objects. When an object disappears from our sight, for example, we do not assume that it has thereby gone out of existence. In other words, we do not confuse our own actions towards another object—our seeing it, hearing, touching it, and so on—with the physical existence of that object, and hence we do not think it automatically becomes annihilated once we lose behavioral contact with it. It *might* lose its integrity as an object (e.g., burn up) during its absence from us, of course, but it normally will not; above all, it will not become nonexistent merely *because* it is not currently being perceived or manipulated by us. "Out of sight" may mean "out of mind," but it certainly does not imply "out of existence" for someone who possesses the Piagetian object concept.

Finally, we believe that the object's behavior is also independent of our psychological contact with it, just as its existence is. We know that once gone from our sight, for instance, the object could perfectly well move or be moved from one location to another. It may or may not continue to await us at the place where we last saw it; we may or may not have to look elsewhere for it. In summary, we all possess an implicit, unarticulated conception of objects which asserts that other physical objects and ourselves are equally real and "objective," volume-occupying inhabitants of a common spatial world, and that the existence and behavior of other objects is fundamentally independent of our perceptual and motor contact with them.

Piaget made three rather startling claims about the object concept, again based upon observations of his own three infants' sensory-motor development. First, he claimed that this utterly basic, "obvious" conception of objects is not inborn but needs to be acquired through experience. Second, its acquisition is a surprisingly protracted one, spanning the entire sensory-motor period of infancy. Finally, this process consists of a universal, fixed sequence of developmental stages or subacquisitions, the infant picking up different aspects or components of the full concept at different stages. Thus, there is a sense in which it could be said that a 1 year old has "more of," or a "different level of," this concept than a 6 month old, for instance, although the 1 year old has not yet achieved the final, complete version of it.

It is almost inconceivable that anyone writing a textbook on cognitive development nowadays would fail to include something on the evolution of the Piagetian object concept. In the first place, the concept itself is so utterly basic and fundamental. If any concept could be regarded as indispensable to a coherent and rational mental life, this one certainly would be. Imagine what your life would be like if you did not believe that objects continued to exist when they left your field of vision. Worse yet, imagine how things would be if *nobody* believed it. It also happens that Piaget's developmental story here is just plain interesting to most people; it is simply one of the very best tales in the developmentalist's anthology. Moreover, a number of researchers are currently trying to clarify our understanding of just how this development proceeds, because there still remains a number of intriguing questions and puzzles concerning it. Some of this recent research is mentioned here, some in the next section. It is not merely an interesting story, therefore, but one that changes somewhat with each new telling.

Piaget assumed that the development of the object concept is intimately linked to sensory-motor development as a whole, and he therefore used the same six-stage framework in describing it. It might be helpful to preface this stage-by-stage account of object-concept development by recalling two earlier points having to do with objects. First, as he develops, the Piagetian infant becomes progressively more cognitively extroverted or external-world-oriented—that is, he becomes more concerned with exploring and discovering the real, objective properties of external things. Second, Werner and Kaplan (1963) postulated a progressive differentiation or distancing of person from referent, such that "ego-distant objects-of-contemplation" are eventually constructed by the developing mind as replacements for initial "ego-bound things-of-action." It is important to recognize that both of these developmental trends are essentially paraphrases of Piagetian object-concept formation—namely, of the gradual mental differentiation of objects from ego's actions upon these objects, such that these objects, and also ego itself, eventually come to be conceived of as autonomous, independent, "objective" entities inhabiting a common space.

Stages 1 and 2 (Roughly 0 to 4 Months)

During this early period, the infant characteristically will try to follow a moving object with his or her eyes until it disappears from view—for instance, until it goes behind a screen of some kind. Whereupon, the infant will immediately lose interest and turn away or, at most, continue to stare for a short time at the place where it was last seen. There is as yet no behavior that could be interpreted as visual or manual search for the vanished object, and more generally, no positive evidence to suggest that the infant has any mental representation whatever of its continuing existence, once visual contact with it is lost.

Stage 3 (Roughly 4 to 8 Months)

The infant shows some progress during this stage in differentiating object-as-independent-entity from self's-action-towards-object, but it will become apparent that the differentiation process still has a long way to go. There are several positive accomplishments. By the end of Stage 2, the infant has become quite accomplished at tracking objects with his eyes, visually pursuing them when they move and visually fixating them when they stop moving (Bower & Paterson, 1972). During Stage 3, he begins to anticipate their future positions by extrapolating from their present direction of movement. If an object falls from his crib to the floor, for instance, he is now apt to lean over to look for it rather than simply stare motionlessly at the spot where it was before it disappeared from sight (he will, to be sure, lose interest and give up searching if he does not locate it right away). Similarly, after some experience in watching a toy train repeatedly enter and leave a tunnel on a circular track, babies in this age range begin to anticipate visually the train's reemergence from the tunnel rather than to only look towards the exit when the train actually appears (Nelson, 1971). The Stage 3 child may also recognize and reach towards a familiar object even if only a part of it is visible, something he could not do earlier. For instance, he might recognize and grasp at his bottle even when all but the nipple end of it is covered by a washcloth or some other opaque screen.

If this very same bottle should slowly and perceptibly disappear once again behind the opaque screen, however, it is an astonishing fact that he will *not* manually search for it (push the screen aside, etc.), even though he is physically competent to do so. The reaching hand can often be seen to drop in midflight once the desired object wholly disappears from view. Herein lies the essential limitation of Stage 3: The baby will exhibit brief and limited *visual* search for objects that have disappeared from sight, but he will show no *manual* search whatever. If the object is placed under a transparent cover, the Stage 3 child will try to retrieve it, but not if it is placed under an opaque cover (Bower, 1974, pp. 204–205). Incredibly, he will not retrieve the object *even when he has already grasped it*, if you quickly cover both object and grasping hand with a washcloth (Gratch, 1972; Gratch & Landers, 1971). Instead, he is likely either to continue to hold onto the object and idly look around as if unaware that he has anything in his hand, or else to let go of it, remove his empty hand, and show no further search behavior. If a transparent cover rather than an opaque one is placed over hand and object under these conditions, he will continue to retrieve it in the normal way. The studies using transparent covers thus show that the baby's inability to retrieve the hidden object is not due to a basic lack of manual skill (Harris, 1983). Piaget believed that in Stage 3 the object is not yet credited with an enduring life of its own, apart from and independent of the subject's perceptual contact with it.

Stage 4 (Roughly 8 to 12 Months)

The child will now manually search for and retrieve an object that he sees someone hide under a cloth or some other cover. The younger, debutant member of Stage 4 will do so only if the object is covered up while he is already engaged in the act of reaching for it, whereas the older, full-fledged Stage 4 child will retrieve it even if it is hidden before he can begin his reaching response (Gratch, 1972).

There is, however, a most peculiar limitation on this newly developed ability to find hidden objects. The child watches you hide object X under cover A and he gleefully pulls off the cover and grabs it. You repeat the hiding a few times; he repeats the finding each time. Then you very slowly and conspicuously hide X under cover B, located to one side of cover A, making sure that the child watches you do it. Quite often, the Stage 4 child will immediately search under A once again and then abandon the search when he fails to find anything there. Why on earth would he do such an odd thing? What level of object-concept development might this bizarre-looking behavior reflect?

Piaget believed that the Stage 4 child does not yet have a clear and conscious mental image of X quietly abiding beneath a cover. He may instead have evolved in this situation a little sensory-motor habit or behavioral "rule" that says, in effect, "Search over there, under that, and you'll have an interesting visual-tactile-manipulative experience." The object of the inter-esting sensory-motor experience (i.e., X) is psychologically embedded in the experience itself and remains secondary to it. According to Piaget's interpre-tation, the differentiation between self's action and object is not yet complete; X is not yet the genuinely action-independent "object-of-contemplation" it will eventually become.

Stage 5 (Roughly 12 to 18 Months)

As Stage 4 draws to a close, Piaget believed that the balance begins to shift from previous motoric success to present perceptual evidence, and the Stage 5 child gradually learns to search at whatever place the object was most recently seen to disappear. In the AB setup described previously, this, of course, means going directly to B when X is hidden at B, even though X had previously been hidden and found at A. Transitional responses between Stages 4 and 5 may include paying more visual attention to B than formerly, being in conflict as to which of the two places to search, and searching at B only after initially failing to find X at A (Gratch & Landers, 1971; Webb, Massar, & Nadolny, 1972).

Piaget argued that the Stage 5 child has progressed further than the Stage 4 child in the crucial matter of differentiating the object per se from his actions towards it. The older infant can read the visual evidence of X's present location more or less objectively (no pun intended); he is no longer locked into a rigid dependence on previous patterns of successful action-toward-object. There is, however, one final limitation to be overcome: The Stage 5 infant cannot imagine or represent any further changes of location the object might have undergone after it disappeared from his view. Let us suppose you put a small object in a felt-lined cup, turn the cup upside down, slide it under a large cloth, silently deposit the object underneath the cloth, and withdraw the empty cup (Miller, Cohen, & Hill, 1970). The prototypical Stage 5 child is incapable of searching for the object anywhere but in the cup, presumably because the cup rather than the cloth was the place where he saw it disappear. As yet, he cannot represent any unseen but readily (to us) inferable movement of the object when inside the cup. In Piaget's words, the child can cope with *visible displacements* but not yet with *invisible displacements*. More precisely, he can infer X's present location from its most recent visible displacement (as the Stage 4 child could not do, you recall, when under the baleful influence of previous visible displacements), but cannot infer X's invisible displacement on the basis of the visible displacements of its container.

Stage 6 (Roughly 18 to 24 Months)

The just-mentioned limitation is gradually overcome in this stage, with the child gradually acquiring the knack of using the visual evidence as a basis for imagining or representing X's unseen itineraries and hiding places. The really accomplished Stage 6-er can be very, very good at it. You put X inside your closed fist and move your fist first under cloth A, then under B, then under C, and then open it up, *sans* object (you have actually left it under cloth A). Many a 2 year old will grin with anticipation and then systematically search each possible hiding place, sometimes in the reverse order from your hiding—that is, first under C, then under B, and finally under A. He may also spontaneously try the same game on you, with his doing the hiding and your doing the finding (and it would be a coldhearted experimenter indeed who would not let him do it). The full-fledged object concept is so clearly "there" in such a child that you feel you can virtually mind-read it. You are *sure* that he is somehow mentally representing that object during its invisible perambulations, and *sure* that he implicitly regards it as an external entity that exists and may move about in complete independence of his own perceptual or motor contact with it. But, of course, he is now in sensory-motor Stage 6, and the essential accomplishment of that stage is precisely that of being able to evoke internal symbolic representations of absent objects and events (recall deferred imitation and symbolic play).

Are humans the only animals that develop any semblance of a Piagetian object concept? Definitely not. Cats clearly show a rather human-like, step-by-step development up through Stage 4 but do not seem to progress further (Gruber, Girgus, & Banuazizi, 1971). Rhesus monkeys pass through the same sequence, but they also go on to develop what looks like genuine Stage 6 competence (Wise, Wise, & Zimmerman, 1974); the same has been claimed for squirrel monkeys (Vaughter, Smotherman, & Ordy, 1972). As for chimpanzees and other apes, Stage 6 competence is undoubtedly only one of their many cognitive talents (e.g., Premack, 1976).

The Object Concept as an Example
of Invariant Formation

The acquisition of the object concept fits into a larger developmental context that merits brief mention. The growth of the human mind partly consists of the successive attainment or formation of cognitive *invariants* (cf.

Gibson & Spelke, 1983). As its name suggests, an invariant is something that remains the same while other things in the situation change or undergo various transformations. The identification of constant features or invariants in the midst of flux and change is an absolutely indispensable cognitive activity for an adaptive organism, and it is particularly characteristic of human rationality.

Perceptual constancies represent one class of invariants. Present evidence suggests that at least two of them, *size constancy* and *shape constancy*, initially become functional during the first year of life (Caron, Caron, & Carlson, 1979; Cohen et al., 1979; Day & McKenzie, 1977; Gibson & Spelke, 1983; McKenzie, Tootell, & Day, 1980). As you probably know, a smaller object situated closer to you can actually produce a visual image on your retina equal in size to a larger object presented farther away, and yet you effortlessly and correctly perceive the one object as smaller and closer and the other as larger and farther away. Therefore, the perceived size of an object remains roughly invariant or constant (hence, "size constancy") despite continual changes or transformations in the size of its retinal image as you or it move in relation to one another. Additionally, the shape of the retinal image of the object constantly alters with changes in the object's spatial orientation with respect to you, and yet you ordinarily have little trouble in perceiving the object's true shape (hence, "shape constancy").

Such perceptual constancies are themselves early invariants, and together they help the infant achieve another invariant that might be termed *object constancy*. This refers to the ability to recognize an object as being the same one seen a moment ago, despite intervening changes in its orientation and distance with respect to the observer and all the modifications in retinal size and shape produced by these changes. The motto of this invariant would be something like, "Despite substantial changes in retinal impression, I know this is the same thing (or the same perceptual experience) as before." The Piagetian *object concept* is another, more conceptual invariant, and its verbal expression would be something like, "Despite a change from retinal image to no perceptual image at all (or more generally, from sensory-motor contact to no contact), the entity that produced that retinal image probably still exists out there in space, in the same or in a different place than where last seen." As we shall see, additional invariants-amid-transformations are identified or constituted during the postinfancy years. The child comes to see himself and significant others as retaining their identity as specific individuals, despite momentary or enduring changes in mood, behavior, physical appearance (e.g., aging, sickness). He also discovers certain quantitative invariants-amid-transformations that Piaget has made famous (the so-called *"conservations"*), for instance, that the amount of clay I have in my hand remains exactly the same when I mold the clay into different shapes, providing only that none gets lost in the process. As you can see, getting straight just what does and what does not stay the same under this versus that salient change is a ubiquitous and extremely important task for a developing mind.

RECENT THEORY AND RESEARCH

A great deal of research on infant cognitive growth has been done since Piaget's pioneering observations of his own three children. In fact, infant cognition is currently one of the most exciting and productive research areas in all of psychology. Useful reviews of recent work in this area include Bower (1974), Brainerd (1978a), Caron and Caron (1982), Gibson and Spelke (1983), Gratch (1975), Haith and Campos (1977), Harris (1975, 1983), Mandler (1983), Uzgiris (1976, 1981), and Uzgiris and Hunt (1975).

What has this recent work shown? Above all, it has clearly shown that Piaget and the rest of us had underestimated the young infant's information-processing capabilities (see Chapters 6, 7, and 8 for a fuller account). It turns out that young infants can perceive and retain in memory surprisingly complex and abstract patterns of information in the environment. Moreover, the astonishing precocity of some of these capabilities—this one detectable at birth, that one at 2 months of age—forces us to believe that they must be largely innate rather than constructed through experience. It is at least roughly accurate to say that, whereas Piaget would think of these abilities as the gradually emerging products of infant development, many present-day infant researchers would instead construe them as the initial cognitive tools that make this development possible (Gibson & Spelke, 1983; Harris, 1983).

Piaget underestimated the young infants' cognitive competencies for two related reasons. One is purely methodological. Without the special experimental techniques now available to infant researchers (see Chapter 6), one simply cannot find out what information young babies are capable of perceiving and processing. What one can see all too well, and be unduly swayed by, is their output incapacities—their inability to speak, gesture, manipulate objects, and so on. They just *look* incompetent to the naked eye. The second reason is that Piaget misestimated the relative potencies of motor activity and perceptual activity as generators of cognitive growth. He thought that motor activity plays a larger and more essential role in infant cognitive development than it probably does in reality, and he underestimated the formative power of perceptual experience. Psychologists Eleanor and James Gibson have now convinced most of us that perceptual learning is a more important source of cognitive growth than Piaget gave it credit for. I discuss their contributions and other important studies of infant perception in Chapter 6.

All this is not to say, however, that we should henceforth dismiss Piaget's account of general sensory-motor development and of the more specific developments (object concept, imitation, play, and others) included in it. As a general description of what follows what in early ontogenesis, Piaget's account has proven to be quite accurate (Brainerd, 1978a; Harris, 1983; Uzgiris, 1976; Uzgiris & Hunt, 1975). It is safe to predict that the general developmental sequences you have been reading about in this chapter will continue to populate such chapters for some time yet to come—and rightly so. On the other hand, many investigators have questioned Piaget's interpretations of various behavioral phenomena, particularly in the case of object-concept development.

The Object Concept

Far more follow-up research has been done on object-concept development than on any other Piagetian infant acquisition, and possibly more than on all the others combined. For reviews of this research see Bower (1974),

Brainerd (1978a), Gratch (1975), Harris (1975, 1983), Haith and Campos (1977), Uzgiris (1976), and Uzgiris and Hunt (1975); the recent review by Harris (1983) is especially useful. Unfortunately, a clear and simple picture of this fascinating development does not emerge from these recent findings. They do not tell an integrated, coherent, and consistent developmental story, at least so far as I can discern. There is consensus and clarity with respect to some things but not others. Major points of agreement include the folowing: Virtually everyone now agrees with Piaget that the infant is not born with the object concept and therefore must somehow acquire it. Because it is so counterintuitive that any living creature could lack an object concept, this agreement is a very important scientific achievement. Virtually everyone also agrees that the development of the object concept as Piaget defined it takes place during the period of infancy and is essentially completed by the end of this period, if not earlier. As mentioned earlier (Stage 6), the full concept is so compellingly present in the average 2 year old that it almost seems visible inside her head. Finally, Piaget's empirical findings have been largely confirmed by other researchers. Several teams of investigators, using sizable samples of infants and longitudinal as well as cross-sectional research methods, have consistently observed roughly the same behavior patterns Piaget described, and observed them to occur in essentially the same age sequence he reported (e.g., Uzgiris & Hunt, 1975). Thus, Piaget's basic findings in this area are replicable as well as arresting.

Consensus and clarity begin to fade, however, when we examine specific behavior patterns more closely and, above all, when we try to explain them. Consider, for example, the most famous of them—the Stage 4 AB error. Recall that this error consists of continuing to search for the hidden object X under cover A, where it has been hidden and found on previous trials, even though the infant clearly sees the experimenter put it under cover B on this trial. This was a particularly important behavior pattern for Piaget because it seemed to suggest so strongly that the infant of 9 months or so does not yet represent the hidden object as a permanent, objectified entity out there in the environment, clearly differentiated from and independent of her own action of retrieving it. From the infant's perspective, Piaget thought, what has been learned on the previous trials is a response that will reinstate a pleasureful sensory-motor experience—that will "recreate" the object's existence as a thing-of-action.

Some striking research findings support Piaget's interpretation of the Stage 4 error. Infants may still continue to search at A when some *new* object Y, rather than X, is now hidden at B (Evans & Gratch, 1972). Even though object Y has never been associated with location A, infants continue in robot fashion to search at A. What are they searching *for*? Piaget would probably have argued that they are not searching for either X or Y, as object-out-there-somewhere, but instead are simply trying to reproduce an interesting sensory-motor experience. Incredible though it may seem, infants will also sometimes even search at location A when they can see that there is no object there at all, can see that desired object X is actually at location B, or both (Butterworth, 1977; Harris, 1974).

However, there are also arguments and evidence against Piaget's interpretation, some more convincing than others (Gratch, 1975; Harris, 1975, 1983; Kagan, Kearsley, & Zelazo, 1978). The baby's successful search at A on the *first* trial, when *X* is initially hidden there, cannot be the result of a temporary, recently established sensory-motor set or habit. Why, then, could it not be exactly what common sense would suggest—a deliberate search for a nonvisible but mentally represented objective entity out there in the environment? If the Stage 4 error results from a sensory-motor minihabit along the lines Piaget has argued, the error should be likelier to occur if the infant is given more rather than fewer successful search trials at *A* prior to the hiding at *B*. It should also be likelier to occur if the infant herself does all the object finding at *A*, rather than just watching the experimenter repeatedly hide and find the object there. These both seem to be reasonable inferences or predictions from Piaget's theory. However, it turns out that most experimental attempts to test these predictions have not confirmed them. Finally, the Stage 4 error does not seem to behave quite like one would think a major developmental stage or landmark should. On the one hand, it has a somewhat fragile, now-you-see-it-now-you-don't quality about it. Infants in the appropriate age range do not always show it. It is also likely not to occur if the infant is allowed to search immediately after the object is hidden in *B*, rather than being forced to wait a second or more. On the other hand, it may even occur in infants of 15 months of age, who should be well past Stage 4, if the information-processing demands of the *AB* task are slightly increased—for example, by increasing the hiding-searching time delay a bit, decreasing the perceptual discriminability of the two covers, making the covers a little more time consuming to remove, adding extraneous covers, and the like. In contrast, infants as young as 7 months of age may not show the error if the *AB* task demands are reduced (Opaluch & Rader, 1980).

The Stage 4 error is not the only locus of empirical uncertainty and theoretical controversy; there are others as well. It would be nice if we could be relatively clear about *something* within this complex and many-faceted topic—that is, if we could get at least *one* developmental story fairly straight here. It might be possible to do this by narrowing our inquiry. Recall that Piaget believed the object concept to be an undissociable mix of several conceptual components. The child who has it in full believes that she and other physical objects are substantial, volume-occupying members of a common spatial world, *and* that other objects normally continue to exist as external things when she is not in perceptual contact with them, *and* that their behavior and location are also independent of her action, although sometimes inferable from various perceptual clues. Other psychologists, in the course of studying the genesis of the Piagetian object concept, have extended or added to this list (e.g., Harris, 1983; Moore, Borton,& Darby, 1978; and especially Bower, 1974). Thus, one also reads of the infant's developing search skills, the ability to code and remember object features, spatial representation and spatial frames of reference (egocentric versus objective), and concepts and rules concerning object identity—for example, that the self-same object cannot be in two different places at the same time. All these cognitive achievements are interesting and worth investigating. The development of concepts and rules concerning object identity seems a particularly promising area of research (Harris, 1983). Moreover, developmental advances in each one probably often facilitate and are facilitated by the others; they are undoubtedly not wholly independent developments. Nevertheless, it may be profitable to focus on just one of them in isolation, even while accepting the view of Piaget and others that the underlying reality is a complex nexus of interacting codevelopments.

The acquisition on which I would like to focus is that of the object permanence or existence component of Piaget's object concept. Piaget's claim that young infants do not represent the continued existence of objects as substantial, "out-there" things when not in sensory-motor contact with them is probably the one that most people find most intriguing and important. Moreover, the ability to form mental representations of absent objects, like the ability to mentally represent absent events (e.g., as in Piaget's deferred imitation), is an expression of Piaget's semiotic or symbolic function, the most important cognitive acquisition of the infancy period. Indeed, one could even argue that it is the most important single acquisition in all of human cognitive growth.

How might we investigate the infant's knowledge of object permanence? Taking our lead from Bower (1974) and others, we would do well to try to test for object permanence using tasks that do not simultaneously test for the other acquisitions mentioned previously. It is more than possible that an infant could mentally represent the continuing existence of a recently visible but now nonvisible object without knowing where it is or how to retrieve it. Furthermore, if the infant did not adequately store in memory the identity or appearance of the object, he might not even recognize the same object, on reappearance, as the one he saw disappear. The essential minimum here would seem to be the baby's basic ability to somehow represent internally the enduring existence, out there somewhere, of a substantial something that was previously in view. Piaget's Stage 4 to 6 visible and invisible displacement tasks certainly assess the infant's ability to locate and retrieve hidden objects, and this ability is certainly worth studying. It seems very doubtful, however, whether these tasks also provide adequately sensitive tests of the basic ability under discussion. As Harris put it: "Instead, we can simply conclude that the infant is easily muddled about where an object is to be found without reaching the more radical conclusion that the infant believes the object's existence and location is dependent on previous actions (Harris, 1983, p. 725)."

I believe there is considerable evidence to suggest that infants have acquired some semblance of this basic ability by about 9 months of age, and perhaps even earlier. There is also reason to believe that it continues to develop in subsequent months, although the exact nature of this development is not altogether clear from present evidence. Perhaps the ability becomes better consolidated, more easily and widely applied, and better connected to other response systems, such as search routines.

Following is some of the research evidence for these beliefs. A horizontally moving object disappeared behind the first of two separated screens and then reappeared on the far side of the second screen. Miraculously, however, it did *not* appear in the empty space between the two screens in the interim, as if it did not continue to exist throughout its whole trip (Moore et al., 1978). The visual tracking of 9 month olds was disrupted by this eerie event. For example, they would look back and inspect the edges of the first screen, as if seeking to find the object there. In contrast, the visual tracking of 5 month olds was not disrupted. Similarly, babies of 4 or 5 months of age are unlikely to look or act surprised to see nothing in front of them after an experimenter covers an object placed on a high-chair tray, spirits the object away while under the cover via a trap door in the tray, and then removes the cover (Charlesworth, 1966). Babies of 8 months and older are apt to look puzzled or startled, show a change in affect, and engage in visual and manual search for the missing object. Comparable results are obtained when, instead of unexpectedly finding no object in the hiding place, the infant unexpectedly finds a different object than the one that had been hidden there (LeCompte & Gratch, 1972; Ramsay & Campos, 1975, 1978). Infants of 8 or 9 months of age usually act puzzled or confused on encountering the new object and may even search for the old one. Older infants are likely to show even more clearly that they have active mental representations of perceptually absent objects.

Evidence for a growing belief in object permanence can also be found in more naturalistic settings. As young children learn to comprehend the meaning of object names, they often show strong evidence of this belief by fetching out-of-sight objects in response to requests like "Where's your dolly?" It is very clear that the 16-month-old boy referred to in the following passage has a very solid grasp of the concept of object permanence:

> The argument that words lead the child to recall the properties of objects in the absence of those objects is strongest in the case where the object named occupies a temporary position out of view. For example, consider the time when Craig spilled cookies on his living room floor. When we were in the kitchen later, we asked Craig for a cookie and he went directly to the living room and got them. To do this, I would argue, he must first have recalled information about *cookies*, and second have recalled the location of those particular cookies (Huttenlocher, 1974, p. 363).

I suspect that one could also obtain observational evidence of the following sort, although I have seen nothing exactly like it reported in the research literature (cf. Ashmead & Perlmutter, 1980; Brody, 1981; Mandler, 1983). A 1 year old, say, is busily engaged in play and some internal or external event "calls to mind" some absent object. Perhaps she sees something often associated with the absent object and this nonverbal cue triggers a mental representation of the object. She may then abruptly stop playing and go directly and purposefully to where the object is located. A child who did that must surely be actively mentally representing that absent object—recalling it in its absence rather than just recognizing it in its presence. Such a child must also surely believe that this recalled object exists out there in the world. The following observation by Piaget seems almost as convincing:

> At 0; 9 (13) [9 months and 13 days of age] she [one of Piaget's daughters] tries to grasp with her left hand a bottle which I place beside her head. She succeeds only in grazing it by turning her face slightly. She gives up shortly and losing sight of the bottle pulls a coverlet in front of her. But suddenly she turns around to reapply herself to her attempts at prehension. It all happens as if she has retained the memory of the object and returns to it, after a pause, believing in its permanence (Piaget, 1954, p. 27).

Piaget believed his daughter was still in Stage 3 of object-concept development at this time and therefore he did not believe she really had the object-permanence knowledge referred to in the last sentence of this quoted passage. However, evidence of the sort just reviewed leads me to believe that he could well have been wrong.

SUMMARY

The human cognitive system undergoes truly momentous changes during the period from birth to the end of infancy. The cognition of the infant is *sensory-motor* rather than *symbolic-representational* in nature. Hers is an unreflective, practical, perceiving-and-doing sort of intelligence. It is not the conceptual, self-aware, symbol-using kind that words like "cognition," "thought," and "intelligence" usually connote.

According to Piaget's theory, much of infant cognitive development consists of the elaboration and intercoordination of cognitive units or structures called *schemes*. Schemes refer to classes or categories of organized, repeatedly exercised action patterns. Examples include sucking, listening, looking, striking, grasping, dropping, and pushing aside. External data (objects and events) are *assimilated* to sensory-motor schemes, and schemes simultaneously *accommodate* to these data. If assimilation and accommodation are roughly in balance and of roughly equal importance in a given scheme-data encounter, the child's cognitive act is said to be one of *adapted intelligence*. In contrast, the act is referred to as *play* if assimilation outweighs or dominates accommodation, and as *imitation* if the reverse happens.

A kind of mnemonic device or memory aid was proposed to help you remember essential points concerning *cognitive motivation:* Ask yourself what propensities or dispositions a human cognitive system ought to have built into it if it is to have a reasonable chance at learning the enormous number of things human beings do typically learn. First and foremost, the system should be disposed from the outset to do a lot of spontaneous information processing, even when there is no tangible objective to be gained by it (e.g., securing food). There is so very, very much to learn that the system cannot be allowed to remain unplugged except in moments of urgent organismic need. It should therefore be outfitted with its own, built-in, *intrinsic* motivation to function repeatedly and frequently, and thereby to learn and develop with reasonable speed. It should also be disposed to focus its attention on those external data that are likely to be most informative to it, given what it already knows. Accordingly, we shall preset it to notice and further investigate movement and contour, and especially inputs that are novel, surprising, puzzling, curious, or otherwise discrepant from and not immediately assimilable to existing cognitive structures (during infancy, this means to existing sensory-motor schemes). We shall also pretune it to inputs to which a young human being should be attentive, such as human speech. Finally, we cleverly endow the system with a pleasureful sense of personal competence in achieving and repeatedly reasserting its mastery over the previously unassimilated situation, thus giving the resulting cognitive progress a chance to solidify.

Piaget's six stages of general sensory-motor development provide a fairly good, overall picture of how the human mind changes from birth to age

2 or so. Most of what was said about this sequence of stages is summarized in Figure 2-1 (p. 29) and need not be repeated here. However, two facts should be borne in mind. Figure 2-1 deals only with the development of adapted intelligence, omitting that of imitation and play, and it seriously underrepresents the text on the development of symbolic representation (Piaget's *semiotic function*).

The two most important generalizations about the evolution of imitation and play during infancy are probably these: (1) Each becomes more and more clearly differentiated and easily distinguishable from adapted intelligence as the infant progresses from stage to stage; (2) the development of the capacity for symbolic representation in Stage 6 makes possible interesting new forms of each—namely, deferred imitation and symbolic play.

Symbolic-representational thought is vastly more rapid, mobile and far ranging, abstract, truth and knowledge oriented, self-reflective, and communicable than sensory-motor intelligence. The semiotic function makes use of a variety of symbolic media, of which natural language ultimately becomes the most important. General intelligence begins its development well before language does, however, and most psychologists now believe that it also remains the more fundamental process of the two, with language development and language use being more derivative or dependent on it than the other way around. Werner and Kaplan describe the development of symbolic ability as a gradual differentiation or "distancing" of person from referent, and of symbol from referent. In the former case, there is a progression during infancy from a reality consisting of "ego-bound things-of-action" to one populated by "ego-distant objects-of-contemplation"; this progression is virtually synonymous with the development of the Piagetian object concept. In the latter case the developmental trend is for symbol and referent to become more physically dissimilar (e.g., the printed symbol "dog" versus the animal to which it refers) and more spatially and temporally separated (e.g., imitating something that is no longer physically present).

The Piagetian object concept is the implicit, common-sensical belief everyone has that we are all physical objects in a common space, and that our fellow objects continue to exist and may move about in this space even when we have lost perceptual contact with them—for instance, after an object has disappeared from sight behind a screen. Surprisingly, so fundamental and "obvious" a conception of objects seems to require nearly the whole first 2 years of a person's life to become fully established.

The highlights of its gradual establishment are described next, using Piaget's sensory-motor stages as a framework. As in all developmental chronologies, the ages given are *very* rough estimates, subject to considerable variation from child to child and also heavily dependent on the particulars of the testing situation. Whenever you cannot remember both, be sure always to concentrate on the sequence of any set of developmental events rather than the rough age norms associated with that sequence.

STAGES 1 AND 2 (ROUGHLY 0 TO 4 MONTHS). The baby tracks a moving object until it disappears, then immediately loses interest or stares briefly at the point of disappearance.

STAGE 3 (ROUGHLY 4 TO 8 MONTHS). The baby can now extrapolate from the moving object's itinerary and extend his visual tracking beyond the point of its disappearance (e.g., leaning over to look for a fallen object). He can also recognize an object on the basis of seeing only a part of it sticking out from behind a screen or cover. If he sees it completely disappear behind the screen, however, he does not retrieve it with his hands even though physically capable of doing so.

STAGE 4 (ROUGHLY 8 TO 12 MONTHS). The baby now manually retrieves a covered-up object. After a few trials at finding it under a given cover, however, he will continue to search under that same cover even though he has just watched you place it under a different one.

STAGE 5 (ROUGHLY 12 TO 18 MONTHS). The baby searches for the object only in the place where it was most recently *seen* to disappear—for example, under the second cover in the preceding example. Thus, if the object is first inserted into a small container, then conveyed to the cover inside the container, and finally released from the container underneath the cover so that the container comes out empty, the child will look inside the container for the object but not under the cover, since it was last *seen* disappearing inside the container.

STAGE 6 (ROUGHLY 18 TO 24 MONTHS). The child can now use his newly developed symbolic skills to represent to himself possible *invisible displacements* of the hidden object instead of only being able (as in Stage 5) to operate in terms of its seen or *visible displacements*. He can eventually solve a wide variety of container-inside-cover problems. The object concept is but one of a number of cognitive *invariants* that get formed in the course of human development. The perceptual *constancies* are earlier invariants; the various *conservations* (of mass, length, weight, etc.) are later-developing examples.

Recent research has confirmed much of Piaget's description of infant cognitive growth. However, it has also shown that Piaget and other early investigators underestimated the infant's information-processing capabilities, especially his ability to perceive, categorize, and retain in memory complex and abstract patterns of environmental input. The development of the Piagetian object concept has been an especially popular research topic during the past decade. Most investigators agree with Piaget that children lack this concept at birth and gradually acquire it during the infancy period. There is less agreement, however, as to exactly what tacit knowledge and beliefs about objects, and exactly how much ability to represent and recall them in their absence, children possess at various ages during this period.

Early Childhood

The 6 year old is a much more mature thinker and knower than the 18 month old. Her cognitive functioning clearly shows a number of positive (i.e., developmentally progressive) attributes when compared with that of a youngster just entering the early-childhood period. On the other hand, the 6 year old, and even more obviously the 4 and 5 year old, seems to present cognitive immaturities of her own when compared with the 10- or 14-year-old child. These apparent immaturities have played an important role in Piaget's and other theorists' accounts of childhood cognitive growth, with the unfortunate result that the mind of the preschool child has often been described in primarily negative terms. In Piaget's theory, for example, the 1 year old is "sensory-motor," the 10 year old "concrete-operational," and the 15 year old "formal-operational"—all good, positive-sounding designations. The poor 3 year old, on the other hand, gets labeled "preoperational" (even at times "preconceptual"), and all too often our description of her thinking has been little more than a dreary litany of her wrong answers to concrete-operational tests.

A more positive characterization is called for, one that stresses the developmental achievements of this period. Until quite recently, it would have been difficult to provide such a characterization because we did not possess research evidence for many early-childhood cognitive competencies. The picture is dramatically different now, thanks to the work of Rochel Gelman and many other investigators (Donaldson, 1978; Gelman, 1978, 1979). Just as we underestimated the infant's cognitive capabilities in past years (Chapter 2), so now does it appear that we also underestimated the young child's. As in the infant case, the reasons for the underestimation are partly methodological. As researchers probed the young child's mind with new and more sensitive diagnostic tasks, they turned up an impressive number of competencies—often fragile, to be sure, but genuine nonetheless. Furthermore, many of them were of the Piagetian concrete-operational genre—that is, they were the sorts of competencies we had previously believed were not acquired until the middle-childhood years. To illustrate, preschoolers have recently been shown to possess more mature abilities in the area of number than we used to believe (see the *Basic Numerical Abilities* section of this chapter).

The results of these recent studies are important for at least two reasons. First, as Gelman and Gallistel (1978, pp. 3–9) have pointed out, it is easier to theorize about a development that progresses from one well-defined set of early competencies to another, more advanced set, than about a development that progresses from the absence of any competencies to the presence of the advanced set. The main reason is that the number of imaginable developmental routes to the advanced set is much reduced in the former case. Therefore, discovering what preschoolers have, instead of only what they lack, may ease the developmentalist's theoretical task considerably.

These studies are also important because they make us rethink our previous beliefs about childhood cognitive development. If preschoolers have at least the rudiments of abilities previously found only in older children, and are generally more competent than we used to think, then important questions arise: Is it really accurate to characterize the young child's mind as "preoperational" (let alone "preconceptual")? Similarly, is the older child's mind clearly "concrete-operational" in a sense that the young child's clearly is not? Finally—the key question that these two questions imply—are middle-childhood minds, and even adolescent and adult ones, as radically and qualitatively different from early childhood ones as Piaget believed? It seems that the recent "focus on the preschooler" (Gelman, 1978, p. 298) has presented us with some uncertainties and perplexities about childhood cognitive development that we were spared in the heyday of Piagetian developmental psychology. (Such are the joys of scientific progress!) We now examine some of the most important positive accomplishments of the early-childhood period, deferring to Chapter 4 a consideration of these uncertainties and perplexities.

KNOWLEDGE STRUCTURES

Mandler (1983) and others have distinguished two senses of the term *representation*. In one sense, the term refers to what a person knows and how that knowledge is structured or organized in memory. In the other, more familiar sense, it refers to the use of symbols (the semiotic function described in Chapter 2). To illustrate, a young child is likely to have some stored knowledge of what happens on a typical day at nursery school. The structure of that knowledge in his head is likely to be partly temporal—that is, organized in terms of what usually happens first, what happens next, and so on. This knowledge structure is an instance of representation in the first sense. In contrast, if the child talked about one of these happenings, or drew a picture of it, he would be engaging in representation in the second, symbol-use sense. Representation in the first sense is necessary but decidedly not sufficient for representation in the second sense. That is, a child obviously must know something in order to represent that knowledge symbolically, but he need not and will not be able to represent symbolically *everything* he knows. The extreme case of this asymmetry is the sensory-motor infant, who clearly possesses considerable organized knowledge without being able to express any of it in symbols. Representation in the first sense is the subject of this section; representation in the second sense, the subject of the next.

Among the most interesting sense 1 representations are the general organizations or structures of knowledge that have variously been called *schemes* (in Piaget's theory), *schemas, frames, scripts,* and *grammars* (e.g., Mandler, 1983). They can be thought of, roughly, as mental forms, molds, or templates that help us assimilate and accommodate to environmental inputs. To illustrate, consider the organized representations of story structure sometimes referred to as *story schemas* or *story grammars.* Even a simple, garden-variety story has a complex underlying structure that is relatively fixed:

> The general notion of the story grammars is that stories have an underlying structure consisting of a setting component in which the protagonist and background information are introduced, followed by one or more episodes which form the skeletal plot structure of the story. Each episode has some kind of beginning, or initiating, event, to which a protagonist reacts. Typically, the protagonist formulates a goal in response to the beginning event, although in traditional stories the goal is frequently obvious enough that it is omitted from

the surface structure of the story. Nevertheless, it is assumed to be present in the underlying structure, since the protagonist and his or her goal form the core around which an episode is built. There follows next an attempt to attain the goal, and the outcome of that attempt (success or failure). The episode comes to a close with an ending, which may consist of a statement of the long-range consequences of the episode, responses of the protagonist or other character to the events that have taken place, or an emphatic statement, such as "They lived happily ever after." As can be seen from this brief description, the constituent units (often called nodes) of an episode are both temporally and causally connected to each other; each constituent is the cause of the next, which follows it in correct temporal sequence (Mandler, 1983, p. 461).

People have an internalized, implicit representation (sense 1) of story structure. Furthermore, they use that representation in a variety of ways:

> People use story structure to provide inferences about information not actually stated in the text; consequently false recognition of expected, but not presented, material tends to be high. Disruptions in comprehension occur when events are described in other than their expected order or when parts are deleted. As for recall, since what is retained is the underlying gist of the story, many details of the surface structure are lost. Recall is, thus, schematic rather than exact. Further, people use the ideal schema to infer appropriate material if they forget the details of content of some unit, leading to intrusions in recall. Events are recalled in their correct order when stories are told in canonical form and when they are told in scrambled or mix-up form, recall tends to approximate the ideal order as well. Finally, people use the underlying structure to summarize the gist of a story. A number of studies have documented these claims (Mandler, 1983, pp. 461–462).

Mandler (1983) also cites evidence suggesting that children begin to acquire and use a story schema during early childhood. Its existence and use in the early school years is even more apparent, as a study by Mandler and DeForest (1979) nicely illustrates. Eight year olds, 11 year olds, and adults heard a two-episode story in interleaved or interwoven presentation order. That is, after first hearing the story title and story setting, the subjects heard the initial story-schema unit of the first episode (its initiating event), then the initial unit of the second episode, then the second unit of the first episode (the hero or heroine's reaction to the initial event, say), and so on in this interleaved fashion through the rest of the story. Some of the subjects at each age level were asked to recall the story in the interleaved order in which they heard it, others to recall it in normal order—that is, all of episode one, then all of episode two. Subjects found it easier to recall the story in normal than in interleaved order. This was especially true of the 8 year olds, who were essentially incapable of retelling the story in other than normal, story-schema form. This and other investigations show not only that young children have acquired something akin to a story schema, but also that they use it automatically— indeed, even obligatorily—when comprehending and recalling stories.

A story is only one instance of a larger class of temporally ordered happenings—namely, events. Recent research has shown that young children have also acquired knowledge structures or sense 1 representations that help them interpret and remember other types of events (Mandler, 1983). They are likely to have laid down in permanent memory organized representations of how concrete, familiar events or routines typically unfold in time (Nelson & Gruendel, 1981). For example, they are likely to have *scripts*, as such routine-events representations are sometimes called, for what usually follows what at lunch at the day-care center, when grocery shopping, at bedtime, and so on. Like story schemas, to which they are closely related (Nelson & Gruendel, 1981), these script representations are general mental templates or molds that tell the child how things are "supposed to go" in such familiar routines.

Since young children are sensitive to the order of events it is not surprising that they also appear to have at least a rudimentary schema for causal relations (Gelman, 1978). For example, Bullock and Gelman (1979) have shown that preschool children know that physical causes precede rather than follow their effects. Their 3- to 5-year-old subjects saw the following sequence of events: One hand puppet dropped a ball onto a runway; the ball rolled down the runway and into a hole; a jack-in-the-box popped up and another hand puppet simultaneously dropped a ball on another runway; that ball traversed its runway and dropped into another hole. The two holes were at equal distances from where the jack appeared, so spatial proximity was not a cue to the causal source. The younger subjects often and the older subjects almost always identified the first, prior-to-effect event rather than the second, subsequent-to-effect event as the cause of the jack's jumping up. For instance, when asked to make the jack jump up themselves, most of the children elected to drop the ball down the first hole rather than the second. Bullock and Gelman (1979) also showed that children of this age seem not to expect physical causes to act at a distance—that is, without any kind of direct or indirect physical contact with their effects.

Young children have also been shown to possess knowledge structures concerning objects in space (Mandler, 1983). Recent evidence suggests that, like their elders, they usually represent the locations of objects in familiar surroundings objectively, in spatial relation to one another, rather than (or in addition to) subjectively, in relation solely to their own bodies. Thus, they too tend to use a spatial code or frame of reference that is external, or *allocentric*, rather than only self-defined, or *egocentric*. For instance, they are apt to represent and remember that the coffee table and rocking chair are located in the living room and right next to each other (allocentric spatial coding), rather than merely that the table is on their right as they come into the room (egocentric spatial coding). In contrast, there is some evidence to suggest that young infants tend to rely on an egocentric rather than an allocentric representation, especially in less familiar environments (e.g., Acredolo, 1979). However, this tendency to fall back on an egocentric frame of reference when in an unfamiliar environment probably remains with us all our lives (Mandler, 1983).

Young children also have well-developed schemas for what familiar classes of objects look like, such as the arrangement of features in a human face. Similarly, they possess "scene schemas" (Mandler, 1983) for how places look. As a simple example, they know that a kitchen is likely to contain a stove, situated on the floor. Even 2 year olds have recently been shown to possess this kind of knowledge about space and objects (Ratner & Myers, 1981).

We have just seen that young children have internal representations of temporal and spatial regularities, stored representations that importantly structure and guide their cognitive interactions with their everyday worlds. Do they also have adult-like representations of the hierarchical, taxonomic organization of familiar classes or categories? For example, are they, as we are, likely to group different kinds of dogs together mentally as subcategories of the same "basic-level" (Rosch, Mervis, Gray, Johnson, & Boyes-Braem, 1976) category of "dogs"? Are they also likely, as we are, to clump dogs, cats, and so on, together cognitively as categories included in the superordinate category of "animals"? The question here is not what young children know about the meanings of and relationships among specific *words* like "hound," "dog," and "animal," although that is also an important question. The issue is, rather, how they mentally group together the underlying *concepts* these words designate. In the past, Piaget, Vygotsky, Bruner, and other theorists have argued that the nature and organization of young children's mental categories differ qualitatively from those of adults (Gelman & Baillargeon, 1983; Horton, 1981; Mandler, 1983). However, here, as in most other areas of early-childhood cognition, recent evidence suggests fewer and less fundamental differences between the two age groups. The issue is a very complex and difficult one, with the nature and extent of child-adult differences claimed being partly dependent on exactly how claims like "possesses hierarchical, class-inclusion representations" are defined and assessed experimentally.

I believe the weight of evidence currently favors the following, somewhat simplistic conclusions (cf. Carey, 1982; Gelman & Baillargeon, 1983; Horton, 1981; Mandler, 1983): Young children probably have sense 1 representations of class-inclusion relations that are, in most important respects, not qualitatively different from those of older people. That is, their basic conceptual organization is probably not radically different from that of adults. However, they have less explicit and general or abstract knowledge about these representations, and consequently are less able to talk and reason about class hierarchies and class-inclusion relations than older people are. Also, they may not use these representations in everyday thinking as much or as fully as adults do, although I am less sure of this conclusion than of the other two.

We have already seen in Chapter 2 that even by late infancy children have some category-like representations (the Ross study described on pp. 30 to 31). There is also increasing evidence that young children have at least some knowledge of class hierarchies and class-inclusion relations. A striking demonstration of this knowledge has been reported by Smith (1979), who showed that 4 year olds can sometimes make valid inferences based on class-inclusion representations. For instance, most of her subjects correctly said "yes" to questions like "A pug is a kind of dog, but not a German Shepherd. Is a pug an animal?" and "no" to questions like "A yam is a kind of food, but not meat. Is a yam a hamburger?" Some subjects even justified their answers in ways that strongly suggest some class-inclusion knowledge: for the German Shepherd question, for example, justifications like "Yes, you said it was a dog" and "Yes, dogs are animals." In contrast, even middle-childhood subjects are apt to have great difficulty correctly answering quantitative class-inclusion questions of the sort Inhelder and Piaget (1964) made famous: After establishing with an 8 year old that, say, a bunch of sixteen flowers consisting of ten red ones and six blue ones are "all flowers," this child is asked "Are there more red flowers or more flowers?" A child of this age is likely to compare the red flowers with the blue flowers, rather than with the entire bunch, and incorrectly reply "More red flowers" (Winer, 1980). Markman (1978) found that even children who pass this test may view the greater numbers of superordinate (e.g., flowers) than subordinate (e.g., red flowers) class members as an empirical fact rather than as a logically necessary fact. For example, they may say "yes" when asked questions like, "Could you make it so that there will be more spoons than silverware on the table?" The logical impossibility of a subordinate class containing more members than its superordinate class is a good example of the explicit, generalized knowledge about the structure of class hierarchies that develops after early childhood.

Class inclusion is not the only way that concepts can be related to one another. Markman (1981b) has done a number of interesting studies contrasting children's abilities to deal with *classes* versus *collections*. Those tall things that squirrels climb constitute the class "trees" but, when a number of them cluster together, they also constitute the collection "forest." Markman has shown that children tend to find it easier to operate conceptually on collection structures than on class structures. For instance, they are surer that one would necessarily have more wood if one chopped down the _____ than if one chopped down the oaks, when the blank is filled with the word "forest" (collection term) than when it is filled with the word "tree" (class term). That is, they can grasp the logic of the inclusion relation more easily when the including whole is described as a collection rather than as a class.

Recent research evidence suggests, then, that the young child has a variety of knowledge structures available to help her predict and understand the world in which she lives. This obviously does not imply that she has no more developing and learning to do in subsequent years. However, it does imply that the young child's mind is more coherent, better organized, and generally less confused than we used to think it was, when our image of her was more exclusively pre-this and pre-that. The recent "focus on the preschooler" has done a lot for the preschooler's image in developmental-psychological circles.

SYMBOLIC-REPRESENTATIONAL SKILLS: PRETEND PLAY AND THE APPEARANCE-REALITY DISTINCTION

We have seen in Chapter 2 that sense 2 representations, or symbolic-representational skills, begin their development during infancy. These skills also show a great deal of additional growth during early childhood. The most obvious and important example is the explosive increase in language competence that occurs during this period (Chapter 8). The ability to use numbers to represent quantities is another example that is taken up later in this chapter. Children also begin to acquire skills in drawing and other forms of artistic representation in this period (Freeman, 1980; Gardner, 1973). The ability to engage in *pretend* or *symbolic play* is a further example, briefly alluded to in Chapter 2 (p. 28). Expressions of this symbolic-representational skill include such acts as pretending to drink out of an empty cup, pretending that a block is a car, and pretending that you are the Mommy and your playmate is the baby.

Several facts about the development of pretend play make it worth discussing in a section on early-childhood cognitive growth. For one thing, it has the unusual property of being largely confined to this particular age period (Fein, 1979). Children younger than 1 year of age are not capable of pretend play; children older than 6 years or thereabouts have largely given it up in favor of other forms of play (games, sports, hobbies, etc.); the ability and disposition to engage in it grow prodigiously in the years between. In fact, much of this growth takes place between 1 and 3 years of age, a period of cognitive development about which we generally know relatively little. Pretend play is also interesting because the impetus for its development seems to come mainly from within the child. I suspect it is one of those biologically evolved activities that, like language, is spontaneously practiced in all cultures but formally taught in none. Our cousin in evolution, the chimp, also appears to be capable of understanding pretense (Premack & Woodruff, 1978). Not surprisingly, the nature and development of this intriguing activity has attracted the attention of some of the field's best minds. Piaget (1962) made important contributions to our understanding of it, for example, as did Vygotsky (1967) and other notables. There has also been some good recent research on the topic (e.g., Elder & Pederson, 1978; Fein, 1975; Golomb & Cornelius, 1977; Jackowitz & Watson, 1980; Overton & Jackson, 1973; Ungerer, Zelazo, Kearsley, & O'Leary, 1981; Watson & Fischer, 1977, 1980).

Pretend play is also an intriguing activity because it has family resemblances and possible developmental links to a wide variety of seemingly unrelated phenomena (cf. Fein, 1979). Consider a prototypical instance mentioned earlier: The young child knows a block is not a car but deliberately pretends it is. If the child also calls the block "a car," as she might well do, she has created something very like a *metaphor*—that is, she has deliberately used the name of one thing to refer to another thing that resembles it in some way (Winner, McCarthy, Kleinman, & Gardner, 1979). Mentally transforming object and word meanings in this manner is reminiscent of imagination and creative thinking, and it is possible that pretend play and early metaphor are developmental precursors of these prized cognitive activities. Recall that pretend play can also consist of the child's making believe that she is another person, that a friend is also another person, and that these two fantasied persons are interacting. Such *sociodramatic play*, as social pretend play is sometimes called, could provide valuable practice in differentiating the self from others, in taking the perspective of others, in trying on social roles (e.g., parent, salesperson), and in interacting socially with others. Thus, it could assist social and social-cognitive development as well as cognitive growth in the strict, narrower sense.

The Appearance-Reality Distinction

Finally, the young child who can pretend has made a start towards grasping an exceedingly important and general conceptual distinction—namely, the distinction between *appearance* and *reality* (Braine & Shanks, 1965a,

1965b; Golomb & Cornelius, 1977; Morison & Gardner, 1978). Consider just a few of the many instances of this distinction (besides pretend play itself) that the growing child may encounter. He will learn early on that dreams seem real but are only appearances (they only "pretend" to be real experiences, one might say). He will also learn that perceptual appearances can deceive. In Piaget's famous conservation tasks, perceptual appearances and inferable conceptual realities are always pitted against one another. In a number-conservation task, for example, the experimenter might initially set two rows of ten buttons each in visual one-to-one correspondence, with one of the two equal-length rows placed directly above the other. After the child agrees that the two rows contain the same number of buttons, the experimenter lengthens one of the rows, thereby causing that row to appear to the child to have more buttons than the other. The child shows conservation of number by stead-fastly maintaining that the two rows are still numerically equal. Whatever else the child may need to know in order to make a number-conservation judgment here, it would seem he must at least know that perceptual appearance and conceptual reality can differ in such situations (Braine & Shanks, 1965b).

If the child does not conserve, but says that the elongated row has more, we could say that he erroneously reported a perceptual appearance when asked to report a conceptual reality. We might label this kind of mistaking-appearance-for-reality error *phenomenism*, after Piaget (Flavell, 1963, p. 256). Interestingly, young children may also sometimes make the opposite error. That is, when asked to indicate exactly how something appears visually from a certain spatial perspective or viewing position, they may erroneously indicate everything that is really there—the nonvisible (from their perspective) as well as the visible. This opposite tendency to print out reality when only appearance is requested is called *intellectual realism*. A study by Liben and Belnap (1981) illustrates intellectual realism. In one of their tasks, children of 3 to 5 years of age saw the experimenter create a block arrangement in which two smaller blocks were placed directly behind a larger one, with the result that only the larger one remained visible to the children from where they sat. They were then shown a series of pictures of block arrangements and were asked to "point to the picture that shows exactly what you see [of the block arrangement] from where you are sitting." Thus, the children were clearly asked to report visual appearance, not reality. Nonetheless, they tended to point to a picture that showed all three blocks (reality) rather than a picture that showed only the one visible block (appearance).

Research by Flavell, Flavell, and Green (1983) indicates that young children may show both phenomenism and intellectual realism in the same task setting. In one part of their procedure, 3 to 5 year olds were presented with an extremely realistic-looking fake egg. The children first clearly estab-lished its real identity as an object (a piece of stone that somebody painted), its real size (small), and its real color (white). The experimenter then said: "Okay, now I'm going to ask you two different questions. I'm going to ask you what it *looks* like to your eyes right now, and I'm going to ask you what it *really, really* is." She then held up the fake egg and asked whether it looked like an egg or a stone, and whether it really, really was an egg or a stone. She also asked the same two two-choice questions about its real and apparent size when it was viewed through a strong magnifying glass and thus looked big rather than small, and about its real and apparent color when it was viewed through a deep blue filter and thus appeared blue rather than white. The experimenter repeated this whole procedure with three other fake objects.

We found that some children as young as 3 years of age show an elementary grasp of the distinction between real and apparent identity, size, and color, much as their skill in pretend play and other cognitive abilities would lead us to expect. However, they also make a number of errors of both types—that is, phenomenism and intellectual realism. For example, the very same child might say that one fake object really was what it looked like (phenomenism) but that another fake object looked like what it really was (intellectual realism). This suggests that their command of the appearance-reality distinction was still poorly consolidated and unstable.

However, the distribution rather than the number of errors proved to be most interesting. The children tended to be phenomenists when asked about object *properties* (size and color) but intellectual realists when asked about object *identity*. When asked about the properties, they were likely to say that the object looked big and blue to their eyes (correct) and also really, really was big and blue (incorrect). Recall that this is the familiar type of error young children make on Piaget's conservation tasks with respect to number and other properties. Other investigators (e.g., Braine & Shanks, 1965a, 1965b) have also found that preschoolers act like phenomenists when questioned about object properties such as size and shape. When questioned about object identity, on the other hand, our subjects tended to say that the object really, really was a stone rather than an egg (correct) and also looked like a stone to their eyes (incorrect). This was the kind of error Liben and Belnap's (1981) subjects made, also with regard to what objects actually were present versus what objects appeared to be present. Subsequent research by Flavell et al. (1983) also suggests that when the properties of color, size, and shape are at issue, preschoolers generally tend to give appearance answers to both appearance and reality questions, and that when what objects or events are present is at issue, they often give reality answers to both questions.

Why do young children show this curious error pattern? We do not know for sure yet. Perhaps they sometimes implicitly define object properties in terms of immediate, here-and-now perceptual appearances; maybe "big" sometimes is taken to mean "looks big now" to them. In support of this interpretation, some children said the egg would be small if we took the magnifying glass away. In contrast, preschoolers may be accustomed to ferreting out what object is really there or what event is really taking place despite appearances, possibly as the result of rich previous experience with hidden objects (object permanence; see Chapter 2), disguised objects (Halloween costumes, etc.), pretend actions and events, and other pretense or pretense-like situations. Why, then, do they often go on to say that the egg also *looks* like a stone, even though—as with our fake egg—it looks exactly like an egg and nothing at all like a stone? It may be partly the result of the just-mentioned disposition's being carried too far; the child overdoes it in his effort to show that he knows what thing is really there. Another possible reason is that the young child is not yet very good at mentally sorting out and examining different sources or "channels" of information. He is less able than an older child to think that, although "stone" is *known* (one channel) to be present over there, all that is actually *visible* (another channel) is "egg." Thinking about perceptual appearances as such may be difficult for him. Whatever the explanation, I can testify that it is an eerie experience to see a 4 year old peer at an imitation egg that would fool the most discerning hen and solemnly indicate that it *looks* like a stone to his eyes right now.

It is hard to overstate the importance and ubiquity of the appearance-reality distinction and its close kin in our everyday lives, and accordingly, its significance as a subject for developmental research (cf. Braine & Shanks, 1965a). Consider some examples. People, like fake eggs, present external appearances that may differ from their underlying realities. People may not really be, think, feel, want, and so on, what surface appearances suggest. They may intentionally or unintentionally deceive others about almost anything imaginable. They also deceive themselves and are deceived by other people, objects, and events. It appears that W means thus and so, that X is true, that Y is the cause of something, and that Z will occur; but the reality often turns out otherwise. And there are many perceptual situations like the fake egg: What we took to be a star turned out to be a plane flying towards us; what we thought to be a Picasso proved to be a forgery; what looked like an innocent conversation from a distance was actually a robbery in progress. Finally, all theory and research in all fields of scholarship amounts to an effort to find new realities hidden beneath new and old appearances (Carey, 1982). The need for erasers in this world has no limits. The discovery and understanding of appearance-reality contrasts in domain after domain is undoubtedly among the child's most important cognitive-developmental odysseys, and pretend play appears to be one of its early instances.

Development of Pretend-Play Skills

The development of pretend-play skills during early childhood has been fairly well mapped by Piaget (1962) and subsequent researchers. Fein (1979) suggests that this development "reveals the phasing in and coordination of several discrete strands of mastery that seem to reflect the growth of the symbolic function" (p. 202). She calls these developmental strands *decontextualization, object substitutions, self-other substitutions,* and *symbol socialization.*

DECONTEXTUALIZATION. The development of pretend play consists in part of detaching behavioral routines and objects from their customary, real-life situational and motivational contexts and using them in a playful fashion. The child who really goes to sleep usually does so in bed, at bedtime, and when sleepy. The child who pretends to go to sleep will do so in other places, times, and psychological states; the routine is disconnected from its usual situational and psychological context. Early in development, pretend actions are fleeting and hard to diagnose as such; the child makes a brief eating gesture with an empty spoon, for example. In time, they become decontextualized in another way: The child shows clearly that she *knows* she is pretending. A grin can be suggestive evidence for this knowledge. A verbal declaration ("I'm playing house!") is irrefutable evidence for it. The child also becomes able to step back and forth between play and reality, keeping straight all the while which world she is in. For example, she may tell her playmate what the playmate's next move should be in the play scenario they are acting out together ("Now you're supposed to cry").

OBJECT SUBSTITUTIONS. Perhaps the best-documented fact about the development of pretend play is that the child becomes progressively less dependent with age upon concrete and realistic props (e.g., Elder & Pederson, 1978; Fein, 1975; Jackowitz & Watson, 1980; Overton & Jackson, 1973; Ungerer et al., 1981; Watson & Fischer, 1977). At first, an object must be present in its familiar form in order to be used in pretend play. For example, the neophyte pretender can only pretend to feed himself if he uses a real spoon or something quite spoon-like in appearance. In contrast, the intermediate-level player can make do with most any object that can be brought to mouth in a spoon-like fashion—for example, a little stick—but he still requires some concrete prop. Finally, the expert player—3 years old, perhaps—can dispense with real objects altogether, using only a spoonless spoon-feeding gesture. There is even additional development at this expert, "Look Ma, no object" level. A 3 year old is likely to comply with a request to pretend to brush his teeth by extending his index finger and using it as a substitute toothbrush, while an 8 year old will "hold" an imaginary toothbrush in the usual way and "brush" vigorously with it (Overton & Jackson, 1973).

SELF-OTHER SUBSTITUTIONS. At first, the child is both agent and recipient of pretend actions. For instance, he (agent) pretends to feed or wash himself (recipient). Later, other persons and objects can be included in play episodes, first as recipients, then as agents. For example, Watson and Fischer (1977) found the following developmental sequence in a study of 14-, 19-, and 24-month-old children's pretend actions: First, the child uses himself as an active agent—for example, he puts his head on a pillow and pretends to go to sleep. At a later age, he uses another object as a passive agent—he places a doll on the pillow and pretends that it goes to sleep. Still later, he uses the other object as an active agent—he has the doll lie down on the pillow and go to sleep, as if the doll itself were actually carrying out the action. These two kinds of substitutions reflect what Werner and Kaplan (1963; see Chapter 2) called the developing child's progressive "distancing" or differentiation between symbol and referent (object substitutions), and between person and referent (self-other substitutions).

SYMBOL SOCIALIZATION. Pretend play becomes increasingly socialized in the course of its development in early childhood. It does so in two respects. First, role-appropriate actions and objects become standardized or conventionalized. In the child's play, "babies drink from bottles, cry, and curl up; adults drink from cups, talk on telephones, make dinner, and wheel baby carriages" (Fein, 1979, p. 207). Second, solitary pretend play gives way to social sociodramatic play. Fein's (1979) observations suggest that children under 30 months of age seldom initiate sociodramatic play with peers and, on the rare occasions when they do, the play episode is apt to be brief and unsuccessful. The capacity for sociodramatic play increases dramatically in subsequent months and years, however (Watson & Fischer, 1980): "By 2½ years of age, the beginnings of sociodramatic play appear and, by the age of 5 years, what began as a few simple gestures begins to encompass intricate systems of reciprocal roles, ingenious improvisations of materials, increasingly coherent themes, and weaving plots" (Fein, 1979, p. 199). Fein (1981, p. 312) also makes the point that, as more young children spend more of their time in group-care settings, the functions of sociodramatic play and techniques for supporting it become increasingly important areas of scientific study.

COMMUNICABILITY: INFORMATION AND CONTROL

One of the most striking differences between the 6 year old and the 1½ or 2 year old is the 6 year old's vastly superior ability to communicate with others, especially by means of spoken language. A truly extraordinary amount of language development gets accomplished during the early childhood period—in fact, we have only recently begun to appreciate just *how* much (Chapter 8). The older child is therefore much more accomplished than the younger one both in sending messages and in receiving them—that is, both in verbally expressing his or her own thoughts and in comprehending the verbalized thoughts of others. Likewise, his capacity for sending and receiving various types of nonverbal communications is greatly superior to that of the younger child. This marked increase in communicative prowess is associated with some equally pronounced changes in his overall cognitive life. A distinction between two types of communication will help clarify the nature of this close association between communicative development and intellectual growth during early childhood.

Some communications are primarily *informative* in character; their content consists largely of facts and ideas of one sort or another. As the child's communicative skills improve, he becomes increasingly able to receive, transmit, and otherwise manipulate information about the world around him. First and probably foremost, he acquires the crucial ability to learn by absorbing information conveyed to him by others through language or other communicative media. Conversely, he becomes able to transmit information to others, a vital means of getting corrective feedback from others as to the adequacy of his facts and ideas. Finally, he develops the ability to "communicate" to himself—for instance, to symbolize, store or retain, and think about the products of his own daily experiences. All of these abilities make for profound changes in the child's cognitive life. Much more than was true of the infant, the young child becomes an "open system" with respect to information flow. Information of all sorts flows into, out of, and inside of the system at a rate and in a manner impossible for any purely sensory-motor, presymbolic organism.

Other communications have a primarily *controlling* rather than *informative* intent. Their main aim is not so much to impart ideas and facts as to control the actions of the recipient. Their function and objective is to impel, inhibit, direct, guide, shape, or otherwise influence the recipient's behavior. The young child's growing communicative competence helps to make him an increasingly active trader in behavioral control as well as in information. Moreover, the patterns of flow are much the same as in the informative-communication case—that is, other-to-self, self-to-other, and self-to-self.

First, a 6 year old is intellectually much more able than a 2 year old to comply with another's request, demand, instruction, behavioral demonstration (which serves as a model for the child to imitate), or any other control-oriented communication. Such communicative inputs are capable of producing increasingly detailed and fine-grained effects as the child grows older. Instructions to carry out complex behavior sequences may elicit precisely those sequences in a willing 6 year old, for example, whereas the most acquiescent of 2 year olds may simply lack the cognitive equipment to comply with such instructions.

Control-oriented communications from child to others also exhibit marked age changes during early childhood. Quite obviously, 2 year olds can and do "control" the behavior of those around them in myriad ways. Again, however, they show nothing like the 6 year old's ability to elicit desired behaviors in compliant others through purposeful and sometimes fairly elaborate verbal instructions, gestures, physical demonstrations, and the like.

Finally, the growing child becomes increasingly capable of exercising control over his own behavior. He develops at least some ability: (1) to initiate a behavioral intention, plan, or set and then sustain it over a period of time; (2) to deliberately inhibit tempting but forbidden or otherwise situation-inappropriate behaviors; (3) to wait and suspend action; (4) to postpone and delay gratification; (5) and a variety of other types of self-management. Thus, late infancy and early childhood are the periods in which numerous forms of *self-control* begin to develop (Kopp, 1982). The word "begin" needs emphasizing, since even the first grader's capacity for self-regulation is, of course, far from absolute (as is the adult's, for that matter); his self-control is sometimes absent, often precarious and short-lived, and usually quite variable in quality from situation to situation. Nonetheless, the emergence of a considerable capacity for voluntary self-control is clearly one of the really central and significant cognitive-developmental hallmarks of the early-childhood period.

As you would expect, the nature and development of self-control is a complicated and many-sided affair (e.g., Kopp, 1982; Maccoby, 1980, Chapter 5; Mischel, 1981; Zivin, 1979). First, as just mentioned, there are various types of self-control. Furthermore, the development of these different types appears to be influenced in various complex ways by parental child-rearing practices and numerous other environmental forces. In addition, different types and developmental levels of self-control are probably mediated or undergirded by different cognitive and social competencies within the child, including, for example, the capacity for symbolic representation and a growing awareness and conception of the self. All things considered, it is not an easy topic to discuss briefly. The present discussion is kept brief, nonetheless, by the expedient of focusing on only one important set of self-control acquisitions: the ability to resist temptation and delay gratification.

Development of the Ability to Resist Temptation and Delay Gratification

During the second year of life the average child acquires some ability to inhibit or briefly delay actions she wants to carry out (Kopp, 1982). Most commonly, the inhibition or delay is instigated by an adult command, such as

"Don't touch!" or "Wait!" Occasionally, one even sees self-initiated attempts to resist temptation. For instance, a child of 13 months was observed to reach for a plant, shake her head, say "No!" to herself, and then withdraw her hand (Kopp, 1982). In general, however, the ability to resist temptation and delay gratification is definitely not the 1 to 2 year old's long suit. As any toddler's parent will tell you, behavior like that 13 month old's is as rare as it is prized.

Recent research has shown that considerable progress in self-control occurs during the third year of life, however. In a longitudinal study, Golden, Montare, and Bridger (1977) tested the same group of children at 24 months and again at 30 months for their ability to delay gratification in response to an adult's request. A cookie was put in a box and each child was told, "Wait until I blow the whistle, then you find the cookie." The experimenters had previously made very sure that the children understood these instructions, thereby ensuring a fair test of the extent to which the children could or would comply with them. There were ten of these delay trials; the time between the instruction to wait and the blowing of the whistle varied from 5 to 50 seconds. The children were much better at holding their cookie-eating urges in check at 30 months than at 24 months. For example, about twice as many of them succeeded in waiting out the full 50 seconds at 30 months as did so at 24 months. Kopp and her co-workers (Vaughn & Kopp, 1981) also observed a marked improvement with age in this kind of self-control in 18 to 30 month olds.

Some years ago, the Soviet psychologist Luria (1959, 1961) proposed a famous theory of the development of self-regulation during the preschool years. This theory stressed the vital role of the child's own self-produced verbalizations in inhibiting and otherwise controlling her own motor actions. Although the theory inspired interesting research and continues to be influential (Zivin, 1979), there are reasons to believe that the psychological mechanisms that mediate self-control are less exclusively or fundamentally verbal in nature than Luria's theory claimed (e.g., Flavell, 1977). For example, that 13 month old who withdrew her hand from the forbidden plant might well have been able to do it even *without* saying "No!" to herself. On the other hand, no one disputes Luria's more general claim that children continue to make very impressive gains in their capacities for self-control during the period between 2 and 5 years of age.

A more demanding test of the child's ability to resist temptation and postpone gratification on her own, without adult help, was devised by Mischel (1958, 1974). In his experimental situations, the child is usually given the choice of obtaining a less desirable reward immediately or else waiting for a more desirable, delayed reward. The ability to select and adhere steadfastly to the high road of delayed reward in situations like this continues to improve with age well into the middle-childhood years (Mischel & Metzner, 1962).

Some subject behaviors and task conditions have been shown to make the task of waiting more bearable than others (Mischel, 1981; Mischel & Mischel, 1979). For example, Mischel and other researchers have found that the task of waiting for a delayed reward is made easier: (1) if the delayed reward is not physically present as a visible temptation during the delay period; (2) if the children distract themselves from the reward by thinking pleasant thoughts about something else; (3) if they engage in "cool" rather than "hot" ideation concerning the reward—for example, if they think about a food reward's abstract and emotionally neutral properties rather than about its yummy taste; (4) if they think about the act of waiting and its virtues rather than engage in "hot ideation" about the reward itself. More interesting is the Mischels' finding that, as they develop, children *themselves* gradually discover some of these very same "rules of delay" (Mischel, 1981) and sometimes use them as deliberate strategies to enhance their self-control:

> We (Mischel & Mischel, 1979) have been finding that children's spontaneous delay strategies show a clear developmental progression in knowledge of effective delay rules. A few preschoolers suggest a self-distraction strategy or even rehearsal of the task contingency. Most children below the age of five years however, do not seem to generate clear or viable strategies for effective delay; instead they tend to make waiting more difficult for themselves by focusing on what they want but cannot have. By the age of five to six years they know that covering the rewards will help them wait for them while looking at them or thinking about them will make it difficult. By third grade children spontaneously generate and reasonably justify a number of potentially viable strategies and unequivocally understand the basic principles of resistance to temptation: For example, avoid looking at the rewards because: "If I'm looking at them all the time, it will make me hungry . . . and I'd want to ring the bell." Often they focus on the task and contingency, reminding themselves of the task requirement and outcomes associated with each choice ("If you wait you get _____ ; if you don't, you only get _____ "). They also often indicate the value of distraction from the rewards or of negative ideation designed to make them less tempting ("Think about gum stuck all over them"). A small minority still suggest that positive ideation about the rewards ("The marshmallow looks good and fluffy") will help, and one wonders if these are the very youngsters for whom delay is likely to be most difficult. Most third graders clearly know that task-contingency ideation helps delay more than hot reward ideation but they still do not know that cool reward ideation is better than hot reward ideation. By the time they reach sixth grade, the children's spontaneous strategies (just like their formal preferences), show considerable sophistication. At this age most of these youngsters seem to clearly recognize the advantage of delay of cool rather than hot ideation about the rewards. The basic delay rules have been firmly mastered.
>
> Perhaps, most important, we are finding the same meaningful developmental sequence in children's growing knowledge of effective self-control rules when we explore the everyday self-control situations they deal with in their lives (waiting for birthdays, cookies, Christmas, the family ski trip) as we find when we examine their delay knowledge in our experimental situations (Mischel, 1981, pp. 266–267).

What sixth graders know about effective self-control is all very well and good, but this is a section on early-childhood acquisitions in this area. The following excerpt from Mischel, Ebbesen, and Zeiss (1972) about the behavior of 4 to 5 year olds in the Mischel task should convince you that there really are some:

> When the distress of waiting seemed to become especially acute, children tended to reach for the termination signal, but in many cases seemed to stop themselves from signaling by abruptly creating external and internal distractions for themselves. They made up quiet songs ("Oh this is your land in

Redwood City"), hid their heads in their arms, pounded the floor with their feet, fiddled playfully and teasingly with the signal bell, verbalized the contingency ("If I stop now I get _____ , but if I wait I get _____)," prayed to the ceiling, and so on. In one dramatically effective self-distraction technique, after obviously experiencing much agitation, a little girl rested her head, sat limply, relaxed herself, and proceeded to fall sound asleep (Mischel et al., 1972, p. 215).

BASIC NUMERICAL ABILITIES

The development of basic numerical abilities is an absorbing subject of study for several reasons. People spend years and years in school improving and building upon these basic skills, and years and years after they leave school putting them to practical use in everyday life. Numerical abilities are surely core, "ecologically significant" cognitive acquisitions if any abilities are. As a consequence, they are of concern not only to psychologists but also to educators, parents, and others.

The fact that numerical concepts and skills are the objects of so much formal education would suffice to make them interesting to most people. However, they are of additional interest to the student of cognitive development because some of these concepts and skills are also informally picked up and extensively practiced on the child's own initiative prior to formal schooling, during the period of early childhood. That is, there is considerable informal, spontaneous learning in this area during the preschool years. More intriguing yet, some startling recent evidence suggests that these abilities may have developmental roots and origins earlier still, during the first year of life. These and other facts have led Gelman (1980, 1982) to suggest that, like language skills (see Chapter 8), basic numerical skills may be natural and universal human abilities. That is, they may be abilities that homo sapiens has somehow evolved a special aptitude and disposition to acquire. We examine this provocative idea later.

Much of the earlier, ground-breaking research on the development of basic numerical abilities was done by Piaget and his co-workers (Piaget, 1952; see also Flavell, 1963, pp. 309–316). A good deal of exciting work on this topic has also been done during the past decade by Gelman (1972b, 1980, 1982; Gelman & Gallistel, 1978) and others (e.g., Brainerd, 1979; Ginsburg, 1977; Klahr & Wallace, 1976; Schaeffer, Eggleston, & Scott, 1974; Siegler & Robinson, 1981). This section focuses on the most important and widely known of this recent work, that of Gelman and her collaborators.

Gelman's research has dealt mostly with numerical abilities that emerge during the early-childhood, preschool period. She and others have convincingly demonstrated that preschoolers do in fact possess more knowledge and skill in the domain of number than Piaget's pioneering research had suggested. Findings from one of Gelman's so-called "magic" studies (Gelman, 1972a; see also Gelman, 1980) serve to illustrate this point. Gelman's subjects ranged in age from 3 to 6½ years. Each subject saw two plates, each with a row of mice on it. There were three mice in one row and two in the other. For some subjects at each age level, the lengths of the rows were identical, with the two-mouse row naturally being less dense than the three-mouse one (since the middle mouse was missing). For others, the densities or spaces between the mice were identical, with the three-mouse row consequently being longer than the two-mouse row. The child's initial task was simply to learn which plate was the "winner" (always the one containing three mice) and which the "loser" (always the two-mouse plate). Notice that the child could learn to identify winners and losers in this task without paying the slightest attention to number and number differences. In the first group, the winner row was denser as well as more numerous; in the second group, it was longer as well as more numerous. The child was reinforced for correctly identifying winner and loser plates but was never told why a given choice was correct. The experimenter never made any reference to number, length, or density, although she did on three randomly chosen trials ask the child why a given plate was winner or loser.

After a series of such trials, the experimenter surreptitiously ("magically") made a change in the winner row before exposing the plates to the child. For some subjects in each group, she removed one mouse from the center or end of that row, thereby making the two rows numerically equal. For others, she shortened or lengthened the winner row. Surprise reactions were noted and the children were subsequently asked various questions about what happened.

Gelman's results are startling to anyone acquainted with the older research literature on Piagetian number conservation (a description of Piaget's number-conservation task was given earlier in this chapter, in the section *Symbolic-Representational Skills*). That literature indicated that young children are apt to respond in terms of row length (or, sometimes, row density) when asked questions about the comparative numerical value of two rows; indeed, the child arrives at his nonconservation response by attending to these irrelevant dimensions instead of number or quantity. Gelman found, however, that even her 3- and 4-year-old subjects conceptualized the winner and loser rows in terms of number rather than length or density. For example, twenty-nine out of thirty-two 3 year olds gave number descriptions of the rows at some point in the experimental proceedings, often using the terms "three" and "two"; in contrast, not one ever referred to differences in length or density. Reactions following the experimenter's surreptitious change in the winner row also clearly showed that number, not length or density, was what the children were attending to in this task situation. When length of row was changed (and number not changed), the children showed little surprise and continued to identify the three-mouse row as a winner, even when it had been made shorter than the two-mouse row. When a mouse was removed from the three-mouse row, on the other hand, they showed surprise, were uncertain as to which row was now the winner, asked where the missing mouse was or searched for it, and the like. It was also apparent that most of Gelman's subjects had some understanding of the fact that addition reversed the effect of subtraction in this situation, an obviously important component of mature number knowledge (see p. 67).

Why this striking discrepancy between Gelman's results and those of most number-conservation studies? Gelman makes a good argument that successful management of the classical conservation task requires more in the way of cognitive processes and skills than the number knowledge it was designed to measure. Since, according to her argument, task solution here is the result of the integrated functioning of number knowledge X *plus* skill Y, concept Z, and so on, a young child could, of course, possess X, lack Y, Z, and so on, and hence still give a nonconservation response. In support of her position, children of the same age as those who did so well on her mouse task were found to do poorly on a standard conservation task that made use of rows *containing only three items* (Gelman, 1972a).

What types of numerical knowledge and skills are acquired during early childhood? Gelman and Gallistel (1978) have identified two major types: *number-abstraction abilities* and *numerical-reasoning principles.* Number-abstraction abilities refer to processes by which the child abstracts and represents the numerical value or numerosity of an array of objects. For instance, the child could count the array and thereby achieve the representation that it contains "four" objects. Numerical-reasoning principles include those that allow the child to infer the numerical outcomes of operating on or transforming sets in various ways. For example, these principles will allow her to infer that the numerical value of a set of objects is not changed by merely spreading the objects out (spreading out is a number-irrelevant transformation), but is changed—more specifically, increased in value—by adding one or more objects to the set (a number-relevant manipulation). In brief, the abstraction abilities help the child establish numerical values and the reasoning principles help her make inferences about, and operate further upon, the numerical values thus established.

Counting Principles

Gelman has paid special attention to the number-abstraction process of counting. Her studies suggest that young children use counting as their principal method for obtaining representations of numerosity. She also shows that their counting activity comes to be governed and defined by five *counting principles.* The first three principles tell the child *how* to count properly, the fourth principle tells him *what* can be counted, and the fifth principle involves a combination of features of the first four. The five principles and evidence for their early-childhood acquisition are presented next.

1. THE ONE–ONE PRINCIPLE. According to this principle, a counter must successively assign one and only one distinctive number name to each and every item to be counted. The first item attended to is ticked off as "one," the next as "two," and so on through the entire set of countables. The person counting should not skip any items that should be counted, should not count any item more than once, should not use the same number name more than once, and should stop the counting sequence precisely when the last item has been enumerated. Thought of in this way, it is clear that accurate counting is a surprisingly complex and demanding process of precisely coordinating the sequential production of number names with the sequential designation of items to be counted. As the process unfurls in this carefully coordinated fashion, both number names and items are progressively "used up" and cannot be reused during that counting act. Although preschoolers do make counting errors that violate the one–one principle, especially when trying to

enumerate larger sets of items, there is good evidence that even 2½ to 3 year olds are likely to have at least some implicit grasp of the one-one principle. For example, Gelman (1982) reports that young children will notice and correct their own violations of the principle and also detect violations of it deliberately made by another (e.g., the experimenter's puppet). Thus, their violations seem to reflect performance problems more than lack of tacit knowledge of the one–one principle. That is, they seem to know how counting should be done but they cannot always do it without error because of information-processing overload or other difficulties.

2. THE STABLE-ORDER PRINCIPLE. When counting out a set of items, one should always recite the number names in the same order. For instance, one should not count out a three-item set "one, two, three" some times and "three, one, two" other times. Gelman found that young children usually honor this principle, despite other—and often amusing—limitations in their counting abilities. For example, a 2 year old might enumerate a set of two objects by saying "two, six," or even "*A, B,*" but would still use that same stable order of counting tags the next time he counted two objects. Older preschoolers sometimes produce longer idiosyncratic but stably ordered strings, such as "one, two, three, four, eight, ten, eleben" (Gelman & Gallistel, 1978, p. 93).

3. THE CARDINAL PRINCIPLE. This principle simply asserts that the final number name uttered at the end of a counting sequence gives the cardinal-number value of the set. For example, I would use it this way in toting up the number of counting principles described so far: "one, two, three—*three.*" Gelman's research indicates that, as with the one–one principle: (1) Young children often do act as if they are following the cardinal principle when counting out sets of items, especially small sets, when they have good command of the relevant number words; (2) the information-processing demands of counting may sometimes interfere with the use of the principle, and thereby lead us to underestimate the young child's grasp of it (Gelman, 1982). As an example of (2), the child himself may not succeed in counting to *n* and then correctly indicating that there are *n* things there. On the other hand, he may well spot a puppet's mistake when the puppet counts up to *n* and then says there are *n* + 1 things here. Similarly, if the experimenter rather than the child assumes the processing burden of counting out a set of items and then asks the child how many there are, even a 2½ to 3 year old can often use the cardinal principle and give the last number word the experimenter said.

4. THE ABSTRACTION PRINCIPLE. The three principles just discussed are how-to-count principles. This one is a what-to-count principle. It stipulates that anything is a potential countable; we may enumerate events, inanimate objects, animate objects, intangible and abstract objects (minds, Gelmanian counting principles)—any sort of entity whatever. Although no 4 year old has yet been observed to enumerate the Gelmanian counting principles, children of this age do not seem to actively exclude any particular type of entity from the potentially countables. Likewise, they are willing to try to count up all the objects in a room without worrying about their heterogeneity (e.g., animates lumped together with inanimates), treating them as if they were all identical, featureless "things" for purposes of counting.

5. THE ORDER-IRRELEVANCE PRINCIPLE. This principle states that it does not matter in what order you enumerate the objects you are counting. For example, in counting out a set consisting of a dog, a cat, and a mouse, you will end up with the same numerical value (three) whether you begin with the dog and call it "one" or end with the dog and call it "three." Recall that the stable-order principle says that the order of the *number names does* matter; it must always be "one," "two," "three," and so on. In contrast, the order-irrelevance principle says the order of the *items* to which this stably ordered enumeration process is applied does *not* matter; the items can be counted out in any order you please.

Clever studies by Gelman and her colleagues (Gelman, 1982; Gelman & Gallistel, 1978) have shown that 5 year olds have fairly explicit knowledge of the order-irrelevance principle and that even 3 year olds probably understand it implicitly. In one of their testing procedures, the experimenter had the child begin by counting out a row of four or five objects from left to right; a toy baby was located in the second from leftmost position in the row. The experimenter then asked the child to count the objects again but this time to "start counting with the baby and make it number one" (Gelman & Gallistel, 1978, p. 151). The child was subsequently asked to recount the same set making the baby number two, to recount again making a different object number one, and so one. These strange requests did not faze Gelman's 5-year-old subjects one bit; they tried and usually succeeded in counting the objects in any order the experimenter asked them to. In another procedure, a puppet maneuvered the child into recounting a small set of objects such that every object eventually got to be called "one." The puppet then said, "I tricked you, I made you make them all number one!" The experimenter asked the child if this was so and how it could be. The 4 and 5 year olds' explanations were not as articulate as an adult's would have been, but they did testify to a fairly explicit understanding of the order-irrelevance principle. One explanation was: "Because if you move them around, you have to start with one" (Gelman & Gallistel, 1978, p. 151). Another child even said, "It could be 1 or 2 or any number, like 6, 10, and even 14" (Gelman, 1982). The 3 year olds were not as accomplished as this, but they also showed no evidence of thinking that a particular *number* name was permanently wedded to a particular object over successive recountings. In marked contrast, they stoutly objected to moving around nonnumerical, *object* names in this fashion—for example, calling the baby "baby" on one occasion and "doggie" on another. They clearly thought one should not play musical chairs with objects and object names but seemed to assume it was all right to do so with objects and number names.

Numerical-Reasoning Principles

Gelman and others (Gelman, 1980, 1982; Siegler & Robinson, 1982) have shown that youngsters acquire numerical-reasoning principles as well as number-abstraction abilities during the early-childhood period. By the end of this period they are likely to have learned that merely changing the color or identity of a set of items, or just moving the items around in space, are not transformations that alter the number of items in the set. They are also likely to have learned that, contrariwise, adding items increases the set's numerical value, subtracting items decreases it, and first adding one item and then subtracting one item leaves the numerical value unchanged. They can also determine the numerical equality and inequality relations between two sets— that is, they can infer that sets *A* and *B* contain the same number of items and that set *C* contains more items than set *D*. They are apt to rely heavily on counting to determine these relations and, as with number abstraction, are generally better at numerical reasoning when the sets involved are small, easily countable ones.

Older preschoolers can even exploit their counting prowess to do simple addition and subtraction (Gelman, 1982; Siegler & Robinson, 1982). Starkey and Gelman (cited in Gelman, in press) tested 3 to 5 year olds on a variety of mental addition and subtraction tasks. The experimenter would hold, say, four pennies in her open hand, ask the child to count them, then close her hand and say: "Now I'm putting two pennies in my hand. [She put two more in the same closed hand.] How many pennies does this bunch have?" Or she might say at the end, "Now I'm taking three pennies out . . ." The majority of Starkey and Gelman's 5-year-old subjects could solve problems that involved starting with one to six items and then adding or subtracting one to four items. As predicted, they usually used counting as a solution aid.

Later Acquisitions

Of course, children's numerical abilities continue to improve and expand during the middle-childhood and adolescent years as a direct consequence of formal teaching in school. However, some of the learning in this area continues to be largely spontaneous and informal, rather than the direct result of specific teaching efforts. One such developmental trend has already begun during the preschool years: Children's knowledge about how to abstract and reason about numbers becomes more explicit (Gelman, 1982); we have already seen an example of this trend in the case of the order-irrelevance principle. Whereas younger children can sometimes detect errors in counting or numerical reasoning, older children can go on to reflect on them and explicitly indicate why they are errors, what effects they have on the outcome, and the like. It is not hard to imagine carrying on a meaningful and articulate dialogue about Gelman's five counting principles with a child of 10, say. In contrast, we surely could not do this with a child of 3, even though the 3 year old might also abide by these principles when actually engaged in counting small sets.

Evans (cited in Gelman, 1980, 1982) has studied the informal acquisition during middle childhood of a very fundamental generalization about numbers: There is no largest number because one can always use the counting system to generate still a larger one. The 5- to 9-year-old subjects tested in this study had not been taught about the concept of infinity in school. Nevertheless, many of the older subjects showed a clear understanding of this generalization when questioned about the biggest number they could think of, about the effects of adding one to that number, and the like. For instance, one 7 year old was asked this question: "If someone tells you that there is a biggest number, what would you say?" Her answer was letter perfect: "No there isn't, because numbers never end and there's always a bigger number" (Gelman, 1980, p. 65). Interestingly, some of the younger subjects grasped one part of the generalization but not the other: They recognized that one can always keep on adding one to get larger and larger numbers but they still believed (quite understandably, in my view) that there *must* be a largest number out there *somewhere*! It is fun to speculate about how children might arrive at this generalization. Gelman (1980, 1982) suggests that their own spontaneous practice with counting and their own private "thought experiments" concerning the number series may play important roles—that is, through trying to count to the highest number they can, and always finding that they can keep on counting higher still, or other self-produced experiences like that, they may induce the generalization themselves or else be led to question their elders and acquire it that way.

Earlier Foundations

At the beginning of this section, I mentioned that recent evidence suggests that numerical abilities "may have developmental roots and origins . . . during the first year of life." More concretely, the evidence in question suggests that infants are sensitive to the dimension of number and, even more mind-boggling, they may spontaneously engage in some sort of nonverbal "counting" activity when presented with sets of two or three stimuli. Let us examine this evidence.

An experiment by Starkey, Spelke, and Gelman (1980) capitalized on the fact that even young infants are capable of showing habituation and dishabituation of attention (see Chapter 6). If infants are presented with the same stimuli on trial after trial, they are likely to attend to them less and less over trials, as if getting bored with perceiving the same old thing; this is called *habituation*. If one then presents new stimuli, and the infants can perceptually discriminate these stimuli as being new and different from the previous ones, their attention is apt to increase once again; this is called *dishabituation*, or *recovery from habituation*. Starkey et al. (1980) showed 6- to 9-month-old infants a series of slides of three-item displays until the infants habituated to them. The items shown were common household objects such as a memo pad, a comb, and a scraper. The three objects on any one slide were different from the three on any other slide and also differed in their spatial arrangement; it appears, therefore, that the only thing the object arrays had in common was their numerical value—their "threeness." After the infants had habituated to these slides they were presented with an alternating sequence of three-item and two-item slides. These slides also contained new household objects in varying spatial configurations. Starkey et al. (1980) found that the infants looked longer at the slides that showed the new numerical value (the two-item slides) than at those showing the old one (the three-item slides). That is, they appeared to exhibit continued habituation of attention to displays of three things but dishabituation to displays of two things. This in turn suggests that they must have perceptually discriminated between the two types of displays. Other infants of the same age who were first presented with two-item slides and then with two- and three-item slides in alternation showed the same psychological pattern: They subsequently looked longer at the novel, three-item slides. In view of the surprising and counterintuitive nature of these findings, it is important to note that a very similar study carried out independently and concurrently in a different laboratory obtained strikingly similar results (Strauss & Curtis, 1981). There is nothing like a successful independent replication to render hard-to-believe results believable.

Starkey et al. (1981) then went on to discover something even more surprising. The experiment I report to illustrate what they found did not employ the habituation-dishabituation method, but a related one that assesses detection of similarity across sense modalities. On each of a series of thirty-two trials, infants of 6 to 8 months were presented with two visual displays side by side, one containing two household objects and the other three. As in their previous study, the nature and spatial arrangement of the objects differed from one display to the next. On some trials the infants heard a sequence of two drumbeats while viewing the displays, on others a sequence of three drumbeats. Over the course of the thirty-two trials, the infants developed a weak but statistically significant tendency to look longer at the three-item display than at the two-item display when three drumbeats sounded, and to look longer at the two-item display when two drumbeats sounded. That is, they acted as if they came to detect some sort of abstract, sense-modality-independent equivalence between sets of stimuli as physically dissimilar as visual displays and auditory sequences. It is difficult to imagine what the abstract equivalence could be other than numerical equivalence. It is also difficult to imagine how that equivalence could be detected except by some neurological process akin to nonverbal counting (Gelman, 1982). Starkey et al. (1981) obtained essentially the same results in three other experiments. There is also evidence from recent studies that infants can detect other (i.e., nonnumerical) intermodal or across-sense-modality equivalences (Gibson & Spelke, 1983; see also Chapters 2 and 6). All the same, it would be nice to see Starkey et al.'s (1981) striking finding replicated by other investigators. When we have to look at the infant's mind through the badly smudged research windows currently available to us, there is always the danger of seeing things that are not really there.

These recent studies suggest that the development of basic numerical skills may build on cognitive sensitivities and abilities already present during infancy. This immediately raises an important question for future research: What developmental changes in numerical competencies take place between midinfancy and age 2½ to 3 years, the age when some implicit knowledge of Gelman's counting and reasoning principles can first be reliably demonstrated (cf. Langer, 1980; Siegler, 1979a)? At present we have scarcely a hint as to what these changes might be.

Basic Numerical Skills: Natural Human Abilities?

These infant studies are also taken by Gelman (1980, 1982; see also Keil, 1981a) as additional support for her belief that basic numerical skills may constitute natural and universal abilities for members of our species. There are several grounds for this belief (Gelman, 1980, 1982): First, as we have just seen, human beings appear to be both able and disposed to process numerical information as early as midinfancy. In contrast, although a fairly close relative of ours and an otherwise intelligent creature, the chimpanzee seems to have surprisingly little aptitude for learning about number (Premack, 1976;

Woodruff, Premack, & Kennel, 1978). Second, young children show both high motivation and high aptitude to acquire basic numerical knowledge and skills on their own, without adult pressure or tutelage. In young children, Gelman's counting principles function very like a Piagetian scheme (Gelman & Gallistel, 1978). Like a sucking or prehension scheme, they spontaneously and voraciously assimilate countable objects and new number words to their own structures. Young children seem to go around counting things and learning new numbers for the sheer pleasure of it. Finally, some form of counting procedure is found in most cultures, including those in which there is no formal schooling. Thus, Gelman believes that, like speech (see Chapter 8), basic numerical processing is just something human beings are born to do. Although her arguments and evidence for this belief may not be wholly compelling, the belief itself is both reasonable and thought provoking.

SUMMARY

The developmental psychologist's portrait of cognition during the period of early childhood (roughly 1½ to 6 years of age) used to be rather negative and unflattering. For example, preschool children's thinking was often characterized as "preoperational," or even "preconceptual." However, recent research has shown that an impressive number of fragile but nonetheless genuine competencies have been acquired by the end of this period. It seems that we had underestimated the young child's abilities, just as we had underestimated the infant's (Chapter 2).

Young children's cognitive attainments include a variety of *knowledge structures* or *sense 1 representations* that greatly assist them in predicting and making sense of their everyday worlds. These structures, variously termed *schemes, schemas, frames, scripts,* and *grammars,* can be thought of as mental forms, molds, or templates that help us assimilate and accommodate to environmental inputs. Children begin to acquire such "mental templates" for the structures of simple stories during this age period and use these story schemas or story grammars when comprehending and recalling stories. They gradually build up scripts for representing and anticipating the usual sequence of events in preschool, at bedtime, and during other familiar routines. Young children have acquired at least a rudimentary schema for causal relations—for instance, they are likely to know that physical causes precede rather than follow their effects. Like older people, they are capable of representing the locations of objects by means of an *allocentric* (external, object-referenced) spatial frame of reference, as well as by means of an *egocentric* (self-referenced) one. Preschoolers also have well-developed schemas for what familiar classes of objects and places look like. In past years, several theorists have claimed that the nature and organization of young children's mental categories differ qualitatively from those of adults. However, recent work suggests that—here as in other areas of cognition—the differences may not be that radical. Although young children's conscious knowledge and ability to reason about classification hierarchies and class-inclusion relations are clearly limited, they may possess sense 1 representations of these hierarchies and relations that are not fundamentally different from those of their elders.

Symbolic-representational skills, or facility with *sense 2 representations*, undergo a great deal of growth during early childhood. For example, there is a marked increase during this age period in children's abilities to engage in *pretend* or *symbolic play*. The development of this ability includes a number of subdevelopments described under the categories of *decontextualization*, *object substitutions*, *self-other substitutions*, and *symbol socialization*. For example, with increasing age children become less dependent upon concrete and realistic props in their pretend play (object-substitutions category). A closely related acquisition of considerable scope and real-world significance is the conceptual distinction between *appearance* and *reality*. Recent research shows that even some 3 year olds may show a beginning ability to make the distinction correctly. However, preschoolers often err on appearance-reality tasks and are susceptible to two types of errors when they do: (1) reporting appearance when reality is requested (*phenomenism*); (2) reporting reality when appearance is requested (*intellectual realism*).

There is enormous progress in all aspects of *communicability* during early childhood. Some communications function primarily to *inform* their audience, others to *control* their audience's behavior. Both kinds of communication can flow from others to self, self to others, and self to self. That is, as they grow older, children become increasingly capable of responding appropriately to both informative and control-oriented communications from others, capable of sending both types of communication to others, and capable of "sending" both to themselves—that is, informing and controlling themselves. This last, the increasing capacity for voluntary self-control, is clearly one of the major cognitive-developmental hallmarks of the early-childhood period. One important set of self-control acquisitions is the ability to resist temptation and delay gratification. Studies have shown marked increases with age in children's ability to resist the temptation to take a less desirable but still attractive reward now in favor of enduring the wait for a more desirable reward that can only be had later. Children also acquire and make effective use of knowledge about how to make this Spartan task of delay more bearable. For example, they learn to put Satan behind them by covering up the alluring immediate reward, by deliberately focusing their attention on something else, and by using other clever strategies.

The acquisition of basic numerical abilities is of compelling interest for several reasons, not the least of which is their great ecological significance. Here, as in other areas, Piaget was the main pioneer. In addition, a great deal of exciting research on this topic has been carried out during the past decade by Rochel Gelman and others. Gelman's research findings strongly suggest that Piaget's number-conservation task underestimates preschoolers' knowledge and skill in the domain of number. Gelman distinguishes between young children's *number-abstraction abilities* and their *numerical-reasoning principles*. Prominent among the number-abstraction abilities is the preschooler's developing command of five *counting principles*: (1) assign one and only one number name to each and every item that is to be counted (*one–one principle*); (2) when counting, always recite the number names in the same order (*stable-order principle*); (3) the final number name uttered at the end of a counting sequence denotes the total number of items you have counted (*cardinal principle*); (4) any sort of entity may be counted (*abstraction principle*); (5) it does not matter in what order you enumerate the objects you are counting (*order-irrelevance principle*). One of the numerical-reasoning principles that children acquire is the number-conservation rule that merely spreading a set of objects out does not change the number of objects in the set.

It is not surprising to learn that children's numerical abilities continue to develop after early childhood. The apparently spontaneous acquisition of the concept of infinity by elementary school children who have not yet received any classroom instruction on it is an intriguing case in point that has recently come to light. However, it certainly *is* surprising to learn that numerical abilities may begin their development *before* the early-childhood period. Recent research suggests that infants are sensitive to the dimension of number and, incredible though it sounds, may even engage spontaneously in some sort of nonverbal "counting" activity when presented with sets of two or three stimuli. These astonishing findings raise the possibility that basic numerical processes may—like walking and talking—be activities we humans are predisposed through evolution to learn and do.

Middle Childhood and Adolescence

Exactly how do the minds of older children, adolescents, and adults differ from those of young children? Despite the existence of thousands of research studies comparing the cognitive performance of early-childhood and older subjects, we still lack a wholly satisfactory answer to this basic question. It is not that these studies fail to show marked age differences in cognitive performance; they almost always do. Rather, the problem is to know how best to describe and explain the age differences found. It is easier to discuss this problem after describing the information-processing approach to the study of cognitive growth, conceived by most contemporary developmentalists as an important alternative or supplement to Piaget's approach (Siegler, 1983b).

THE INFORMATION-PROCESSING APPROACH
TO THE STUDY OF COGNITIVE DEVELOPMENT

At the present time, "the information processing approach is arguably *the* leading strategy for the study of cognitive development" (Siegler, 1983b, p. 129). In this approach, the human mind is conceived of as a complex cognitive system, analogous in some ways to a digital computer. Like a computer, the system manipulates or processes information coming in from the environment or already stored within the system. It processes the information in a variety of ways: encoding, recoding, or decoding it; comparing or combining it with other information; storing it in memory or retrieving it from memory; bringing it into or out of focal attention or conscious awareness, and so on.

The information manipulated in these ways is of different types and is organized into units of various sizes and levels of complexity or abstraction. As to types, some of the information that is processed is more "declarative" in nature, consisting of knowledge of word meanings, facts, and the like. Other information is more "procedural" in type, consisting of knowledge of how to do various things. As to sizes and levels, some units of information are small and elementary, such as an encoded perceptual distinctive feature that helps the individual recognize a stimulus as a particular letter of the alphabet rather than as some other letter. Other units are organized wholes comprised of elementary units and are at higher levels of abstraction, such as the meaning of the written sentence that contains the just-mentioned letter. More interesting higher-order units include the sense 1 representations or knowledge structures described in Chapter 3—schemes, schemas, scripts, and so on—as well as plans, strategies, and rules used in thinking and problem solving. Thus, an episode of information processing may involve retrieving or assembling a complex plan or strategy for solving a problem, attempting to execute that plan or strategy, revising it if it proves inadequate, and so forth.

The information-processing approach has several other distinctive characteristics. Its primary objective is to provide an explicit, detailed understanding of what the subject's cognitive system actually *does* when dealing with some task or problem, here and now or "on line." It attempts to answer such questions as: What does the system do first, at the onset of the information-processing episode? What is the second thing it does, and the third? Are some of these processing steps carried out simultaneously (parallel processing) rather than successively (serial processing)? Which ones? An episode of information processing is thus conceived as a kind of odyssey of information flow: Where does the information go first and what happens to it there? What is its next destination and adventure, and so on? The ideal goal of the information-processing approach is to achieve a model of cognitive processing in real time that is so precisely specified, explicit, and detailed that it can actually be run successfully as a working program on the computer. The model should also make specific predictions about how the subject (and computer) would behave under specific task conditions or constraints, and in response to specific inputs. Some information-processing psychologists make heavy use of computers to simulate the hypothesized operations of the human cognitive system; they use computer simulation as a tool for testing and revising their information-processing models (e.g., Klahr & Wallace, 1976). Others do not use it much or at all, but still share the information-processing approach's paramount goal of producing an explicit, testable model of here-and-now cognitive functioning.

Proponents of this approach stress the fact that the human cognitive system has important processing limitations. As examples, there are severe limitations on the number of units of information that can be attended to and processed simultaneously, and cognitive operations such as encoding, comparing, and retrieving information from memory all require time to execute and usually have to be performed serially. It is therefore possible for a task to overload the system—that is, to impose processing demands that exceed its processing capacity. For instance, if a task required a subject to keep five units of information in mind at once and that particular subject was only capable of keeping four in mind, we would have a case of information-processing overload and the subject would likely fail the task. As we shall see, the concept of information-processing limitations is emerging as an important one in our thinking about cognitive development.

Finally, practitioners of the information-processing approach use a variety of analytic methods to test their ideas about how the human cognitive system functions (Siegler, 1983b). Patterns of response latencies or reaction times can provide evidence about the time course of information processing. Verbal reports by a subject may reveal the conscious plans and strategies the subject used during problem solving. Eye-movement data can yield information about the subject's attentional patterns over time. Inferences about functioning can be made from what the subject remembers and forgets of the information presented. Finally, as we shall see presently, analyzing patterns of correct answers and errors over a carefully selected set of tasks can tell us much about the nature and development of the child's knowledge and reasoning. More generally, great emphasis is placed on analytically decomposing tasks into their components and trying to infer what the cognitive system must do to deal adequately with each component.

An Example of an Information-Processing Approach to Cognitive Development: Siegler's Rule-Assessment Approach

A good deal of information-processing-oriented work has been done in the area of cognitive development during the past few years (e.g., Anderson & Cuneo, 1978; Case, 1978, 1985; Fischer, 1980; Gelman & Gallistel, 1978;

Halford & Wilson, 1980; Keating & Bobbitt, 1978; Klahr & Robinson, 1981; Klahr & Wallace, 1976; Pascual-Leone, 1970; Siegler, 1981; Sternberg & Nigro, 1980; Trabasso, 1975; Trabasso, Isen, Dolecki, McLanahan, Riley, & Tucker, 1978). Much of this work builds directly on Piaget's pioneering accomplishments. Some investigators, like Pascual-Leone and Case, have attempted to modify Piagetian theory so as to take into account information-processing considerations. Thus, one sees "neoPiagetian" theories with an information-processing look about them. Numerous others have restudied cognitive-developmental phenomena initially discovered by Piaget, such as conservation and class inclusion, but using concepts and methods from the information-processing tradition (e.g., Klahr and Wallace, Trabasso). Robert Siegler's investigations using his *rule-assessment approach* (e.g., 1976, 1978, 1981, 1983a, 1983b) are of the latter type and represent a good example of how cognitive growth can be profitably studied from an information-processing perspective.

Siegler believes that much of cognitive growth can be usefully characterized as the sequential acquisition of increasingly powerful rules for solving problems (Siegler, 1981). In studying cognitive growth within a particular conceptual domain, Siegler begins by predicting the different problem-solving rules that children of different developmental levels might use. These hypotheses about the developmental ordering or sequence of rules are usually based, in part at least, on prior research findings by Piaget. It is in this sense that Siegler's work can be said to build on and extend Piaget's. Siegler's next step is to administer a special, very carefully selected set of problems in that domain to subjects of different ages. A subject's pattern of responses across this set of problems may then help to determine which of Siegler's hypothesized rules, if any, the subject is using. One response pattern might suggest that rule A had been used, another that rule B had been used, and so on. More fine-grained analyses usually follow. For example, Siegler might go on to determine that two subjects who use the same problem-solving rule may nonetheless differ in how adequately they attend to or encode the critical features of the problem situation. He might then be able to show that the subject who encoded these features better will progress more quickly and easily to the next higher problem-solving rule in the sequence. He might then further show that the other subject will similarly progress once taught to encode more adequately. Siegler's immediate goal in each study is to gain more precise and solid information about how development proceeds in the specific conceptual domain investigated. His ultimate and more ambitious goal is to use his research findings from a variety of domains to draw general conclusions about the nature and development of the human cognitive system.

Let us now examine Siegler's rule-assessment approach more concretely and specifically. In one series of investigations, children of different ages were presented with a simple balance scale that had four equally spaced pegs on each side of the fulcrum (Siegler, 1976, 1978), a device similar to one used by Inhelder and Piaget (1958) in a study of formal operational thinking. The arm of the scale could fall down to the left or right, or remain horizontal and balanced, depending on the number and distribution of equal-sized weights that were placed on the pegs. Weights were never placed on more than one peg on a side on each trial, to simplify the problem. The subjects' task was to predict which, if either, of the two sides would go down if a lever that kept the scale from moving were released.

Siegler hypothesized that the knowledge children of different ages would have about the balance scale could be represented as four developmentally ordered, increasingly complex rules. The simplest and earliest-acquired rule, Rule I, takes into account only the number of weights (thus, the total weight) on each side of the fulcrum. If the number of weights is the same on both sides, Rule I users always predict that the scale will balance; and if the number of weights is greater on one side, that side is always predicted to go down. Rule I subjects completely ignore the distances the weights are from the fulcrum on each side. Subjects who follow Rule II also predict solely on the basis of which side has the greater number of weights, except when the number is equal on both sides. When that happens, and only then, the distances from the fulcrum are correctly taken into account. That is, Rule II subjects predict balance if the two distances are equal. If they are not equal, these subjects predict the descent of whichever arm has its weight located farthest from the fulcrum. In contrast, subjects who follow Rule III always try to consider both weight and distance equally in making their decisions. If both dimensions are equal on both sides, balance is predicted. If one dimension is equal and the other not, the decision is based on that other dimension. For instance, if the weights are equal but the distances are not, the subject predicts that the side with the weights farthest out will go down. And, of course, if both are unequal and favor the descent of the same side, that side will be predicted to go down; thus, if one side both has more weights than the other and also has them placed on a peg that is farther from the fulcrum, that side will be judged to go down. However, if both dimensions are unequal but favor the descent of different sides, Rule III subjects have no recourse but to guess. For example, Rule III subjects do not know what to predict if the left side has three weights situated two pegs out from the fulcrum and the right side has two weights situated four pegs out. They just have to guess—"muddle through," as Siegler puts it. Finally, Rule IV subjects know how to compute the torques on each side. That is, they multiply the distance (expressed as the number of pegs out from fulcrum) by the number of weights placed at that distance, and correctly predict that the side with greater product (torque) will tip down. In the problem just mentioned, for instance, they would correctly predict that the right side would go down ($2 \times 4 = 8$) and the left side would go up ($3 \times 2 = 6$).

Siegler tested for the presence of these four rules in subjects' thinking by presenting them with the following six types of problems:

1. Balance problems, with the same configuration of weights on pegs on each side of the fulcrum.
2. Weight problems, with unequal amounts of weight equidistant from the fulcrum.
3. Distance problems, with equal amounts of weight different distances from the fulcrum.
4. Conflict-weight problems, with more weight on one side and more "distance" (i.e., occupied pegs farther from the fulcrum) on the other, and the configuration arranged so that the side with more weight goes down.
5. Conflict-distance problems, similar to conflict-weight except that the side with greater distance goes down.

6. Conflict-balance problems, like other conflict problems, except that the scale remains balanced (Siegler, 1978, p. 114).

Table 4-1 shows how a user of each rule would be predicted to behave on each of the six types of tasks. For example, it shows that Rule I children should be correct only on problems for which attending to weight alone happens to yield the right answer—namely, those problems in which weights and torques always correspond (balance, weight, and conflict-weight problems). In contrast, users of Rule III should be correct on all problems in which the weights and distances do not conflict or suggest different answers but they should be reduced to chance responding (33 percent) on all problems in which they do conflict. Notice that inferences about rule use are based on the subject's *pattern* of responding over the entire *set* of problem types, rather than on how any single problem is handled, because it is only the pattern as a whole that discriminates among the four rules. Notice also that Siegler's model predicts that more cognitively advanced (Rule III) subjects will actually do *worse* than less advanced (Rules I and II) subjects on conflict-weight problems—not the usual "older-children-do-better" developmental prediction.

How well does the rule model fit subjects' response patterns across this set of different scale-balance problems? Very well indeed, it turns out. In one of Siegler's studies (1976), 120 children of ages 5, 9, 13, and 17 years were given the just-described set of problems. Of these 120, fully 107 (89 percent) consistently responded in accord with one of the four rules: twenty-nine used Rule I, twenty-two Rule II, forty-eight Rule III, and eight Rule IV. Children's verbal descriptions of how they solved the problems were also highly consistent with their response patterns, and thus provided additional corroborating evidence that the children were using Siegler's rules. All the 5 year olds who could be classified as rule users employed Rule I. Most of the older children used one of the other three rules; among these older subjects there

TABLE 4-1   Predictions for Percentage of Correct Answers and Error Patterns for Subjects Using Different Rules

	RULE				COMMENT
Problem Type	*I*	*II*	*III*	*IV*	
Balance	100	100	100	100	
Weight	100	100	100	100	
Distance	0	100	100	100	Rule I predicts "balance"
Conflict-Weight	100	100	33	100	Rule III performance at chance (33%)
Conflict-Distance	0	0	33	100	Rules I and II fail to take into account greater effect of distance than weight; Rule III performance at chance
Conflict-Balance	0	0	33	100	Same comments as Conflict-Distance

From Sternberg, R. J., & Powell, J. S. The development of intelligence. In J. H. Flavell & E. M. Markman (Eds.), *Handbook of child psychology: Cognitive development* (Vol. 3), p. 387. Copyright © 1983 by John Wiley & Sons, Inc. Reprinted by permission of John Wiley & Sons, Inc.

was also a slight increase with age in the tendency to use more advanced Rules III and IV. In a similar study using 3 to 5 year olds, Siegler (1978) found that almost all of the 5 year olds used Rule I, about half the 4 year olds did, and almost none of the 3 year olds did. Moreover, the younger children who did not employ Rule I seemed not to be using any consistent rule, rather than to be using some other, alternative rule.

Siegler (1978, 1981) has applied his rule-assessment approach to a wide variety of other Piagetian problem-solving tasks, with generally similar results. That is, a small set of rules closely analogous to those just described nicely models the performance of children of age 5 and older on many tasks; 3 year olds typically show no evidence of consistent rule use on any task. These results led Siegler to the interesting hypothesis that the development of scientific reasoning in children may be roughly divisible into two phases: one prior to about age 5, during which children develop from nonrule-governed to rule-governed approaches to problems, and the other from about age 5 to adulthood, during which increasingly sophisticated rules are employed (Siegler, 1978, p. 147).

Siegler (1976) has also shown that children who use the same rule in a problem area may still differ cognitively from one another in ways that affect their subsequent learning and development in that area. For example, Siegler found that groups of 5 year olds and 8 year olds, both of whom consistently used Rule I on scale-balance problems at the beginning of the experiment, nevertheless differed in how much they profited from additional experience with conflict-distance and conflict-weight problems—that is, the 8 year olds advanced to the use of Rules II or III following this additional experience, whereas the 5 year olds continued to use Rule I. Subsequent research suggested an explanation for this age difference in responsiveness to a learning opportunity: The younger children were encoding the distance dimension less adequately than were the older ones; they were not attending to it and storing it in memory as well. For instance, Siegler showed that the younger children were less likely than the older ones to notice and remember how far out on each side the weights were placed on any given problem. Once 5 year olds had been trained to encode the distance dimension adequately, they too advanced in rule use following additional experience with conflict problems—that is, once their encoding problems were remedied, they benefited from the same learning experience that had previously benefited only 8 year olds. This strongly suggests that inadequate encoding had been at least the proximate cause of their inability to learn. Siegler has also found a similar close relation between encoding adequacy and ability to learn at other developmental levels and on other kinds of problems. For example, 4 year olds spontaneously encode weight more adequately than 3 year olds do. Similarly, they acquire Rule I when given appropriate experience, whereas 3 year olds do not. However, 3 year olds can also learn Rule I if first trained to encode weight adequately (Siegler, 1978).

As was stated earlier, Siegler's ultimate objective is to use the specific research findings generated by his rule-assessment approach as a basis for making broader generalizations about the nature and development of the human cognitive system. The following illustrate the sorts of generalizations Siegler's research has suggested so far (Siegler, 1978, 1981, 1983a, 1983b):

1. Children's cognitive performance on a variety of tasks and at a variety of age levels appears to follow rule-like patterns. Their grasp of many concepts progresses through a sequence of qualitatively distinct rules, such as the four described previously in connection with the scale-balance task.

2. For any given concept, later-developing rules are more highly correlated than earlier-developing ones with the correct rule in their predictions over the whole range of tasks testing for that concept. A rule that more often makes the same prediction that the most advanced rule does will be acquired later than one that makes the same prediction less often. In the case of scale-balance problems, for instance, later-developing Rule III will lead to the same prediction as Rule IV more often than earlier-developing Rule I will, over the entire range of these problems.

3. There is more similarity in reasoning across concepts when children (or adults) have relatively little knowledge about the concepts than when they have more. When they have little knowledge, they may rely on more general, all-purpose rules—Siegler calls them "fall-back rules." On the balance-scale problem, for example, 5 year olds act as if they are following a general, fall-back rule that says one should reason and predict only on the basis of the most salient or important-seeming dimension present—in this case, the weight dimension. Siegler and others have found that children of this age also tend to respond in a similarly "unidimensional" manner in other conceptual areas where they lack sufficient knowledge, such as Piagetian conservation tasks (Siegler, 1981, 1983a). When their knowledge increases, however, the rules they evolve will increasingly conform to the structure and demands of the conceptual area and therefore are likely to be different for different areas. Expressed in Piaget's terminology, Siegler's argument seems to be that when children know little about a concept area they will assimilate it to very general, all-purpose rules. As they learn more about its particularities their rules will increasingly accommodate to these particularities. As mentioned earlier, Siegler further believes that very young children may not even use general fall-back rules when dealing with many problems—that is, the very tendency to approach problems in any sort of consistent, systematic, rule-governed fashion is itself an important product of development.

4. Limited encoding can be an important obstacle to developmental progress. As we have seen in the case of the scale-balance problem, children who do not adequately encode a relevant stimulus dimension may not profit from experiences designed to help them acquire more advanced rules that properly take that dimension into account. Improved encoding leads to improved ability to learn and thus could be considered a mechanism of cognitive development.

Like all theoretical approaches, Siegler's has its problems and limitations and is subject to criticism (Siegler, 1983b; Strauss & Levin, 1981; Wilkening & Anderson, 1980). Perhaps the most important question about it is how much of a person's knowledge and thinking can be adequately expressed or captured in rules, whether of the type Siegler posits or of any other type. Whatever the final verdict will be on his rule-assessment method and the generalizations about intellectual development it has spawned, Siegler's work represents an interesting and well-articulated example of recent information-processing approaches to cognitive growth.

PROBLEMS IN DEMONSTRATING FUNDAMENTAL
DEVELOPMENTAL CHANGES IN THE HUMAN
COGNITIVE SYSTEM
DURING THE POSTINFANCY YEARS

Let us now return to the question with which we began this chapter: Exactly how do the minds of older children, adolescents, and adults differ from those of young children? Although other developmental psychologists would undoubtedly disagree with me, I think a good case could be made for Piaget's claim that infants have cognitive systems that are fundamentally different in some ways from those of older humans, including very young children. In particular, a cognitive system that uses symbols just seems on that account alone to be radically, drastically, qualitatively different from one that does not and cannot. So great is the difference that the transformation of one system into the other during the first 2 years of life still seems nothing short of miraculous to me, no matter how much we learn about it.

Are subsequent changes that basic, that fundamental? Do they also seem nothing short of miraculous, or do they rather seem something short of miraculous, although no doubt still considerable? Piaget thought they were very fundamental indeed, as did other major developmental theorists like Vygotsky and Werner. In Piaget's theory, for instance, the sensory-motor period of infancy is only the first of several major qualitatively distinct stages in the ontogeny of the human mind. Not only is the infant's cognitive system portrayed as radically and qualitatively different from the young child's, but differences of a similarly dramatic and qualitative nature are also said to hold between the young child's and the older child's system, and again between the older child's and the adolescent's. However, there is growing doubt in the field as to whether postinfancy age changes in people's cognitive systems are as fundamental, momentous, qualitative, and stage-like as Piaget and others believed (see Flavell, 1982a, 1982b). Some of the reasons for these doubts can be made clear if we consider what typically happens when people acquire a great deal of knowledge, skill, and general expertise in some specific conceptual domain (e.g., Carey, 1982; Chi, Glaser, & Rees, 1982).

As children grow older and accumulate learning experiences, they gradually change from being novices to experts or near-experts in many conceptual domains. What effects does becoming experts in a domain tend to have on the nature and quality of their cognitions in that domain? Recent research suggests that these effects can be surprisingly powerful and pervasive. Becoming an expert in a domain can greatly increase a person's cognitive capacities and skills when dealing with problems in that domain. All the relevant concepts and the words that refer to these concepts are highly familiar and well learned. The problems the person encounters in the domain are also apt to be highly familiar and therefore can be rapidly recognized and represented as belonging to one of a limited set of well-understood problem types (Chi, Feltovich, & Glaser, 1981).

When concepts, technical terms, problem patterns, and other domain-specific data are highly familiar, they require less time and mental energy to process. This in turn means that more of them can be attended to or held in working memory at one time, effectively increasing the person's attentional or short-term-memory capacity. This increase in capacity has at least two beneficial effects. First, since more units of information can be held in focal attention or working memory at the same time, more of them can be compared and related to one another. As Siegler's scale-balance problems illustrated, complex tasks often demand the active interrelating of a number of dimensions or other pieces of information. Second, this functional increase in information-processing capacity creates some unused mental work space or mental energy that can be devoted to higher level, "executive" or "metacognitive" processing. The person has some capacity left over for selecting problem-solving strategies, for regulating their activity, for monitoring their effectiveness, and for other vital managerial activities. The fact that the expert can quickly and automatically recognize different problems as belonging to familiar, frequently encountered types also means that he or she is likely to know what solution strategies to try and to be able to use these strategies efficiently and effectively (Larkin, 1981). Unlike the 5 year old in Siegler's studies, our expert does not have to resort to simple "fall-back rules" which are not closely tailored to the specific requirements of a specific problem type.

The evidence is beginning to suggest, then, that having a great deal of knowledge and experience in an area has all sorts of positive, beneficial effects on the quality of one's cognitive functioning in that area. Unlike the novice, the expert attends to and keeps in mind all the right features of the problem situation (Siegler's "adequate encoding"), selects the right problem strategies and uses them in the right ways, and generally engages in sustained feats of reasoning that appear highly logical in quality. In short, the expert looks very, very smart—very, very "cognitively mature"—when functioning in her area of expertise.

If, as is often the case (Brown & DeLoache, 1978), the novice in any given domain is a young child and the expert is an older child or adult, what may we be led to conclude? We may think we are witnessing a fundamental developmental shift of the infancy-postinfancy variety. It may appear that the younger novice and the older expert are in qualitatively different stages of intellectual development and that we are dealing with two very different cognitive machines. However, several considerations may lead us to temper that judgment. The older person may appear to be a much less mature and logical thinker when operating in domains in which she lacks expertise. Both everyday observation and a good deal of recent research (Nisbett & Ross, 1980; Shaklee, 1979) attest to the fact that even highly intelligent and well-educated adults often fail to process information adequately and to think rationally and logically. Even if it is in her area of expertise, a particularly complex and difficult problem might at least temporarily overtax an older person's information-processing system and thus greatly diminish the quality of her reasoning and problem-solving activity on that problem.

Conversely, a young child may show cognition of distinctly better quality in those few domains in which he has already achieved some expertise.

Even in domains in which he is a relative novice, he may at least show glimmerings of good thinking, especially on very easy problems. We can usually make a problem easier for a young child by (1) stripping away all but the most essential elements of the problem; and (2) making the problem setting and problem elements as familiar and meaningful to the child as possible (Brown, Bransford, Ferrara, & Campione, 1983). Both procedures reduce the information-processing demands the problem makes on the child or, which amounts to the same thing, increase the child's capacity to process information effectively. Recall from Chapter 3 that recent research has demonstrated unexpected competencies in young children. These competencies have usually surfaced only in task situations made easier by these procedures.

If the cognitive differences between young children and their elders proved to be largely due to differences in knowledge, we would hesitate to speak of qualitatively different "stages" of cognitive development. First, "differences in knowledge" has more of a quantitative than qualitative sound to it. It suggests one kind of mind with two different amounts of accumulated knowledge rather than two basically different kinds of mind. It does not suggest a fundamentally different intellectual modus operandi, as is at least arguably the case for the infant as contrasted with the child and adult. Second, neither younger children nor their elders would be completely and consistently "in" any single stage, in the strong sense of always functioning cognitively in the general manner and at the general level specified by that stage (Flavell, 1982a, 1982b). In domains in which they have considerable knowledge, both age groups would perform above their usual levels. In domains in which their knowledge is skimpy or nonexistent, they would perform below those levels—sometimes well below. Neither group would be consistently enough like itself, nor consistently enough unlike the other group, to warrant a sharp division into two different "stages." The recent trend in the field has been to highlight the cognitive competencies of young children (see Chapter 3), the cognitive shortcomings of adults, and the cognitive inconsistencies of both, effectively pushing from both ends of childhood towards the middle and blurring the difference between the two groups (Siegler, 1979a).

Does all the foregoing mean that cognitive development in the postinfancy years is definitely not stage-like in any meaningful sense? Does it also mean that we cannot identify any important cognitive-developmental changes that take place during this period? I believe that the answer to both questions is no. It is true that the concept of stage in general and Piaget's stages in particular have come under heavy fire in recent years (e.g., Brainerd, 1978a, 1978b; Flavell, 1971c, 1982b). Nevertheless, the issue remains controversial and some still continue to believe that a viable stage theory of cognitive growth may yet be possible (Case, 1981, 1985; Flavell, 1982a; Halford & Wilson, 1980). Furthermore, it is very far from certain at present that all important postinfancy developmental changes can be explained by appeal to age increases in domain-specific knowledge (Markman, 1979). As to the second question, we certainly can identify some very important and substantial changes in thinking and knowledge that typically occur during the middle childhood and adolescent years; the task of the rest of this chapter is to describe such developmental trends. The main purpose of the present section was to suggest why the conservative term *trends* seems to be a more realistic descriptor than the more radical term *stages*, at least until some future Piaget can convince us that postinfancy developmental changes in the cognitive system are as truly fundamental and deep-lying as those that take place between early infancy and early childhood.

DEVELOPMENTAL TRENDS DURING MIDDLE CHILDHOOD AND ADOLESCENCE

As you will surely guess, there exists no "official list" of such trends that all developmentalists know and upon which all developmentalists agree. The set of trends presented here is simply my best try, based on the presently available evidence and some educated intuitions. For an interesting alternative set, see Sternberg and Powell (1983).

Information-Processing Capacity

As already indicated, the human cognitive system is known to have significant limitations on its information-processing capacity: Each processing step requires a certain amount of time and cognitive resources for its execution; only a small number of units or "chunks" of information can be kept active in working memory at once, and so forth. An awareness of these limitations is one of the most important legacies of the information-processing approach to the study of cognition. A number of developmental psychologists have argued that these limitations are even more severe in children than adults, that there is a gradual increase with age in processing capacity, and that this increase makes possible more complex and higher-order forms of cognition. This argument has been presented and critically examined in many publications (e.g., Case, 1978, 1985; Chi, 1978; Chi & Rees, 1983; Dempster, 1981; Fischer, 1980; Fischer & Bullock, 1981; Flavell, 1978a, 1982a; Halford & Wilson, 1980; McLaughlin, 1963; Pascual-Leone, 1970; Scardamalia, 1977; Siegler, 1983b; Trabasso & Foellinger, 1978). The general idea is that below a certain age children may find it difficult or impossible to engage in certain types of mental activity, acquire concepts of a certain level of complexity, and the like; the reason is that doing so would require them to attend to and cognitively interrelate more pieces of information than their working-memory capacities can handle. As capacity gradually increases with increasing age, such interrelating of information becomes possible and cognitive growth can occur. Pascual-Leone (1970) has explicitly tied this idea of a growing processing capacity to Piaget's stage theory of development, claiming that an increase in capacity is a necessary precondition for developmental movement to the next higher Piagetian stage. For example, Pascual-Leone argues that the developmental transition from the late preoperational stage to the early concrete-operational stage requires an increase of one information chunk or "scheme" in the child's working memory capacity or "central computing space"; until the child's capacity increases by that one unit, the transition cannot be made. Others have also conceptualized cognitive development as basically stage-like in nature, with the transitions from stage to stage dependent upon increases with age in the child's information-processing capacity (Case, 1978, 1985; Halford & Wilson, 1980; McLaughlin, 1963).

This general position raises several questions, some easier to answer than others. One that is easy to answer is whether the quality of a person's cognitive performance on a task can in fact be strongly affected by the task's information-processing capacity requirements. As already indicated, it certainly can be. If the task demands overload one's working memory or overtax one's attentional capacity, the result is very likely to be a lower level of intellectual performance on that task (e.g., Baddeley & Hitch, 1974; Hunt, 1978). Another easy question is whether performance on conventional tests of short-term memory improves with age. The answer is that it clearly does. For example, consider the digit-span task, a well-known procedure for estimating a person's short-term-memory capacity. If I were to administer this test to you, I would read aloud a random sequence of digits at the rate of one per second. Your task would then be to reproduce that sequence exactly, just as soon as I stopped reciting it. I might begin, for instance, with "4-9-1-2," and you would immediately respond "4912." I would then try a five digit series, then a six-digit one, and so on, until you reached your limit, traditionally referred to as your *memory span* for this kind of input. Performance on this and other memory-span tasks definitely improves with age during childhood. For instance, a 4 year old is likely to have a digit span of about three or four, a 12 year old one of about six or seven.

Other questions are harder to answer. Precisely what should we take "processing capacity" to mean in this context? What is it, exactly, that improves or increases with age? There are two possibilities. To illustrate them by a rough analogy, consider the case of a physical capacity, such as muscular strength. Obviously, two people could differ in "raw muscle power" as evidenced, for example, by how hard they could push or squeeze something. We could say that the person with more raw muscular strength had more *structural* physical-strength capacity than the other. However, two people with identical structural physical-strength capacities might nevertheless differ considerably in their *functional* (usable, actual, effective) capacities in specific physical tasks. Experts at karate, boxing, wrestling, shotputting, weightlifting, golf, and the like can deploy and exploit their structural capacities far more fully and effectively in their areas of skill than can physically identical nonexperts. They know how to deliver the maximum force possible at precisely the right moment and place and can thereby get considerably more mileage (functional capacity) than nonexperts can out of a fixed and limited physical potential (structural capacity).

A similar distinction between structural and functional capacity can be made in the area of mental activity (Case, 1978). Psychologists have conceptualized structural or "raw" information-processing capacity in several different ways (Dempster, 1981; Siegler, 1983b). For example, it often used to be thought of as akin to the number of "slots" in a person's short-term or working memory "box." The more slots the box has, the more processing capacity the person has. It is more commonly conceptualized nowadays as the amount of attentional energy the individual has available for information processing over any brief span of time. The analogy between physical and cognitive capacity holds best for this more current, attentional-energy conceptualization. Here, structural capacity would refer to your total reservoir of potentially available attentional energy—how much "raw attentional muscle power" you have, so to speak. In contrast, functional capacity would mean how skillfully and effectively you can deploy that reservoir. It would mean how much and how well you can do with what you have.

What could one do to increase one's functional information-processing capacity without increasing structural capacity? Several possibilities have been suggested (e.g., Brown et al., 1983; Case, 1978; Chi, 1978; Dempster, 1981). One possibility would be to find a way to expend less attentional energy on each processing step. A processing step could be any sort of basic cognitive operation: encoding or recognizing an item, comparing it with another item, storing it in memory, retrieving it from memory in order to process it further, and so on. One way to expend less attentional energy per step would be to execute each step more rapidly. If each step could be performed more quickly, then more steps could be performed per unit time. That would amount to an increase in functional capacity, because it would allow the individual to keep more items or processes "alive" in active, working memory at once. In fact, research evidence does suggest that an increase in functional capacity can be achieved by increasing processing speed. The evidence shows that people have larger memory spans for items that they can identify more rapidly, when speed of naming is used as a measure of speed of identification. For example, digits can usually be named (identified) more quickly than words, and one's memory span for digits is usually larger than one's memory span for words (Dempster, 1981). In general, there seems to be a consistent positive correlation between span, an index of functional capacity, and speed of processing, an index of attentional expenditure: The faster the processing, the greater the span (Case, Kurland, & Goldberg, 1982; Chi & Gallagher, in press; Dempster, 1981). But how can speed of processing be increased? Through practice and experience. Items can be identified or otherwise processed with greater rapidity as they become highly familiar. Similarly, operations that are highly practiced can be performed quickly and with little expenditure of attention; in fact, some have claimed that operations can become so overlearned and automatic that they require virtually no attentional outlay at all (Shiffrin & Schneider, 1977).

Let me now reprise the structure of this argument, but this time in reverse order. Operations can be performed more rapidly and with less expenditure of attention after they become highly practiced and the items on which they operate become overlearned and highly familiar. When opera tions can be performed more rapidly, then more can be executed per u time. Thus, more can be "on stage" at once in one's attentional fie cognitive workspace, which amounts to an increase in one's fun information-processing capacity.

It is also possible to increase functional capacity without structural capacity through the use of information-processing other high-level, "executive" maneuvers (e.g., Brown et al., 1 Siegler, 1983b). One such maneuver would be to allocate o limited attentional resources over items and operations in task-adaptive fashion. On a memory-span task, for deliberately rehearse previous items in the series whil of the next one. Or one might correctly sense that one item needs more atten-tion than another in order to be recalled, understood, or whatever the task calls for, and therefore allocate more attention to that item. Like skilled athletes, skilled information processors deploy their limited resources in effi-cient, "cost-effective" fashions.

Still another method of amplifying functional capacity without changing structural capacity is to make judicious use of external attentional and mnemonic aids, such as pencil and paper, libraries, computers, and other people's minds (Flavell, 1982a; Flavell & Wellman, 1977; Larkin, McDermott, Simon, & Simon, 1980). The skillful use of such external aids or "mental prostheses" can greatly increase the amount of information and information processing an individual can manage per unit time. There is a physical-capacity analogue here also, although it is a bit absurd: An athlete could lift much heavier weights than his structural capacity permits by enlisting the aid of his friends or, better still, by using a crane.

What, then, increases with age during childhood? Structural capacity, functional capacity, or both? It seems certain that at least functional capacity increases with age, by the three means described previously: (1) Many opera-tions undoubtedly become faster or otherwise less capacity-consuming in the course of years of practice, experience, and accumulation of knowledge; (2) children do gradually acquire a variety of strategies for intelligently deploying and allocating the limited capacities they have; (3) they also gradually learn how to supplement internal capacity with external aids to processing. However, the everpresent possibility that these factors may be at work in any task situation makes it very difficult to find out whether structural capacity also increases with age. On any given task in which older children behave as if they command more information-processing capacity than younger children, it is hard to be sure that functional-capacity factors like processing speed and strategy use are not the sole causes. In other words, it is possible that there is in fact little or no maturationally based increase with age in structural, "hard-wired" capacity and that the apparent increases that we see are produced by the sorts of knowledge- and experienced-based functional-capacity changes just discussed. Thus, the question of whether structural capacity also increases with age simply cannot be answered one way or the other on present evidence (Dempster, 1981; Siegler, 1983b). Whatever its causes, however, age increases in children's effective, usable information-processing capacities appear to constitute a very important, "core" developmental trend during the postinfancy years.

Domain-Specific Knowledge

Another important developmental trend during childhood and adoles-cence is the acquisition of a great deal of knowledge and skill in many specific areas or domains. As indicated earlier in this chapter (pp. 82–84), in the course of years of learning and experience children gradually change from being novices to being experts or near-experts in a wide variety of domains. The view that at least a good deal of human cognitive growth might be conceptualized as the gradual acquisition of expertise in many specific domains is currently receiving considerable attention in the field of cognitive development, thanks to the efforts of Michelene Chi and others (e.g., Carey, 1982; Chi et al., 1981; Chi & Glaser, 1980; Chi et al., 1982; Larkin, 1981; Simon & Simon, 1978). It may seem puzzling to you that this trite-sounding view could be regarded as either new or interesting. Surely, the idea that cognitive development might consist largely of the accumulation of knowledge would not surprise many psychologists past or present; I also cannot imagine my grandmother being exactly bowled over by it either, for that matter. It just sounds like common-sensical, layperson-type developmental theory, if anything does.

However, there is a good reason why the present incarnation of this old developmental saw deserves our serious attention (cf. Markman, 1979). The reason is that its proponents are doing more than just affirming it as a possible alternative to Piagetian-type stage theories (pp. 82–85). They are also painstakingly trying to build up, through careful research, a precise and detailed picture of exactly what the acquisition of expertise in a domain does to and for our heads—that is, they are trying to discover everything that the acquisition of domain-specific knowledge does to the nature of our problem-solving and other information-processing activities in that domain. The search has only recently begun and there is naturally a great deal that we still do not know about the cognitive consequences of knowledge acquisition.

Much of the research in this area has examined cognitive differences between adult novices and experts in the domain of elementary physics, a richly structured area of knowledge. Consequently, most of the concrete examples cited here are from that domain. Chi and Glaser (1980) have recently summarized some important differences between novices and experts in physics. They begin by making a rough distinction between two components of human information processing: (1) a knowledge structure or content component that can be conceptualized as a network of concepts and relations; and (2) a set of processes or strategies for performing a sequence of cognitive actions on the content.

Chi and Glaser then identify several novice-expert differences within the knowledge structure or content component. First and most obvious, the expert simply knows more different domain-specific concepts than the novice does. In the domain of physics, for example, whereas the novice might be able to define and recognize a few concepts such as mass, density, and acceleration, the expert also commands many others (e.g., force, momentum, coefficient of friction). In addition, the expert's stored representation of each concept is apt to be richer than the novice's, in that it contains more conceptual relations and features. For the novice, mass may only be represented as related to the concepts of weight and density. In contrast, the expert's mental representation of mass may additionally include acceleration, force, and other related concepts. This means that each of the expert's concepts is closely connected in long-term memory with many other concepts. As a consequence, there are multiple routes from each concept to each other concept in the expert's stored conceptual network; we might say that each concept is multiply cross-referenced in the expert's mental dictionary of physics concepts. This greater density of interconcept links in the expert's conceptual network in turn means that the probability is higher of any one concept's evoking other, related concepts—that is, thinking of one concept is more likely, in the expert's case, to cue the retrieval from memory of related concepts and concept features. Consistent with this claim is Larkin's (1979) finding that an expert in physics is more likely than a novice to recall small groups of conceptually related equations in rapid bursts, with pauses in between groups, as if related equations were stored together as chunks in the expert's long-term memory.

Chi and Glaser (1980) also describe differences between novices and experts in the cognitive processes or strategies they use in solving problems (component 2 earlier). For example, experts are apt to be more planful. They are more likely to analyze and categorize a problem before attempting to solve it. This initial processing may then provide the expert with an effective plan of action to execute in the actual solution of the problem. Here also, the expert's vast and richly organized memory store of knowledge gives him many advantages over the novice. For instance, a very effective way to solve a new problem is to notice its similarity to some other problem that one already knows how to solve. The noticing is a matter of memory (recognition memory) and so is the knowing how to solve it (stored procedural knowledge). Obviously, this "memory method" of solving problems can be used much more often by the expert than by the novice because the expert has traces of many more previously solved problems stored in long-term memory.

This example illustrates a significant point about how experts differ from novices. We usually think of the expert as the more able reasoner of the two, as the one who is more capable of extended chains of complex inferences or judgments (within his area of expertise). Although this is undoubtedly true, it is also true that the experts often solve problems by quick and easy remembering that novices must try to solve by slow and laborious reasoning. In such instances, the expert appears more cognitively mature and sophisticated than the novice because his mental processing is so fast, effortless, and effective. In reality, however, his processing may have been more "mnemonic" than "rational" in nature, more a matter of recognition and recall memory than of complex reasoning and fancy mental computation. And, of course, the expert's processing was not fast, effortless, and effective *despite* the fact that it involved "mere remembering" rather than "sophisticated ratiocination." Rather, it had these qualities precisely *because* of this fact—that is, because it involved the relatively automatic processes of detection of familiar problem patterns and execution of overlearned solution procedures. It normally takes many years for a person to become expert in any complex domain. During that extended period the person may gradually acquire the ability to recognize and respond adaptively to a surprisingly large number of domain-relevant problem patterns. For example, the work of Herbert Simon and his colleagues suggests that chess experts have learned to recognize and react appropriately to some 50,000 chessboard patterns (Anderson, 1980). Thus, if one benefit of expertise is the ability to think better in the area of one's expertise, another is the ability to solve many problems in that area without having to think much at all. As Anderson describes it:

> To become an expert in any problem-solving field requires years of study. The effect of this study is to transform solution by creative problem solving into

solution by the simple retrieval of stored answers. One becomes an expert by making routine many aspects of a problem that require creative problem solving for novices. Thus, one's behavior is less error prone and more attention can be focused on those aspects of the problem that cannot be routinized (Anderson, 1980, p. 292).

In what domains are children and adolescents likely to build up complex knowledge structures through years of experience and learning? The physics example makes us think first of those domains in which they receive extensive formal schooling. In this vein, Carey (1982) has recently shown that major changes in the content and structure of children's biological knowledge take place between the ages of 4 and 10 years. Piaget and others had observed that young children tend to attribute the properties of life and consciousness to certain nonliving things, especially things that are capable of autonomous movement (e.g., Flavell, 1963, pp. 280–283). For example, they might say that a fire is "alive." Piaget referred to this tendency as *animism* and believed that it reflected an early developmental stage of thinking. However, Carey (1982) argued that "alive" is a theoretical term in biology and adduced evidence suggesting that young children's animistic responses reflect a lack of domain specific (i.e., biological) knowledge rather than a more general, stage-type level of cognitive ability.

Many other candidate domains are also less closely associated with formal education. As examples, children gradually build up elaborate knowledge structures through countless hours of experience and practice with various sports, games, hobbies, all sorts of cultural artifacts and institutions, and numerous forms of social interaction and exchange. In later years they will similarly build up knowledge structures in the occupational domains they enter. The social-interaction example implies that the development of social as well as nonsocial cognition can be conceptualized in terms of domain-specific knowledge acquisition. As in the domains of physics, chess, and so on, a vast store of organized social knowledge allows us to recognize and respond appropriately to a very large number of specific patterns of input from our everyday "social chessboard." This memory-based pattern-recognition process often allows us to behave reasonably in many complex social situations without benefit of much, if any, complex social reasoning (cf. Higgins, 1981; Shantz, 1983). Thus, in all the many and different domains in which the growing individual may acquire at least some measure of expertise, this expertise makes possible high-level, developmentally mature-looking cognitive performance. In some cases, complex and sophisticated reasoning, inferences, or other forms of mental computation may produce this high-level performance. In other cases, however, the performance may be largely mediated by more automatic, memory-based processes.

At this point the reader may wonder if there is anything more to post-infancy cognitive development than the acquisition of knowledge in many specific domains. Many cognitive developmentalists are currently wondering the same thing, and the issue is far from settled (see Carey, 1982, for a thought-provoking discussion of this question). My own intuitions are that the acquisition-of-expertise model will *not* account for all of cognitive growth. My reasons are similar to those given by Ellen Markman:

It is an important alternative to stage theory to postulate that growth in expertise is the only major change and then to see how much that can explain. Can striking developmental differences such as children's limited memory spans, their failure to use strategies, their ineffective problem-solving skills, and their inability to sustain attention be explained by growth in knowledge? Already, there are some empirical studies and plausible arguments that suggest expertise may go a long way in accounting for these differences. Yet it is hard to believe that this can be all there is. Are novice adults really tantamount to children? Imagine adults confronted with a new situation, bewildered by the novelty. It seems likely that their attempts to acquire relevant information, their search for clarification, in fact, even their sensitivity to and analysis of their confusion will differ dramatically from a child's. So when this line of argument is pushed as far as it can go, I suspect that important developmental differences will persist that cannot be explained by expertise. At that point, we will have to reconsider the question and ask what else develops (Markman, 1979, p. 964).

Concrete and Formal Operations

Piaget's theory postulates the following sequence of major stages or periods of cognitive development: (1) the sensory-motor period of infancy; (2) the preoperational subperiod of early childhood, conceived as a period of preparation for concrete operations; (3) the concrete-operational period of middle childhood; (4) the formal-operational period of adolescence. Piaget's theoretical treatment of concrete-operational and formal-operational thinking was much more formal and abstract than that of sensory-motor cognition. In the former case, he constructed formal theoretical models which incorporated logical and mathematical concepts and structures. These models were intended to be rigorous and precise characterizations of the distinctive, stage-specific cognitive competencies of children and adolescents. For example, Piaget invented a formal structure called a *grouping* to model concrete-operational thinking. A grouping incorporates properties from two well-known mathematical structures, the *group* and the *lattice*. A Piagetian grouping is thus a kind of hybrid group-lattice structure.

An intelligible presentation of Piaget's formal models of middle-childhood and adolescent thinking would require too much space to be attempted here; detailed descriptions of them can be found in Brainerd (1978a), Brown and Desforges (1979), Ennis (1975), Flavell (1963), Keats, Collis, and Halford (1978), and Osherson (1974). These sources also provide the evidential basis for what seems to be a growing conclusion in the field concerning these models. The conclusion is that they are in varying degrees unclear, incorrect, and incomplete as theoretical descriptions of the thinking capabilities of children and adolescents:

> As to clarity, its [Piaget's theory's] stage-specific mental structures are often not clearly and consistently defined, and exactly what they are intended to refer to in children's actual cognitive abilities and activities is often obscure or uncertain. As to correctness, classical Piagetian tasks such as the various conservation problems may not necessarily or even frequently be solved by the operations that constitute Piagetian structures. As to completeness, the logic-like mental activities the theory postulates may play a more restricted and limited role in the child's overall mental life than the theory assumed. That is, Piagetian operations

may simply not be the basic, general, deep-lying, and all-pervasive "cardinal traits" of childhood thinking that the theory claimed they are. As the field of cognitive development has grown and extended its scope, developmentalists have identified new knowledge structures, processes, strategies, and the like in such areas as communication, comprehension, attention, and social cognition. In consequence, it is only natural and to be expected that the intellectual attainments described by Piaget will seem to account for progressively "less of the variance" in children's mental worlds as this proliferation of new cognitive acquisitions continues (Flavell, 1982a, pp. 2–3).

It is, of course, always possible that other mathematical models, different from Piaget's but of the same general type (e.g., Halford & Wilson, 1980; Keats et al., 1978), will prove to be more adequate theoretically.

Although Piaget's formal models of concrete and formal operations currently seem inadequate, some of his more informal generalizations about postinfancy cognitive growth seem very insightful and likely to prove at least roughly correct. Although these generalizations may not add up to a credible stage theory of development, they do at least constitute a highly interesting set of possible developmental trends. To communicate these trends more clearly I present them as two sets of contrasts: (1) contrasts between early-childhood and middle-childhood cognition; (2) contrasts between middle-childhood and adolescent-adult cognition. However, these should be thought of as rough age trends, not as sharp and clear contrasts among three entirely different and discontinuous mentalities. Also note that what follows is not a review of the vast research literature on concrete- and formal-operational thinking. Reviews of some of this literature can be found in Acredelo (1982), Beilin (1971), Braine and Rumain (1983), Brainerd (1978a), Dasen (1977), Flavell (1970a), Gelman and Baillargeon (1983), Keating (1980), Kuhn (1979), Neimark (1975), and Silverman and Rose (1982).

Contrasts between Early-Childhood and Middle-Childhood Cognition.

Perceived appearances versus inferred reality. Piaget's test for conservation of liquid quantity illustrates the meaning of this and the other contrasts: (1) The child first agrees that two identical glasses contain identical amounts of water; (2) the water from one glass is poured into a third, taller and thinner glass, with the child watching; (3) the child is then asked if the two amounts of water are still identical, or whether one glass now contains more water than the other. The typical preschool nonconserver is apt to conclude, after the liquid has been poured, that the taller and thinner glass now has more water in it than the other glass. Why? One reason is that it *looks* like it has more to her, and she is more given than the older child to make judgments about reality on the basis of the immediate, perceived *appearances* of things (Acredelo, 1982). More than her school-age counterpart, the preschool-age child is prone to accept things as they seem to be.

The middle-childhood conserver, on the other hand, may also think that the tall glass *looks* like it contains more water because the liquid column is higher, but she goes beyond mere appearances to *infer* from the available evidence that the two quantities *are really* still the same. That is, she makes an inference about underlying reality rather than merely translating perceived appearances into a quantity judgment. More generally, the older child seems to be more sensitive to the basic distinction between what seems to be and what really is—between the phenomenal or apparent and the real or true (see Chapter 3). Of course, this is not to suggest that young children never make inferences about unperceived states of affairs or that older children never base conclusions on superficial appearances. It is to suggest, however, that there does exist a rough age trend in this respect across this broad segment of childhood.

Centration versus decentration. The foregoing contrast emphasizes the younger child's heavy reliance on perceptual input when dealing with conceptual problems like Piaget's conservation-of-liquid-quantity task. But, of course, the older child also is carefully attending to the perceptual input throughout that task, even though he or she recognizes that the task ultimately calls for a conceptual rather than a perceptual judgment. Moreover, he is apt to be distributing that attention in a more flexible, balanced, and generally task-adaptive way than the younger child is. The preschooler is more prone to concentrate or *center* (hence, *centration*) his attention exclusively on some single feature or limited portion of the stimulus array that is particularly salient and interesting to him, thereby neglecting other task-relevant features. In the present example, the difference in the heights of the two liquid columns is what captures most of his attention (and "capture" often does seem the apposite word), with little note given to the compensatory difference in column widths.

In contrast, the older child is likelier to achieve a more balanced, "decentered" (hence, *decentration*) perceptual analysis of the entire display. While, of course, attending to the conspicuous height differences, just as the younger child does, he also carefully notes the correlative differences in container width. He therefore attains a broader and more inclusive purview of the stimulus field. He is likelier to notice and take due account of *all* the relevant perceptual data—in this case, the lesser width as well as the greater height of the new liquid column. Piaget (e.g., 1970b, p. 52) believed that the younger child's centration tendency often takes the form of relying heavily on *order* or *ordinal* information in making quantitative judgments. If one of two identical pencils is slid ahead of the other, for example, it is apt to be judged as longer than the first (nonconservation of length). Ordinal relationships like "ahead of," "first," "out in front," "*X* has passed *Y*," and so on, are very salient for the preoperational child and are often used inappropriately as the sole basis for quantitative comparison.

By using a special camera that records the child's eye movements during task solution, O'Bryan and Boersma (1971) have actually succeeded in measuring "live," ongoing patterns of visual centration and decentration in various conservation tasks. Their data lead them to conclude that:

> There seems little doubt that the nonconserver centrates on the dominant part of the visual display, and that the transitional S displays a type of dual centration on both parts, shifting infrequently between the two. By contrast, the conserver appears to have overcome the perceptual distortion presented by the transformed element in that she displays many shifts of fixation and seems completely decentered (O'Bryan & Boersma, 1971, pp. 167–168).

States versus transformations. The test of conservation of liquid quantity can be thought of as comprising two *states*, one initial and one final, plus a *transformation* or process of change that links these two states together. In the initial state, two identical glasses of water contain identical amounts of water. In the final state, two dissimilar glasses contain identical amounts of water (identical in "reality," if not in "appearance"). The transformation that links them together is, of course, the process of pouring water from one glass to another. The act of pouring is a dynamic event that changes, in the course of a brief time period, one static situation into another static situation; it is a transformational process that produces or creates a later state out of an earlier state.

Piaget made the profound observation that younger children, to a greater degree than older ones, tend to focus their attention and conceptual energies on states rather than on state-producing transformations, and also on present states more than on past or future ones. When solving problems of all sorts they are less likely to call to mind or keep in mind relevant previous states of the problem, or to anticipate pertinent future or potential ones. In particular, Piaget argued they are both undisposed and relatively unable to represent the actual, detailed processes of transition or transformation from one state to another. Thus, they exhibit a kind of "temporal centration" analogous to the spatial one just discussed. They center their attention on the present spatial field or stimulus state to the exclusion of other relevant states and state-linking transformations in the "temporal field," which consists of the recent past, the immediate present, and the near future. They do this just as, within the present spatial field itself, they center their attention on a single, privileged segment of that field. To put it more briefly and concretely, the preoperational subject tries to solve the conservation problem by attending only to the present stimulus field ("temporal centration") and, within it, only to selected, highly salient stimulus features ("spatial centration"). In contrast, the conserver is likely to make spontaneous reference to initial state and intervening transformation when asked to justify her conservation judgment. She might say that the two quantities had, after all, been identical at the outset (initial state), or that the experimenter had merely poured the water from one container to the other, and without spilling any or adding any (intervening transformation). The older child might even say that the continuing equality of amounts could be proved by pouring the liquid back into its original container (future or potential transformation, yielding new state equal to initial state). The conservation task is a conceptual problem rather than a perceptual one precisely *because* of the real or potential existence of such nonpresent states and transformations of states. The older child is more attuned to these background, not-now-perceptible factors and uses them in producing a conceptual solution to this and other, similar conceptual problems.

Irreversibility versus reversibility. According to Piaget the middle-childhood subject possesses *reversible* intellectual operations; his thought is said to exhibit the property of *reversibility*. Contrariwise, the preschool child's mental operations are *irreversible*, and his thought is said to show *irreversibility*. In the particular conservation problem we have been using as an example, the older child can exhibit reversibility of thought or reversible mental operations in two distinct ways.

On the one hand, he may recognize that the effect of the initial pouring of the water into the tall thin glass can be exactly and completely undone or negated by the inverse action of pouring the water back into its original container. The older child readily senses the possible existence of such an inverse, wholly nullifying action that changes everything back to its original state, and he may cite this possibility as a justification for his conservation judgment. A middle-childhood mind is more sensitive than an early-childhood one to the fact that many mental and physical operations have opposites that exactly—in a rigorous, precise, quantitative way—negate them, and thereby reset the whole situation to zero, so to speak.

On the other hand, the older child similarly recognizes that something equivalent to situation zero can also be achieved by an action that compensates for or counterbalances the effects of another action, rather than one that literally undoes it in the manner of the inverse or opposite action just described. For example, the child might justify his belief in conservation by pointing out that the increase in height of the liquid column which results from the pouring transformation is exactly offset or compensated for by the accompanying decrease in column width. According to this kind of reversible thinking, the column loses in width what it gains in height, and hence the quantity must remain the same. The width decrease obviously does not literally wipe out or annul the height increase, as actual repouring would. It has the same effect and cognitive significance (i.e., it provides a rational justification for a conservation verdict), but it does so by virtue of constituting an indirect compensation rather than a direct, literal negation. As with direct negation, the older child is more attuned than the younger one to the potential existence of such indirectly countervailing, compensation-type factors, and he better understands their utility in making rigorous quantitative inferences.

Other examples of these two forms of reversible thinking abound in Piagetiana. Recall that conservation of length can be assessed by first placing two identical pencils (sticks, rods) side by side so that their ends exactly coincide and then, after the child agrees that they are equal in length, sliding one a bit to the right, so that its end leads or is ahead of the other's end on that side. The younger child focuses "irreversibly" on this "transformation"-produced, immediately perceptible "state" of the sticks ("temporal centration") and, within that state, equally irreversibly "centers" his attention on the right-hand portions of the sticks ("spatial centration"); mistaking "appearances" for "reality," he then concludes that the rightmost stick is now longer than its companion. (Whereby is it demonstrated that all four of our early-childhood–middle-childhood contrasts can be insinuated into a single sentence, although the use of the semicolon does admittedly represent a bit of fudging on my part.) In the same situation, the older conserver may exhibit reversible thinking, either by appealing to the results of the inverse, directly negating act of realignment of the pencils, or by suggesting that the length gained by the displaced stick at its right end is exactly compensated for by the length lost at its left end. These two types of concrete-operational reversibility are often referred to by Piagetians as *inversion* and *compensation*, respectively; the terms *reciprocal* and *reciprocity* also are frequently used in describing reversible operations of the latter, compensatory type (e.g., Piaget & Inhelder, 1969, pp. 98, 102).

Research evidence suggests that a real sensitivity to compensating factors in conservation or conservation-like task settings is, in fact, not often seen in the preschool period; indeed, it may still have some developing to do at the end of middle childhood. In one study (Gelman & Weinberg, 1972), for instance, children were presented with a standard beaker which already contained a certain quantity of water and a second, empty beaker which was either taller and narrower or shorter and wider than the standard. Each subject was given a pitcher of water and was told to pour the same amount into the second beaker ("so that both of us have as much to drink in our glasses"). He was also questioned afterwards as to how he knew he had poured the same amount. Not until third grade did a majority of their subjects pour in even a roughly compensatory way—for example, producing any lower-than-standard-beaker water level in the shorter and wider beaker, rather than simply matching the two water levels. Moreover, only a minority of their *sixth*-grade sample (mean age 11 years, 9 months, and the oldest subjects tested) provided clear and explicit compensation-type explanations for their equalization efforts. However liberally or conservatively diagnosed, this sort of flexible, reversible, quantitatively oriented thinking does appear to be a relatively late-emerging developmental outcome. For interesting research reviews concerning the relationship between compensation and conservation, see Acredelo (1982) and Silverman and Rose (1982).

CONTRASTS BETWEEN MIDDLE-CHILDHOOD AND ADOLESCENT-ADULT COGNITION. An experimenter and a subject face one another across a table strewn with poker chips of various solid colors (Osherson & Markman, 1975). The experimenter explains that he is going to say things about the chips and that the subject is to indicate whether what the experimenter *says* (i.e., his *statements*) is true, false, or uncertain ("can't tell"). He then conceals a chip in his hand and says, "Either the chip in my hand is green or it is not green," or alternatively, "The chip in my hand is green and it is not green." On other trials, he holds up either a green chip or a red chip so that the subject can see it and then makes exactly the same statements.

Middle-childhood subjects are very likely to try to assess the truth value of these two assertions solely on the basis of the visual evidence. They focus on the concrete, empirical evidence concerning poker chips *themselves* rather than on the nonempirical, purely logical properties of the experimenter's *statements* about the poker chips. Consequently, they say they "can't tell" on the trials in which the chip is hidden from view. When it is visible, both statements are judged to be true if the chip is green and false if it is red. In other words, if the color (green) mentioned in the statement matches the color of the visible chip, the statement is said to be true; if there is a mismatch, it is judged false; and if the chip cannot be seen, its truth status is uncertain. What middle-childhood subjects fail to appreciate is that such "either-or" statements are always true and such "and" statements always false, regardless of the empirical evidence. Logicians call the former a *tautology* and the latter a *contradiction*, and they are true and false, respectively, solely by virtue of their formal properties as propositions.

Adolescent and adult subjects, on the other hand, are likelier to focus on the verbal assertions themselves, and to evaluate their internal validity as formal propositions. They appear to have a better intuition than the younger subjects do of the distinction between abstract, purely logical relations and empirical relations. These more mature thinkers recognize that one can some-times reason about propositions as such, instead of always "seeing right through them" to the entities and states of affairs to which they refer. Thus, Osherson and Markman's data hint at some of the important changes in the nature and quality of thought during the adolescent years proposed by Piaget (Inhelder & Piaget, 1958).

Real versus possible. Piaget argued that adolescents and adults tend to differ from children in the way they conceive of the relation between the real and the possible. The elementary school child's characteristic approach to many conceptual problems is to burrow right into the problem data as quickly as possible, using his various concrete-operational skills to order and inter-relate whatever properties or features of the situation he can detect. His is an earthbound, concrete, practical-minded sort of problem-solving approach, one that persistently fixates on the perceptible and inferable reality right there in front of him. His conceptual approach is definitely not unintelligent, much less nonsymbolic, and it certainly generates solution attempts that are far more rational and task-relevant than anything the preoperational child ever produces. It does, however, hug the ground of detected empirical reality rather closely, and speculations about other possibilities—that is, about other potential, as yet undetected realities—occur only with difficulty and as a last resort. A theorist the elementary school child is not.

An adolescent or adult is likelier than an elementary school child to approach problems quite the other way around, at least when operating at the top of her capacity. The child usually begins with reality and moves reluctantly, if at all, to possibility; in contrast, the adolescent or adult is more apt to begin with possibility and only subsequently proceed to reality. She may examine the problem situation carefully to try to determine what all the *possible* solutions or states of affairs might be, and then systematically try to discover which of these is, in fact, the *real* one in the present case. For the concrete-operational thinker, the realm of abstract possibility is seen as an uncertain and only occasional extension of the safer and surer realm of palpable reality. For the formal-operational thinker, on the other hand, reality is seen as that particular portion of the much wider world of possibility which happens to exist or hold true in a given problem situation. Possibility is subordinated to reality in the former case, whereas reality is subordinated to possibility in the latter case.

Empirico-inductive versus hypothetico-deductive. This subordination of the real to the possible expresses itself in a characteristic method of solving problems. The formal-operational thinker inspects the problem data, *hypothesizes* that such and such a theory or explanation might be the correct one, *deduces* from it that so and so empirical phenomena ought logically to occur or not occur in reality, and then tests her theory by seeing if these predicted phenomena do in fact occur. More informally put, she makes up a plausible story about what might be going on, figures out what would logi-cally have to happen out there in reality if her story were the right one, checks or does experiments out there to see what does, in fact, happen, and then accepts, rejects, or revises her story accordingly. If you think you have just heard a description of textbook scientific reasoning, you are absolutely right. Because of its heavy trade in hypotheses and logical deductions from hypotheses, it is also called *hypothetico-deductive* reasoning, and it contrasts sharply with the much more nontheoretical and nonspeculative *empirico-inductive* reasoning of concrete-operational thinkers.

Notice that this kind of thinking begins with the possible rather than the real in two senses. First, the subject's initial theory is only one of a number of possible ones that she might have concocted. It is itself a possibility rather than a reality, and it is also only one possibility among many. Second, the "empirical reality" predicted by or deduced from her initial theory is itself only a possibility, and also only one possibility among many. Actual, concrete reality only enters the scene when the subject tries to verify her theory by looking for the "reality" it has predicted. If it is not found, new theories and new theory-derived realities will be invented, and thus the sampling of possibilities continues. It is important to emphasize that these theories and theory-derived realities are purely conceptual entities, not physical ones. They are complex objects of thought constructed by a mature, abstract reasoner on the basis of a careful analysis of the problem situation; they are not mere representations of the perceived situation itself.

What would really good, vintage hypothetico-deductive thinking sound like if it were verbalized aloud? Following are two made-up examples:

> Well, what I have just seen gives me the idea that W and *only* W *might* have the power to cause or produce Z, that the presence of X *might* prevent W from causing Z, and that Y *might* prove to be wholly irrelevant to the occurrence of Z. Now if this idea is right, then Z should occur *only* when W is present and X is absent, whether or not Y is also present. Let's see if these are, in fact, the only conditions under which Z does occur . . . . Oh no, that idea is shot down, because I've just found that Z also occurs sometimes when neither W nor X is present. I wonder why. Hey, I have another idea . . . .

> I am a college student of extremely modest means. Some crazy psychologist interested in something called "formal-operational thinking" has just promised to pay me $10 if I can make a coherent logical argument for the proposition that the federal government should under no circumstances ever give or loan money to impecunious college students. Now what could a nonperson who believed *that* possibly say by way of supporting argument? Well, I suppose he *could* offer this line of reasoning . . . .

Intrapropositional versus interpropositional. The child of elementary school age can construct mental, symbolic representations of concrete reality and can also evaluate their empirical validity under many circumstances. He might, for example, quite explicitly formulate the proposition that there is still the same number of objects in the two rows after one has been spread out (number conservation test), and then he might prove it to you by counting the objects in each row. Although the term *propositional* is often applied to formal-operational reasoning to distinguish it from the concrete-operational type, middle-childhood subjects can indeed produce, comprehend, and verify propositions. There is, nonetheless, an important difference between the two in the way they deal with propositions. The child considers them singly, in isolation from one another, testing each in its turn against the relevant empirical data. Since what is confirmed or infirmed in each case is but a single claim about the external world, Piaget calls concrete-operational thinking *intrapropositional*—that is, thinking within the confines of a single proposition. Although a formal-operational thinker also naturally tests individual propositions against reality, she does something more that lends a very special quality to her reasoning. She reasons about the logical relations that hold *among* two or more propositions, a more subtle and abstract form of reasoning which Piaget terms *interpropositional*. The less mature mind looks only to the *factual* relation between one proposition and the empirical reality to which it refers; the more mature mind looks also or instead to the *logical* relation between one proposition and another.

The first of the two examples of hypothetico-deductive reasoning given in the previous section illustrates this distinction particularly well. The individual's initial theory asserts ("proposes") that the logical relation called *conjunction* holds between three propositions: W is the sole cause of Z *and* (conjunction relation) X neutralizes W's causal effect *and* (conjunction relation) Y is not causally related to Z at all. Conjunction is also used to interconnect a set of hypothetical propositions or predictions about external reality: The conjunction of W present and X absent produces ("conjoins with") the presence of Z, and none of the other logically possible conjunctions involving the presence or absence of W and X will yield Z. Moreover, the conjunction of Y's presence or absence with the foregoing changes nothing. There are other logical relations which our imaginary subject might also apply to various combinations of these propositions, although she would not necessarily use the logician's terminology in describing them. For instance, she would understand that, within her theory, the presence of Z (one proposition) *implies* (logical relation) the presence of W (another proposition), whereas the reverse implication, W implies Z, does not hold due to the *incompatibility* (logical relation) between X and Z. Above all, the "if . . . then" phrasing in her second sentence shows that she knows that the entire complex of conjoined propositions which constitutes her theory logically *implies* the entire complex of conjoined propositions which constitutes her predicted reality. That is, she establishes a logical relation between two *sets* of propositions, the constituent propositions of each of which she has already knitted together by logical connectives. This is certainly "interpropositional" thinking in the fullest sense.

It should now be clear why this kind of reasoning is also called *formal*. To reason that one proposition "logically implies" ("contradicts," etc.) another is fundamentally to reason about the relation between a pair of *statements*, not about any *empirical phenomena* to which these statements might refer. The statements in question may not be factually correct assertions about the real objects and events to which they refer; they may not refer to real objects and events in the first place; or indeed they may not even refer to anything at all, real or imaginary. Consider the following bit of formal reasoning: If A is true in all cases where B is true, then B will be false in all cases where A is false (or equivalently, if B implies A, then not A implies not B). This is logically valid reasoning, but its validity has to do with the way the statements are related, not with the referential meaning of A and B (they have been given none). It is now apparent why the Osherson and Markman (1975) questions might differentiate a formal reasoner from a concrete one. The formal reasoner knows that the experimenter is asking about the logical truth or falsity of pairs of statements as a joint function of what they state (affirmation, negation) and how they are logically linked (conjunction, disjunction); she knows that the experimenter is not really asking anything about the color of chips.

The second of the two hypothetical hypothetico-deductive reasoners described in the previous section illustrates a closely related insight—namely, that one does not have to believe something is either true or just in order to argue for it (although it sure helps). Formal-operational thinkers understand that logical arguments have a disembodied and passionless life of their own, at least in principle. Concrete-operational thinkers have enough trouble seeing what logically follows from credible premises, let alone from premises that actually contradict one's knowledge, beliefs, or values.

Finally, formal-operational reasoning is an abstract, derivative-type of mentation by virtue of its interpropositional nature, in that it entails thinking about propositions rather than about reality directly. As Piaget put it, whereas concrete operations are "first degree" operations that deal with real objects and events, formal operations are "second degree" operations that deal with the propositions or statements produced by the first degree, concrete ones (Inhelder & Piaget, 1958, p. 254).

Quantitative Thinking

This developmental trend is also owed primarily to Piaget's work. As we saw in Chapter 3, children do acquire some basic numerical skills during the preschool period. Furthermore, a series of studies by Bryant and Kopytynska (1976) has shown that children of 5 to 6 years are even capable of simple measurement operations under some task conditions. Asked to find out which of two holes was deeper, their young subjects spontaneously used a stick as a measuring device. Nevertheless, most of what people come to know about mathematics and measurement is acquired after early childhood. Although there is not as much research evidence for this claim as one might wish, it does seem that older children have a more quantitative, measurement-oriented approach to many tasks and problems than younger children do. The younger child's approach appears to have a more global, qualitative cast to it. The older child seems to understand better than the younger one that certain problems have precise, specific, potentially quantifiable solutions, and that these solutions may be attained by reasoning in conjunction with well-defined measurement operations. The younger child often lacks the cognitive equipment to do other than guess or make simple perceptual estimates. In contrast, the older child has come to understand that wholes are potentially divisible into unit parts of arbitrary size, and that these parts can serve as units of measurement in making a quantitative judgment about the whole.

Once again, Piaget's conservation problems are useful in illustrating this difference between a qualitative, "guestimate"-minded approach and a quantitative, measurement-minded one. Six wooden matches are placed end-to-end but nonlinearly, so that they form a jagged, angular "road" on the table. An objectively shorter (e.g., only "five matches long") but perfectly straight stick representing a second road is placed directly above the first. Because it is straight, the crow's-flight distance between its end points is actually longer than the distance between the end points of the other, crooked road. Who makes the longest trip, the experimenter asks, the person who drives the entire length of the crooked road or the person who drives the entire length of the straight road? The second person, says the nursery school child, centering only on the end points. The first person, says the fourth grader, carefully attending to what lies *between* the end points. Unlike the younger subject, he recognizes that total lengths (distances, areas, volumes, etc.) are composed of, and are conceptually divisible into, subparts of any arbitrary desired magnitude. He understands that whole lengths are potentially fractionable into so-and-so many length segments of such-and-such size, or alternatively, into some different number of segments of any other, arbitrarily selected size. If asked to prove that the crooked road was actually longer than the straight road, appearances notwithstanding, he might, of course, simply straighten it out, align the two and point to the difference. He might instead, however, use one of the matches as a convenient, preformed unit measure, and prove that the crooked road was "one match longer" than the straight one. Equivalently, he could use a ruler, or a meter stick, or a hairpin, or anything else that would allow him to arrive at a rigorous, exact, quantitative solution to the problem. Such a child we would say, has a metric, genuinely quantitative conception of length. He has what Bearison (1969) has termed a "quantitative set," and it allows him to envision exact solutions to a variety of quantitative problems.

A possible developmental trend towards quantitative thinking is worth highlighting because quantitative thinking is applicable to such a very wide range of situations. Quantification and measurement obviously do not apply only to one or a few specific knowledge domains. They are, as Carey nicely puts it, "tools of wide application" (Carey, 1982). The ability to read is another one. The acquisition of such tools must indelibly color one's cognitive life, it seems to me (Flavell, 1982a).

A Sense of the Game

This putative developmental trend is based more on intuition than on solid research evidence and consequently you should be appropriately skeptical about it. As children develop, they gradually learn more and more about what "the game of thinking" is like and about how it is supposed to be played (cf. Flavell, 1977, 1982a). We have seen (Chapter 3) that young children acquire schemas and scripts for "how things are supposed to go" in stories, daily routines, and the like. It seems likely that as they grow older they also build knowledge structures concerning "how things are supposed to go" in cognitive enterprises.

They might learn the following things, and doubtless many more. Tasks and problems usually have solutions. One normally has to engage in some sort of cognitive activity in order to solve them—that is, cognitive activity is the usual means to achieving ("scoring") goals in cognitive games. Some cognitive outcomes or end products are of better quality than others. They are likely to be of better quality (more true, more adaptive, more in accordance with the rules of the cognitive game) if they were arrived at by plausible or logically valid reasoning, if they can be justified or explained by appeal to sound evidence or compelling arguments, if they are not incoherent or self-contradictory, and the like. One is not playing by the rules of the cognitive game if one just picks an answer or solution at random, reasons illogically, ignores crucial evidence, tolerates contradictions or inconsistencies, and so on. Cognitive games do not have to have real-world meaning or significance to be playable (cf. Donaldson, 1978). They are legitimate cognitive games even if they have no ecological significance or practical value. A cognitive game may be as decontextualized and unrelated to "real life" as a conundrum in a bridge or chess column, a problem in a logic text, a question on an intelligence test, and a cognitive task in a psychological experiment.

The fact that one has acquired a sense of the cognitive game does not imply that one will play it well. Although older children, adolescents, and adults usually do engage in higher-quality cognitive play than young children do, it is nevertheless true that the quality of their play is often not very high. As mentioned earlier in this chapter (p. 83), even very bright and well-educated adults often fail to process information adequately and reason intelligently (Braine & Rumain, 1983; Nisbett & Ross, 1980; Shaklee, 1979). In fact, the major message of a large body of research in the field of cognitive psychology is that adult cognition is frequently of poor quality—sometimes of surprisingly, even shockingly poor quality. Nisbett and Ross (1980) convincingly document many of the cognitive shortcomings of adult thinkers. But there are yet others, as Miller and Cantor (1982) point out in their review of the Nisbett and Ross (1980) book:

> If the authors' purpose had been to belittle human reasoning, they would have had much ammunition available they did not use. Years of research on reasoning and problem solving have uncovered many glaring weaknesses unrelated to probability or statistical decision theory: pursuit of false analogies; preference for positive instances; neglect of alternative hypotheses; overreliance on familiar content; functional fixedness; the treatment of conditionals as biconditionals and the pervasive fallacy of asserting the consequent; the tendency to delete, change, or add premises; and so on. Nisbett and Ross have not tried to compile a list of all the ills that reason is heir to. *Human Inference* treats a limited aspect of human inference (Miller & Cantor, 1982, p. 87).

To say that the reasoning of adults is often not as fully "logical," "scientific," or "formal-operational" as the situation calls for is an understatement.

Yet, the fact that most of us can understand and appreciate the force of these claims—namely, that we often play the thinking game quite poorly—suggests to me that we *have* acquired a fair sense of what the game is about and how it *should* be played. I do not think that preschool children possess this sense. They have not yet learned about explanation, justification, evidence, hypotheses, proof, logical necessity, contradiction, and other intellectual creatures that figure importantly in the game (cf. Bullock, Gelman, & Baillargeon, 1982; Carey, 1982).

Metacognition

Preschool and elementary school subjects were instructed to study a small set of items until they were sure they could recall them all (Flavell, Friedrichs, & Hoyt, 1970). The older children studied them for a while, judged that they were ready, and usually were: They then usually went on to recall every single item correctly. The younger children studied them for a while, judged that they were ready, and usually were not: They usually failed to recall some of the items. It seems that the preschoolers could not monitor and evaluate their current memory capabilities as accurately as the older children could. Monitoring and evaluating one's current memory capabilities is an example of *metacognition*, and the study by Flavell et al. (1970) is only one of many showing marked developmental advances in metacognitive skills during middle childhood and adolescence (see Chapter 7).

The nature and development of metacognition has been a very popular research topic in recent years: "It is surely fair to say that one of the more influential conceptual developments in cognition during the last decade has been the notion of metacognition, which highlights the individual's own awareness and consideration of her or his cognitive processes and strategies" (Masters, 1981, p. 129). Following are some of the sources that contain useful discussions of the concept: Baker (1982), Baker and Brown (1984), Brown (1975, 1978, 1979), Brown et al. (1983), Brown and DeLoache (1978), Cavanaugh and Perlmutter (1982), Chi (1984), Flavell (1976, 1978c, 1978d, 1979, 1981a, 1981b, 1984b), Flavell and Wellman (1977), Hakes (1980), Kluwe (1984), Markman (1981a), Meichenbaum and Asarnow (1979), Paris (1978b), Paris and Lindauer (1982), Siegler (1983b), Sternberg and Powell (1983), Wellman (1983, in press), and Yussen (in press).

What is metacognition? It has usually been broadly and rather loosely defined as any knowledge or cognitive activity that takes as its object, or regulates, any aspect of any cognitive enterprise (e.g., Flavell, 1981a). It is called *meta*cognition because its core meaning is "cognition about cognition." Metacognitive skills are believed to play an important role in many types of cognitive activity, including oral communication of information, oral persuasion, oral comprehension, reading comprehension, writing, language acquisition, perception, attention, memory, problem solving, social cognition, and various forms of self-instruction and self-control. Because of its broad applicability, the concept is reintroduced several times in subsequent chapters. Metacognition or related concepts (e.g., executive processes) have also recently seen service in the fields of cognitive psychology, artificial intelligence, human abilities, social-learning theory, cognitive behavior modification, personality development, gerontology, and education, as well as in the field of childhood cognitive development. Metacognition and its conceptual relatives are much in vogue nowadays in psychology and education. Although the term metacognition is of recent coinage, the idea that knowledge and cognition can take cognitive as well as noncognitive objects is by no means new; for a good history of the concept, see Brown et al. (1983). As one example, Piagetian formal-operational thinking is clearly metacognitive in nature because it involves thinking about propositions, hypotheses, and imagined possibilities—cognitive objects all. The "sense of the game" described in the previous section is also clearly a form of metacognition, by the way; it was given a section of its own only because I wanted to highlight it.

Different theorists have conceptualized and classified the domain of metacognition in somewhat different ways (cf. Brown, 1978, 1979; Brown et al., 1983; Chi, 1984; Flavell, 1979, 1981a, 1984b; Kluwe, 1984; Markman, 1981b;

Paris, 1978a; Wellman, 1983, in press). The key concepts in my own conceptualization are *metacognitive knowledge* and *metacognitive experience* (Flavell, 1979, 1981a, 1984b).

METACOGNITIVE KNOWLEDGE. This refers to the segment of your acquired world knowledge that has to do with cognitive matters. It is the knowledge and beliefs you have accumulated through experience and stored in long-term memory that concern not politics or football or electronics or needlepoint or some other domain, but the human mind and its doings. Some of this stored knowledge seems more declarative ("knowing that") than procedural ("knowing how")—for example, your declarative knowledge that you have a rather poor memory. Other metacognitive knowledge seems more procedural than declarative—for example, your procedural knowledge of how and when to supplement that poor memory by the use of shopping lists and other external memory aids (cf. Chi, 1984). Your knowledge of any given metacognitive item could, of course, be both declarative and procedural. For example, you might both know as a verbalizable fact that writing shopping lists is a good memory strategy and also "know to" write them on appropriate occasions. Metacognitive knowledge can be roughly subdivided into knowledge about *persons, tasks,* and *strategies.*

The person category includes any knowledge and beliefs you might acquire concerning what human beings are like as cognitive processors. It can be further subcategorized into knowledge and beliefs about cognitive differences within people, cognitive differences between people, and cognitive similarities among all people—that is, about universal properties of human cognition. Examples of the within-people subcategory might be your knowledge that you are better at psychology than physics or your belief that your friend learns better by reading than by listening. An example of the between-people category could be your belief that your parents are more sensitive to the needs and feelings of others than many of their neighbors are (a belief about others' social-cognitive skills). The cognitive-universals subcategory is the most interesting of the three. It refers to what you have come to know or believe about what the human mind in general is like—any person's mind. For instance, you did not have to read this book to sense that everybody's short-term memory is of limited capacity and highly fallible. Similarly, you are aware of the important fact that sometimes people understand, sometimes they do not understand, and sometimes they understand incorrectly, or *mis*understand. You also know that what you cannot recall now you may be able to recall later and that what you can recall now you may not be able to recall later. More generally, you have learned that the human mind is a somewhat unpredictable and unreliable cognitive device, although still a remarkable one. I believe that people the world over must acquire considerable metaknowledge of this subcategory and also must make important use of it in managing their lives. Try this thought experiment to convince yourself of its usefulness: Imagine how well you would fare as an adult in any human society if you were incorrigibly ignorant of the fact that you and other people sometimes misunderstand or forget things.

The task category has two subcategories. One subcategory has to do with the nature of the information you encounter and deal with in any cognitive task. You have learned that the nature of this information has important effects on how you will manage it. For example, you know from experience that complex and unfamiliar information is liable to be difficult and time-consuming for you to comprehend and remember. You have also learned that having only skimpy and unreliable information at your disposal implies that judgments and conclusions based on this information are apt to be wrong. The other subcategory concerns the nature of the task demands. Even given the exact same information to work with, you have learned that some tasks are more difficult and demanding than others. For example, you know that it is easier to recall the gist of a story than its exact wording. You also know that it is generally easier to recognize something when you see it than to recall it outright; recognition memory is usually better than recall memory.

As for the strategy category, there is much you might have learned about what means or strategies are likely to succeed in achieving what cognitive goals—in comprehending X, remembering Y, solving problem Z, and so on. For instance, if someone asks you what a person might do to memorize a phone number you could no doubt tell him that the person might try rehearsing it (declarative knowledge about rehearsal as a memory strategy). And, of greater practical importance, if actually faced with the task of memorizing a phone number you would probably automatically, from long habit, start rehearsing it (overlearned procedural knowledge of when and how to use rehearsal as a memory strategy). You also probably have at least procedural knowledge of more sophisticated cognitive strategies, such as the strategy of spending more time studying more important or less well-learned material than less important or better-learned material. A rough distinction can be made between straightforward cognitive strategies and metacognitive strategies. The main function of a cognitive strategy is to help you achieve the goal of whatever cognitive enterprise you are engaged in. In contrast, the main function of a metacognitive strategy is to provide you with information about the enterprise or your progress in it. Two examples of metacognitive strategies are skimming a textbook chapter to get some feeling for how hard it will be to learn and double checking your solution to some problem to make sure it is right. We might say that cognitive strategies are invoked to *make* cognitive progress, metacognitive strategies to *monitor* it. Monitoring one's progress in a task is a very important metacognitive activity. The study by Flavell et al. (1970) described on pp. 103 to 104 illustrates this activity.

Finally, the bulk of your metacognitive knowledge actually concerns combinations of, or interactions among, two or three of these three categories. To illustrate knowledge of an interaction between strategy and task, you would undoubtedly select a different preparation strategy if your task were to give a talk on some topic than if you only needed to follow a talk on that topic given by someone else.

Its exotic and high-sounding name may suggest to you that "metacognitive" knowledge must be qualitatively different from other kinds—perhaps a different species of knowledge altogether. However, there is no good reason to think it actually is fundamentally different. In fact, there is reason to wonder if the choice of the "meta" prefix was an altogether felicitous one, since it may suggest that the knowledge in this domain is more separate and special than is really the case (cf. Brown et al., 1983). There are several ways in which metacognitive knowledge seems similar to other kinds of knowledge. Like much other knowledge, a given bit of metacognitive knowledge may be declarative, procedural, or some of both. As with other knowledge acquisitions, metacognitive knowledge is probably accumulated in a slow and gradual fashion through years of experience in the "domain" of diverse sorts of cognitive enterprises. Also like the other stored knowledge, it is frequently activated automatically and nondeliberately through recognition and response processes that detect and appropriately respond to familiar cognitive situations. Much as the chess expert automatically recognizes a familiar chessboard situation and automatically retrieves from memory a set of possible responses, so too may you recognize and respond appropriately to a familiar type of cognitive situation. You may categorize and respond to it as a situation that is going to be very difficult and time-consuming to get through, as one that is basically easy but needs careful attention to detail, as one that you will not be able to solve without outside help, as one that needs clearer specification, and so on. Like the chess expert, you too may have learned through years of experience to recognize and react appropriately to a large number of input patterns relevant to the conduct, course, and outcome of cognitive enterprises (cf. Chi, 1984). Finally, just like your knowledge about other things, your knowledge about cognitive enterprises can have various shortcomings. A given segment of your metacognitive knowledge may be insufficient, inaccurate, not reliably retrieved and used when appropriate, or otherwise flawed. Thus, although metacognitive knowledge is an important kind of knowledge, it is not a mysterious, qualitatively different kind.

METACOGNITIVE EXPERIENCES. Metacognitive experiences are cognitive or affective experiences that pertain to a cognitive enterprise. Fully conscious and easy-to-articulate experiences of this sort are clear cases of this category but less fully conscious and verbalizable experiences should probably also be included in it. Metacognitive experiences can be brief or lengthy, simple or complex in content. For instance, you may sense only a momentary flicker of uncertainty or puzzlement, or you may obsess at considerable length about whether you *really* understand what your friend is like, "deep down." Metacognitive experiences may also occur at any time before, during, or after a cognitive endeavor. For example, you may think that you did very well on the first half of the final exam but feel pessimistic about how you are going to do on the second half. As these examples suggest, many metacognitive experiences have as their ideational content where you are in a cognitive enterprise and what sort of progress you have made, are making, or are likely to make. They seem especially likely to occur in situations that would be expected to engender careful, conscious monitoring and regulation of one's own cognition. Examples include novel roles or situations in which you have to feel your cognitive way along, step by step, and those weighty decision problems for which the penalty for cognitive missteps is high. Trying to decide whether to marry someone, for instance, may entail both a lot of cognition and a lot of rumination about the quality of that cognition (metacognitive experiences).

Metacognitive experiences can serve a variety of useful functions in ongoing cognitive enterprises. For instance, the sudden realization that you are not understanding what you have just been reading may instigate any of several adaptive actions: As examples, you may reread the passage, rethink what you already understand (or *thought* you understood), read ahead to see if something further on clarifies the muddle, enlist someone else's help, or try to modify your task objective in such a way as to reduce the importance of the problem (cf. Collins & Smith, 1982). Metacognitive experiences are presumably informed and shaped by whatever relevant metacognitive knowledge you have acquired. For example, when you were a young child you may not have clearly understood what your metacognitive experiences of noncomprehension signified, nor what you should do about them when they occurred. There is, in fact, research evidence to suggest that young children do not adequately attend to such experiences and do not fully appreciate their meaning and behavioral implications (see the section on *metacommunication* in Chapter 8). As an adult, you possess the metacognitive knowledge necessary to properly interpret and act upon them. Conversely, metacognitive experiences must also contribute information about persons, tasks, and strategies to one's developing store of metacognitive knowledge: The ideas and feelings you experience when engaged in cognition must contribute to your knowledge about cognition, just as the ideas and feelings you experience while watching or playing, say, tennis must contribute to your knowledge of tennis.

It seems likely that metacognitive knowledge, metacognitive experience, and cognitive behavior are constantly informing and eliciting one another during the course of a cognitive task. To illustrate, imagine what might happen if I gave you the problem of thinking of a possible social-cognitive example of the task-demand subcategory of metacognitive knowledge. You automatically "know to" begin problem solution by trying to achieve the subgoal of understanding what that particular subcategory means; this automatically activated "know to" is procedural metacognitive knowledge of the strategy category. The cognitive behavior of trying to understand may at first trigger the metacognitive experience of not feeling quite sure you understand what that subcategory does mean. This experience in turn instigates the cognitive behavior of looking back through this chapter to see where and how I have described it. Additional interactions among these three processors (plus others such as the activation of nonmetacognitive knowledge) may yield this plausible instance of the subcategory: your metacognitive knowledge that you need to know more about a person's ability and character to decide whether to make her your business partner than to decide whether to hire her to keep your shelves stocked during the holiday rush.

As indicated earlier, the just-described scheme is not the only way to conceptualize and categorize the domain of metacognition, nor is it necessarily the best, most scientifically productive way. To briefly illustrate other ways, Brown and her coworkers (Baker & Brown, 1984; Brown, 1978, 1979; Brown et al., 1983) parse the domain into *knowledge about cognition* and *regulation of cognition* (see also Paris, 1978b; Wellman, 1983). Brown et al. (1983) also argue that the phenomena typically included in this broad domain may be collectively just too heterogeneous, just too different in both nature and developmental course, to warrant the use of any single cover term, such as *metacognition*. They think we might be better off retiring the term, or else restricting its use to stable and statable knowledge about cognition, and then studying various forms of cognitive regulation (monitoring, self-directing, etc.) as separate executive processes "without the addendum, metacognition" (Brown et al., 1983, p. 125). Wellman and Johnson take a different tack (Johnson & Wellman, 1980; Wellman, 1983, in press). They study the development of the child's implicit "theory of mind" (see also Bretherton, McNew, & Beeghly-Smith, 1981). This "theory" includes, in addition to the sorts of knowledge and cognition already discussed in this section, the insights that we all have minds, that there are distinguishable mental processes (e.g., reasoning, remembering, dreaming), and that these processes are also related to each other in various ways. They are particularly interested in the first stirrings of this metaknowledge in early childhood.

One reason why many of us are currently interested in metacognition is that we believe it has important applications in the field of education (e.g., Baker, 1982; Baker & Brown, 1984; Brown et al., 1983; Flavell, 1979, 1981a; Markman, 1981a; Paris, Lipson, Jacobs, Oka, DeBritto, & Cross, 1982). Consider the cognitive activity of reading, for example. Baker (1982) cites research evidence that younger/poorer readers may show metacognitive or metacognitive-like deficits in no fewer than nine areas: (1) understanding the purposes of reading; (2) modifying reading strategies for different purposes; (3) identifying the important information in a passage; (4) recognizing the logical structure inherent in a passage; (5) considering how new information relates to what is already known; (6) attending to syntactic and semantic constraints—for example, spontaneously correcting errors in the text; (7) evaluating text for clarity, completeness, and consistency; (8) dealing with failures to understand; (9) deciding how well the material has been understood.

As an example of (2), there is some evidence that older/better readers are more likely than younger/poorer ones to expend additional effort on more demanding reading assignments, such as the assignment to study a text versus that of only skimming through it to find one specific piece of information (Forrest & Waller, 1979). Younger/poorer readers thus appear less sensitive to the need to tailor their reading activities to the specific demands and objectives of the reading task (Brown et al., 1983). More generally, they are less likely to allocate and reallocate their efforts and attention in an efficient, task-adaptive fashion over time. For instance, they do not concentrate most of their study efforts on those segments of the material that are currently least well learned and hence currently most in need of study, and then strategically reallocate their study efforts to other, still-unmastered segments when those segments are mastered (Brown et al., 1983). The ability to deploy and redeploy one's cognitive forces intelligently over time in accord with changing needs and circumstances seems an essential one for adapting successfully to the complex and changeable life situations most of us face—both in school and out.

You have just read a passage and now need some information from it that you cannot recall. What do you do? The answer is obvious for you—go back and look. However, Garner and her colleagues (Garner & Haynes, 1982; Garner & Reis, 1981) have shown that it is not so obvious for younger children and poor readers. In one of her studies (Garner & Haynes, 1982), students in fourth, sixth, eighth, and tenth grade first read a brief passage and then were asked questions about it, an "ecologically valid" task similar to those the children often experienced in the classroom. They were explicitly told they could look back at the passage if they wanted to and, in fact, some of the questions required rereading to be answered correctly. Garner and Haynes found a significant and regular increase with age in the amount of spontaneous rereading observed, each grade group doing more of it than its predecessor.

If metacognitive skills are useful in school learning and if students, especially younger ones, are deficient in them, an intriguing possibility arises: Perhaps these skills could and should be directly taught to children, as an integral part of the school curriculum. Ann Brown, Scott Paris, and others are currently investigating this possibility with respect to metacognitive skills in reading comprehension (Brown et al., 1983; Paris et al., 1982). Although these investigations are still in progress at this writing, preliminary results indicate that the skills can be successfully taught and that learning them markedly improves children's reading comprehension.

Even more than is true of quantitative thinking (p. 102), metacognition is a "tool of wide application" and its development gains additional importance and interest because of that fact. True, metacognitive development can be conceptualized as the development of domain-specific knowledge. It is correct to say that, during the years of childhood and adolescence, we gradually acquire some "expertise" in the "domain" of cognition. Yet, it seems wrong to think of cognition as just another domain of knowledge, distinct and separate from all the others. By definition, cognition comes into play whenever we operate intellectually in *any* domain, and where there is cognition there can also be metacognition. Consequently, metacognitive knowledge and experiences can serve their usual regulatory function when we play chess, or solve physics problems, or engage in mental activity in any other knowledge domain. A great deal of metacognition can be usefully employed in any domain—for example, in double-checking one's cognitive procedures and products. Thus, although metacognition can be construed as domain-specific knowledge, it should be remembered that its "domain" spans all others. However, I do *not* further metastasize "metas" by labeling it a "metadomain."

Improving Existing Competencies

When we think of cognitive development we naturally think of the acquisition of new knowledge and skills. However, cognitive development also consists of the further growth of knowledge and skills that already exist in the child's repertoire but only in rudimentary or immature form. We saw in Chapter 3 that preschoolers have more knowledge and skills than we used to think they had. However, virtually all of these competencies are still quite immature at this age and will undergo considerable further development during middle childhood and adolescence (Brown et al., 1983; Gelman & Baillargeon, 1983; Wellman, 1982):

> In the current trend to prove the early emergence of almost any cognitive capacity, we should not overlook the obvious fact that 6 and 7-year-olds are able to show their understanding in a wider range of situations, including the much-maligned laboratory task. The cognitive competence of the grade-school child is

far more robust; it is manifested on many criterial tasks. This compares sharply with the fragile nature of the preschooler's fleeting moments of insight (Brown et al., 1983, p. 95).

Similarly, competencies which first appear during middle childhood continue to develop in subsequent years. In fact, the period of time between first budding and final blooming of a cognitive acquisition can sometimes be surprisingly long (Flavell, 1971c). Thus, the final developmental trend discussed here is the prosaic but important one of further developing what you have already acquired.

In the course of development a cognitive competency can be improved or perfected in a number of closely related ways (cf. Brown et al., 1983; Flavell, 1972, 1982b; Siegler, 1981; Wellman, 1982). As it develops, a competency may become more reliably accessed and used in any given task that calls for it. When the competency first emerges it may be activated and properly used on one presentation of a task but not on the next presentation of that very same task. On an appearance-reality problem (see pp. 54–57), for example, it is possible that a young child would correctly say that the fake egg *looks* like an egg but *really, really* is a stone on one presentation of the fake egg but then fail to access his fragile and precarious grasp of the distinction on a subsequent presentation of the same fake object. Embryonic competencies tend to have this unreliable, "now-you-see-them-now-you-don't" quality.

They also tend to be highly restricted and limited in their range of application, often seeming tightly bound or "welded" (Brown et al., 1983) to a few specific task situations. Here are two examples: (1) Young children might at first be able to make an appearance-reality distinction in only a few familiar task situations; (2) preschoolers may be able to apply some of their number knowledge (see Chapter 3) only to small sets—for example, sets of two to four objects (Siegler, 1981). Thus, as a competency develops it not only becomes more reliably and dependably applied in any single appropriate situation, but it also extends its range of application to more and more appropriate situations. In addition to this extension of range, or generalization, there may also be some restriction of range, or differentiation. That is, children may initially apply a competency to some situations in which it should not be employed and then later restrict its use to appropriate situations only.

A competency may also further develop by changes in the relative weightings given by the child to different problem-solving rules or procedures and to different stimulus information in the task environment. For example, a younger child might possess two competing procedures for dealing with appearance-reality problems. That is, if asked to report what the object really is or, alternatively, how it appears, the child may either: (1) use her budding understanding of the appearance-reality distinction to attend to and report correctly whichever of the two is requested; or (2) simply report whichever happens to be uppermost in consciousness when the question is asked—that is, whichever of the two is more cognitively salient to her at that particular moment. For the young child, these competing strategies might have roughly equal weights, on average, and whichever wins out on a given task may depend on specific stimulus features or other properties of that task. As knowledge about the appearance-reality distinction improves, however, strategy (1) would become increasingly dominant. A similar change in rule weightings probably occurs in the development of Piagetian conservations (Acredelo, 1982). For example, the child may truly have some grasp of the rule that the number of elements in a row remains the same so long as no elements are added or taken away, even though the rule he usually follows is that of relying only on the length of the row. It is apparent that such developmental changes in dominance relations among rules or strategies are closely related to the other changes described earlier. For instance, as the "correct," task-appropriate strategy becomes increasingly dominant over its competitors, it will be more reliably accessed and used on any given relevant task and also will be applied to an increasing number of such tasks.

Still other changes in existing competencies are related to these and to one another. For instance, competencies may become linked with other competencies to form larger systems of interrelated knowledge and skills. Competencies may also become more accessible to conscious reflection and verbal expression. Such changes may constitute or engender further development of these competencies. For example, once we become able to reflect on and deliberate about the distinction between appearance and reality, we may become capable of generating new ideas about the distinction and of identifying new and more subtle instances of it (Flavell, Flavell, & Green, 1983).

Finally, concomitant with or in consequence of the just-mentioned changes, acquisitions that were fragile and unstable in early or middle childhood may become consolidated and solidified in adolescence or adulthood. Consider, for example, the Piagetian concepts of conservation of weight and transitivity of weight. To assess these competencies, the experimenter takes two identical balls of clay and puts one on each pan of a balance scale. The two pans remain horizontal—that is, in equilibrium—and the subject agrees that the two balls weigh the same. The balls are then removed from the scale and one of them is deformed in some way—for example, flattened into a pancake or rolled into a sausage shape. The subject would fail to evidence a belief in conservation of weight if he denied that the two pieces of clay would necessarily still weigh the same and still depress the two scale pans equally. A nonconserver of weight is therefore someone who does not understand that object weight remains unchanged when object shape is changed. An individual would fail to show a recognition of the transitivity property of weight if, having established by using the balance that object A weighs the same as object B and that object B weighs the same as object C, he denied that A had to weigh the same as C. The same would be true if "less than" or "more than" were substituted for "the same as" in the foregoing sentence. Hence, a person is said to recognize the transitive nature of weight relations if he understands that, for any weights A, B, and C, $A = B$ and $B = C$ always implies $A = C$, that $A < B$ and $B < C$ always implies $A < C$, and that $A > B$ and $B > C$ always implies $A > C$.

There is evidence that subjects' beliefs in both conservation and transitivity of weight, initially acquired during middle childhood, may become firmer as they move into adolescence and adulthood (Miller, 1973; Miller & Lipps, 1973; Miller, Schwartz & Stewart, 1973). Recall from Chapter 2 (pp. 42–43) that infants' tacit beliefs in the permanence of objects have been assessed by presenting them with trick conditions which apparently violate the object-permanence rule. An infant who believes in object permanence ought to be and is surprised and perplexed if an object that had just been covered is nowhere to be seen when the cover is removed. Miller and his colleagues have similarly put older subjects' beliefs in weight conservation and transitivity to very severe tests by similar machinations. Their trick is to rig the scale balance with electromagnets so that it gives false weight information on any trial the experimenter chooses. What does a subject who has previously demonstrated both beliefs say when confronted with, for example, a flattened ball that now inexplicably appears to weigh more than what had just been its exact duplicate, or a series of pairwise weighings of three objects that yields the startling information $A = B$, $B = C$, and $A < C$? In the case of the conservation belief, only a minority of elementary school subjects who had initially been diagnosed as weight conservers continued to maintain this belief in the face of such apparently disconfirming evidence. College students, on the other hand, showed considerably more fidelity to the conservation concept, although some of them did succumb. Transitivity of weight proved to be a sturdier concept. A minority rather than a majority of Miller's younger elementary school subjects abandoned it when given false feedback, and a significantly smaller proportion of his older elementary subjects abandoned it. College students' beliefs in weight transitivity were not assessed in these studies, but presumably they would have been sturdier yet. Miller et al.'s (1973) conclusions speak to the idea of postchildhood consolidation and solidification of childhood acquisitions:

> . . . there may be developmental changes in the certainty with which a concept such as conservation of weight is held, changes which extend well beyond the point at which the child is usually considered to "have" the concept (p. 316).

SUMMARY

Some acquaintance with the currently popular *information-processing approach* to cognition is useful in trying to understand the nature of cognitive growth during middle childhood and adolescence. In this approach, the human mind is conceptualized as a cognitive system in which units of information of differing magnitudes and complexity are processed in various ways—for example, encoded, recoded, retrieved, and compared. Information-processing psychologists try to construct detailed and testable theoretical models of what the system actually *does*—step by step, in real time—when dealing with a specific cognitive task or problem. Some of them also try to simulate hypothesized sequences of processes on a computer to help evaluate the theoretical adequacy of their processing models. One of their most important contributions to our thinking about cognitive development has been their demonstration that the human cognitive system has severe limitations on its ability to process information and that the quality of an individual's cognitive performance is likely to suffer greatly when these limitations are exceeded—that is, under conditions of information overload.

Robert Siegler's *rule-assessment approach* provides a good contemporary example of how cognitive development can be investigated within an information-processing perspective. Siegler argues that much of cognitive development consists of the sequential acquisition of increasingly powerful rules for solving problems. He begins his investigation of any given problem area by predicting the different problem-solving rules that children of different developmental levels would use in that area The next step is to administer to subjects of different ages a very carefully designed set of problems. The specific pattern of responses each subject produces across the entire set of problems then suggests which of Siegler's hypothesized rules, if any, that particular subject used to try to solve these problems. Siegler has been quite successful in his efforts to predict and find orderly and plausible-looking developmental sequences of rule acquisitions in several problem areas, most notably in his work with a scale-balance problem involving the concept of torque. In addition, he has shown that the more adequately subjects attend to and store in memory the task information pertinent to a rule they have not yet acquired, the more easily they can learn that rule. Siegler's rule-assessment research has also led him to other intriguing conclusions about the nature and development of the human cognitive system.

It can be argued, with Piaget, that the cognitive systems of infants are indeed fundamentally and qualitatively different from those of older humans. Although Piaget also believed that the cognitive systems of early-childhood, middle-childhood, and adolescent-adult thinkers are likewise qualitatively different from one another, there is growing doubt in the field that these differences, too, are that radical and stage-like. Older minds may appear to be more qualitatively different from younger ones than they really are. One reason for this is that older minds have accumulated much more organized knowledge, or *expertise*, in many more knowledge domains than younger ones have, and we now know a number of specific ways that the possession of expertise in a domain can dramatically improve the quality of one's cognitive functioning within that domain. We would hesitate to say that older minds truly are qualitatively different from younger ones—constitute distinct and different cognitive systems—if disparities in domain-specific expertise were largely responsible for the appearance of qualitative difference. For one thing, the older mind might look almost as immature as the younger one when operating in domains in which it, too, is an utter novice. More generally, both child and adult minds can vary considerably over domains and occasions in the quality of their cognitive performance. At present, therefore, it is difficult to identify really clear-cut, stage-like "cognitive metamorphoses" during the childhood and adolescent years. It is far easier, instead, to defend and document the existence of very important and substantial "developmental trends" during these years. Seven such trends are proposed in the remainder of the chapter.

1. INFORMATION-PROCESSING CAPACITY. A distinction can be made between *structural* and *functional* information-processing capacity. Structural capacity refers to our "hard-wired," neurologically based processing capabilities. It might be interpreted as the number of "slots" in our short-term or working memory "box," or as the total amount of attentional energy we can expend during any brief span of time. Functional capacity refers to the processing we are actually able to carry out in specific task situations, by using

our basic structural capacities plus whatever other resources we may command, such as greater processing speed due to well-practiced operations or familiar stimuli, internal information-processing strategies, and external attentional and mnemonic aids. There is widespread agreement that older children and adolescents have more functional information-processing capacities in most task situations than younger children do, and also that this greater capacity may be at least partly responsible for their frequently superior cognitive performance. However, we do not yet know if hard-wired structural capacity also increases with age and thereby contributes significantly to this age increase in overall functional capacity.

2. DOMAIN-SPECIFIC KNOWLEDGE. As previously indicated, older children have accumulated more knowledge in more different knowledge domains than younger ones have, and this greater expertise makes for better cognitive performance in these domains. Precisely how it does so is the subject of much recent research. One thing that the possession of expertise does is to permit us to solve many problems more by memory processes than by complex reasoning processes—that is, by recognizing familiar problem patterns and responding to them with overlearned solution procedures. The domains of knowledge in which the growing child gains expertise include those taught in school plus many others, such as social-cognitive domains. Just how much of postinfancy cognitive development can ultimately be accounted for by the acquisition of domain-specific knowledge is currently one of the "hot issues" in the field.

3. CONCRETE AND FORMAL OPERATIONS. Although Piaget's logical-mathematical models of *concrete-operational* (middle-childhood) and *formal-operational* (adolescent and adult) thought currently appear to be theoretically inadequate, many of the developmental trends he described still seem very insightful and largely on the mark. Development from early to middle childhood exhibits the following closely related trends. In conservation and other tasks, younger children are apt to base their judgments on *perceived appearances*, older ones on *inferences* that go beyond surface appearances to the underlying *reality*. Younger children are prone to *center* their attention on a single, highly salient task element (*centration*), older ones to *decenter* their attention and distribute it more equitably across all important task elements (*decentration*). Younger children focus on problem *states*, especially the current state, whereas older ones also take note of the *transformations* that link one state with another. Finally, younger children's thinking tends to be *irreversible*; older children's thinking is more *reversible*, showing an understanding of *inversion* and *compensation*. Development from middle childhood to adolescence and adulthood also shows a set of trends that are closely linked to one another. In scientific reasoning problems, especially, the elementary school child begins with the *real* and moves reluctantly, if at all, to the *possible*; the adolescent may begin by trying to imagine all that is possible in the present situation and then try to find out which of these possibilities actually obtains in this situation. Therefore, the child's approach is more *empirico-inductive* in nature, whereas the adolescent's is more *hypothetico-deductive*. The child considers propositions singly,

in isolation from one another (*intrapropositional* thinking); the adolescent reasons, in addition, about the logical relations (e.g., logical implication) that hold among two or more propositions (*interpropositional* thinking).

4. QUANTITATIVE THINKING. The acquisition of the concept of a unit measure makes it possible for older children and adolescents to make exact, quantitative measurements. Together with their greater knowledge of mathematics, this knowledge probably leads them to approach many tasks and problems with a more *quantitative, measurement-oriented set* than is true of younger children. This hypothesized developmental trend gains additional importance from the fact that quantification and measurement are cognitive tools that are widely applicable in many different knowledge domains.

5. A SENSE OF THE GAME. As children develop, they may gradually increase their knowledge about what "the game of thinking" is like and about how it should be played. This does not imply that they will always play the game well, even when they reach cognitive maturity; on the contrary, considerable research evidence suggests that adult cognition is frequently of poor quality. Unlike the young child, however, older individuals have some sense of what it means to think well versus poorly, and that sense seems like an important cognitive attainment in its own right.

6. METACOGNITION. *Metacognition* ("cognition about cognition") includes any knowledge or cognitive activity that takes as its object, or regulates, any aspect of any cognitive enterprise. Metacognitive abilities undergo considerable development during middle childhood and adolescence. A distinction can be made between *metacognitive knowledge* and *metacognitive experiences*. The former refers to your accumulated *declarative* and *procedural* knowledge concerning cognitive matters, and can be divided into three categories: *person, task*, and *strategy*. The person category includes your knowledge and beliefs about people as cognitive processors. The task category refers to your knowledge about the cognitive-processing implications of task information and task demands. The strategy category includes your knowledge about cognitive and metacognitive strategies. Its high-sounding name notwithstanding, metacognitive knowledge is assumed to be similar in important respects to the other classes of knowledge that children acquire. Metacognitive experiences are cognitive or affective experiences that pertain to a cognitive enterprise, such as the sudden feeling that you do not understand something you just read. Metacognitive knowledge and metacognitive experiences are assumed to interact with one another as they influence our cognitive activities. There is reason to believe that metacognitive skills play important roles in reading and other areas of school learning, and therefore reason to try teaching them directly to children. Even more than is true of quantitative thinking, metacognition is a cognitive tool with very broad applicability.

7. IMPROVING EXISTING COMPETENCIES. An important part of cognitive growth is the further development of recently acquired, immature competencies. A competency may be improved in the course of development by

becoming more reliably invoked and used on any one task, more generalized and differentiated in its use across tasks, more dominant over competing, inappropriate approaches, more integrated with other competencies, more accessible to conscious reflection and verbal expression, and more consolidated and solidified.

Social Cognition

Social cognition takes humans and human affairs as its subjects; it means cognition about people and their doings. Machines, mathematics, and moral judgments are all objects and products of human cognition, for instance, but only the latter would be considered a topic within human *social* cognition. Social cognition deals with the strictly social world, not the physical and logical-mathematical ones, even though all three worlds obviously have people's fingerprints all over them. The scientific investigation of this kind of cognition currently is of great interest to psychologists, but its actual practice has undoubtedly been of even greater interest to practically everybody since the dawn of the species. Numerous motives, ranging from self-preservation to idle curiosity, must continually impel people the world over to try to make sense out of themselves, other people, interpersonal relations, social customs and institutions, and other interesting objects of thought within the social world (Wegner & Vallacher, 1977). And psychologists well ought to be interested in the nature and development of processes which are that significant in everyday mental life.

Social-cognitive development has received a good deal of scientific study, especially in recent years. Good sources on this topic include Butterworth and Light (1982), Chandler (1977), Collins (1980), Damon (1977, 1978), Flavell and Ross (1981b), Glick and Clarke-Stewart (1978), Higgins, Ruble, and Hartup (1983), Keasey (1978b), Lamb and Sherrod (1981), Rest (1983), Selman (1980), Serafica (1982), and Shantz (1975, 1983). The book by Lamb and Sherrod (1981) is the best single source on social-cognitive development during infancy; the review chapters by Rest (1983) and Shantz (1983) provide excellent coverage of postinfancy acquisitions.

THE NATURE OF SOCIAL COGNITION

What are the major classes of objects and events towards which social cognitions are directed? Here is a good list:

> The observations or inferences we make are principally about intentions, attitudes, emotions, ideas, abilities, purposes, traits, thoughts, perceptions, memories—events that are *inside* the person and strictly psychological. Similarly, we attend to certain psychological qualities of relationships *between* persons, such as friendship, love, power, and influence. We attribute to a person properties of *consciousness* and *self-determination*, and the capacity for *representation of his environment*, which in turn mediates his actions (Tagiuri, 1969, p. 396).

I would add: that the persons in question include the self as well as others; that we think about social groups and people in general as well as about particular human beings (e.g., we think about human nature, and we think about governments or other social structures, with their constituent roles, rules, and institutions); that we ponder what individuals and groups *ought* to do (for moral, legal, or social-conventional reasons), and why, as well as what they actually *do* do; and that there are no doubt other interesting classes of social-cognitive phenomena psychologists have not yet identified for study. The possible objects of human social cognition are very numerous and very diverse, and psychology's present representation of them is almost certainly insufficiently rich and inclusive.

At least part of what social cognition includes is schematized in Figure 5-1. S means the self and O means another person or group of persons. The dashed arrows represent acts and products of social cognition. They mainly include a person's inferences, beliefs, or conceptions about the inner psychological processes or attributes of human beings, and are therefore represented in Figure 5-1 as penetrating into the interior of their targets. The solid arrows represent overt social acts rather than covert mental ones, and consequently they cannot "penetrate" their objects in quite this sense. For instance, I may be able to infer what is going on inside your head if given enough clues (social cognition), but I can affectionately pat only the outside of it (social act). The top part of Figure 5-1 shows that the self can have all manner of cognitions about the self as well as about another person or group of persons. The bottom part shows that social cognition can also encompass various relationships and interactions among individuals or groups (Damon, 1977; Selman & Byrne, 1974). It further shows that the self can be one of the interacting individuals the self is mentally representing, and that the inter-actions represented can themselves include covert social cognitions (Flavell, 1981b) as well as overt social acts. Thus, I may think about myself in isolation, about you in isolation, and also about the social acts and social cognitions each of us may carry out with respect to the other.

Another way to characterize the domain is to indicate some very general preconditions for the successful execution of any specific act of social thinking (Flavell, 1974; Flavell, Botkin, Fry, Wright, & Jarvis, 1968/1975). There are at least three such preconditions: *Existence, Need,* and *Inference.*

Existence refers to the person's basic knowledge that a particular fact or phenomenon of the social world exists as one of life's possibilities. In order to think about something in the social world, one obviously first has to be aware of its very existence as a possible object of social cognition. If a young child has not yet become aware that people even *have* such psychological goings on as percepts, thoughts, and motives, for instance, she manifestly cannot try to infer their presence and detailed characteristics in particular people on

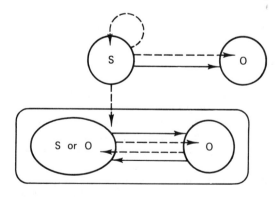

FIGURE 5-1. A representation of social cognition.

particular occasions. The point is a most unprofound one: There scarcely can be any thinking about social-cognitive phenomena if the very existence of such phenomena is not yet represented by the thinker.

Need refers to the disposition or sensed need to attempt an act of social cognition. A person may know perfectly well that she and other people have experiences called feelings (Existence), and yet she may not even try to diagnose them when opportunities arise (Need). She may not think to, may not want to, or may not see any point to making such an effort.

Inference concerns the skill or capacity to carry off a given form of social thinking successfully. The thinking need not involve "inference" strictly defined—any social-cognitive process qualifies (Flavell, 1974). I may know of the existence of the type of thought or feeling you are currently having (Existence), and I may badly want to figure out what you are presently experiencing (Need), and yet I may simply not have the ability to identify it on the basis of the evidence provided (Inference). I can infer, perhaps, that you are feeling something unpleasant, and knowing even that much, of course, requires some Inference ability. However, lack of sufficient evidence, my general inadequacies as a people reader, or both, may prevent my obtaining a more detailed and precise understanding of exactly what sort of unpleasant affect you are experiencing.

The distinction between Existence and Inference is especially clear in the area of cognitions about visual percepts. I sit on one side of a random arrangement of complex objects (e.g., four vases of different shapes and colors, each containing a variety of different flowers) and you sit on the other. My task is to select, from a large number of different photographs of the array taken from different positions, that photograph which shows exactly how the array looks to you, from your vantage point. I am not allowed to walk around and look; I must figure out what you see from where I sit. The problem of computing (Inference) another person's visual perspective in such tasks can range from the trivially easy to the near impossible, depending upon the complexity of the array, the set of photographs used, and so on. Even in the most difficult of these tasks, however, I know perfectly well that you have *some* visual experience of the array, just as I do (Existence). I also know some other things that require little or no on-the-spot computation, and therefore seem more Existence-like than Inference-like. For instance, I know at the onset that you have one and only one view of the array and that, whatever that view is, it is different from my own; consequently, only one photograph in the set can possibly be the right one, and any photograph depicting my own view can automatically be excluded (Flavell, Omanson, & Latham, 1978; Salatas & Flavell, 1976).

To characterize the general nature of social cognition in these ways is implicitly to indicate what the child's developmental task is—what social-cognitive development is the development of. It is the developing awareness and general knowledge (Existence) of the enormous variety of possible social-cognitive objects alluded to in the first part of this section. It is also a developing awareness (Need) of when and why one might or should try to take readings of such objects. Finally, it is the development of a wide variety of cognitive skills (Inference)—still largely unknown—with which to take these readings.

SIMILARITIES AND DIFFERENCES
BETWEEN SOCIAL AND NONSOCIAL
COGNITION

In what respects are social and nonsocial cognition similar to one another? How might they be different, and why? What about possible similarities and differences in their developmental courses? A number of psychologists have wrestled with these important questions recently and the following discussion owes much to their ideas (e.g., Broughton, 1978; Butterworth, 1982; Damon, 1981; Flavell & Ross, 1981a; Gelman & Spelke, 1981; Glick, 1978; Higgins, 1981; Hoffman, 1981; Ross, 1981; Schneider, Hastorf, & Ellsworth, 1979; Shantz, 1983; Shweder, 1980).

Similarities

A little reflection should convince you that there have to be many similarities between social and nonsocial cognition. In the first place, the head that thinks about the social world is the self-same head that thinks about the nonsocial world. All of the basic mental tools described in previous chapters (knowledge structures, symbolic abilities, information-processing capacities, etc.) can be used to categorize, remember, reason about, and otherwise manipulate social data as well as nonsocial data. Thanks to these tools, both the social and the nonsocial world come to be experienced as "structured, stable, and meaningful" (Schneider et al., 1979, p. 10). As with nonsocial cognition, some of our social cognition involves complex reasoning (e.g., elaborate perspective taking) and some of it involves only the recognition of familiar input patterns and the automatic running off of overlearned responses to these patterns.

In addition, social and nonsocial inputs are similar in certain fundamental respects. Things are physical objects in space and so are people. Things participate in events that take place over time and so do people. Things relate to and interact with one another in numerous ways and so do people. Nonsocial concepts can be concrete ("ball") or abstract ("entropy") and so can social ones ("girl," "friendship"). In some cases, we may even have trouble deciding whether the object of our cognition is a "social" or a "nonsocial" one; possible examples include your comatose and moribund great aunt, your pet dog, and a computer that beats you in chess. Not surprisingly, therefore, many of the trends in the development of nonsocial cognition described in previous chapters can also be seen in the area of social-cognitive development. Following are some examples.

SURFACE TO DEPTH. We have seen (pp. 93–94) that cognition about nonsocial phenomena begins with surface appearances alone and only later gets beneath the surface to construct an inferred underlying reality. Social-cognitive development also proceeds from surface to depth. Children begin by reading only the most external, immediately perceptible attributes of themselves, other people, social interactions, and other social-cognitive objects. They pay attention to people's appearances and overt behaviors, but they initially do not use these or other kinds of evidence to make inferences about the covert social-psychological processes, meanings, and causes which underlie them. The dashed arrows in Figure 5-1 initially stop at the boundaries of those circles and ellipses, and only gradually penetrate into the interior.

SPATIAL AND TEMPORAL CENTRATIONS. The social cognition of younger children also shows spatial and temporal centrations (pp. 94–95). They are prone to attend only to the most obvious and highly salient features of a social object or situation, neglecting subtler but possibly more important features (spatial centration). For example, the young child can read the big, obvious signs of gaiety in another, but she will require additional social-cognitive growth before she can also pick up the little, nonobvious signs that indicate that this individual's gaiety is forced and false. Seeing through social facades is not the long suit of young children, any more than seeing through Piagetian-task nonconservation facades is. The same applies to temporal centration. The younger child is likely to hew closely to the immediately present social situation. It is only later that she will spontaneously infer its likely past antecedents and future consequences—for example, what prior social experiences, motives, intentions, and so on, led the people to act as they are now acting, and what will be the likely next steps in the episode. The child only gradually learns to integrate over time and events, to interlink states and transformations, and this is as true in the social domain as in the nonsocial one.

INVARIANT FORMATION. Another parallel has been mentioned already (pp. 37–38)—namely, that there is a good deal of invariant formation in both worlds. Children gradually come to think of themselves and others as stable human beings who conserve, over time and circumstances, their personhoods, personalities, social and sexual roles and identities, and many other attributes. Day to day changes in one's own or another's mood and behavior come to be construed as variations on an enduring theme, rather than as a succession of unrelated melodies. The cognitive construction of these social invariants can, of course, be viewed as a special type of temporal decentration, one which identifies important personal continuities which persist over time.

QUANTITATIVE THINKING. The child was said (pp. 101–102) to acquire a quantitative approach towards physical phenomena, entailing a conception of how to measure things in a precise fashion. Similarly, in the social realm the child develops a quasimetric conception of rewards and punishments. He gradually comes to believe that rewards and punishments should be doled out in strict proportion to the recipient's deserts, however these be ascertained (the criteria become more sophisticated with age). This conception includes ideas about "fair" versus "unfair" distribution or exchange of goods ("fair" shares and "fair" trades), "fair" versus "unfair" punishments, and so on, and all of these ideas seem to have a semiquantitative cast to them.

METACOGNITION. Recall (p. 104) that metacognition was defined as knowledge or cognitive activity that takes as its object, or regulates, any aspect of any cognitive enterprise. Since cognitive enterprises are carried out by people—self or others—metacognition about them clearly represents a form of social cognition (Flavell, 1981b). During the adolescent years, especially, people are likely to develop a heightened consciousness of their own and other people's cognitive enterprises. These enterprises gradually become "objects of contemplation" (pp. 32–33)—things to think about rather than merely things to do. Accordingly, the individual becomes more introspective, much given to scrutinizing his own thoughts and feelings. He also spends more time wondering about those of significant others. In particular, he may wonder what they think of his outer appearance and behavior (self-consciousness), and also what they might know or guess about his inner world.

ABSTRACT AND HYPOTHETICAL THINKING. Similarly, the sometimes abstract and hypothetical quality of mature thinking is also visible when its cognitive objects are social. The person becomes capable of thinking about groups, institutions, and people in general (concepts of "human nature," etc.) as well as about specific individuals. Moreover, specific individuals, both self and others, become endowed with more general, enduring traits and dispositions as well as more specific and transient processes. Likewise, the mature thinker may think about all manner of abstract ideas and ideals in such areas as morality, religion, and politics. Finally, the hypotheses she makes in a Piagetian task situation have their social-cognitive counterparts in the speculations she makes about her personal future. Elkind (1967) has written insightfully about these and other social-cognitive expressions of formal-operational intellectual capacity.

COGNITIVE SHORTCOMINGS. We have seen (p. 103) that even mature thinkers are vulnerable to all sorts of errors and fallacies when reasoning about impersonal phenomena. The same is true for social reasoning. Social psychologists and personality theorists (e.g., Mischel & Peake, 1982; Nisbett & Ross, 1980; Ross, 1981; Schneider et al., 1979) have shown that our inferences about ourselves and other people, although by no means wholly inaccurate, are subject to numerous biases and distortions. For example, laypeople and psychologists alike tend to overestimate the degree to which a person's behavior is consistent over situations—that is, the degree to which the behavior is governed by stable and general internal traits and dispositions versus variable, external circumstances (Mischel & Peake, 1982). This is especially true when trying to explain another's behavior rather than our own (Mischel, 1973, p. 264; Schneider et al., 1979, Chapter 5): You tripped because you are clumsy (a stable trait) whereas I tripped because it was dark (a variable circumstance).

An ailment that particularly bedevils social cognition, however, is what Piaget called *egocentrism*. Piagetian egocentrism can be roughly defined as a failure to differentiate or distinguish clearly between one's own point of view and another's. For instance, my assessment of your opinions and feelings about something is egocentric to the degree that I have unwittingly misattributed my own opinions and feelings to you. Piagetian egocentrism is often assumed to be very prevalent in early-childhood social cognition and to decline thereafter, much like logical errors in nonsocial cognition. Although there is something in this assertion, it does not represent the whole truth about egocentrism, as Piaget and his followers have been well aware (e.g., Elkind, 1967).

The following is only one psychologist's ideas about egocentrism, and should therefore not be read uncritically. Unlike, say, nonconservation of number, I believe we are "at risk" (almost in the medical sense) for egocentric thinking all of our lives, just as we are for certain logical errors. The reason lies in our psychological designs in relation to the jobs to be done. We experience our own points of view more or less directly, whereas we must always attain the other person's in more indirect manners. Our own points of view are more cognitively "available" to us than another person's (Tversky & Kahneman, 1973). Furthermore, we are usually unable to turn our own viewpoints off completely when trying to infer another's. Our own perspectives produce clear signals that are much louder to us than the other's, and they usually continue to ring in our ears while we try to decode the other's. It may take considerable skill and effort to represent another's point of view accurately through this kind of noise, and the possibility of egocentric distortion is ever-present. For example, the fact that you thoroughly understand calculus constitutes an obstacle to your continuously keeping in mind my ignorance of it while trying to explain it to me; you may momentarily realize how hard it is for me, but that realization may quietly slip away once you get immersed in your explanation. Interestingly, the "other" can be oneself in another time and condition, rather than a different person (Flavell, 1981b, p. 275). For example, it can be hard to imagine yourself feeling well and happy next week if you feel terribly ill or unhappy today. Taking the perspective of yourself, when that perspective is different from your current one, can sometimes be as hard as taking the perspective of another person. Thus, we can no more "cure" ourselves of our susceptibility to egocentrism than we can cure ourselves, say, of our difficulties in understanding two simultaneously presented messages. Both cases represent a human information-processing limitation with respect to a certain class of cognitive task.

A SENSE OF THE GAME. Unlike the young child, however, the mature thinker knows that others do have cognitive perspectives which differ from his own, that his own perspective may interfere with his representation of them, and other Existence-type truths about social cognition. Therein lies a final parallel with nonsocial cognition. Grown-ups the world around surely have developed some "sense of the game" of people reading, just as they have in the case of impersonal thinking games (pp. 102–103). As with the latter, the disposition and ability to play this kind of game no doubt shows enormous individual and cultural differences. Once again, however, even the poorer and less motivated players undoubtedly have some sense of the enterprise, and that sense is the product of development.

Differences

People are different from most other objects in a number of ways. Also, our relations with people differ in key respects from our relations with most other objects. These two sets of differences together make for some differences in the content and process of social versus nonsocial cognition. Our social cognition acquires certain characteristic and distinctive qualities from the fact that the objects of this cognition and our relation to them are somewhat distinctive. As Shweder put it, "What one thinks about has some influence on how one thinks" (1980, p. 270).

How are people different from most nonsocial objects? They are sentient creatures who can act spontaneously and deliberately. They can perceive, represent, know, believe, think, mean, intend, want, emote, and learn. They are causal agents who can, within limits, freely and intentionally generate their own mental and physical acts and hence can be held responsible for these acts. Their behavior is often difficult to predict because they respond to internal as well as external events, and also to their own representations and interpretations of external stimuli rather than to the "raw stimuli" themselves. They can deliberately reveal and conceal critical information about themselves, and this further adds to their unpredictability.

Our relations with people are typically very different from our relations with other objects. There is first of all the static relation of similarity. We are very similar to the objects of our social cognition (indeed, we *are* those objects in the case of social cognition about the self). This similarity makes possible the use of cognitive processes that are distinctively social cognitive. There are also the dynamic relations that comprise all the special ways we respond to social objects and they to us. Our interactions with other people are often intricately coordinated, mutual, reciprocal affairs, interactions quite unlike those we have with nonsocial objects. Our thoughts and behaviors concerning another person are apt to be importantly guided by our cognitive representations of the social roles, relations, and behaviors in play between us. Our thoughts and behaviors may also be guided by our representations of the other person's thoughts and intentions concerning us, even including the other person's possible representations of these representations of ours (e.g., "I think she knows I like her ideas"). Thus, the social cognitions of two people can overlap and include one another in complex and changing ways over the course of a social interaction between them (see Figure 5-1).

> Unlike all other components of the world, other people have the capacity to establish mutually intentional relations with the subject. Such relations are composed of a series of interactions in the course of which the subject shares perspectives and coordinates actions and reactions with the other. It is this mutuality of conduct and communication that distinguishes social from merely physical events and that engenders (and requires) a special sort of understanding. The developmental study of social cognition is, in part, a study of this understanding as it grows and changes in the child (Damon, 1981, p. 159).

As indicated, differences in type of cognitive object and in self-object relations make for some differences in the content and process of social as contrasted with nonsocial cognition. The differences in content are obvious and need little comment. Examples of distinctively social-cognitive content include our mental representations of: (1) other people's thoughts and attitudes about us and our behavior; (2) their and our own moral or social-conventional obligations and responsibilities. Obviously, when trying to solve a problem in, say, mechanics, our mental contents do not include inferences about the attitudes and moral responsibilities of the various masses and forces involved.

Possible examples of uniquely or at least predominantly social-cognitive processes have not been very precisely specified as yet by students of social cognition (Dweck, 1981). In general, however, it can be said that we use information about ourselves and our own reactions more often and in a different way when engaged in social cognition than when engaged in non-social cognition (cf. Hoffman, 1981). For example, we may either delib-erately or nondeliberately (i.e., egocentrically) assume that the other person will think, feel, and act in his present situation as we would if we were in that same situation. If we would feel upset in that situation, for example, we might assume that he would too. Furthermore, because people often do respond to the same situation in much the same way, such an assumption will often be correct. Alternatively, if we know or believe that the other person is very different from us in certain respects, we might assume for that reason that he will respond differently than we would—and we may again be right. Of course, both of our assumptions might turn out to be wrong instead, but that is beside the point. The point is that in both instances the social-cognitive process that was employed made heavy and special use of the self as a point of reference and basis for judgment.

Another possible social-cognitive process, also deriving from similarities between ourselves and the objects of our cognition, is that of *empathy*. Empathy includes the process or processes by which affective arousal in another person may automatically and involuntarily elicit affective arousal in ourselves (Hoffman, 1981). In proposing empathy as a social-cognitive process, Hoffman (1981) speculates that our "visceral and somatic responses together provide cues about the fact that another person is affectively aroused and they also provide some rough cues about the particular affect the other is experiencing" (p. 76). It seems unlikely that empathic-type mechanisms see much service in our cognition of nonsocial content. Even when empathic processes are not involved, it is possible that affect plays a more important and varied role in social than in nonsocial cognition. More generally, it would not be surprising if it turned out that our species has evolved at least some distinctive, "domain-specific" cognitive tools for gaining information about social objects, just as it probably has for acquiring natural language (Chapter 8).

It would be unwise to overexaggerate the role of special, domain-specific processes here, however. Most of the basic processes and operations used in social cognition are probably also used in nonsocial cognition. Although what one thinks about probably does influence how one thinks (Shweder, 1980, p. 270), we should also remember that it is the same human mind that does the thinking. All the same, its distinctive objects and contents coupled with whatever special processes it may possess combine to make social cognition seem plenty different enough—different enough, certainly, to warrant giving it its own chapter in this book.

SOCIAL-COGNITIVE DEVELOPMENT
DURING INFANCY

There is now considerable research evidence (Lamb & Sherrod, 1981) that infancy is a rich formative period for social as well as nonsocial cognition:

During the first year of life, the infant makes major strides in the acquisition of knowledge about the social world. Behaviors such as the fear of strangers, the formation of specific attachments, and the onset of communicative skills are all reflections of this. Central to these developments are the infant's emerging concepts of person and specific individuals. During the first year, the infant differentiates persons from other classes of experiences, acquiring knowledge about their common properties. Further, the infant learns the characteristics of specific individuals such as mother and father, and comes to view them and others as individual members of the class of persons. These cognitive achievements are prerequisites for the major landmarks of social development . . . (Olson, 1981, p. 37).

Infant Social-Cognitive Development as a Process of Differentiation

As Olson's summary suggests, part of infant social-cognitive development can be characterized as a process of *differentiation*—differentiation of self from nonself, of human objects from nonhuman objects, and of one human object from another. In the case of self, the child has as one of her major developmental tasks in this area the gradual evolution of a sense of herself as a distinct and separate entity, clearly differentiated from all the other entities, human and nonhuman, that populate her everyday world. She must acquire some conception of herself both as a physical object and as a person among persons. This process of articulation and definition of self, and especially of self as person or psychological subject, has not progressed very far by the end of infancy. A definite beginning has been made, however (Bretherton et al., 1981; Lewis, 1981; Lewis & Brooks-Gunn, 1979).

Infants also make a start at acquiring knowledge about other people. Human objects gradually become distinguished from nonhuman ones in ways such as the following (Gelman & Spelke, 1981; Lamb & Sherrod, 1981). There is research evidence that infants as young as 2 months of age may become upset if a person faces them in an impassive manner, without moving or speaking. This distress probably reflects the learned expectation that people, unlike most other objects, will spontaneously interact and communicate with them. Infants gradually learn that human beings are very special objects with which they can interact in very special ways. Of particular importance, they learn that their own behavior and that of other people are often predictably *contingent* on one another. You the infant act and the other person reacts appropriately. If your action is a request, the other person will function as a means to your goal without your making physical contact with him—that is, he will behave as an active, communicable agent in the service of your needs and wants rather than as a passive, uncommunicable tool or instrument that you must physically manipulate. Reciprocally, the other person acts and you react appropriately. Eventually, you will learn how to manage an alternating sequence of reciprocal actions with him: You take your turn in a simple social game like peek-a-boo or in a baby-style "conversation" of prelinguistic utterances, then you wait for him to take his turn, then you take another turn, and so on.

Infants also gradually become more responsive to other people's facial and gestural expressions of emotion and eventually even learn to use these expressions as guides to prudent actions. For example, it has recently been shown that when a 12 or 18 month old is introduced to a novel and somewhat frightening toy in the company of his mother, he is likely to consult her facial expression before making his next move. If her expression is happy, he will approach the toy; if it is fearful, he will approach her instead (Klinnert, Campos, Sorce, Emde, & Svejda, 1983). Imagine, if you can, an infant's "consulting" the appearance of a nonsocial object in this way. Finally, there is some evidence that children of 2 years of age or even younger may possess at least a rudimentary, dim understanding of the fact that people have inner, psychological states and processes—that people have feelings and can see things, for example (Bretherton et al., 1981; Flavell, 1974; Lempers, Flavell, & Flavell, 1977).

Some grasp of the person-nonperson distinction is definitely achieved by the end of infancy, therefore. Needless to say, a more detailed and penetrating knowledge of the psychological characteristics of personhood (e.g., that people act out of inner motives, that they may not mean what they say, etc.) is still a thing of the distant future for a child of this age.

In addition to distinguishing persons from nonpersons, the infant comes to distinguish one person from another. Certain people, such as his mother and father, become familiar, easily recognizable, and above all, highly significant emotionally. He gradually becomes emotionally *attached* to such people, and they to him. The development of the capacity and disposition to form such affect-laden bonds to selected others is referred to as the development of *social attachment* (Bowlby, 1969). There is more research evidence available on the development of attachment during infancy than on the parallel and intimately related developments of the concept of self and of others as persons (e.g., Alloway, Pline, & Krames, 1977; Maccoby, 1980; Maccoby & Masters, 1970; Waters & Deane, 1982). Moreover, explicit attempts have been made to tie the growth of social attachment to the growth of cognitive skills. Let us look first at the developmental highlights of social-attachment formation, and then examine its possible links to infant cognitive growth.

Development of Social Attachment

Social attachment is always a reciprocal process of social interaction, necessarily involving the feelings and behaviors of both parties in the interaction. I concentrate mainly on the infant's half of the interaction, however, intentionally slighting the parents' own obviously very important attachment feelings and behaviors towards him. Infant social attachment here is taken to refer both to an underlying disposition and to various overt behaviors that implement or express that disposition. The underlying disposition is a strong affection and yearning for one or more specific people, especially the parent or parent substitute. And I do mean *strong* affection:

> Children's attachment to their parents is a passionate thing. When a two-year-old is frightened, the child's small arms cling to the parent's body with surprising strength. When the parent has been away and the two are reunited, the child's smiles and enthusiastic hugs are among the unalloyed pleasures of parenthood, signaling that the child returns the parent's love. On occasion children will protest with all the vigor at their command a separation from their parents (Maccoby, 1980, p. 47).

Many of the overt behaviors which reflect this emotional bond have to do with the maintenance of a suitable (from the child's point of view) degree of proximity or physical nearness to the attachment figure. Depending on his age, the infant does some things which bring or keep him satisfactorily close to this person (clinging, sucking, crawling after), and other things which tend to bring or keep the person near to him (smiling, crying, calling). Again depending on his age, the infant may show signs of acute fear or unhappiness if this desired level of proximity is not achieved or maintained—for instance, if the parent puts him down or leaves him alone in his room. Other indices of attachment may include lack of positive social response or outright fear in the presence of people other than the current object or objects of his attachment (e.g., a strange person), and the use of the attachment object as a source of comfort and security (e.g., retreating to her when frightened or ill, being more venturesome with strange people or objects when she is nearby).

Now to the actual development of social attachment. There is substantial variation from infant to infant, throughout the course of this development, as to what behaviors are exhibited and when. It is *not* a really neat and tidy developmental progression, although general trends can be indicated.

During the first weeks of life, the infant shows no detectable emotional attachment to any object, human or nonhuman. The baby could not be characterized as socially attached in any sense during this early period. People as a class do appear to become especially interesting objects for the infant during the next several months, but there is little apparent emotional differentiation within this class. A 2 month old, for instance, may be capable of a genuinely social smile, but he is likely to be disconcertingly promiscuous in his use of it: He may smile just as winningly at a total stranger as at his mother, although perhaps more broadly at both than at most inanimate objects. Such a child is no longer quite presocial, but his failure to discriminate one person from another emotionally still makes him "preattached."

During or around the age period from 3 to 6 months, the baby will usually begin to smile a bit more brightly and gurgle a bit more happily at one or more familiar people than at the rest of humankind. However, he may still exhibit no fear or poker-faced "sobering" in the presence of strangers, and may show no more tendency to protest when mother leaves him than when anyone else does. Genuine social attachment to specific, individualized persons seems imminent, but perhaps not quite there yet.

Most babies show unmistakable signs of having begun to form specific social attachments sometime during the third quarter of their first year. For example, they may show pronounced negative reactions to the approach of a stranger, especially if in an unfamiliar setting or if a parent is not close by. Stranger anxiety is sufficiently regular in its occurrence to have won the label of "8 months anxiety," but, in fact, not all babies exhibit it, and among those who do, it does not necessarily first occur or reach its peak at that age. They are also likely to show decidedly negative reactions to separation from one or more specific individuals, rather than either showing no such reaction at all or showing it to almost anybody's departure. There is evidence (Kagan, 1976) that such separation protest reaches its peak with some regularity early in the second year of life, even in children reared in quite different cultures. This and other regularities in the nature and sequence of attachment development testify to its biological-evolutionary roots and partly maturational character. Moreover, the child's functional definition of "proximity" versus "separation" changes with age from this period onward. Younger children may require actual physical contact to feel content (negative reaction to being put down), older ones only perceptual contact (negative reaction to seeing parent leave the room), and still older ones only potential or symbolic contact (negative reaction only if parent is known not to be somewhere in the house, or known not to return soon, etc.—otherwise, the child acts as though no *psychological* separation has occurred). "Social attachment" in the somewhat negative, emotionally dependent sense of the term gradually wanes in most children during the preschool and early school years; in the more positive sense of love and affection felt for significant others, however, it may, of course, endure for the rest of one's life.

Cognitive-Developmental Prerequisites for Attachment Development

There is a mutually facilitative, reciprocally mediative developmental relationship between cognitive (perceptual and conceptual) processes and social behavior. This is true during infancy, and it is also true at later periods of development. On the one hand, the infant's social interactions and emotional relations with her caretakers must constitute a nearly indispensable crucible for the formation and development of cognitive processes. It is difficult to conceive how there could be any significant cognitive development at all if the amount and quality of the infant's social relations with other human beings fell below some unknown minimum. Human beings are intrinsically social beings, and human cognitive development requires human social relations.

A little thought will indicate that something like the reverse also has to be true. Social behavior is always partly managed and mediated by cognitive processes, and the developmental level or quality of social behavior that an individual is capable of showing must be at least partly dependent on the developmental level or quality of that individual's cognitive abilities. The latter is conceived as a necessary but definitely not sufficient condition for the former—that is, having achieved a certain general level of cognitive development does not *ensure* the occurrence of a particular kind of social behavior, or a particular kind of social cognition either, for that matter; it only makes it *possible*. For example, I cannot cooperate with another person in some common endeavor (social behavior) unless I have the wherewithal upstairs (cognitive processes) to integrate and coordinate my responses with that person's in such a way as to merit the term *cooperative behavior*. At the same time, the mere possession of the necessary penthouse equipment obviously does not *oblige* me to be cooperative. For want of sufficient cognitive skill, young babies *cannot* cooperate; for want of sufficient motivation rather than sufficient cognitive skill, old misanthropes *can* cooperate but *will not*.

How might the course of infant attachment development reflect or be partly mediated by the course of infant cognitive development, in the necessary-but-not-sufficient-condition sense just described? One very plausible cognitive prerequisite for the formation of specific and focused social attachment is the developing infant's increasing ability to make fine visual discriminations (Yarrow & Pederson, 1972). Until she is perceptually capable of discriminating one looming face from another (no mean achievement, when you think about it), she obviously cannot recognize or identify particular faces as special, recurrent, and familiar ones; and until she can do the latter, she can hardly form social-emotional bonds to particular individuals.

The same argument can, of course, be made with regard to the development of auditory (Horowitz, 1974) and other sensory discriminations. The parent constitutes a complex bundle of sights, sounds, feelings, and smells, and this bundle has to become quickly and easily distinguishable from other, quite similar bundles before the infant can become differentially attached to it.

In fact, some arresting research findings from recent studies indicate that human infants do possess at birth or soon develop just the sorts of perceptual skills and perceptual preferences that could permit and promote the development of social attachments to human objects (Gibson & Spelke, 1983; Olson, 1981; Sherrod, 1981; Spelke & Cortelyou, 1981; see also Chapters 2, 6, and 8). These findings suggest that, like the young of many other species, young human babies are well equipped by evolution to begin the developmental process of becoming attached to conspecifics.

Consider first their visual abilities and preferences. We now know that babies tend to be especially visually attentive to large objects that move, have edges and contours that exhibit high light-dark contrast, and are brightly colored or shiny. And what objects in the baby's environment have those properties in spades? You guessed it—looming and animated human faces displaying high-contrast hairlines and prominent, shining eyes. The claim here is not that human infants have an inborn ability to discriminate between human faces and other objects that have the just-mentioned stimulus properties. The presently available evidence does not suggest that babies are born with "face detectors"—that is, with cognitive templates that resonate solely and specifically to face-like visual inputs (e.g., Sherrod, 1981). On the other hand, babies probably do not need to be provided by evolution with anything much more specific than the visual preferences just outlined to get them preferentially looking at and learning about people. The reason is that people are likely to be the most frequently perceived objects possessing all these visually attractive features.

The available evidence does not allow us to say exactly when infants first become able to discriminate consistently one human face from another, using only visual information (e.g., Olson, 1981). There appears to be solid, positive evidence that they can do so by 3 to 5 months of age. However, the methods commonly employed to assess this ability (e.g., using static, two-dimensional photographs of faces as the visual discriminanda) may well have underestimated the face-discrimination abilities of infants younger than 3 months.

Young human infants' auditory abilities and sensitivities with respect to the human voice appear to be even more stimulus-specific and precocious than their visual abilities and sensitivities with respect to the human face. As indicated in Chapter 8, babies seem to be biologically pretuned and disposed to process human speech sounds: "Speech is attended to strongly and preferentially, it would seem, from birth" (Gibson & Spelke, 1983, p. 23). To illustrate, newborns will suck to maintain the sound of tape-recorded folk songs but not to maintain the sound of white noise, suggesting that they can discrimate between the two and prefer to hear the former (Butterfield & Siperstein, 1972).

Even more impressive auditory abilities and preferences have recently been documented by DeCasper and Fifer (1980). Their subjects were infants of 3 days of age or less who lived in a group nursery, where their general care and night feeding were handled by a number of female personnel. These newborns were fed by their mothers four times a day and, at testing, had had a total of 12 or fewer hours of contact with their mothers. Shortly after delivery, the experimenters tape recorded the mothers as they read a Dr. Seuss children's story. These recordings served as the auditory stimuli in subsequent testing. In three experiments it was found that the newborns tended to suck in such a way as to produce (would "work for") the sounds of their own mothers' voices in preference to that of another mother. The authors concluded from their research and that of Butterfield and Siperstein (1972) that "within the first 3 days of postnatal development, newborns prefer the human voice, discriminate between speakers, and demonstrate a preference for their mothers' voices with only limited maternal exposure" (DeCasper & Fifer, 1980, p. 1176). They also mentioned that not enough is known yet about intrauterine auditory experience in humans to know if prenatal exposure to the mother's voice could have contributed to this discrimination and preference. Whatever the basis, the fact that a creature as mindless looking as the human neonate could make *that* fine and specific an auditory discrimination seems truly extraordinary.

Mehler, Bertoncini, Barrière, and Jassik-Gerschenfeld (1978) have also shown that slightly older babies (1 month olds) discriminate and prefer to hear their own mothers' voices versus another mother's voice, but only if the speech is of the normally intoned, mother-talks-to-baby variety. If the mothers' speech is a nonintonated monotone, the babies show no discrimination between the two voices.

Of course, in the extralaboratory world people do not present themselves to babies as voiceless faces or faceless voices. There is simultaneously a face for the baby to look at and a voice for her to listen to. Moreover, the face and the voice are unified in space and time: The voice and the face share the same spatial location, and the voice's sounds and the face's mouth movements are temporally synchronized. In addition, certain specific faces always co-occur with certain specific voices; for example, the mother's face with her voice, the father's face with his voice. Finally, how each face looks and acts on a given occasion is highly correlated with how its voice sounds; for instance, happy and sad voices usually accompany happy and sad faces, respectively. Detection of these cross-modal relationships between the sights and sounds of people will help the baby recognize, represent, and become attached to specific individuals.

Recent research by Elizabeth Spelke and others has shown that the ability to detect these relationships is present quite early in infancy, as the following sample findings illustrate (see Spelke & Cortelyou, 1981). Young babies will usually look at and visually inspect a person's face if they hear the person speak. Spelke and Cortelyou (1981) suggest that they may do this not because they have learned specifically to expect to see a face whenever they hear a voice. The behavior may stem instead from a more general tendency to become visually attentive whenever they hear any sound and to look in the direction of the sound they hear. But, of course, even this general tendency will help get them simultaneously looking at and listening to people, and doing that will be grist for the development of social cognition and social attachment.

By 4 months of age, babies seem to possess a much more remarkable ability (see Chapter 6): They are somehow able to detect the temporal synchrony that obtains between oral speech movements and speech sounds. In a study of this ability by Spelke and Cortelyou (1981), 4-month-old subjects saw two films playing simultaneously, side by side. Each film showed a different adult female stranger facing the subjects and talking to them in a normal, adult-to-baby manner. Each film had its own sound track. However, only one of the two sound tracks was "on" on any given trial, and it always came from a speaker located midway between the two film screens. This arrangement ensured that the only way a subject could tell which person's voice was playing would be to note the temporal synchrony between the speech sounds and speaker's facial movements, since only one speaker's movements would be "in synch" with the speech heard. Spelke and Cortelyou's infant subjects were apparently capable of detecting this synchrony, as evidenced by their tendency to look primarily at whichever woman had her sound track playing on that particular trial—the woman on the left on some trials and the woman on the right on other trials. A study by Dodd (1979) obtained similar results.

Walker (1982) used a similar method to demonstrate a related ability in infants of 5 and 7 months. In one of her studies, the subjects saw two films of the face of one adult stranger. In one film she was engaged in a "happy" monologue and in the other an "angry" monologue, each complete with appropriate facial expressions and gestures. The two films were presented simultaneously and side by side. The babies heard different things during different periods of the film showing: the angry monologue during one period, the happy monologue during another (both monologues coming from a centrally located loudspeaker), and no sound during another. Walker found that the infants tended to look preferentially at whichever face corresponded in emotional tone to the voice that was playing. For instance, they looked longer at the angry face when the angry voice was heard than when no voice was heard and, similarly, longer at the happy face when the happy voice was heard than when no voice was heard.

Spelke and Cortelyou (1981) and Walker (1982) point out that we do not yet know precisely what perceptual information infants use to detect such correspondences between speech and expressive movements. For the present, we can only marvel at the fact that they are somehow able to carry it off:

> . . . the above studies have uncovered a remarkable perceptual ability. When two people are seen to speak, and a voice is centered between them, infants can discover which of the people is the source of that voice. However they do this, it is clear that they are sensitive to subtle and complex relationships in stimulation to the eye and the ear. Infants have revealed a striking ability to perceive auditory-visual relationships in animate events (Spelke & Cortelyou, 1981, p. 75).

Finally, you will probably not be surprised to learn that babies in this age range have learned that particular familiar voices belong to particular familiar people. Spelke and Owsley (1979) demonstrated this in the following way: Babies of 3½ to 7½ months saw their two parents sitting side by side. While the parents remained motionless, their tape-recorded voices were heard in turn through a speaker located between them. Despite the absence of any temporal synchrony between faces and voices (because the faces did not move), babies at all ages tended to look at whichever parent was heard to speak that moment.

However, the most frequently proposed cognitive prerequisite for attachment development is not a perceptual one but a conceptual one— namely, the Piagetian object concept. The idea that the development of social attachment should be at least partly dependent on the development of object permanence seems plausible on its face. If an infant were too cognitively immature to differentiate external objects from his own actions and to con- ceive of them as independent entities that continue to exist when perceptually absent, he could scarcely either yearn for or search for an absent mother (attachment figure), since she is, of course, also an external object. So long as "out of sight, out of mind" applies to his mother as well as to other objects, one could hardly say that a baby's "social attachment" to her had progressed very far. Conversely, once the object concept is established, he can bridge her physical absences by symbolic-representational means and thereby sustain an enduring affective link to her that we can comfortably refer to as genuine social attachment. Moreover, Piaget and others have suggested that the mothering figure might well become the very *first* of the infant's permanent objects, a most plausible idea in view of her general emotional and attentional salience for him, and in view of the frequency with which he must see her disappear and reappear every day. Constituting the mother as a permanent Piagetian object could be regarded as one of the most important accomplish- ments of infant social-cognitive development.

However, you just do not know the field of psychology unless you know how often perfectly reasonable ideas prove to be either wrong or inordinately hard to demonstrate experimentally. The hypothesized dependence of attachment development on object-concept development has turned out to be a good case in point (Campos & Stenberg, 1981; Flavell, 1977; Haith & Campos, 1977). Most research attempts to demonstrate this dependence have been either unsuccessful or unconvincing and at least some developmentalists (e.g., Campos & Stenberg, 1981) are now persuaded that the whole idea is wrong. My view is that at least part of it has to be right on logical grounds alone. To paraphrase the argument just given, how ever could a child persis- tently yearn and search for a specific other person if the child were still cogni- tively incapable of mentally representing that person in the person's absence? I think the quality of the existing research evidence is more assailable than that logical argument is. An amusing observation by Schaffer (1971), although scarcely "hard evidence," illustrates the plausibility of some such tie between object permanence and social attachment. Schaffer's 6- and 12-month-old subjects seemed a bit uneasy when serving in a visual-perception experiment, so he asked their mothers to sit behind them during the testing. After watching what happened, he quickly found himself recording the number of times the infants turned away from the visual stimulus set before them in favor of looking at the mothers:

> The results are clear-cut. The younger infants hardly ever turned—they tended to behave in a "stimulus-bound" fashion and acted towards the mother in an "out of sight out of mind" manner. The older infants, on the other hand, frequently turned in the course of the experimental session from one stimulus to the other, apparently well able to keep in mind the perceptually absent object, integrating it with other activities, and so showing a much more flexible type of behaviour (Schaffer, 1971, pp. 257–258).

SOCIAL-COGNITIVE DEVELOPMENT DURING THE POSTINFANCY YEARS

Percepts

This topic concerns the child's developing knowledge and inferential ability concerning people's perceptual acts and experiences. She gradually must come to understand, for instance, that other people also see things, and that the nature of another person's visual experience at a given moment can often be inferred from various clues (e.g., the apparent direction of the person's gaze or the spatial relation between the person and what he is looking at). There appear to be at least two, roughly distinguishable developmental levels or stages of Existence-type knowledge about visual percepts (Flavell, 1974, 1978b; Flavell, Everett, Croft, & Flavell, 1981; Hughes, 1975; Hughes & Donaldson, 1979; Masangkay, McCluskey, McIntyre, Sims-Knight, Vaughn, & Flavell, 1974; Shantz, 1975, 1983).

At the higher one, called Level 2, the child has a symbolic-representational (i.e., not merely sensory-motor) understanding of the fact that the self-same object or array of objects presents different appearances when viewed from different spatial locations. The Level 2 child understands the idea of people having different, position-determined perspectives or views of the same visual display. She is aware that even though she and another person both see the very same object, they nonetheless see it differently—have different visual experiences of it—if located at different observation points.

The younger, Level 1 child has acquired the very fundamental and important insight that another person need not always see the same object that she herself currently sees. For instance, she is likely to realize that, if a picture of an object is held vertically so that the picture's face is towards her and its back towards another person seated opposite her, she sees the depicted object but the other person does not. Similarly, she probably would be aware that, if she placed an object on the other person's side of an upright opaque screen, the other person would see it even though she herself no longer could. What she fails as yet to represent, however, is the Level 2 idea that an object which is currently seen by both is seen differently from different spatial perspectives. What is addressed at Level 1 is the global, all-or-none question of *whether* someone does or does not see something; *how* that something looks from here versus there, assuming that it is visible from both positions, is probably not yet a meaningful question. The Level 1 child thinks about *viewing objects*, according to this theory, but not yet about *views of objects*.

Masangkay et al. (1974) found that 2 to 3 year olds can usually solve very simple Level 1-type problems, such as the vertical-picture problem just mentioned. It is not until 4 to 5 years of age, however, that children get to be equally facile with very simple Level 2-type problems, such as the following. Child and experimenter sit facing one another and a side-view picture of a turtle is placed flat on a small table between them. The child is first shown repeatedly that the turtle appears "right side up" (i.e., standing on its feet) to her when the picture is placed in one horizontal orientation, and "upside down" (i.e., lying on its back) when the picture is rotated 180° from that orientation. She is then queried about which of these two perspectives of the turtle she and the experimenter see in each of a series of these 180° picture rotations. Only nine out of twenty-four of Masangkay et al.'s 3 year olds were consistently correct in attributing the upside-down view to the experimenter when they saw the right-side-up view, and vice versa, although all twenty-four were always accurate in describing their own views. In contrast, thirty-five out of their thirty-six 4 to 5½ year olds were consistently accurate in their inferences about how the turtle looked to the experimenter (cf. Flavell et al., 1981). As indicated earlier in our example of the flowers-and-vases perspective task (p. 121), however, it is one thing to know in general that object appearance covaries with observer position (Level 2 Existence knowledge) and quite another to construct an accurate, detailed representation of exactly how something appears from a position other than one's own (Inference skills). The turtles task was the easiest, least-taxing perspective problem Masangkay et al. could think up. Even though it may indeed have required some genuinely Level 2 Existence knowledge for its solution, as intended, it certainly required next to no Inference skill. Numerous other studies (e.g., Coie, Costanzo, & Farnill, 1973; see Shantz, 1975, 1983) have shown how very much more Inference-skill acquisition the 4 year old has ahead of her before she reaches her zenith as a visual perspective taker.

We have also studied the genesis of Level 1-type knowledge and skill, and thus, presumably, the very beginnings of children's cognitions about percepts (Lempers et al., 1977). A large battery of simple tasks was administered to 12- to 36-month-old children in their homes with the help of their mothers. The tasks were designed to assess various skills within each of three major categories of Level 1 ability: (1) *percept production* or provision, where the child causes another person to have a visual percept of an object that the other person did not previously have—for example, by showing him an object picture or pointing to an object; (2) *percept deprivation* or prevention, where the child hides an object or otherwise prevents the other from seeing it; (3) *percept diagnosis*, where the child infers what object the other is visually attending to by interpreting the other's eye or finger orientation, as indicated by the child's looking where the other looks or points, rather than simply staring at his eyes or outstretched finger.

There were a number of interesting results. The favored method of showing pictures at 18 months seems to be to "share" the percept—for example, holding the picture flat or while standing directly beside the other. This method gives way at 24 months to the adult-like procedure of holding the picture vertically, turning it around, and thrusting its face towards the other so that only the other sees it. If the other holds his hands over his eyes at the time, the 18 month old may and the 24 month old will uncover the eyes before showing the picture. The latter can also solve showing problems with which she has presumably had little experience in everyday life, such as showing a picture which is glued to the inside bottom of a hollow cube. Percept-deprivation skills (e.g., hiding objects) are acquired later than percept-production ones, but they seem well developed by age 3 (see also Flavell, Shipstead, & Croft, 1978). Children of 1½ to 2 can usually look where the other looks when the other's eyes and face both point in the same direction, and older children can usually do so even when they are divergent (e.g., face straight ahead but eyes facing to the right). Infants of 12 months point to objects and correctly interpret others' pointing gestures (see also Churcher & Scaife, 1982). In general, the results of this study suggest that at least some elementary forms of cognition about visual percepts may develop towards the beginning of the early-childhood period.

You may have heard the popular rumor or belief that young children egocentrically assume that another person cannot see them when their own eyes are closed. If young children really have as much Level 1 knowledge as the just-described results indicate, that rumor ought to be false. Flavell, Shipstead, and Croft (1980) did two studies to find out. We discovered that 2½ to 4 year olds, but not 5 year olds and adults, would indeed often give an incorrect negative reply to the experimenter's question "Do I see you?" when their eyes were closed, just as the rumor would predict. However, the same young children would also correctly reply that the experimenter did see their arm, did not see their eyes and back, and so on. This strongly suggests that they were in fact making perfectly valid, nonegocentric, Level 1–type inferences about what physical objects (body parts) another person could and could not see, just as our theory would predict. We still do not know exactly why they answered the "you" question incorrectly. We suspect that their incorrect answers may have resulted from a misinterpretation of the meaning of the word "you" in this particular context. Whatever the explanation, the children's correct answers almost certainly mean that the rumor is wrong in substance; young children really are not as egocentric in their percept cognition as the rumor suggests. However, given their incorrect answers to the "you" question, it is not hard to see how such a folk belief got started.

You may have noticed that "percepts" has been unobtrusively rendered as "visual percepts" throughout this section. The reason is that we simply know virtually nothing about the child's developing knowledge and inferential skill concerning audition or other types of perception. More generally, students of social-cognitive development have seldom investigated children's abilities to assess others' *attention* to external stimuli, regardless of the participating sense modality or modalities (cf. Miller & Weiss, 1982). Higher forms of this sort of social cognition would include the ability to detect feigned attention ("You're not *really* listening, Mommy!") and feigned inattention ("You're just *pretending* not to notice, Mommy!").

Feelings

If an 18 month old looks at his mother's face, and then immediately looks where she is staring (Lempers et al., 1977), must we conclude that he is consciously representing the fact that she is having a certain visual experience? Surely not, and we always have to be very careful not to overestimate the young child's social-cognitive competence regarding other people's percepts on the basis of such isolated pieces of evidence. His perception of her demeanor certainly led to his achieving the same visual experience she had, but that alone does not prove that he was aware of the fact and content of her visual experience.

A similar situation occurs in the area of cognitions about feelings. Another person may give conspicuous evidence of experiencing some intense negative feeling, say, and a young child observer may straightaway display a similar feeling. As Hoffman (1972; 1978) and others have pointed out, however, it is possible in such cases that the child's feeling may have not been accompanied by any sort of mental representation whatever of the other's feelings. Simple conditioning mechanisms could plausibly explain the child's distress, for instance. There might even be an innate, unlearned component. On the other hand, such a cognitive representation of the other's feeling might have been present. And if it had been present, it may have been either a cause or a consequence of the child's distress (Feshbach, 1973)—or, conceivably, just a functionally unrelated concomitant of it. It is apparent that there are a number of possibilities here, and I believe they all occur at one age or another, in one interpersonal situation or another.

Three of the possibilities are of particular interest. The first, just illustrated, might be termed *noninferential empathy*: The expression of the other's feelings somehow triggers off similar or related feelings in the child—a sort of emotional contagion phenomenon—but no relevant social cognition accompanies these induced feelings. The child's emotional reaction may, for example, be a "passive and involuntary one, based upon the 'pull' of the cues emitted by the victim which are perceptually similar to cues associated with his own past painful experiences" (Hoffman, 1972, p. 2).

The second could be called *empathic inference* (or inferential empathy). In this case the child has inferred something about the other's feeling state in addition to having some sort of related feeling himself. Of course, the empathy would still be "inferential" even if he happened to be dead wrong about how the other actually felt; inaccurate social cognition is still social cognition. If the child really "felt with" the other, we might be inclined to call his response "empathy," whereas if he only "felt for" the other, we might label it "sympathy"; the differentiation is often a difficult one, however.

The third possibility could be called *nonempathic inference*. It means an inference about the other's feeling unaccompanied by any relevant feeling of one's own, or perhaps by any feeling at all. There might exist a natural and appropriate affective response to the other's feelings (e.g., pleasure at the other's happiness), or there might not (e.g., dispassionately noting that the tennis player on the TV screen appears a bit winded after a longish rally). Even in the former case, the social cognition can be and often is relatively affectless.

Following are some of the main things presently known or surmised about the development of cognition concerning feelings and emotions (Shantz, 1975, 1983). Noninferential empathy probably has its origins in early or middle infancy, and it is certainly observable in very young children

(Hoffman, 1972, 1978). For example, Kreutzer and Charlesworth (1973) found that babies of 6 months and older are likelier to react negatively (e.g., frown, cry) when an adult displays anger and sadness than when the same adult acts happy or neutral; no developmental psychologist I know, however, would interpret that as evidence that 6 month olds can have conscious representations of people's inner emotional states. Although the problem has been studied for many years, there is still actually very little solid research evidence concerning the ability of infants of various ages to detect and respond differentially to the expression of different emotions by others. And we know still less about any nascent ability they might have to interpret them *as* emotional expressions (Oster, 1981).

By preschool age, children show some capacity for both nonempathic and empathic inference. For the former, they can accurately interpret certain facial expressions of emotions, and they can correctly infer how another person is likely to feel when certain things happen to her (Borke, 1971, 1973; Shantz, 1975). These inferences and interpretations can naturally be quite affectless. For example, the child who understands, from strong facial-expression cues, that the stranger in the picture is "happy" is seldom overcome with joy herself in consequence. Why on earth should she be? However, the preschooler's seeming capacity to make such dispassionate inferences and interpretations suggests that, unlike the infant and toddler, when she is observed to feel with or for other children, her feeling may, in fact, be enlightened by some knowledge of their emotional states. Thus, evidence for nonempathic inference in early childhood buttresses evidence for empathic inference. As Shantz (1975) points out, however, the cognitive level of these inferences need not be very high. For instance, the child knows she would feel unhappy if someone took her toy, and hence she assumes that this toyless child feels unhappy.

At first, the child seems only to distinguish global positive affect from global negative affect: In effect, the other "feels good" if she wears a broad smile, or "feels bad" if something obviously unpleasant has happened to her. It is only later that, for instance, the other's negative affect will be differentially interpreted as "mad," "sad," "scared," and so on, depending upon how she looks or what happened to her.

There are also other major changes with age (e.g., Flapan, 1968; Rothenberg, 1970; Savitsky & Izard, 1970). Older children and adolescents are more likely than younger children to try to infer feelings spontaneously, without explicitly being asked to (a development in the Need category). They become increasingly accurate at diagnosing emotional states, and they need fewer obvious cues to do it. They also become more disposed and able to explain the feelings they have diagnosed (Hughes, Tingle, & Sawin, 1981). Furthermore, their explanations will eventually include the actions and feelings of other alters as causes (e.g., "He is unhappy because she doesn't love him") as well as impersonal causes (e.g., "He is unhappy because he lost his watch"). Predictably, their affect inferences can also be more complex, abstract, and broad-ranging. For instance, an adolescent may represent and sympathize with the chronic, silent plight of some distant group as well as the temporary, noisy distress of a familiar individual (Hoffman, 1972, 1978). Finally, they must eventually discover the possibilities of intentionally monitored and guided emotional expression—for example, pretended or disguised feelings, both in themselves and in others. As would be expected, adults differ considerably in their disposition and ability to consciously monitor and shape the expression of their own feelings (e.g., Snyder, 1974).

An interesting developmental theory recently advanced by Harris and Olthof (1982; Harris, Olthof, & Meerum Terwogt, 1981) lends some conceptual coherence to these and other postinfancy developments in this area (cf. Selman, 1980). Their theory is based in part on a study (Harris et al., 1981) in which they interviewed children of 6, 11, and 15 years regarding their concept of emotion. The children were asked a number of questions about the cues by which and the accuracy with which an emotion can be identified, about the strategies that can be used to regulate both the outward display of emotion and the inner experience of emotion, and about the effects of emotion on other psychological processes. The children's replies to these questions indicated a striking age change in their concepts of emotion, particularly between 6 and 11 years.

According to Harris and Olthof's theory, younger children tend to conceive of emotions in a simple stimulus-response (S-R), behavioristic fashion. In this conception, the S represents some familiar emotion-eliciting situation, such as receiving a present or losing a prized possession, and the R refers to a set of nonmental responses, such as facial expressions and behavioral reactions. Older children have a more complex, three-factor conception, in which mental states are believed to mediate or accompany these nonmental responses. Thus, the younger child's "theory" of emotions is behavioristic, whereas the older child's is more mentalistic or cognitivist.

These differing conceptions lead to differences in the way younger and older children think about the identification, regulation, and effects of emotions. Younger children tend to think that if an emotion-producing situation occurs, the resulting emotional reaction is bound to be readily perceptible to an observer. In contrast, older children are likelier to realize that it might not be perceptible because the person experiencing the emotion might decide (mediating mental event) to try to hide or disguise her feelings. For younger children, situations and emotions are tightly linked in a direct, one-to-one fashion. Certain emotions just go with—or even form part of—certain situations (Gove & Keating, 1979). The link is seen as more indirect and unpredictable by the older children because they understand that mental states may intervene. First, older children recognize that people may use their cognitive skills to deliberately modify the inner nature or the outward expression of their emotions. As an example, they are more knowledgeable about "emotional-display rules"—for example, that one can and should try to conceal from the gift giver one's disappointment with an unwanted gift (Saarni, 1979; Selman, 1980). Older children further recognize that a single situation may simultaneously elicit more than one emotion in a single individual (Selman, 1980). For example, you may feel simultaneously happy because you are doing something you really enjoy but also a bit sad because your best friend was unable to do it with you. Such "mixed feelings" are obviously accompanied or mediated by ideation. Although Harris and Olthoff (1982) do not make this point, it is also true that older children better understand that a single situation may elicit different emotions in different people. For instance, they better understand that whereas one child may feel happy when given a dog, another could feel apprehensive (Gove & Keating, 1979). In addition, they know that a person's emotional reaction to a current situation may be colored by a previous emotional experience. For example, they are aware that a person might continue to brood about an earlier unhappy experience and that this mediating mental event could serve to dampen a person's positive feelings about a present happy event. In contrast, younger children only take into account the immediate, present situation in predicting the person's feelings. Finally, although younger as well as older children know some of the effects that emotions can have on people's opinions and social dispositions, older children are likelier to interpret these effects in mentalistic terms—again, the recognition that thoughts and feelings are closely interwoven. Altogether, Harris and Olthof (1982) make a good case for their view that the developing child's increasingly mentalistic concept of emotions makes for profound and pervasive changes in the child's social cognition in this area.

Thoughts

What is there for the developing child to learn about this domain—about thinkers, thinking, and thoughts? The acquirable knowledge and cognition here ranges from the very simple and elementary to the very complex and advanced (see Flavell, 1977; Flavell et al., 1968; Miller, Kessel, & Flavell, 1970; Selman, 1980; Shantz, 1975, 1983). Following are examples from each end of the spectrum.

In a study by Mossler, Marvin, and Greenberg (1976), children of 2 to 6 years of age were individually shown a videotaped film in which much of the information about what was happening was carried by the audio portion. Each child's mother was absent from the room during this initial showing of the film. Each mother then returned and watched the film with her child, but with the audio portion conspicuously turned off (the child's attention was explicitly drawn to this fact). The child was asked questions about the mother's knowledge of various film happenings—for example, "Does your Mommy know whose house the boy went into?" The oldest children were clearly able to infer correctly and nonegocentrically what the mother did and did not know on the basis of her restricted perceptual experience with the film. In contrast, most of the youngest children blithely asserted—probably without any sort of social-cognitive inference at all—that she knew everything that happened in the film. They showed no evidence of attributing any differentiated, individuated knowledge or cognition to her at all. In a study by Abrahams (1979), similarly, 3 year olds clearly knew what another person *saw* from that person's perspective (different from their own) but equally clearly, and in contrast to 5 year olds, could not correctly infer what that person must have *thought*, given what she saw. Other recent studies have also shown a striking improvement during the preschool years in conceptual role or perspective taking of this simple and elementary, "privileged-information" type (see Abrahams, 1979; Brandt, 1978; Selman, 1980; Shantz, 1983).

In a study by Flavell et al. (1968), subjects of 7 to 17 years played a game of strategy that allowed for much more sophisticated knowledge and cognition about thoughts. In this game, the subject was presented with two cups placed upside down on a table. One had a nickel glued to its upturned bottom to show that it concealed a nickel inside; the other was similarly marked to show that it contained two nickels. The subject was told that another person would shortly enter the room, select one or the other of the two cups, and get to keep any money that might be hidden under it (two nickels had not yet inflated to the status of play money when this study was done). The subject's task was to fool the person by taking the money out of one cup, whichever one she thought the person would select. She was also told that the person knew full well that she was going to try to fool him in this way. She was encouraged to think hard, pick a cup, and explain why she thought the person would choose that one.

A few of the older subjects showed some bravura displays of social cognition on this task. For example, one subject first reasoned that the other person would probably select the one-nickel cup because he (the other person) would anticipate that the subject would think he would choose the two-nickel cup (because it contained more money), and hence he would try to fool the subject by selecting the one-nickel cup. (Clear so far?) However, the subject then went on to reason that the other person would anticipate this whole line of reasoning on the subject's part and therefore would switch back to the two-nickel cup in a master stroke of double duplicity. We experimenters could empathize with the subject's struggle to put all this complex thinking about thinking about thinking . . . into words:

> . . . he might feel that we, that we know that he thinks that we're going to pick this cup so therefore I think we should pick the dime cup, because I think he thinks, he thinks that we're going to pick the nickel cup, but then he knows that we, that we'll assume that he knows that, so we should pick the opposite cup (Flavell, et al., 1968, p. 47).

Complex, wheels-within-wheels social cognition of this genre really occurs in life and literature as well as in the laboratory. Here is my favorite example from literature:

> "Does he know I know?" I asked. "No, he doesn't. Does he know you know? Who can tell?"

> "Does he know I know you know they know she knows you know?" Steven asked. (Francis, 1978, p. 206).

These examples hint at the two groups of acquisitions that seem most central and distinctive to this area of social cognition. The key acquisition of the first group is no less fundamental and important for being obvious:

Children will come to understand the basic fact that they and other human beings think as well as perceive and feel, that people know, interpret, understand, remember, believe, judge, infer, and so on. The presently available research evidence suggests that this core, Existence-type understanding probably begins to be acquired around 2 or 3 years of age. However, future studies, using more sensitive and valid assessment methods, might well show earlier precursors and premonitions of it (Bretherton et al., 1981). Related Existence-type insights and Inference-type abilities emerge during early and middle childhood but, because their appearance-nonappearance in task situations depends upon the specifics of the task and situation, one hesitates to date them

© 1962 United Features Syndicate, Inc.

(Shantz, 1983). They may include the recognition that other people's conceptual perspectives may be different from, as well as the same as, your own, even in the same situation; that others' conceptual perspectives are potentially inferable from their perceptual experiences/perspectives or other indirect evidence, rather than being wholly unknowable because internal and nonperceptible; that, nonetheless, limitations of data or of your inferential abilities may lead to unconfident or incorrect conceptual perspective taking; and that there are various strategies and cues you can use to obtain information about other people's conceptual perspectives (cf. Selman, 1980; Shantz, 1983). A mundane but seemingly important strategy here that appears to have been little investigated is that of simply asking others what they are thinking, or asking them to confirm/disconfirm an hypothesis about their thinking that you have already made.

The other group of acquisitions has to do with one of the most intriguing and distinctive properties of thought or mental representation—namely, its potentially *recursive* nature (Miller et al., 1970). An action or process is said to be recursive if it can repeatedly (i.e., recursively) operate upon itself or its own output, thereby creating increasingly longer and more complex self-embedded structures. People's motor and perceptual actions and experiences with respect to themselves and others are not recursive in the way that their conceptual or representational actions and experiences are. For instance, my visual experience cannot literally include your visual experience nor can yours include mine or a third person's. It therefore follows that more complex recursive structures like "my visual experience of [your visual experience of (my/his visual experience . . .)]" make no sense. In contrast, "my mental representation of [your mental representation of (my/his mental representation . . .)]"—for example, "I think that you think that I/he thinks . . ."—and innumerable other structures of the same type are both possible and psychologically real. Recall the mental representations of Flavell et al.'s (1968) subject and Francis' (1978) story characters.

The development of children's understanding of the recursive nature of thinking has been the subject of several research investigations (Barenboim, 1978; Flavell et al., 1968; Landry & Lyons-Ruth, 1980; Miller et al., 1970; see also Selman, 1980, and Shantz, 1983). Although there is evidence for some understanding of it during middle childhood, perhaps even earlier (Shultz, 1980), it is clear that this understanding continues to improve during adolescence (Shantz, 1983). As one example, Miller et al. (1970) found that some of even their oldest subjects (11 to 12 year olds) did not show a full understanding of "one-loop" recursions (e.g., "The boy is thinking that the girl is thinking of him"), and that still more of them had difficulties with "two-loop" recursions (e.g., "The boy is thinking that the girl is thinking of him thinking of her"). As another example, Barenboim (1978) analyzed 10 to 16 year olds' personality descriptions of their peers for spontaneously generated expressions of recursive thinking, defined as any mention by the subject of the peer's thoughts about another person's thinking or about the peer's own thinking. Although younger and older subjects alike often mentioned nonrecursive thinking (the peer thinking about noncognitive matters), only the older ones mentioned recursive thinking with any frequency. In fact, an impressive 65 percent of the 16 year olds did so.

The acquisition of knowledge about the potentially recursive character of thought is obviously not the only important acquisition in this area of social-cognitive development. As an example, there is also the more basic insight that people have thoughts, discussed previously. Nor is the complex perspective taking that trades on knowledge of recursiveness the only important cognitive process in social-cognitive functioning and development, as Shultz (1982) has rightly pointed out. However, there are two reasons why this knowledge could be regarded as an especially noteworthy acquisition.

First, as we have seen, potential recursiveness is a distinctive property of mental representation; it helps set mental representation apart from other human activities. One could hardly be said to have acquired a mature, adult level of knowledge about thinking if one did not know that thoughts can recursively take other thoughts as cognitive objects. Second, a surprising amount of the ordinary, everyday social thought and communication of adolescents and adults seems to presuppose this knowledge. Consider, for example, the sorts of things two people often say to each other when analyzing and clearing up a previous misunderstanding between them: "Oh, you thought I meant X," "I thought you already knew about Y," and even "I didn't realize you thought I really meant it when I said that." Although statements like these are fairly commonplace in adult conversations, they surely reflect a tacit assumption on the speaker's part that thoughts can recursively include other thoughts. In fact, that assumption seems to be in the background of a lot of everyday speaker and listener behavior among mature communicators (Clark & Marshall, 1978). In addition, Shultz argues that knowledge of recursiveness of people's intentions:

> . . . makes possible strategic acts, acts that are performed in order to disguise one's own intentions or to lead others to misinterpret one's intentions. It is likely that this recursive awareness of intention makes social interaction truly interactive in the sense that agents are at that point fully aware of their fundamental similarity to other agents and fully aware that social knowledge can be reciprocal (1980, p. 152; see also Selman, 1980).

Shultz also speculates that "it may well be that recursive awareness of intention is one of those few distinctly human characteristics, serving to make our social interactions not only truly interactive but also essentially human" (1980, p. 156). All things considered, the acquisition of this insight about thinking seems like a cognitive-developmental milestone, and one that would well repay further scientific study.

Robert Selman (1976, 1980) has proposed an interesting theory of the childhood growth of interpersonal understanding that incorporates several of the developmental acquisitions described in this section. Selman describes five developmentally ordered levels (0 to 4) of social perspective taking. Following is a very brief, bare-bones summary of Selman's levels. The age range given for each level is approximate and is meant only as a very rough guide.

At Level 0 (3 to 6 years), children do not yet clearly and completely differentiate between people's physical and psychological characteristics, nor between their own and others' conceptual perspectives. At Level 1 (5 to 9 years), these differentiations are clearly made. Children now believe that each person has a unique, covert psychological life. This new conception of people's inner worlds helps them understand that different people might have different thoughts or feelings about the self-same situation. At Level 2 (7 to 12 years), children can step outside themselves, mentally, and take self-reflective or second-person perspectives on their own thoughts and actions; moreover, they realize that others can do the same thing. This permits children to be aware, for instance, both that they know another person likes them and also that the other person knows they like that person. According to Selman (1980), this is the level in which children first discover the recursive, "I think that he thinks that I think . . ." property of thought. At Level 3 (10 to 15 years), children can also adopt more abstract, third-person or generalized-other-person perspectives that enable them to take interpersonal relationships themselves (e.g., friendships) as objects of reflective thought. Additional knowledge and skills are present at Level 4 (12 years to adulthood), including the ability to consider still more abstract and generalized points of view, such as that of one's whole society. Refer to Selman (1980) for further details about this developmental theory and its applications, and to Shultz (1982) for a critical appraisal of it.

Perspective taking is often characterized as putting yourself in another's shoes. The following excerpt suggests that little perspective takers can imagine putting themselves in the little shoes of little others:

> Tom (10,0): You should take the other person's opinion. Like say you're about to step on an ant, and you get in the ant's shoes and you wouldn't want to be killed or something; so I wouldn't really step on the ant (Selman, Damon, & Gordon, 1973, p. 18).

Intentions

There are at least two reasons why the acquisition of knowledge about intentions is a highly significant development for children. First, it helps them understand how people differ causally from other objects. Unlike the behavior of other objects, some of the behavior of human beings is caused by their intentions (Shultz, 1980). Certain of their actions are voluntary or willed—instigated and impelled by their own inner intentions, motives, and plans. As indicated earlier, people differ from objects in that they are causal agents that can deliberately (i.e., by means of an intention) generate some of their own mental and physical acts. The second reason is that knowledge about intentions is indispensable for understanding responsibility and morality (Shantz, 1983). Children must learn that people deserve to be praised or credited, blamed, or judged to be blameless, depending in part upon whether what they did was intentional or unintentional, and whether the effects of what they did were intended or not intended. Good sources on the childhood development of knowledge about intentions include Gardner (1982), Karniol (1978), Keasey (1978a), Shantz (1975, 1983), Shultz (1980), and Smith (1978).

Most research in this area has been primarily focused on children's use of intention information in making moral judgments, rather than on their knowledge about intentions per se (Shultz, 1980). This research grew out of Piaget's (1932) seminal studies of moral reasoning in children. One of his many findings, subsequently confirmed by others, was that there is a developmental tendency during middle childhood for what he termed *subjective responsibility* to replace *objective responsibility* as a basis for assessing blameworthiness. For example, children were asked which child is naughtier—a child who clumsily breaks one cup in the course of doing something he should not or one who, through a completely unavoidable accident, breaks fifteen cups in the course of doing what his mother told him to. Children of 6 to 7 years of age were apt to say that the second child was naughtier because his action resulted in more objective damage (objective responsibility criterion). In contrast, children of 9 to 10 years were likelier to assert that the first child was naughtier because of his bad intentions.

For a long time we tended to interpret the results of these studies as suggesting that children below 8 or 9 years are either unaware of intentions or do not see their relevance to judgments of moral responsibility (Shultz, 1980). However, it gradually became clear that these studies have serious methodological flaws that preclude the drawing of such conclusions. To illustrate, since *both* children in Piaget's story did their damage accidentally rather than intentionally, we have no way of knowing whether the younger, "objective-responsibility" subjects are or are not cognizant of the intentional-unintentional distinction. Similarly, we could only conclude that they did or did not see the relevance of intentions to culpability if we changed the research procedure so that key variables would not be experimentally confounded. For example, we could use a story in which both children do the same amount of damage, but one clearly does it intentionally and the other accidentally. This avoids confounding the variables of intentionality and amount of damage. In fact, several investigators have used such methods and have found that children even younger than 7 to 8 years are able to recognize that the one who did the damage intentionally is more blameworthy (Shultz, 1980).

It appears that researchers are finally making real progress on what has proved to be the tricky problem of assessing how children of different ages make use of information about intentionality and other variables in making moral judgments (see the literature cited earlier). However, it has been a surprisingly long and difficult struggle. One of the lessons to be learned from it is that if you want to find out about children's developing knowledge about intentions as such, try to study it directly, by itself, rather than try to infer it from children's moral judgments (Shultz, 1980). Only a few studies have adopted this strategy as yet (Berndt & Berndt, 1975; King, 1971; Smith, 1978; Shultz, 1980). I use some of Smith's (1978) and Shultz's (1980) results as a vehicle for describing developmental trends in children's knowledge about intentions.

In Smith's (1978) study, children of 3½ to 4½, 4½ to 5½, and 5½ to 6½ years and adults (college students) were shown two series of videotapes, each depicting a brief action sequence by a young woman. The adult subjects were asked to pretend that the actions were genuine rather than staged. In the first series, the actress displayed voluntary actions (e.g., walked across the room), involuntary actions (e.g., sneezed), and object-like movements (e.g., slipped on a rug and fell into a chair). In the second series, she moved an object from a high place to a lower place in all eight possible combinations of three two-value variables that provide information concerning intentionality: (1) apparent attention to her act (looking at her book versus looking at the object as she moved the object); (2) desirability of the outcome of her act (e.g., garbage—the object—ending up in a garbage can versus on the floor); (3) type of act (moving the object by means of the clearly intentional act of picking it up with her hand versus the possibly unintentional act of knocking into it with her forearm). The eight action sequences of this second series were accompanied by voice-overs describing the action. Thus, for example, in the most unequivocally intentional of these eight sequences, the voice-over said: "There was some garbage on the table. The lady was looking at it, and she picked it up and put it in the garbage can." In the most unequivocally unintentional one, it said: "There was a box of cookies. The lady wasn't looking at it, and she knocked it into the garbage can." After each videotape subjects were asked "What happened that time?" to be sure they perceived and recalled the action sequence correctly; even the youngest subjects usually described it accurately on the first try. They were then asked, in succession, both a "try" and a "want" form of the intentionality question—for example, "Was she trying to sneeze?" followed by "Did she want to sneeze?" As it turned out, subjects usually gave the same answer to both questions.

The results of Smith's (1978) study provided evidence for a clear and interesting developmental progression. The 3½ to 4½ year olds tended to describe all acts/movements (first videotape series) as intentional and all action-produced effects (second series) as intended. At most, some of them recognized that object-like movements were not intentional. The 4½ to 5½ year olds recognized this latter fact even more clearly and, in addition, usually understood that involuntary actions were also not intended; the 5½ to 6½ year olds and adults also made these distinctions, but still more sharply. Moreover, the 4½ to 5½ year olds understood that, whereas voluntary acts are intentional, their effects are not always intended, and could use some of the available evidence in a systematic fashion to decide which effects were intended and which were not. In particular, desirable effects were more often judged as intended than were undesirable ones.

The adults made systematic use of all three types of evidence in a complex, interactional fashion. When the woman picked up and deposited the object (a clearly intentional act), the effect was usually judged to be intended, except in the sequence in which she did it without looking and the end result was undesirable. In that sequence—in which she might well have been acting absent-mindedly—some adults judged the effect to be unintended and some judged it to be intended—that is, there was a division of opinion. If she knocked it with her arm (possibly unintentional act) without looking, the effect was almost always judged to be unintended, whether or not it was undesirable. If she was looking, however, opinion was again divided, with the verdict of "intended" getting more votes if the effect was desirable.

The adult pattern of judgments in this study seems to attest to a subtle and sophisticated conception of what makes an act intentional or unintentional and an effect intended or unintended. Of course, that is not surprising; we would expect bright adults to have a high level of understanding of intentionality. What *is* surprising and quite remarkable is that the 5½ to 6½-year-old subjects also showed this very same pattern of judgments, suggesting that they may have had a similarly sophisticated conception, at least for those aspects of intentionality assessed in Smith's (1978) study.

As Smith (1978) points out, there is much more knowledge and ability to be acquired in this area than his study investigated. For example, there are intentional acts of omission as well as of commission that the developing individual must learn to recognize. Further, a person can intentionally simulate involuntary acts and object-like movements. For instance, the person can feign crying or pretend to bump into someone accidentally. The growing child will need to learn about these as well as other forms of deception in the social world. There are also the important learnable truths that a person may be carrying out more than one intentional act at any given moment (i.e., doing more than one thing at once) and that many action sequences may reflect the existence of a hierarchical structure of subgoals and superordinate goals. Finally, there is the fact that representations of intentions can also have a recursive quality: I can be aware that you are aware that I am trying to divine your intentions (Shultz, 1980). More generally, cognizing all that is going on in the "behavior stream" (Smith, 1978, p. 742) is a formidably complex process, and much of it implicates rich knowledge about intentions.

Recall that Smith's (1978) 3½- to 4½-year-old subjects, in marked contrast to his 5½ to 6½ year olds, showed virtually no knowledge at all about intentionality. Might it be that children of this age possess more knowledge about intentionality than Smith's assessment procedure revealed? Some clever studies by Shultz (1980) suggest that this could be the case. The results of his studies suggest that 3 year olds may have some ability to distinguish intended actions from such nonintentional behaviors as mistakes and reflexes. In one of his tests for the distinction between intentional and mistaken behavior, he asked the subject to repeat normal sentences (e.g., "She lives in a house.") and tongue twisters (e.g., "She sells sea shells by the sea shore."). Of course, the subject was likely to make mistakes in trying to repeat the tongue twisters. Then he would ask either that child, or another 3-year-old bystander who had previously experienced the task, or one who had not, "Did you (he/she) mean to say it like that?" Shultz (1980) found that his 3-year-old subjects could usually answer that question correctly, and about equally so whether in the role of speaker, experienced bystander, or inexperienced bystander. That means that even a child who had not yet tried to repeat a tongue twister knew that another child who repeated it incorrectly did not "mean to say it like that."

In the case of reflexes versus intentional acts, subjects of 3 to 4, 5 to 6, and 7 to 8 years experienced both an elicited knee-jerk reflex (the experimenter tapped the child's knee to elicit it) and a similar-looking voluntary leg movement (the child imitated the experimenter's leg movement). In each case the subjects were asked if the movement was done "on purpose." The subjects in the two older groups usually said the voluntary movement was done on purpose and the reflexive movement was not; the 3 to 4 year olds also showed a tendency to do the same, but the trend was not statistically significant. Again, whether the child made the intentionality judgment while in the role of mover, experienced bystander, or inexperienced bystander had little effect on the correctness of that judgment.

Shultz (1980) also reported some naturalistic observations of 3 year olds using the "not on purpose" argument. For instance, one child accidentally hurt another and was asked to apologize to the crying victim. The child refused, indignantly claiming that he had not done it "on purpose."

Do all these correct uses of "mean to" and "on purpose" by 3 year olds reflect a genuine grasp of the intentional-unintentional distinction, or merely a learned association between these verbal expressions and certain classes of experienced events, such as actions or action-produced effects that are judged desirable or expected versus those that are not? It is hard to decide on present evidence. However, my guess is that if Shultz has not clearly documented a full-fledged, genuine grasp of the distinction in 3 year olds, he has at least documented a beginning, precursive competence in this area.

How do children learn to distinguish between intentional and unintentional actions? As is true for most questions about the "how" of cognitive development, the answer is that we do not know yet. However, Smith (1978) and Shultz (1980) have described some of the internal and external cues that often distinguish the two kinds of actions. It is possible that some or all of these cues may help the child learn to make the distinction. Adults may respond to the two kinds of actions differently—for example, telling the child that her harmful action had been done on purpose, and punishing her for it. Children might work out various rules of thumb for making the distinction. As examples, they might come to assume that an outcome is likely to be intended if it matches the agent's stated intention, if the agent looked like he was trying to achieve it, if it has positive, desirable consequences for him, and if he does not look disappointed, surprised, or puzzled when it occurs. Also, in the case of one's own behavior, intended and unintended actions and outcomes engender very different thoughts and feelings in oneself—very different "metacognitive experiences," to use a concept from the previous chapter (pp. 107–108).

Personality

The counterpart of this section in Shantz's (1975) review of social-cognitive growth has a homely but apt title: "What is the other like?" How, in other words, do children of different ages construe and characterize the personal characteristics of other people? What are the salient developmental changes in the way they describe human personalities? Good reviews of this topic can be found in Hill and Palmquist (1978), Livesley and Bromley (1973), and Shantz (1975, 1983). The Livesley and Bromley book also contains an extensive and insightfully discussed empirical investigation which serves to illustrate the way research is commonly done in this area. The subjects in their principal study were 320 English boys and girls, forty at each of eight age levels between 7 and 15 years. Over a series of sessions the children wrote descriptions of themselves and other people they knew well. They were very carefully and repeatedly instructed to indicate what sort of person the individual is, what he or she is like and what they think of him or her, and *not* to describe the person's physical appearance, clothing, and so on. Although such free-description procedures have their problems (Berndt & Heller, in press; Shantz, 1975), Livesley and Bromley appear to have managed both method and data analyses intelligently; moreover, their results and conclusions seem convincing and also accord well with other research evidence. The following developmental sketch is a synthesis of their findings and those of other studies (e.g., Barenboim, 1977, 1981; Flapan, 1968; Peevers & Secord, 1973; Rosenbach, Crockett, and Wapner, 1973).

The child of 6 to 7 years or younger is very prone to describe the other person's general identity, appearance, family, possessions, environment, and so on, despite the experimenter's explicit instruction to the contrary. Almost 50 percent of Livesley and Bromley's 7 year olds failed to mention even a single psychological quality (1973, p. 210). Likewise, Peevers and Secord found that "kindergarten children scarcely recognized a person as such, and described him in terms that failed to differentiate him from his environment or his possessions" (1973, p. 126). If any personal traits do get mentioned they are apt to be global, stereotyped, and highly evaluative ("He is very bad"). Children of this age are also likely to describe the other in rather egocentric, self-referential terms ("She gives me things"). This excerpt from a 7 year old's description of a woman she likes illustrates some of these properties:

> She is very nice because she gives my friends and me toffee. She lives by the main road. She has fair hair and glasses. . . . She sometimes gives us flowers . . . (Livesley & Bromley, 1973, p. 214).

During middle childhood the subject's descriptions become more focused on traits and dispositions, his trait vocabulary increases considerably, and the trait-descriptive terms he selects seem less global and stereotyped, more abstract, and more precise in meaning than before ("nice" gives way to "considerate," "helpful," etc.). The other person is often endowed with attitudes, interests, abilities, and other psychological qualities seldom found in the younger child's description. The more external types of attributions (possessions, etc.) also occur, however, and will continue to do so into adulthood. (Peevers & Secord [1973, p. 127] make the interesting observation that nonpsychological descriptors do sometimes seem to help create a vivid impression of the essence of an individual.) The middle-childhood subject's character sketch is still likely to be rather poorly organized, however, with different attributions just strung together in a more or less random sequence. In the same vein, opposite or contradictory qualities are simply juxtaposed with no attempt at reconciliation; more generally, there is not apt to be much explanation and integration in his descriptions. Two 10 year olds' descriptions illustrate these points:

> She is quite a kind girl. . . . Her behaviour is quite good most of the time but sometimes she is quite naughty and silly most of the time . . . (Livesley & Bromley, 1973, p. 218).

> He smells very much and is very nasty. He has no sense of humour and is very dull. He is always fighting and he is cruel. He does silly things and is very stupid. He has brown hair and cruel eyes. He is sulky and 11 years old and has lots of sisters. I think he is the most horrible boy in the class. He has a croaky voice and always chews his pencil and picks his teeth and I think he is disgusting (Livesley & Bromley, 1973, p. 217).

Some interesting novelties become increasingly prominent during the adolescent years. The subject flexibly and planfully selects ideas from a wide range of possibilities, and carefully shapes them into an organized, integrated portrait of the other. He knows that his impression of the person is only *his* impression, and may therefore be inaccurate or different from other people's. He is sensitive to the presence of seemingly contradictory traits and of different levels or depths within the individual's personality; the individual may be both this and that, or may appear to be this but really be that "underneath." For example, a 13-year-old acquaintance of mine began his written character sketch of a friend this way (it was an English class assignment, and was therefore judged to require fancy vocabulary—this too represents a bit of social cognition): "He may appear a joker in class because of his unique style of eloquence, but in reality he feels a deep responsibility towards the advancement of his own personal knowledge." The adolescent also feels that a human personality represents a unique blend of qualities and therefore deserves an idiosyncratic, nonstereotypic characterization. Because he is aware of these considerations, he tries to explain and justify, not merely describe, and he tries to particularize and qualify, not just baldly assert. Since there are apparent contradictions within or between levels of an individual's personality, he knows that one must appeal to dispositions, motives, personal history, environmental factors and forces, or other internal and external causes to explain and reconcile them. And since each individual is believed to have a unique personality, he feels one should search out (and explain) unexpected combinations of traits, unusual blends of feelings, and so on. The best examples of these higher forms of personality description are, of course, to be found in great literature, not in Livesley and Bromley (1973). Nonetheless, Livesley and Bromley and other investigators have obtained some fairly impressive specimens from lesser mortals: "She is curious about people but naive, and this leads her to ask too many questions so that people become irritated with her and withhold information, although she is not sensitive enough to notice it" (Livesley & Bromley, 1973, p. 225).

I find Shantz's (1983) précis of developmental changes in the child's "implicit personality theory" both apt and easy to remember:

> If one were to view the "child as a psychologist" who subscribes to certain positions or theories, the developmental changes, broadly put, suggest the following: prior to 7 or 8 years of age, the child conceives of persons largely as one who is both a demographer and a behaviorist would, defining the person in terms of her environmental circumstances and observable behavior; during middle childhood, persons are conceived more as a trait-personality theorist would, ascribing unqualified constancies to persons; and by the onset of adolescence, a more interactionist position emerges in which people and their behavior are often seen as a joint function of personal characteristics and situational factors (p. 506).

Self

The development of knowledge and cognition about the self is one of those topics that is intrinsically and enduringly fascinating to just about everyone—developmental psychologist, nondevelopmental psychologist, sociologist, anthropologist, philosopher, and lay person. It is also a topic that is frustratingly difficult to write intelligibly about, especially briefly, because it is so sprawling and heterogeneous in content, so poorly defined and fuzzily conceptualized, and so difficult to research—and hence, so unevenly researched.

Fortunately, there is one fact about the topic that should make the present, necessarily brief exposition of it more comprehensible than would otherwise be the case: The development of knowledge and cognition about the self closely parallels and overlaps the development of knowledge and cognition about cognition and about other people. In the former case, if you know something about the development of metacognition (Chapter 4) you ipso facto know something about the development of the self system—that is, the acquisition of metacognitive knowledge about persons, tasks, and strategies and of an informed, sensitive awareness of one's metacognitive experiences is, manifestly, an acquisition of significant knowledge and awareness of the self. Similarly, the growing child's attained knowledge, conception, and cognition regarding her own self is usually not very different in developmental level from that regarding other selves. As examples, Livesley and Bromley's subjects' personality descriptions of themselves tended to be on the same cognitive-developmental levels as their descriptions of others (1973, pp. 236–241). Their younger children's self-descriptions showed the same dearth of personal-psychological attributions, for instance, that their descriptions of others did. Characterizations of others also become less global and more differentiated with age, and the same has been shown to be true of characterizations of the self (Katz & Zigler, 1967; Mullener & Laird, 1971).

The implication of the foregoing is that you can predict much of the cognitive-developmental story with respect to the self by consulting the stories you have already read concerning metacognition (Chapter 4) and social cognition in general (this chapter). The remainder of this section consists of a brief description of another way to predict or remember what development in this area comprises, followed by an account of some ingenious recent research on one early and vital segment of this development: the dawning of visual self-recognition. For additional information on this topic, see Lewis (1981), Rotenberg (1982), and especially, Damon and Hart (1982), Lewis and Brooks-Gunn (1979), and Maccoby (1980, Chapter 7).

We can use the concept of differentiation to help us organize the course of development here. Recall the argument made earlier in this chapter (pp. 128–129) that an initial task for the child is to acquire the sense that she is a distinct and separate entity, clearly differentiated from all others. She will learn that she is a physical object that occupies a particular location in space and takes up a certain amount of space, is physically detached and separate from other objects, and has her own distinctive physical properties (physical appearance, voice quality, etc.). She is also a psychological being (a person, a self) as well as a physical one, again to be distinguished from all of her fellow psychological beings; she has her own unique selfhood and they all have theirs. Moreover, this self will be conceived as somehow retaining its own singular, unique identity ("me-ness") over time and the physical and psychological changes that time brings. Later, she may make further differentiations between her own conception of herself and the various conceptions of her that she thinks various other people have. There are also many other self-other and within-self differentiations that will mark this development. She will learn that she is a female rather than a male, a differentiation that will have profound implications for her conception of what and who she is, and will engender many other differentiations. Within the self, but achieved through comparisons with others, she will distinguish between attributes (personality traits, intellectual competencies, moral qualities, etc.) she thinks she has and those she thinks she lacks. She will build up a differentiated psychological profile of herself. These differentiations will in time lead to a greater or lesser differentiation between the self she thinks she is stuck with (actual self) and the one she wishes she owned instead (ideal self). Thinking of the development of self-conceptions as an extended process of making many differentiations will not take us the whole way in understanding this development; for other aspects of this development, see Damon and Hart (1982) and Maccoby (1980, Chapter 7). However, like the metacognition and social-cognition mnemonics described earlier, it definitely helps.

Our account of the development of children's abilities to recognize themselves visually begins with some inspired research on chimpanzees by George Gallup (1977). He observed that, after a few days of experience with a mirror, chimpanzees began to use the mirror to examine and experiment with visually inaccessible parts of their bodies. For example, he saw them grooming parts of their bodies that they could not see, making faces at the mirror, and picking bits of food out of their teeth. Instead of treating the image in the mirror as if it were another creature, as other animals have been observed to do and as they themselves did at first, they seemed to construe it as a *self* image. That is, they acted for all the world as if they recognized themselves in the mirror, and recognized themselves *as* themselves—that is, they knew that the familiar-looking objects they saw were their own bodies.

To test this possibility more rigorously, Gallup anesthetized the chimps and, while they were asleep, applied a bright red, odorless, nonirritating dye to parts of their faces that they could not see without a mirror. After recovery from the anesthesia they were observed for a time in the absence of the mirror to get baseline data on how often they would touch the marked portions of their faces under normal conditions. Gallup then reintroduced the mirror and again counted the number of mark-directed responses. The results were dramatic: The number of mark-directed responses increased to more than twenty-five times that of the baseline period. The chimps did not reach out and touch the directly visible red marks on the surface of the mirror, as they might well have done; instead, they touched the "invisible" red marks on the surfaces of their faces. Significantly, they also examined and smelled their fingers after touching their faces, in an apparent attempt to find out what had gotten onto their faces.

Can other animals recognize themselves as themselves, as assessed by Gallup's mark-on-face method? Research has shown that the orangutan, another great ape, definitely can (Gallup, 1977). Gorillas had not been systematically tested for this ability when Gallup wrote his 1977 paper, but there is every reason to believe that they also possess it (Patterson, 1979). Gallup also wonders about porpoises (and also wonders about how on earth to find out experimentally, given an aquatic, flippered creature as your subject). In dramatic contrast, researchers have decisively failed to find this ability in several species of gibbons, baboons, and monkeys—even after 2400 hours of mirror exposure, in the case of one monkey tested. Experimenters have even tried to train in the skill, but to no avail. Curiously, a monkey *can* learn to look away from a mirror to see an object it had just seen reflected in it. "Still, for some strange reason, they fail to correctly interpret their own reflections" (Gallup, 1977, p. 334). Gallup believes that these startling findings may testify to the presence of some form of self-concept and self-awareness in the great apes, a capability that had previously been thought unique to human beings. Apes who have been taught to use nonvocal, language-like symbol systems can use them to refer to themselves (e.g., Premack, 1976), a finding that also seems to support Gallup's contention.

What would happen if a procedure similar to Gallup's were used with human infants of different ages? Several studies of this kind have now been done and their results are in quite close agreement; see Lewis and Brooks-Gunn (1979) for a review of these studies. A careful and well-controlled investigation by Lewis and Brooks-Gunn (1979) illustrates the method and typical results. Their subjects were infants of 9, 12, 15, 18, 21, and 24 months. They were first observed, unmarked, in front of a large mirror to get baseline data. Then their mothers surreptitiously applied rouge to their noses with a cloth, under the pretense of wiping dirt off their noses, after which they were again placed in front of the mirror. Only two infants touched their noses during the baseline period, whereas thirty did after the rouge was applied. No child younger than 15 months of age showed this mark-directed behavior and there was an increase in age from 15 to 24 months in the number of children showing the behavior. Interestingly, children of all ages touched one or another part of their bodies more after rouge application. This might mean that the younger infants also recognized themselves as themselves but simply could not locate the rouge mark as accurately as the older ones, although other explanations seem at least as plausible to me. In any case, this study and others by Lewis and Brooks-Gunn (1979) provide ample evidence of the self-recognition prowess of older infants (circa 1½ to 2 years of age). In addition to touching their noses they will also say "nose," show clear nonverbal signs of recognizing themselves in videotape replays and still photographs as well as in mirrors, and use their own names to refer to the external images of themselves that they see. The development of a sense of self is, of course, not very far along by 2 years of age, but these studies show that a solid beginning has been made.

Social Relations: The Case of Friendship

There are a number of good reasons why a chapter on the development of social cognition ought to include at least a brief section on children's changing conceptions of friendship. First, most research in the area of social-cognitive growth has concentrated on the development of knowledge and cognition about psychological properties and processes *within* individual persons—for example, about their inner thoughts and feelings. The previous sections of this chapter reflect this fact. In contrast, friendship is a complex relation *between* persons, and such interpersonal relations are also important objects of people's social knowledge and cognition (Damon, 1977). Second, as if in belated recognition of this fact, there is currently a lively and growing research interest in the child's developing thought and understanding concerning friendship (e.g., Berndt, 1981; Bigelow, 1977; Damon, 1977; Selman,

1981; Youniss & Volpe, 1978; for reviews of this work, see Damon, 1977, and Shantz, 1983). Third, there seems to be quite good agreement among different investigators about the typical course of this development. Fourth, like cognition about the self, cognition about friendship changes with age in a manner that is consistent with and partly predictable from the course of social-cognitive development in general. As with the self, if you can remember the latter you can largely reconstruct the former. Fifth, friendship is obviously very important in the lives of children. Children discover that their fortunes with regard to friendship can powerfully affect their present happiness. Developmental psychologists, parents, and other concerned adults know that children's fortunes here can also powerfully affect their future development. Finally, there has recently been some exciting research on a most unusual educational venture—teaching friendless, socially isolated children social skills that will help them achieve the acceptance and friendship of their peers (Asher & Renshaw, 1981; Oden & Asher, 1977). I first describe how conceptions of friendship change with age and then summarize some of this recent educational work.

Most of our knowledge about the development of friendship conceptions derives from interview studies with children. Children are questioned about why children they have named as their best friends are their best friends, what they expect of a friend, how they know if another child is their friend, how one becomes a friend, how friendships end, and the like. The typical course of development is roughly as follows (Damon, 1977; Shantz, 1983).

During the late preschool and early school years, children tend to conceive of friends as peers who are nice and are fun to be with, and with whom one plays and shares material goods. Friendships tend to be regarded as transient affairs, quickly and easily formed and quickly and easily terminated. There is no sense of either liking or disliking particular stable and distinctive personal traits in the other children. Thus, neither the friends' personal characteristics nor the friendship relations themselves are conceived as having an individualized and enduring quality.

During middle and late childhood, friends come to be represented as people who help and trust one another. Reciprocal helping and mutual trust become defining elements of friendship. Children also begin to conceive of friendship as a subjective as well as an objective state of affairs. Friends are no longer represented only as agreeable others with whom one plays, but also as individual persons who have specific traits and dispositions that one likes.

Finally, during adolescence, friends become conceptualized as:

> . . . persons who understand one another, share their innermost thoughts and feelings (including secrets), help each other with psychological problems, and avoid causing each other problems. Compatibility of interests and personality are the bases for selecting one as a friend, and the termination of friendship is viewed likely if one shows bad faith to a friend. Adolescents' reasoning also emphasizes communication as critical to friendship, both as an end in itself and as a means to share and assist one another (Shantz, 1983, p. 531).

It should be apparent that these age changes in children's conceptions of the friendship relations between people reflect developmental changes in their conceptions of people considered as individuals. For example, the "surface to depth" developmental trend for conceptions of people (p. 122) is clearly evident in the case of friendship. There is a change "from defining friendship as a concrete, behavioral, surface relationship of playing together and giving goods to more abstract, internal dispositional relationships in adolescence of caring for one another, sharing one's thoughts and feelings, and comforting each other" (Shantz, 1983, p. 531). To illustrate more concretely how adolescents may conceive of friendship, consider this answer by a 13 year old to the question, "How do you know who to become friends with and who not to?"

> Well, you don't really pick your friends, it just grows on you. You find out that you can talk to someone, you can tell them your problems, when you understand each other (Damon, 1977, pp. 163–164).

One can scarcely imagine a 5 year old, say, thinking about friendship in this deep "psychological" way.

Recent research by Steven Asher and his co-workers (Asher & Renshaw, 1981; Oden & Asher, 1977) suggests that it is possible to increase the popularity of unpopular, socially isolated children by coaching them in social skills that are useful in making friends. In one study (Oden & Asher, 1977), the subjects were third- and fourth-grade children who were identified by sociometric measures as the least popular children in their classes. These children were given five sessions of instruction and actual practice (with other peers) in the nature and use of such social skills as cooperation (e.g., taking turns, sharing materials) and communication (e.g., talking with and listening to a would-be playmate). The results indicated that this coaching program helped the subjects become better accepted by their classmates. More impressive yet, a follow-up assessment 1 year after coaching showed that the subjects had made still further gains in peer acceptance. It is easy to imagine an athletic coach's indirectly increasing the peer acceptance of some unpopular children. Asher's work makes it possible to imagine a "friendship coach's" directly increasing the peer acceptance of many unpopular children. I should also add that Asher's is by no means the only attempt to teach social skills to children; there is a surprisingly large literature on the subject (Shantz, 1983; Shure & Spivak, 1978).

Morality

The development of moral reasoning is a fascinating and scientifically vigorous area of social-cognitive development, thanks in large measure to the influential theories of Jean Piaget (1932) and Lawrence Kohlberg (e.g., 1976). However, it has also become a very large and complex area—too much so, unfortunately, to be covered adequately in a book of this size. Fortunately, it is summarized in virtually every introductory text on introductory psychology and developmental psychology, and more advanced treatments are also plentiful. A recent and comprehensive review chapter by Rest (1983) is particularly useful. It is also useful for conveying the magnitude of the morality area in relation to the rest of social-cognitive development: Our volume on cognitive development (Flavell & Markman, 1983) contains one chapter on the development of moral thinking by Rest (1983) and one chapter on the remainder of social-cognitive development by Shantz (1983). Rest's is longer.

SUMMARY

Social cognition is cognition about people and what they do and ought to do. It includes thinking and knowledge about the self and others as individuals, about social relations between people, about social customs, groups, and institutions. Figure 5-1 (p. 120) is one representation of what social cognition entails. Another emphasizes three preconditions for successfully identifying any social-cognition object (e.g., another person's feeling state): knowing that such states can exist in people (*Existence*); being motivated or disposed to identify them (*Need*); being able actually to identify them on the basis of the available evidence (*Inference*).

There are both similarities and differences between social and nonsocial cognition. There are inevitable similarities stemming from the fact that it is the self-same head that does both social and nonsocial cognition and from the fact that social objects and concepts are similar in some respects to nonsocial ones. As a consequence of these similarities, many of the developmental trends in nonsocial cognition described in previous chapters can also be seen in social cognition. Like its nonsocial counterparts, social-cognitive growth proceeds from *surface* (people's appearance and behavior) to *depth* (their inner thoughts, feelings, etc.), and also shows *invariant formation*; immature social thinking is plagued with *spatial* and *temporal centrations*; mature social thinking is *abstract, hypothetical, metacognitive*, and sometimes *quantitative*, has characteristic *cognitive shortcomings* (e.g., *egocentrism*), but clearly has *a sense of the game* of people reading.

People are different from most other objects in several ways. Unlike other objects, they are sentient beings who can intentionally behave and reveal/conceal information about themselves. Our relations with people are also usually very different from our relations with other objects. As examples, we are similar to other people and our relations with them entail mutual and reciprocal coordination of actions, communication, and perspective taking. There are also some distinctively social-cognitive processes, such as empathy and using information about ourselves to make inferences about others.

Infancy is a rich period of growth for social as well as nonsocial cognition. Part of infant social-cognitive development can be characterized as a process of *differentiation*—of self from nonself, of human from nonhuman objects, and of one human object from another. One important thing infants gradually learn about people is that their own behavior and that of others are often predictably *contingent* on one another.

The best-researched aspect of infant social development is the growth of *social attachment*, which involves differentiation of person from nonperson, and, especially, of one person from another. On the infant's side of the social interaction, attachment refers to the formation of a strong emotional bond to one or more specific people, and to the constellation of behaviors and feelings that testify to the existence of that bond. For instance, the baby engages in certain behaviors (crying, crawling, etc.) which tend to maintain a desired level of physical proximity to the object of her attachment—her father, say— and exhibits certain feelings (pleasure, fear, etc.) when that level of proximity is achieved or lost. The development of social attachment during infancy normally proceeds something like this: at first, no detectable emotional attachment to any object, human or nonhuman; then, particular attention and interest to people as a class but no significant differentiation among people; next, the recognition of certain people as familiar and especially pleasureful objects; finally, unmistakable and intense emotional attachment to one or a select few clearly differentiated and identified people, complete with strong protest when separated from such people and, frequently, when other people approach too closely ("stranger anxiety"). The general course of attachment development appears to be quite similar cross-culturally, attesting to its biological-evolutionary roots and partly maturational character.

Social behavior mediates cognitive growth and cognitive skills mediate social development. As examples of the latter, recent research findings show that babies are born with or soon develop precisely the sorts of perceptual skills and preferences that could help mediate the development of social attachment. They appear to have innately given preferences to look at objects that possess the stimulus properties people do—for example, movement and contours exhibiting high light-dark contrast. Babies also seem to be innately disposed to attend to and discriminate human speech. For instance, there are data suggesting that even newborns can learn to discriminate their own mothers' voices from that of another mother. During the first half year of life babies also become able to detect cross-modal (auditory-visual) temporal correspondences between the speech they hear a person produce and the mouth movements and other gestures they see that person make at the same time. Another cognitive acquisition that ought to help mediate the development of social attachment is the development of the Piagetian object concept; however, research attempts to demonstrate such mediation have not been very successful thus far.

Social-cognitive development during the postinfancy years can be described under such (overlapping) headings as *percepts, feelings, thoughts, intentions, personality, self,* and *social relations* (e.g., that of *friendship*).

Recent theory and research suggest that there are at least two developmental levels of cognition concerning visual *percepts*: At Level 1, the young child represents *whether* another person sees a given object; at Level 2 she also represents *how* an object that the person sees looks to that person from his particular spatial perspective. Some Level 1 understanding seems to be present towards the beginning of early childhood, some Level 2 understanding towards the end of this period. A Level 1 3 year old is quite good at inferring when another person does and does not see an object; one interesting example of this is her ability to recognize that her body is still visible to your eyes when her eyes are closed. Unlike a Level 2 5 year old, however, she is liable not to realize that an object that looks right side up from her perspective may appear upside down from yours.

Preschool children can correctly attribute global positive and negative *feelings* to another person on the basis of his facial expression or his immediately prior experience (e.g., someone just gave him a present). The intellectual processes mediating these attributions may not be very high level, however. As the child grows older, he progressively differentiates the emotional domain ("bad" is partitioned into "sad," "mad," "afraid," etc.), becomes more attuned to others' affects, seeks to explain as well as describe people's feelings, and can abstractly represent the plight of a whole group of unfortunates (e.g., the populace of some distant country which is stricken with drought). He also will probably learn to monitor and shape his own affective expression (e.g., consciously feign a certain emotion), as well as to detect such behaviors in others. According to a recent theory, younger children tend to conceive of emotions in a simple S-R, behavioristic fashion, whereas older children have a more mentalistic or cognitivist conception, in which mental states are believed to mediate between the emotion-eliciting S and the affected person's behavioral or expressive R.

Two groups of acquisitions seem most central and distinctive to social-cognitive development concerning *thoughts*. The core acquisition of the first group is the basic recognition by young children that they and other people think (know, understand, remember, etc.) as well as perceive and feel. Other insights and abilities in this group emerge during early and middle childhood. These include the recognition that others' conceptual perspectives may be different from your own, even in the same situation, and that their perspectives are potentially inferable from their perceptual experiences or from other indirect evidence. The other group of acquisitions includes the recognition that thought is potentially *recursive*—that is, one thought can subsume or take as its object another thought, and that thought can simultaneously include yet another, and so on, to create complex and extended chains of inference: "I think that you think that he thinks . . ." Coming to understand that thought or mental representation is recursive seems an important developmental acquisition, both because recursiveness is a distinctive property of representation and because much everyday social thought and communication seems to presuppose this understanding. A recent theory of the development of interpersonal understanding incorporates several of the acquisitions concerning thoughts just described.

Recent studies have clarified and added to our understanding of children's developing knowledge about *intentions*. They suggest that even 3 year olds may have some ability to distinguish intended actions from such nonintentional behaviors as mistakes and reflexes. For instance, they may understand that someone who made mistakes in trying to repeat a tongue twister did not "mean to say it like that." By the age of 6 years, children may evince an unexpectedly subtle and sophisticated conception of what makes an act intentional versus unintentional and what makes the effect of an action intended versus unintended. Other, as yet little studied, acquisitions in this area of social cognition include the knowledge that people can commit intentional acts of omission as well as commission, can pretend to do things unintentionally, and can be carrying out more than one intentional act at any given moment, as well as the insight that representations of intentions, like other representations, can be recursive. Proposals have also been made recently as to how children might gradually learn to distinguish intentional from unintentional actions.

There are striking ontogenetic changes in the way children conceptualize and describe another individual's *personality*. Up to 6 to 7 years or there-abouts, a child is likely to characterize another person in terms of "surface" rather than "depth"—the person's appearance, possessions, overt behavior (especially towards the self), and so on, rather than his inner, psychological qualities. During middle childhood there is considerably more emphasis on these internal aspects, and the child acquires a larger and more differentiated set of trait-descriptive terms, but his personality descriptions still tend to lack organization. They become increasingly well organized and integrated during adolescence, however. The other's seemingly conflicting and idiosyncratic combinations of traits are mentioned, and attempts are made to explain, justify, and qualify what is said about him.

The development of knowledge and cognition concerning the *self* closely parallels and overlaps the development of knowledge and cognition about cognition (metacognition) and about other people (social cognition in general). For example, conceptions of both self and others become more differentiated and more "psychological" with increasing age. In fact, much of the development of self conceptions consists of making key differentiations— for example, between one's self and other objects and selves, and between one's real or actual self and one's ideal self. Research has shown that apes (but not monkeys) are capable of recognizing their images in a mirror as images of their own bodies, suggesting that they possess at least a rudimentary form of self-concept or self-awareness. Subsequent studies have suggested that human beings acquire a similar sense of bodily self or "me-ness" towards the end of infancy.

Social-cognitive growth includes the development of children's knowl-edge about between-person *social relations*, such as *friendship*, as well as about the within-person processes already discussed (percepts, feelings, thoughts, etc.). Recent investigations have shown that the ontogenesis of friendship conceptions, like that of self-conceptions, is consistent with and partly predictable from the course of social-cognitive growth in general. For instance, as they mature cognitively children increasingly come to conceive of friendship as a subjective, "psychological" affair entailing mutual assistance, trust, and intimate communication. Other recent studies have shown that it is actually possible to increase the popularity of unpopular children simply by coaching them in social skills that are useful in making friends.

six

Perception

THE ROLE OF INNATE AND EXPERIENTIAL
FACTORS IN PERCEPTUAL DEVELOPMENT

As Gibson (1969) defines it:

> Perception, functionally speaking, is the process by which we obtain firsthand
> information about the world around us. It has a phenomenal aspect, the aware-
> ness of events presently occurring in the organism's immediate surroundings. It
> also has a responsive aspect; it entails discriminative, selective response to the
> stimuli in the immediate environment (p. 3).

What is the origin of that "process," that "awareness," that "discriminative, selective response"? The question has been asked for centuries, and the
answers given have ranged from those of extreme nativism to those of
extreme empiricism (Hochberg, 1962; Pick & Pick, 1970). Are our adult
perceptual abilities and our perceptual knowledge of objects, events, and
space provided by initial, inborn biological "nature" (nativism), or are they
the products of years of postnatal psychological "nurture" (empiricism)?
They might be available right at birth or they might require a shorter or longer
period of biological maturation to become completely functional; in either
case, the extreme nativist assigns no developmentally formative role to
experience. Alternatively, the organism might begin with the classical empiricist's tabula rasa, or blank slate, and have to construct all perceptual abilities
and knowledge through countless experiences with the external environment.
Which view of perceptual development is the correct one, the nativist's or the
empiricist's?

When stated in such extreme and uncompromising terms, neither view is
correct. All perceptual processes (like all other psychological processes) are
mediated by biological structures evolved by the species and inherited by the
individual. Conversely, these structures usually require some sort of sensory
input from the world if the processes are to function and develop. Recall the
favorite cliché of introductory psychology texts: Development is always a
matter of heredity *and* (or *times*) environment, never heredity *or* environment. The nativists and empiricists of old were clearly addressing a real issue,
however, even though their questions and answers concerning it now may
strike us as too extreme, too much all nature or all nurture. Contemporary
students of human and animal perceptual development would prefer to get
answers to more precise and differentiated questions such as the following:
How much of exactly what kind of experience during exactly what period of
ontogeny is necessary and/or sufficient for the emergence of exactly what
component of perceptual knowledge or skill? Is a lot of experience needed, or
only a little? Will any of a wide variety of experiences do the developmental
job, or is a particular, specific kind required? Is there a so-called "critical" or
"sensitive" period involved—namely a particular age period during which the
experience has its maximum influences on the development in question?

Possible Roles of Experience in Perceptual
Development

Very seldom are we able to answer questions as precise as these in the
case of human perceptual development. Nevertheless, it is important to keep

these ancient issues in mind and to formulate them as clearly as we can. A conceptual scheme for characterizing some of the many different roles that experience can play in perceptual development should be helpful in this regard. Gottlieb (1981) has provided the beginnings of such a scheme and Aslin (1981) has elaborated it further. Part of the scheme is illustrated in Figure 6-1 (Aslin, 1981). The lines to the left of the vertical dashed line represent the level or degree of development that the perceptual ability or preference has attained prior to the introduction of the experience. (Aslin uses the geneticist's term *phenotype* for whatever is undergoing development—here, some perceptual ability or preference.) For example, the phenotype might be human binocular vision and the experience might be normal, everyday visual input to both eyes, introduced at birth when the baby's eyes open. The lines to the right of the vertical dashed line represent the subsequent course of

FIGURE 6-1. Five roles of experience in the development of a phenotype. From R. N. Aslin, J. R. Alberts, & M. R. Peterson (Eds.), (1981), *Development of perception: Psychobiological perspectives.* Vol. 2: *The visual system.* New York: Academic Press, p. 50. By permission.

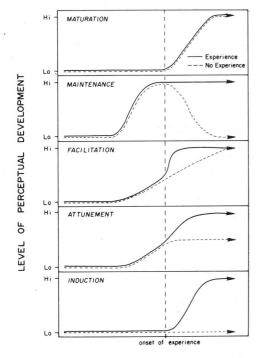

ROLES OF EARLY EXPERIENCE

development of the phenotype with (solid line) and without (dashed line) exposure to the experience in question.

The effects of experience on perceptual development are increasingly potent and specific as one moves down the figure from (a) to (e). In the limiting case of pure *maturation*, experience—especially, specific experience—is assumed to play little or no developmental role. The development is believed to "unfold" according to a genetically programmed maturational schedule and independently of any specific kind or amount of experience. Aslin, Pisoni, and Jusczyk (1983) cite a possible example: Fantz, Fagan, and Miranda (1975) have shown that a preference for patterned visual stimuli by full-term and premature human infants is positively correlated with gestational age (i.e., time since conception) rather than with postnatal age (i.e., time since birth and, therefore, amount of visual experience).

In the *maintenance* case, the phenotype is already fully developed when the relevant experience first becomes available. Since development is already complete, of course the experience cannot engender any additional development. However, the experience does serve to maintain and stabilize the fully developed phenotype. If the experience is not provided, the ability or preference declines, perhaps permanently. In kittens, for example, the full complement of cortical cells responsible for binocular vision is present when their eyes first open. It is likely, therefore, that their capability for binocular vision is essentially fully developed at that time. If they are subsequently deprived of visual input to one of their two eyes (monocular visual deprivation), this capability will decline, which suggests that visual imput to both eyes serves to maintain or stabilize binocularity (Aslin, 1981).

Facilitation is said to occur when the experience hastens the subsequent development of a partly developed phenotype but does not influence its final form or level of development. Thus, it increases the rate of development without affecting the final outcome of development. If, instead, the experience increases the final developmental level or otherwise modifies the final developmental outcome, Aslin (1981) speaks of *attunement*. Hearing their high-pitched vocalizations late in the embryonic period appears to play a facilitation role in the development of young ducklings' ability to respond to the higher frequencies of the maternal call (Gottlieb, 1976). If they are prevented from vocalizing, this development still occurs, but it takes longer. Postnatal visual experience apparently plays an attunement role in the development of depth perception in rats. Although visually deprived rats do develop some depth perception, they do not develop it to the fine degree shown by visually experienced rats (Gottlieb, 1976).

Finally, *induction* describes the case in which the fact and form of the development are heavily dependent upon the presence and specific nature of the experience. The well-known phenomenon of *imprinting* illustrates induction. The mother duck's movement induces the duckling to follow and, more specifically, to follow only her. If some other object serves as the moving stimulus object at the critical time, the duckling will develop a perceptual preference for that object instead. Similarly, learning to understand or read a specific first language obviously requires perceptual experiences with that specific language.

Although this scheme highlights important complexities in the nature-nurture issue of which you might not have been aware, there are yet others

(Aslin, 1981). For example, one can readily imagine intermediary forms among these five "ideal types"—for instance, between facilitation and attunement and between attunement and induction. The scheme also does not adequately take account of the fact that the effect of a given kind of experience on a phenotype may depend upon *when* it is introduced. There may be a *critical* or *sensitive period* for the development considered. A critical or sensitive period is a stretch of time in the organism's life during which the phenotype is maximally sensitive to the developmental influence of the experience. The developments of a number of perceptual functions have been shown to have sensitive periods (Mitchell, 1981). Moreover, the heightened sensitivity can be to a broader or a narrower class of experiential inputs, a variable which further complicates the developmental picture (see Aslin, 1981, for still further complexities). Finally, the same analysis of the possible interactions between innate and experiential factors could be applied to nonperceptual aspects of cognitive development, and also to noncognitive or less cognitive aspects of psychological development.

INFANCY

In 1962, Hochberg said that it would be highly desirable to study young infants' visual abilities, but that "the human infant displays insufficient behavior coordination to permit its study to give us very much useful information" (Hochberg, 1962, p. 323). Or as Bower (1977) so graphically put it, "infancy was like the dark side of the moon" (p. 5). Since that time, Robert Fantz and other developmental psychologists have developed a variety of ingenious methods for assessing the perceptual abilities and dispositions of infants—even newborns. It is no exaggeration to say that we have witnessed a methodological revolution here in the past two dozen years. The new order it produced is a flourishing area of psychological inquiry called infant perception, currently one of the "hottest" research areas in the whole field of developmental psychology. The recent flood of articles, chapters, and books dealing with infant perception would have been virtually unimaginable when Hochberg wrote those words. Several excellent, comprehensive surveys of research in this area are now available (Aslin et al., 1983; Banks & Salapatek, 1983; Gibson & Spelke, 1983; Harris 1983; Olson & Sherman, 1983). Other good sources include Aslin et al. (1981), Cohen et al. (1979), Haith and Campos (1983), and Rosinski (1977).

What has all this recent research taught us about infants' perceptual capabilities? You can probably anticipate the short answer to this question from what I have already said about infant nonsocial (Chapter 2) and social (Chapter 5) cognition: Infants' perceptual capabilities are a good deal more impressive than we used to assume they were. I think there may have been three reasons why we tended to underestimate their perceptual competencies.

1. We made an unwarranted generalization from babies' motor abilities to their perceptual abilities. Young infants have very poor motor skills. They cannot control and coordinate well the movements of their heads, trunks, and, especially limbs. On the motor side, they fairly radiate behavioral incompetence. What could be more natural, then, than to assume a similar level of

incompetence on the perceptual side? It was, in fact, an easy and natural assumption to make.

2. There has been a strong tradition in philosophy and psychology to assume that we begin life with very minimal capabilities and only slowly and gradually, through months and years of experience, construct these capabilities (Gibson & Spelke, 1983). According to this view, we start with next to nothing (virtually a tabula rasa, or blank slate) and build all we have from the ground up, brick by brick. All developments would therefore be instances of *induction*. "Empiricism," "associationism," and "traditional learning theory" are some of the terms associated with this tradition. This view—dominant in psychology during the middle decades of this century—certainly could have contributed to our negative estimate of infants' perceptual skills, and I believe it actually did.

3. Although psychologists in past decades were not able to study infant perception for want of adequate research methods, they could and did study perceptual development in the postinfancy years. These investigations usually found improvements with age in perceptual skills, with young children often performing rather poorly on the particular tasks given. A bit of downward extrapolation from such results easily led to the assumption that infants' perceptual abilities must be very poor indeed.

Methods of Studying Infant Perception

As to the methodological breakthrough, the key to studying infant perception proved to be the experimental exploitation of nonverbal response patterns, patterns that partially track or reflect infants' perceptual activities. Infants naturally cannot report on these activities, as older subjects can; as you can imagine, that was the principal reason why the effective study of infant perception was such a late scientific development. However, perceptual stimulation may elicit behavioral and physiological response patterns that can tell us much that the babies themselves cannot.

The main behavioral responses used in this way have been looking (eye movements and eye fixations), sucking, head turning, and reaching. Let us first examine how looking patterns can be used to gain information about infant perception and attention. An object is moved across the infant's field of vision and the infant follows it with his eyes. The experimenter displays a certain stimulus figure and a special camera or a human observer provides evidence that the infant's eyes almost always scan and fixate particular parts of the figure rather than other parts. She displays two figures simultaneously and discovers that the baby systematically tends to look at one of them more quickly, or more often, or for a longer period of time, than the other. The experimenter repeatedly shows pairs of figures, one member of which always remains the same while the other keeps changing from pair to pair—that is, consists of a new figure on each presentation trial. As the trials continue, the baby devotes more and more of his looking time to the novel figure, as if he had gotten used to and bored with the unchanging figure. More technically and less anthropomorphically, we would say that the infant "habituated" to it (Chapters 3 and 5). Similarly, if the experimenter presents only one figure for trial after trial, looking time to that figure will also gradually diminish.

This process of *habituation* also figures importantly in the experimental use of behavioral responses such as sucking and physiological responses such as heart rate. The infant is given a pacifier nipple to suck on and his baseline sucking rate is recorded. Then, every time he increases his sucking rate above a certain predetermined level, he is reinforced by the presentation of a particular sound, say. This leads to an increase in sucking rate. Even young babies seem happy to "work" in such ways (increased sucking, head turning, etc.) for purely auditory or visual wages. Similarly, using heart rate rather than sucking rate as an indicator, special recording devices might indicate a slowing down of the infant's heart rate when the sound is presented. Except in very young infants, such heart-rate deceleration seems to reflect an orienting, attentional response. (In contrast, heart-rate *acceleration* would mean startle, upset, etc.) After repeated presentation, however, perceptual interest in that sound may gradually appear to wane (habituate), as evidenced by a gradual decrease in sucking rate or a gradual increase in heart rate to their initial, prestimulus levels. The experimenter then presents a new and different sound. The infant may signal his recognition of the change and his heightened interest in the new sound by once again increasing sucking rate or decreasing heart rate. As noted in Chapter 3, this is referred to in the trade as *recovery from habituation*, or *dishabituation*. Even a newborn baby is capable of habituating to a repeated stimulus, and then dishabituating when it is replaced by a new one.

Without saying exactly what we mean to attribute to the infant psychologically in using the term, it is useful to think of all these measures as indices of infant perceptual "preferences." The measures may variously show that he "prefers" to look at or listen to this rather than that stimulus or stimulus component, or "prefers" a newly presented stimulus to the very same stimulus after it has been presented repeatedly (habituation). Such preferences tell us two very important things about the infant's perceptual system. First, they tell us what the system can perceptually distinguish or discriminate. Preferences logically imply discriminability: An organism could not systematically attend to ("prefer") one thing rather than another unless it could somehow perceptually discriminate one from the other. If an infant prefers to look at a pattern of fine black and white stripes rather than at a homogeneous gray pattern of equal total brightness, for instance, that preference tells us that she has at least sufficient visual acuity to see the stripes. Her visual acuity may, of course, be better than that, but it must be at least that good or there could have been no perceptual preference for the one pattern versus the other. Second, preferences tell us about themselves—that is, what the infant is more and less disposed to attend to, and thereby something about the design of the infant's perceptual-attentional and related psychological systems. Recall the discussion of cognitive motivation in Chapter 2 (pp. 15-20). It was said that human beings may be designed to be selectively attentive to certain absolute and relative properties of stimuli, such as movement and novelty. If a young infant usually looked at a moving object rather than an identical stationary one, we could say both that she can perceptually discriminate movement from nonmovement and that her visual system is so constructed as to be more attentive to movement than nonmovement. In summary, research methods now exist that can detect systematic attentional preferences in infants of different ages, including neonates. Inferences about both the powers and the propensities of the infant's perceptual system can then be made from these preferences.

I should also mention that habituation of attention implies at least some sort of recognition-type memory capability. If the baby's cognitive system could not somehow code the fact that the repeated stimulus has been perceived before—could not "recognize" it, in some sense, as old or familiar—the system could not habituate to it (see Chapter 7). It is, after all, a physically identical stimulus from one trial to the next. Thus, these research methods can actually give us information about three things rather than just two: (1) infant perceptual-discrimination abilities; (2) infant perceptual preferences or sensitivities; and (3) infant recognition-memory abilities.

Some other behavioral and physiological indices of perceptual processing are mentioned only briefly. Infants can show their abilities to locate a sound source by turning their heads in the direction of the sound. Conditioned head turning can also be used as an index of perceptual processing. Even young babies may show some capacity for depth perception by blinking or moving backwards when a large object continues to move towards them, as if about to collide with them. Somewhat older infants may show their abilities to discriminate depth by reaching for objects if they are within reach and refraining from reaching for them when they are farther away. Finally, still older infants may signal their perception of depth of a drop off under a glass surface (a "visual cliff") by refusing to crawl onto the surface. Additional physiological measures include the recording of the electrical activity of neurons at auditory or visual centers during perceptual stimulation via electrodes attached to the infant's scalp. Such recordings are called *evoked potentials*. It should now be clear what the methodological dictum of today's infant researcher is: Measure and try to interpret anything the baby will do in response to sensory input.

In this brief description of current methods I have, as always, made things sound more simple and straightforward than they really are. The recording and interpretation of looking, sucking, heart-rate, and other response patterns in infants are fraught with problems; see Aslin et al. (1983), for example, for a good discussion of the strengths and weaknesses of existing methods for assessing infant auditory functioning. Young babies are unstable little creatures, subject to changes in physiological state from one time period to another. Imagine how that fact can complicate the interpretation of, say, changes in heart rate over time. The evidence obtained from one measure may not always accord with that obtained from another. The infant may, in fact, be able to discriminate between two stimuli perceptually but not show any attentional preference for one versus the other, with the result that his discriminative ability goes undetected—preference logically implies discrimination but discrimination certainly does not logically imply preference. This is clearly a very important methodological limitation. Even if it can be shown (e.g., by preference data) that the infant can discriminate one thing from another, it still may be very difficult to establish the exact basis on which the discrimination was made. Stimuli are likely to differ from one another in a variety of ways simultaneously, and it may be very hard to prove to exactly which differentiating feature or combination of features the baby is responding (Banks & Salapatek, 1983). Any given research method may be a better, more sensitive measure of perceptual functioning at one age level than another during infancy (Aslin et al., 1983). Moreover, some methods that are good measures at certain age levels cannot be used at all at other age levels. As two examples, very young babies cannot reach for objects, and 1 year olds are usually not willing to sit quietly for trial after trial, looking or listening to the same stimulus; they obviously have discovered more interesting things to do in this world. These problems make it very difficult to trace the development of a perceptual capability. Finally, the available methods—being nonverbal—cannot tell us exactly what conscious perceptual experience the infant is having, or what meaning and significance the percept has for him. Indirect measures, however clever, are still indirect measures.

Despite these problems, the new methods have produced a number of provisional facts about infant perceptual development. Most of the evidence concerns vision and audition, the two most important sensory instruments of human learning and development. Therefore, the following synopsis deals almost exclusively with infant auditory and visual development.

Audition

This summary owes much to a recent, very comprehensive review of the research literature in this area by Aslin et al. (1983). It is apparent from this and previous reviews (e.g., Pick, Frankel, & Hess, 1975) that we know less about infant audition than about infant vision, partly because of special methodological problems that plague the assessment of infant auditory functioning.

HEARING. Evidence from fetal and prematurely born infants suggests that the auditory system begins to function at least several weeks prior to the normal term of birth. However, there are three reasons why we do not presently know exactly what the fetus does and does not hear inside its uterine world or how whatever it might hear would sound to it.

1. We do not know how sensitive the fetal auditory system is to sounds of different frequency spectra (pitch and tone quality).
2. Sounds from the outside have to pass through the mother's body tissues and through the fluid of the amniotic sac before they can reach the fetus's ears. Under these conditions, sounds can provide vibratory stimulation to the fetus's skin as well as to its auditory system. Consequently, a fetal behavioral reaction to a sound is always open to the interpretation that, in effect, the fetus felt something rather than heard something. On the other hand, recent evidence does indicate that sounds of frequencies below 1000 Hz (cycles per second) are transmitted from the external environment to the amniotic sac with little attenuation, whereas the intensities of sounds of higher frequencies are reduced considerably in the transmission process (Aslin et al., 1983). The most important frequency range for human speech is from about 500 to 2000 Hz, and thus important components of speech sounds could reach the fetal ear.
3. Recent data indicate that the ambient noise level in the intrauterine environment is surprisingly high (Aslin et al., 1983)—85 decibels, which is roughly that of the interior of a noisy factory. That is an important finding that should be verified by other investigators.

These findings appear to suggest that, even if we could assume fairly good auditory sensitivity, the fetus might well not be able to hear ordinary conversational speech at all. This further implies that parents who want to "communicate" with their infants before birth will, at the very least, have to speak up.

They should not have to speak up after birth, however. Almost all existing studies suggest that the newborn's auditory threshold is only about 10 to 20 decibels higher than the adult's (Aslin et al., 1983); that is about the magnitude of hearing loss you have when you have a head cold. It is always possible, moreover, that the relatively crude measures that must be used in assessing auditory thresholds in infants underestimate their auditory acuity. It is not known when this (apparent) age difference in auditory sensitivity disappears. As to auditory-discrimination ability, what little evidence exists shows that babies of 6 to 12 months of age can make quite fine intensity and frequency (roughly—loudness and pitch) discriminations. Finally, there is now good evidence that even newborns can localize sounds, at least to the extent of discriminating whether a sound came from the extreme left or the extreme right. That is, if the head is properly supported so that head movements are easier to make, infants will fairly reliably turn their heads to the right when they hear a sound coming from the right, and to the left when they hear a sound coming from the left (Aslin et al., 1983).

PERCEIVING SPEECH. In Chapter 5 (pp. 133–135) I presented recent evidence indicating that the favorite auditory diet of even very young babies appears to be the human voice. I cited studies by DeCasper and Fifer (1980) and Mehler et al. (1978) showing that 0 to 1 month olds can discriminate their own mothers' voices from those of other mothers, and prefer to hear the former. Recall that Mehler et al. (1978) also found that their young infants could make this discrimination only if the speech was of the sort normally directed to babies by mothers. What is this sort of talk like? Aptly named "motherese" (see Chapter 8), one of its hallmarks is greatly exaggerated intonation; it has a strongly "up and down" quality. Recent studies described by Aslin et al. (1983) show that 4 month olds would rather listen to tape-recorded motherese than to tape-recorded adult-to-adult talk, even when the voice is that of a female stranger rather than the child's mother. Interestingly, they would even rather listen to *nonspeech* sounds that have expanded pitch contours than nonspeech sounds that do not.

Far and away the most dramatic research on infant speech perception, however, has to do with the perception of elementary phonological speech units, such as consonant sounds. Studies by Eimas, Siqueland, Jusczyk, and Vigorito (1971) and others in this area can only be described as astonishing. It is necessary to say something about the nature of speech perception in adults before the infant findings can be understood and appreciated. Someone once told me that there are only two levels of understanding of the field of international trade and finance: One takes about five minutes to achieve and the other about five years. The same is true of speech perception. I only try for the five-minute variety here; you are referred to Aslin et al. (1983) and the sources they cite if you want to get started on the five-year course.

The purely physical, acoustic difference between an auditory stimulus that sounds like "ba" and one that sounds like "pa" is a completely quantitative, continuous one. The acoustic dimension involved is a continuum, just like length or weight. Supposing we were to vary the auditory stimulus on that dimension. We start on the "ba" end of the dimension and gradually, continuously change the stimulus until we get to the "pa" end, much as we might gradually, continuously lengthen a line by slowly moving our pencils along a straightedge. What should happen perceptually? The "ba" should come to sound more and more "pa"-like, and there should be a broad zone in the middle of the dimension where the listener cannot easily say which of the two consonants the sound most resembles. He might be inconsistent in his choice from trial to trial within this broad zone, or report blends of "ba" and "pa."

A major discovery of speech-perception research is that adults do not perceive certain speech sounds in this expected, continuous fashion. What happens instead is that suddenly, abruptly—almost at a single point on that continuous dimension—the stimulus is heard as "pa" instead of "ba." As the stimulus continuously varies, the listener discontinuously reports . . . "ba," "ba," "ba," "pa," "pa," "pa" . . . . Thus, consonant perception tends to be discontinuous or "categorical" rather than continuous, in marked contrast to most other forms of perception. For instance, a tiny change in light-wave length does not abruptly change the color category reported—for example, from a clear, unequivocal blue to a clear, unequivocal green. Similarly, my pencil line will not suddenly and thereafter be perceived as "long" rather than "short" when it reaches, say, 8.23 inches.

What Eimas and other investigators have shown is that very young infants (e.g., 1 month old) also exhibit categorical perception of consonantal sounds (Aslin et al., 1983). To illustrate the nature of their evidence, let us suppose that our "ba"-"pa" acoustic dimension was arbitrarily marked off into equal physical segments, like this: 1-2-3-4-5-6. Let us further suppose that adults hear stimuli 1, 2, and 3 as "ba" and stimuli 4, 5, and 6 as "pa," since the dimension's small transition zone lies between stimuli 3 and 4. Even though sounds 1 and 3 are no more different from each other from the physicist's standpoint than 3 and 5 are from each other, a listener hears the members of the first pair as the same sound ("ba") and the members of the second pair as two different sounds ("ba" and "pa"). This is a clear instance of categorical speech perception. If a young infant is exposed to 1 until she habituates to it, she will continue to show habituation if 1 is replaced by 3. In contrast, if initially habituated to 3 and then presented with 5, she shows dishabituation. In other words, the baby acts as if she does not hear the difference between 1 and 3, just as adults do not, but as if she does hear the difference between 3 and 5, just as adults do.

It used to be believed that infants learned to discriminate speech sounds only gradually, through months of experience listening to their own babbling and the speech of others. However, there is now a great deal of evidence showing that they are capable of perceptually discriminating between many acoustically similar speech sounds during early infancy. As Aslin et al. (1983) put it: "After a decade of research on infant speech perception, it is fair to say that every phonetic contrast presented to infants has been shown to be discriminated prior to 12 months of age" (p. 646). Furthermore, many of those discriminations are categorical rather than continuous in nature.

Could the early ability to make those many perceptual discriminations possibly be the result of perceptual learning—that is, could it be acquired by infants through experience listening to the speech they hear around them? There are several reasons why that cannot be the case (Aslin et al., 1983). First, the ability to make at least some of these contrasts is present as early as one can test for it (e.g., 1 month of age). This suggests that it may well be present at birth, and thus prior to any speech-perception experience. Second, young babies who live in different speech communities and consequently hear different languages are nevertheless very similar to one another in the phonetic contrasts they can discriminate perceptually. They also tend to make discontinuous categorical discriminations at about the same points on the various acoustic continua. In the example given earlier, that is tantamount to saying that young babies would discriminate between sounds 3 and 5 but not between sounds 1 and 3, even if the language they heard others around them speak did not make use of that particular contrast. If a language does not use a phonetic contrast, the adult speakers of that language may not be able to hear that contrast, at least not without some training and practice. We would expect, therefore, that young babies might be able to hear some speech contrasts that their parents could not easily hear. In fact, the research evidence strongly suggests that precisely that could happen. To illustrate, Trehub (1976) tested the ability of young infants from English-speaking homes to discriminate a phonetic contrast that occurs in Czech but not in English. The infants showed clear evidence of being able to make the distinction. A group of English-speaking adults, on the other hand, had considerable difficulty hearing the contrast. Needless to add, no one thinks young infants are attaching any linguistic meaning to the contrasts they can hear; they merely are capable of hearing them as different sounds.

Findings such as these led to the hypothesis that we are equipped from birth with a highly specialized mode of perception, a so-called "speech mode," designed solely and specifically to help us acquire and use the phonological distinctions found in human natural languages. Auditory perception in the speech mode, in contrast to other auditory perception, is categorical rather than continuous in nature; that is the main distinguishing characteristic of this evolved capacity. This hypothesis suggests two predictions: (1) Since only humans acquire human speech, only humans should show categorical, speech-mode-like auditory discriminations; (2) since it is a "speech mode," humans should use this capacity only when perceiving speech sounds.

Experimental tests of these two quite reasonable-looking predictions yielded a very surprising outcome, however: The evidence ran counter to *both* predictions (Aslin et al., 1983). The first prediction was initially disconfirmed in a particularly shocking fashion: *Chinchillas*, of all creatures, also turn out to show categorical perception of human speech sounds (Kuhl & Miller, 1975). Subsequently, macaque monkeys were also found to do the same (Kuhl & Padden, in press). In addition, even the absolute location of the category boundaries along the acoustic continua tested proved quite similar for chinchillas, macaques, and humans. That would be as if, using our earlier example, the category boundary lay between 3 and 4 for all three species. The second prediction was confirmed by the finding that certain nonspeech-like sounds are also perceived categorically rather than continuously, both by adults and by infants (Aslin et al., 1983). (One would expect that chinchillas and macaques would also perceive these same sounds categorically, but I do not think this has actually been tested yet.) Although the issue is still controversial among the experts and the story could change next year, present evidence seems to support the conclusion that categorical auditory perception is—contrary to what many used to think—neither species-specific nor speech-specific.

If the capacity for categorical auditory perception is neither species-specific nor speech-specific, what are we to make of it? One highly speculative line of reasoning is the following (cf. Aslin et al., 1983): It is a general auditory capacity (thus, not restricted to speech perception) that other mammals also share (thus, not restricted to humans). Since other mammals also possess it, it may have been acquired quite early in our evolutionary history—earlier than the capacity for human oral speech. More speculative yet, maybe the sound structure of human language then evolved to fit the particular processing characteristics (e.g., proclivity for categorical perception) of this general auditory capacity. To put it another way, it is at least conceivable that human speech sounds are as they are partly (probably *only* partly) because our mammalian auditory system is so constructed that it can easily discriminate and categorize them. If all this were true, we would expect that infants as well as adults would possess this capacity, because it will help them discriminate and eventually learn human speech sounds, and we should not be surprised to discover that other mammals also possess it, because it evolved so early, in the eons when we were mammalian but not yet human.

One more speculation about infant speech perception before examining infant vision: Perhaps infant speech perception is a bit like infant face perception (see Chapter 5, p. 132). Just as infants are probably not born with highly specific and specialized "face detectors," so also are they probably not born with highly specialized "speech-sound detectors" (a "speech mode"). On the other hand, infants probably are born with perceptual preferences and/or abilities that are specific enough to help them with the vital tasks of people learning and language learning.

Vision

The first section on audition (*Hearing*) dealt mostly with *how well* human infants can *hear*. It described what might be called the basic sensory capacities of the infant auditory system. In contrast, the second section (*Perceiving Speech*) was concerned with *what* meaningful events in the world infants can *perceive* through the use of these auditory capacities. Very roughly, we could say that the first section dealt with lower-level auditory *sensation* and the second with higher-level auditory *perception*. This rough distinction is also useful to make in describing developmental aspects of infant vision. At the lower-level, "sensation" end, we can ask how well infants of different ages can see. Can their eyes scan, fixate, and focus effectively? How good is their visual acuity or "eyesight"? What about their ability to see colors, forms, patterns, and movement? At the higher-level, "perception" end, we can ask what important information about the world babies of different ages can obtain by using these visual capacities. According to Gibson and Spelke

(1983), one can use one's visual system to obtain all manner of information and knowledge about objects, events, and places, either real, physically present ones or pictorially represented ones (thus, picture perception). This distinction between lower-level "sensation" and higher-level "perception" is somewhat forced and can lead to conceptual muddles if taken too literally. Although not quite right, the distinction is—as a friend of mine used to say about such distinctions—good enough for government standards. Above all, it is useful in segmenting this chapter section.

SEEING. This summary makes heavy use of Banks and Salapatek's (1983) comprehensive review chapter. A number of neural systems subserve human visual functioning: the retina, the lateral geniculate nucleus, the visual cortex, and the superior colliculus. None of these systems appears to be fully developed at birth; all seem to be immature to a greater or lesser degree. As a consequence, very little if any of the neonate's visual functioning is of the quality it will be in later infancy and early childhood. This is not to say that neonates cannot see at all—they certainly can. On the other hand, it is clear that their visual system has a good deal of developing to do. Several theories of early visual development have been proposed (e.g., Bronson, 1974). Since none of them appears to be wholly satisfactory as a theory (Banks & Salapatek, 1983) I do not describe them here. It is worth noting, however, that all of them agree on one important point: Many of the changes that take place in early visual development reflect biological growth or maturation of these neural systems—especially of the visual cortex.

The fovea, located at the very center of the retina, has much higher visual acuity than more peripheral retinal areas. Consequently, we often have to move our eyes to bring object images into sharp and clear foveal fixation. There are several different kinds of eye movements that accomplish this. If an object appears in peripheral vision, a very rapid eye movement called a *saccade* is made to fixate it. If the object moves across the visual field, smooth pursuit movements are made to maintain continuous focal fixation on it. Other kinds of eye movements (vestibular-controlled, optokinetic) are designed primarily for use when we try to achieve or maintain fixation on objects while we ourselves are in motion. The saccadic eye movements of newborns and very young infants tend to be slow and imprecise. Young infants commonly undershoot the visual target on the initial saccade and then have to initiate a second saccade to get them the rest of the way to the visual target. Similarly, their smooth pursuit movements are usually far from smooth. Rather, they tend to consist of a jerky series of saccadic "catch-up" refixations of the moving stimulus. Thus, newborns are apt to have some difficulty both in fixating stationary objects and in maintaining fixation on moving ones. The eye-movement systems that are most useful when one is moving about in space are more mature at birth than those that are most useful when one is stationary. This is a curious state of affairs, in view of the fact that young babies are less mobile than older ones and consequently have less immediate need for the former systems than for the latter ones.

To add to the very young infant's problems in achieving and maintaining fixation, her eyes do not always converge on the same visual target. As you might imagine, two eyes looking in different directions could present a problem for the researcher who is trying to determine to what the baby is attending. (The problem is sometimes solved by covering one eye during testing.)

The eye can only be sharply focused for one viewing distance at a time. If a nearby object is in focus, a far-away object will look blurred, and vice versa. Objects at different depths are brought into visual focus by automatically changing the curvature of the eye's lens, a process called visual accommodation. Like Piagetian cognitive accommodation (Chapter 1), visual accommodation involves adapting one's own structure to the properties of stimuli. Very young infants often make focusing errors, accommodating too much or too little for a given target distance. Curiously, these errors may lead to less blurred vision for them than they would for us. The reason is that they appear to have a greater depth of focus than we do—that is, a greater distance through which an object can be moved without accommodative change in lens curvature and still remain in focus (Banks & Salapatek, 1983). All of the basic processes just described—the various kinds of eye movements, convergence of the two eyes, and visual accommodation—become much more adult-like during the first few months after birth.

Vision not only provides information about external events but also about the observer's own movements. For example, if you fell over backwards, you would perceive an increase in distance between your eyes and the wall in front of you. What if, while you were just standing there facing the wall, the wall itself moved backwards, away from you? Experiments by Lee and co-workers (Lee & Aronson, 1974; Lishman & Lee, 1975) have shown that this visual experience leads adults and 11 month olds to feel that they are falling backwards; to compensate, they tend to fall forward. Because they are more unsteady on their feet than the adults, the 11 month olds often actually fall down. The question arises whether this sort of reaction is inborn or acquired—that is, gradually learned through repeated experience in seeing how objects in front of you look when you fall. Subsequent research by Butterworth and his colleagues suggests that it is probably not learned (described in Gibson & Spelke, 1983): Two month olds make similar compensatory movements of their heads in response to a moving wall, even though they cannot even sit up without support, much less stand up.

Fixating and focusing on objects via eye movements and accommodation mechanisms are, of course, only the initial, preparatory steps in the visual process. There remains the main task of detecting and discriminating all the complex visual information that the objects can present. This includes information about pattern, color, motion, and depth. Pattern is the most complex of these, comprising information about contours, figure-ground relations, texture, form or shape, object elements, objects, and relations among any of these (e.g., configurations of contours).

Two closely related visual capacities important in detecting and discriminating patterns are visual acuity and contrast sensitivity. Your visual acuity is defined technically as the highest spatial frequency you can detect. It can be measured by using patterns of alternating black and white stripes of equal width. The narrower the stripes, the higher the spatial frequency of the pattern, and the harder it becomes to see the stimulus as striped rather than unpatterned—that is, a uniform grey. Thus, the higher the spatial frequency

(= narrower the stripes) of the pattern you can still see as striped rather than grey, the better your visual acuity. Good visual acuity permits you to identify small or far-away objects or object parts, read fine print, and the like.

Your contrast sensitivity refers to your capacity for discriminating differences in light intensity (light-dark differences). Suppose that the stripes in the stimulus were broad rather than narrow, and therefore posed no visual-acuity problem. The stimulus would obviously still become harder and harder to see as striped rather than unpatterned as the intensity differences between the stripes become smaller—that is, as the black and white stripes both change in intensity towards a common grey. Intensity differences tend to be concentrated at the edges or contours of objects and object parts. They help tell you where figure stops and ground begins, or where this object part ends and that one begins. Therefore, you use your contrast-sensitivity capacity to detect and discriminate contours, figure-ground, shape, object parts, objects, and configurations of these. In short, you use it to perceive patterns, large ones as well as small ones. Atkinson and Braddick (1981) characterize these two related capacities as follows:

> Almost every visual perceptual function depends on the visual system transmitting information about the spatial pattern in the incoming optic array. Visual acuity is a measure of the finest detail that is transmitted. The contrast sensitivity function . . . provides a more complete description of how the visual system transmits spatial information, as it is not restricted to the sensitivity to fine detail that is measured as acuity, but also quantifies the sensitivity to the broader distribution of light and dark in a spatial pattern (pp. 245-246).

Considerable research evidence has now accumulated on the development of visual acuity during infancy. The main facts are the following (Banks & Salapatek, 1983). The newborn's visual acuity is surprisingly poor—perhaps as poor as 20/600 Snellen. That is a rather startling figure when you realize that normal adult visual acuity is about 20/20 and that a person whose uncorrected visual acuity is poorer than 20/200 would usually be categorized as legally blind. Thus, the resolving power of the neonatal visual system appears to be only about 1/30 that of the normal adult. Visual acuity improves considerably during the first half year of life, although it is still definitely below the adult level at 6 months of age. The improvement appears to be due largely to maturational changes rather than to experience looking at objects and events. For example, the visual acuity of premature babies has been shown to match that of full-term babies of the same gestational rather than postnatal age, suggesting that it is time from conception rather than time in the world, looking, that most influences acuity. Maturational changes in what? In neural structures, most probably, since the strictly optical properties of the newborn's eyes seem quite good. With increasing age, the photoreceptors (cones) in the fovea become more densely packed and the spatial resolution of retinal, lateral geniculate, and cortical neurons also probably improves (Banks & Salapatek, 1983). Either or both of these changes could markedly improve the infant's visual acuity. Like visual acuity, contrast sensitivity is also quite poor at birth and improves considerably during the first half year of life.

What can the newborn see and how well can she see it, given these substantial deficits in visual acuity and contrast sensitivity? Well, she certainly could not see well enough to read or make needlepoint samplers, but we would not exactly consider that a catastrophic disability for a newborn baby. On the positive side, visual detection and discrimination would probably be at least tolerably good for objects that are not overly small, that have contours exhibiting high light-dark contrast, and that are presented fairly close to her eyes. People meet these requirements, and so do many other everyday objects and events of potential interest to a young baby (Banks & Salapatek, 1981, 1983). And, of course, infant person perception is further helped along by the fact that people provide other perceptual cues besides pattern; for instance, they also come in living color, complete with sound and animation (Chapter 5).

The existence of systematic infant pattern preferences is now very well established. Young infants, even newborns, clearly prefer to fixate some visual patterns over others. However, the precise description, prediction, and theoretical explanation of these preferences has turned out to be an exceedingly difficult and frustrating scientific task (Banks & Salapatek, 1983). One early sensible-sounding hypothesis was that the stimulus complexity of the pattern determines preference. The complexity hypothesis predicted that a certain level (an "optimal" level) of complexity will be most preferred at a given age, and that this optimal level will increase as the infant grows older (see Chapter 2). However, "stimulus complexity" can be defined in several different ways and none of the definitions tried has been very successful in predicting preferences. Others have suggested that the size and number of pattern elements determines preferences, but this, too, has proved to be an unsatisfactory predictor. Karmel (1969) hypothesized that young infants prefer to look at those patterns that possess greater contour density, defined as the total length of contour contained in a pattern divided by the total area of that pattern. Karmel's contour-density model has proved to be a better predictor of infant preferences than either the complexity model or the size-number model. However, it also fails to account for some known preferences. For example, it cannot explain why young infants often prefer to look at patterns containing unconnected pattern elements that are irregularly rather than regularly arranged, since contour density is unaffected by regularity-irregularity of arrangement. Finally, Banks and Salapatek (1981, 1983) have recently presented and tested an explanatory model that takes account of the young infant's relatively poor contrast-sensitivity capacity. This capacity allows only some of the pattern information present in the stimulus to reach "decision centers" in the baby's central nervous system. Banks and Salapatek make their preference predictions on the basis of the information that reaches these centers—roughly speaking, on the basis of what the baby actually sees rather than what the stimulus presents. For the complicated details on how this is done, see Banks and Salapatek (1981, 1983). Their model appears to me to be superior to Karmel's, but it is too new to be sure just how adequate it will prove to be. Unlike good wine and infant vision, theories seldom improve with age.

Two questions remain concerning infant pattern preferences. First, what developmental function might these very early, undoubtedly unlearned pattern preferences serve? One possible answer was suggested in Chapters 2 and 5: Young infants may be biased to attend to the information in the environment that is most important for them to learn about (e.g., information about people). Their visual pattern preferences may be one expression of this built-in bias. Another is suggested by Banks and Salapatek (1983). Exposure to patterned information—not just light, but patterned stimuli—is known to maintain and/or facilitate the normal development of the cat visual cortex. The same may be true in humans, and thus "human infants' looking behavior may reflect a fixation strategy which tends to expose the central retina to salient patterns in order to provide the stimulation required for cortical development to proceed optimally" (Banks & Salapatek, 1983, p. 507).

The second question is: How do pattern preferences change with age and experience? You can probably guess the answer. As an infant comes to recognize and learn more about specific objects and events in her environment, memory and meaning become much more important determinants of visual preferences than built-in processing biases or the need for cortical stimulation. For example, through experience she will come to prefer faces to nonsense patterns of equal contour density and, subsequently, familiar faces to unfamiliar ones. As Salapatek (1977) describes it: "The infant is changing from an organism that began by selecting patterns and shapes solely on the basis of amount and size of contour present towards a conscious human with memory for visual events who now selects where he will look, on the basis of memory as well as reflexes" (p. 453). Or, in Bronson's (1974) words, "the infant becomes an internally directed, historically guided, pattern-organizing individual" (p. 887).

Other facts about what young infants look at and see can be summarized briefly (Banks & Salapatek, 1983). Newborns usually do not scan a figure very extensively. Their gaze tends to get "captured" by a single feature or part of the figure, and they may continue to stare at that one part for quite a long time. Predictably, the part that preempts their attention is likely to have high light-dark contrast and contour density—for instance, one corner of a black triangle, where two contours meet. They also tend not to scan the interior of figures, confining their fixations instead to the outside contours. Thus, they are apt to look at only the exterior pieces of patterns. These scanning tendencies should serve to reduce their fixations on the interior features and feature arrangements of the human face, although any such reduction should be counteracted in part by the fact that these features have other attention-getting properties, such as movement. These scanning limitations are largely overcome during the first 2 to 3 months of life. By about 3 months of age also, babies can distinguish patterns on the basis of their shapes or forms alone, which must represent a giant step in the development of object perception. Important also for object perception is the acquisition of size constancy and shape constancy (Chapter 2), both of which seem to be largely accomplished by about 6 months of age.

Assessing infant color vision has long been extremely difficult to do (Banks & Salapatek, 1983; Teller, 1981). The biggest methodological problem has been to find ways to distinguish cleanly between infant discriminations based on wave length (what you are after) and infant discriminations based on brightness (a correlated, confounding variable that you want to control for). Some clever recent studies appear to have largely overcome this problem, however. The results of these studies suggest that: (1) Considerable development in this area of visual functioning occurs during the first 3 months of life;

(2) by 2 months of age, infants definitely can make some wave-length discriminations (indeed, some that adults with the two most common types of color blindness cannot); (3) by 3 months, many fundamental aspects of color vision appear to be quite adult-like; (4) there may well be further developments after this age—for example, in the precision with which color differences can be discriminated. In this area of basic visual functioning, as in the others we have examined, it is clear that a lot of developmental progress gets accomplished during those first few postnatal months.

PERCEIVING THE WORLD

The Gibsonian movement. There have been two major movements in the history of infant perceptual research. The first, already described, began with the methodological innovations of Robert Fantz. This movement has generated and continues to generate a wealth of important information about the more sensory or sensation-like capacities of infants of different ages. With the exception of the discussion of infant speech perception, this chapter has thus far dealt solely with the work of this movement. The second movement was initiated by Eleanor Gibson and James Gibson (Gibson, 1966, 1969). Researchers in the Gibsonian tradition are primarily concerned with higher-order perceptual processing. They tend to study infants' abilities to perceive events, objects, places, and pictures (Gibson & Spelke, 1983), rather than their abilities to detect sounds, contours, colors, movement, and the like. The Gibsonians have made some very exciting discoveries in the past few years (see Gibson, 1982; Gibson & Spelke, 1983) and their work is currently having a profound effect on our thinking about infant perceptual capabilities. Some of these discoveries were described in Chapter 5 (the work of Spelke and others on infant cross-modal perception of face-voice synchronisms); others are described presently.

The flavor of the Gibsonian approach and how it differs from that of the other movement may be conveyed by examining a prototypical Gibsonian "stimulus": a looming object. Consider the invariant features in the visual input that specify perceptually that an object is coming directly towards you at a roughly constant rate of speed, as when someone throws a basketball at your face, hard, from ten feet away. Optically, the features consist of a continuous, symmetrically expanding closed contour, with the expansion accelerating at a certain rate (Gibson, 1969, p. 271). If the expansion is not continuous, the movement will be seen as jerky (hardly the behavior of a thrown basketball). If the expansion is not symmetrical, within the visual field, the ball will be perceived as heading to one side, about to miss you. If the expansion of the contour is uniform in speed, or insufficiently accelerative, you will perceive the ball as magically slowing down more and more as it nears your face. Compare this sort of visual input with the sort employed to test a basic sensory capacity—for instance, a striped pattern used to assess visual acuity. First, the Gibsonian stimulus is more complex. Second, part of its greater complexity lies in the fact that it is extended in time and undergoes complex changes during its time course. It is a dynamic, unfolding event in time rather than a static, "frozen" stimulus display. Finally, it is an ecologically significant, biologically meaningful event. Obviously, the ability to perceive that something is about to collide with you, or you with it, is needed to evade predators and missiles and to avoid bumping into objects while moving about. It is just the sort of ability that a species might evolve and that consequently might well be inborn or early matured by members of that species.

That is the type of perception in which the Gibsonians are most interested: the perceptual pick-up of complex, often temporally extended patterns of sensory stimulation, especially patterns that specify objects and events in the environment that are meaningful and ecologically significant for the species doing the perceiving. As Gibson and Spelke (1983) put it:

> We approach the problems and the literature of perception by beginning with the ecology of an animal, its way of life as a species, and the biological structures with which it has been endowed by nature. Every species has evolved in a habitat, and in the long course of evolution, its niche and its biological structures have developed in reciprocity with one another. The perceptual systems developed in the context of this mutual relationship. They have adapted to enable the perceiver to extract the information that he needs for survival in the kind of world he lives in, especially to extract information about the affordances of things (p. 3).

Because they are concerned with very complex, high-order perceptual skills that presumably have evolved to serve the adaptation of a species to its habitat, the Gibsonians are prepared to find these skills already functional in the young infant. Eleanor Gibson has long been a student of perceptual learning, and consequently the fact that some important perceptual skills might only be acquired later in ontogenesis, through experience, poses no problem for the Gibsonian approach. Nevertheless, the Gibsonians' most important scientific discoveries in the area of infant perception owe much to their readiness to believe that *very* powerful, mature-seeming perceptual competencies might well be present at birth or soon after. Because the Gibsonians could imagine that such competencies might be present very early, they have thought to look for them; and thinking to look, they have often found some remarkable things.

OBJECTS. The world around us is populated by a wide variety of objects of different sizes, shapes, colors, and textures. As we look at them from any given perspective, they may be related spatially to one another and to other surfaces in several ways. For instance, objects A and B are seen side by side in the frontal plane and flush up against each other. In contrast, object C is behind object D from our perspective but sticks out on both sides of it, thus permitting us to see the two ends of C but not its middle part. Object E is suspended in front of but not touching a background surface (e.g., a wall), object F rests on a horizontal surface (e.g., a larger, flat object), object G moves across the visual field, and so on.

As adults, we are remarkably adept at perceiving each object in the visual field as a unitary, continuous, bounded entity, separate and distinct from the other objects or surfaces that touch or partly occlude it. We instantly see A and B as two objects, not one. We automatically perceive C as one continuous object rather than as two discrete and separate objects, one on each side of *D*. It would be natural for a Gibsonian to be interested in the developmental history of a perceptual ability as ecologically significant and adaptive as the ability to perceive objects; indeed, Elizabeth Spelke and her colleagues have recently done some ingenious experiments on infant object perception (Spelke, 1982). Their research has addressed the infant's ability to perceive an object (1) as distinct from the background surfaces behind it (e.g., object *E*); (2) as continuing behind any surfaces that partly hide it from their view (object *C*); and (3) as a separate entity from any surfaces that touch it (*A* and *B* seen as two different objects).

In the case of (1), it has been surprisingly difficult to get firm scientific evidence on the basic question of when or whether young babies perceive single objects suspended in front of them as unitary, bounded entities, distinct and separate from background surfaces (Spelke, 1982). By the time they are 4 or 5 months old, infants will reach for suspended objects. They will also adjust their reaching to certain spatial properties of the objects. For instance, they will more often reach for nearby objects than ones farther away, and will reach differently for large objects than small ones. The behavior of younger infants is harder to interpret.

In one series of experiments, Spelke and Born (Spelke, 1982) tried to find out if 3 month olds tacitly expect that objects can move independently of their backgrounds but, being unitary, bounded entities, must do so by moving as wholes. In one experiment, the infants first saw an orange cylinder suspended in front of a flat, blue surface. On some trials subsequently, they saw the cylinder as a whole move forward, towards them, while the background surface remained still. On other trials, the movement broke the object in half; half of the object moved forward in tandem with an adjacent portion of the background. The investigators "reasoned that if infants perceived the object as unitary and separate from the background, they would be surprised or puzzled when the object broke apart and moved together with part of the background" (Spelke, 1982, p. 412). The infants did in fact exhibit more apparent surprise or puzzlement in the latter trials than in the former ones. Subsequent research showed that infants of this age do not exhibit more surprise or puzzlement on trials of the latter, abnormal-movement kind when object and background are both two dimensional and initially form part of the same surface, as in a picture, rather than being separated in depth from each other. Spelke (1982) interprets these results as indicating that infants of this age probably do see as unified, bounded wholes objects that are clearly separated in depth from their backgrounds. Although one would like to see additional controls in this study, its results are consistent with what I think the weight of evidence in this area suggests: By 3 months of age, babies can perceive objects as unified entities under favorable perceptual conditions.

As to (2), Spelke (1982) also reports some clever experiments by Kellman and Spelke of 4 month olds' abilities to perceive partially hidden objects as unitary entities and to represent correctly the probable shapes of their occluded parts. The stimulus display consisted of a straight black rod positioned vertically behind a tan block. The rod's top and bottom segments were clearly visible but its middle section was of course occluded by the block. Adults looking at this array effortlessly and automatically perceive the rod as a single, continuous object located behind another object. Kellman and Spelke used an habituation-of-looking method to try to ascertain whether 4 month olds would also perceive the rod as a single object, or, in a more "sensation-like" way as two rods separated by a space, as the image of this stimulus on one's retina would specify. The infant subjects were first habituated to the sight of the original stimulus display and then saw two test displays: (1) the complete rod and (2) two rods separated by a space—that is, the retinal projection of the occluded rod. If the infants perceived the occluded rod in the original display as a single unitary entity, as adults do, they should look more at the two rods separated by a space than at the complete rod, because the two rods would be perceived as a novel stimulus and the complete rod as a familiar, previously seen one. If, instead, they perceived the occluded rod as two separate objects, they should look more at the complete rod, because that would constitute the novel stimulus for them. Appropriate control groups were also included in the research design. Much to the investigators' surprise, the babies did not look more at either test display. They acted as if they had no expectations one way or the other as to what was behind the block. Another study using a different occluded object yielded the same results and suggested the same interpretation. Thus, even though the two visible parts of the occluded rod were identical in width, color, and texture, and were oriented along the same straight line, the babies apparently did not use these cues to single-object-ness to perceive the rod as one object partly hidden by another.

On the other hand, additional experiments by Kellman and Spelke showed that infants of this age are able to use another visual cue to single-object-ness very effectively—namely, common movement of object parts or, as the Gestalt psychologists called it, "common fate." Kellman and Spelke found that if 4 month olds saw the rod moving back and forth behind the block, they definitely acted as if they perceived it as one continuous object rather than as two discontinuous ones. Even if the two visible parts of the occluded object differed from one another in size, shape, color, texture, and alignment (e.g., a thin rod visible above the block and a broad polygon visible below the block), 4 month olds still appeared to perceive them as being connected behind the block, provided only that both parts moved in unison.

Finally, Prather and Spelke have done a preliminary study of (3)—that is, of infants' abilities to perceive two adjacent, touching objects as two objects rather than one (Spelke, 1982). They capitalized on the fact (see Chapter 3) that young infants can sometimes become habituated to the number of objects in a display, provided that the number is small—for example, "one" or "two." Some of their 3-month-old subjects were initially habituated to a series of two-object displays and others to a series of one-object displays. The subjects were then shown on some trials two adjacent, touching objects and, on other trials, two objects clearly separated in depth, one partly occluding the other. Subjects acted as if they correctly perceived the latter pair of objects as two objects. That is, if initially habituated to two objects they continued to show habituation when presented with this pair ("two objects again—how boring"), but if initially habituated to one object they showed dishabituation to this pair ("ah, something new"). In contrast, they acted as if the pair of adjacent, touching objects had been perceived as a single entity—as an array of "one" rather than of "two." Objects placed flush up against one another seemed to be seen by 3 month olds as one entity, not two.

Spelke (1982) makes some intriguing conjectures about the possible development of object perception in infancy based on this set of studies. She suggests that we may be born with two organizing principles for perceptually carving up visual scenes into objects. One, the *common movement principle*, states that "two surfaces lie on the same object if they undergo a common translation throughout the layout: a movement that carries the surfaces from one place to another without destroying the connection between them" (Spelke, 1982, p. 426). The other, the *connected surface principle*, "states that two surfaces pertain to the same object if they touch each other directly or through other object surfaces" (Spelke, 1982, p. 426). These unlearned principles are subsequently used to help us learn additional ways of estimating where one object ends and another begins. For example, we can use them to help us learn that abrupt changes in color or texture are apt to signal transitions from one object to another. Spelke further argues that these two principles reflect *essential* properties of objects, whereas other principles we use reflect *characteristic* properties of objects—that is, typical properties but not necessary ones. This in turn leads Spelke (1982) to a very provocative hypothesis about the development of our knowledge and perception of objects:

> Knowledge about the characteristic properties of objects may be acquired gradually over infancy and childhood, as children encounter objects and explore them. But knowledge of an object's essential nature may be shared, in part, by the youngest infant. It may first be expressed through the infant's perception of objects in visual scenes (p. 428).

Some very impressive feats of object and event perception by young babies have also been documented recently by other researchers. Suppose I attach a total of ten luminous dots to the hip, arm joints, and leg joints of a person, ask the person to face to the left or right and start running in place, turn off all the lights, bring you in, and ask you what you see. Although all that is visible to you are ten dots darting this way and that, you will say you see a person running. This is called the "perception of biological motion" and adults have been found to be very good at it. Fox and McDaniel (1982) wanted to find out if infants were also capable of this sort of perception. In one of their experiments, a videotape of the just-described, running-in-place biological motion display was presented side by side with a control display that consisted of ten dots moving in independent, randomly determined directions. The subjects were infants of 2, 4, and 6 months of age. Each of the two older groups showed a significant visual preference for the biological-motion display over the control display; the youngest group showed no looking preference.

In a second experiment using new groups of 4 and 6 month olds, the biological-motion display was again the same running-in-place event. This time, however, the control pattern was such as to gladden the heart of the fussiest methodologist: the very same event shown upside down. In the sober and measured prose of scientific journal writing, Fox and McDaniel inform us

that: "For adult observers, such inversion severely impairs veridical perception of the human form" (1982, p. 486). It undoubtedly impaired it for the
infants as well, for once again subjects of both ages significantly preferred to
look at the normal, right-side-up event. Other investigators have obtained
similar results (Gibson & Spelke, 1983).

At the close of their article, Fox and McDaniel (1982) write:

> These data force us to conclude that young infants are sensitive to biological
> motion. This supports the hypothesis that the mechanism responsible for such
> sensitivity is largely intrinsic rather than acquired slowly through experience.
> Yet it is not obvious why the youngest infants did not exhibit this sensitivity.
> Perhaps a postnatal period of growth is required before such a mechanism
> becomes functional (p. 487).

Notice that the authors do not favor any sort of learning interpretation here.
They probably find it implausible that infants could have accrued the necessary perceptual experiences (frequently seeing people running in place?)
or acquired the necessary perceptual learning abilities by 4 months
of age. I find a learning account implausible too, but some psychologists
might disagree.

If videotapes of two natural events are superimposed on the same
screen, adults and elementary school children can easily follow visually one
event while ignoring the other. Bahrick, Walker, and Neisser (1981) hit upon a
very clever method of finding out whether 4 month olds could do the same.
Their method is too space-consuming to describe here. However, the two
events they superimposed on a screen were: (1) a rhythmic hand-clapping
sequence which showed the hands and forearms of two adults, clapping together and onto an empty box; (2) a pair of gloved hands manipulating a
"slinky" toy (tightly wound plastic spiral). You guessed it: The infants could
and did attend visually to one event while ignoring the other. That is object
and event perception of a high order.

PLACES. According to Gibson and Spelke (1983):

> Places are segregated parts of the layout of the world at which surfaces meet one
> another, often forming an enclosure. Places may have vistas and paths that can
> be seen or walked through, walls that constitute obstacles and conceal things, a
> ground that can be walked on, and dropoffs that must be avoided (p. 2).

For Gibson and Spelke (1983) "perception of places" includes perception,
representation, or knowledge of all aspects of the spatial environment.
Among its many constituent topics are infants' and children's perception of
obstacles, openings, supporting surfaces and dropoffs, all undergirded by
their ability to perceive depth and distances and their perception; and knowledge of spatial layouts and spatial frames of reference, including their ability
to find their way around, to search for and locate hidden objects, and other
spatial abilities. In this section I discuss only two of these topics: (1) the perception of looming objects (a type of obstacle); (2) the perception of a solid
surface of support as contrasted with a dropoff.

It is possible to present the critical optimal information that specifies a rapidly looming object about to hit you by using a shadow caster and a screen. If the shadow is made to expand on the screen continuously, symmetrically, and at a certain rate of acceleration, you will perceive it as a "loom." If the very same visual event is run off in the reverse order, you will perceive the resulting optical contraction pattern as a rapidly receding object, or a "zoom." Since the optical change is identical in the two patterns, except for direction, the "zoom" pattern provides a very good experimental control for the "loom" one.

Schiff (1965; see also Yonas, 1981; and Gibson & Spelke, 1983) presented these two patterns to animals of several species (e.g., kittens, chicks, and fiddler crabs). In most of the species tested, the animals tended to back away from the loom pattern but not from the zoom pattern. Additional experiments with chicks showed that their tendency to retreat from an optical flow pattern specifying impending collision was clearly innate rather than acquired through experience with looming objects.

Since, unlike chicks, young human infants are not very mobile, it has been difficult to find out how early they perceive an optical loom pattern as if it were something about to hit them, and also whether or to what extent experience plays a role in the acquisition of this ability. The matter has been the subject of a running controversy between two distinguished infant researchers, T. G. R. Bower (Bower, 1974, 1977) and Albert Yonas (Yonas, 1981); see also Gibson and Spelke (1983). It may be useful to give some of the flavor of this controversy, because it illustrates how tricky a scientific enterprise the pursuit of the infant psyche can be.

The typical sequence of events in this controversy (see Yonas, 1981) has been for Bower and colleagues to obtain what looks like strong evidence for this ability in very young infants (under 1 month of age, say), and then for Yonas and colleagues either to fail to observe the same phenomena Bower observed or to find plausible alternative explanations for them. For instance, Bower found that very young infants would often move their head backwards as the shadow pattern expanded, as if to defend themselves against a perceived impending collision. Yonas then showed that the infants might instead only be following with their eyes the upward moving top contour of the expanding shadow; as they look upward, their heads automatically retract. Next, to show that Yonas's rising-contour interpretation was incorrect, Bower provided research evidence that young babies still retract their heads in response to a loom pattern that does not present a rising top contour. Then Yonas, in his turn, was unable to replicate this finding of Bower's.

However, in this and other studies Yonas (1981) did find that infants would often blink their eyes in response to a loom, even though they might not consistently retract their heads or show other defensive-looking behavior. Yonas makes a plausible case for the idea that this minimal, "lightweight" response can be used as a fairly reliable index of the infant's perceptual sensitivity to collision information (1981). He also obtained three findings of interest using this response. The first is that 3 month olds quite consistently blink to a normal (accelerating) loom pattern but not to a zoom pattern. More important, they also do not blink to a steady, nonaccelerating expansion pattern. Recall that this latter pattern gives the perceptual impression of an object that is slowing down as it gets closer to you, not one about to hit you in the face.

This finding suggests that 3 month olds do perceive the optical loom pattern—that very specific pattern and not others—as indicating that something is about to hit them. The second finding is that 1 month olds likewise tend to blink more to a normal loom than to a zoom, but they also tend to blink more to the nonaccelerating, "slow-down" expansion pattern as well. Yonas thinks that collision and approach may not yet be perceptually distinguished at this early age. The third finding is that 6 week olds born 3 to 4 weeks late (after normal term) blink more frequently in response to a loom than biologically younger, normal-term 6 week olds, even though both groups have had the same number of weeks of looking experience. This result suggests that maturational factors probably play a role in the functioning of this perceptual capability as they do in the case of others. Yonas (1981) thinks that perceptual learning might also play some developmental role here, perhaps serving to differentiate and tune the response more exclusively to a loom pattern (see the second finding just discussed).

Not every expanding contour (appropriately symmetrical, accelerating, etc.) specifies an approaching obstacle; some specify approaching openings or apertures. Walking towards a closed door illustrates the first type of perceived optical expansion pattern; walking towards an open doorway illustrates the second. Carroll and Gibson (1981) showed that 3 month olds can distinguish these two patterns perceptually. If a solid panel approaches them on a hit path, they respond appropriately—that is, as if something were about to contact their face. This, of course, confirms the findings of Bower, Yonas, and others that infants of this age can read loom patterns correctly. If an opening in a larger panel, identical in size and shape to the solid panel, approaches them, they again respond appropriately—that is, they show no defensive or avoidant behaviors. Well before they can move about on their own, infants can discriminate perceptually between obstacles that obstruct straight-ahead locomotion and open paths that allow it.

We have just seen that human beings and other animals possess special visual-perceptual capabilities that serve the adaptational function of helping them avoid collisions with objects. Similarly, we can also use our eyes to keep only to solid-looking surfaces and avoid going over cliffs or other dangerous dropoffs (Gibson & Spelke, 1983). We are capable of making four closely related responses when we encounter deep dropoffs. First, our depth-perception mechanisms enable us to see them instantly *as* deep dropoffs—as edges with slopes receding sharply downward to bottoms that are a considerable distance away. Second, we avoid stepping off those edges. Third, we experience fear if we do go off them, or even perhaps if we get too close to them. Fourth, we understand that they are dangerous and can evaluate intellectually the probable consequences of falling into the abyss. As in the case of looming, it is natural to wonder when and how humans and other animals come by such response capabilities.

Eleanor Gibson and Richard Walk invented a device called a "visual cliff" to explore this developmental problem (Gibson & Walk, 1960; Walk & Gibson, 1961). On one side of the device, a horizontal plate of glass rests just above a patterned surface. On the other, deep or "cliff" side, the patterned surface lies a considerable distance beneath the covering glass. Gibson and Walk and other investigators have found that newborn animals of some species (goats, rhesus monkeys, chickens) would readily descend from a center board onto the shallow side but would not venture onto the deep side. For these species, clearly, perceptual detection of a dropoff and avoidance of it is innate. Detection and avoidance do not require either experience with dropoffs or a period of postnatal maturation to be fully functional. On the other hand, the young of some other species (cats, rabbits) do not avoid the deep side initially; they only do so after a few weeks of visual experience (Campos, Hiatt, Ramsay, Henderson & Svejda, 1978; Walk, 1966). For these animals, perception and avoidance of dropoffs might be the product of postnatal biological maturation, experience, or some combination of the two.

Young human infants cannot be tested in the usual manner on the visual cliff because, unlike the very young of many other species, they are too immature motorically to be able to locomote. Once they are mature enough to crawl, the method usually used is something like the following (Rader, Bausano, & Richards, 1980): The baby is placed on the center platform facing its mother across the deep or the shallow side. The mother calls the baby to cross. (It seems vaguely immoral . . .) If the baby does not cross within 2 minutes, the mother shows the baby a familiar toy and continues to coax for another 2 minutes. The same procedure is then repeated for the other side. Human infants also show some tendency to avoid the deep side under these testing conditions. Whether this avoidance tendency is mediated by maturational processes, learning processes, or both is currently a matter of controversy between infant researchers Nancy Rader and Joseph Campos. Rader emphasizes the importance of maturational processes (Rader & Ashley, 1983; Rader et al. 1980; Richards & Rader, 1981, 1983) and Gibson and Spelke (1983) find her arguments and evidence persuasive. In contrast, Campos emphasizes the importance of learning processes, especially experiences associated with crawling or other forms of self-locomotion (e.g., Campos et al., 1978; Campos, Svejda, Bertenthal, Benson, & Schmid, 1981; Caplovitz & Campos, 1983). Let us examine and try to evaluate the relevant evidence.

Infants usually begin to crawl somewhere around 7 months, give or take a few months. (There is a great deal of individual variation here—a point that is seen to be important in what follows.) Before they reach this age, however, most babies probably have become capable of perceiving the bottom of the deep side of the visual cliff as "far," although they may not be able to perceive how deep it is (or depths in general) as accurately as older infants. The developmental literature on the ages at which infants first become responsive to various types of depth cues (Banks & Salapatek, 1983) makes this assumption seem reasonable. There is also more direct evidence on the matter. Campos and his research colleagues have found that prelocomotor infants show greater heart-rate deceleration when placed on the deep side of the visual cliff than when placed on the shallow side, suggesting that they can perceptually discriminate between the two (Campos et al., 1978). More convincing yet, when slowly lowered towards the glass on the shallow side, prelocomotor babies put their hands out just prior to touchdown; they do not make this placing response just prior to reaching the glass on the deep side, strongly suggesting that they perceive that they still have some distance yet to go (Svejda & Schmid, 1979).

Assuming, then, that infants can perceive dropoffs as dropoffs prior to any instructive experiences crawling towards and perhaps falling off them, the question arises as to whether infants of this age show any fear of them. If the tendency to avoid dangerous dropoffs were innate or early maturing in humans, we might expect infants to show such fear. They do not show it, however. If placed over or on the deep side their faces appear calm, they do not cry, and—as just mentioned—they show heart-rate *de*celeration, signifying attentiveness rather than fear (Gibson & Spelke, 1983). In contrast, older, crawling infants have been found to show heart-rate *ac*celeration in this situation, indicating fear (Campos et al., 1978; Svejda & Schmid, 1979; Richards & Rader, 1983).

Another fact worth noting is that not all older, self-locomoting babies avoid the deep side of the visual cliff (Gibson & Spelke, 1983). Not all of them avoid real cliffs, either (Campos et al., 1978): Parents often report that their babies will happily take off from the tops of staircases, beds, and other high places and, one presumes, not so happily land. Rader and Ashley (1983) outfitted twelve 7- to 10-month-old crawlers with safety harnesses and put them on the edge of the deep side of a visual cliff. The glass had been removed, making it a *real* cliff. No fewer than five of the twelve succumbed to the mother's siren call or the lure of the beloved toy and set sail into the void. We would not expect such things to happen if, like goats, people were either born with, or early acquired through some purely endogenous maturational process, a powerful, unlearned inhibition against venturing over the edges of abysses.

From what has been said so far you would be entitled to conclude that, in our species in contrast to some others, avoidance and fear of deep dropoffs must be wholly learned—entirely a matter of nurture rather than nature. Things may not be quite that simple, however. Some of those babies who so fearlessly sally forth over glassed visual cliffs, glassless visual cliffs, and the real article at home have had weeks or months of self-locomotion experience. If experience were the whole story, one might expect that all infants would quickly learn to avoid going over dropoffs once they had learned to crawl and suffered a few painful falls. Yet this is not what seems to happen, at least for a number of babies. At the very least, there ought to be a strong positive correlation within any group of infants between the amount of crawling experience they have accumulated (time between onset of crawling and testing on the visual cliff) and their tendency to avoid the deep side. Campos and his associates do find such a positive association between crawling experience and avoidance (Caplovitz & Campos, 1983) but Rader and her associates do not (Rader et al., 1980; Richards & Rader, 1981). The reason for this discrepancy in results is not readily apparent, but it at least suggests to me that the association between crawling experience and avoidance may not be as strong or dependable as a straightforward learning explanation would predict.

Another finding that might be regarded as problematic for a purely learning account has also been reported by Rader et al. (1980). One would think that babies who avoid crawling onto the deep side do so because they have learned that locomoting over the edge of deep dropoffs is associated with pain and fear experiences. However, if these same babies are locomoting in a "walker" (a locomotor aid that the babies are used to and skilled at using) rather than crawling when tested on the visual cliff, almost all of them unhesitatingly propel themselves right onto the deep side. This suggests that avoidance tendencies at this age may not be mediated by conditioned fear or by conceptual appreciation of danger, and also that they may be tied specifically to biologically natural means of locomotion—namely, crawling.

However, the strongest evidence that some sort of maturational process might be at work here comes from another curious finding by Rader (Rader et al., 1980; Richards & Rader, 1981). She discovered that the best statistical predictor of visual-cliff avoidance is age of onset of crawling. However, the direction of the relationship is exactly opposite to what a learning interpretation would lead us to expect: Rader found that babies who learned to crawl *late* tended to *avoid* the deep side and that babies who learned to crawl *early* tended *not* to avoid it. How on earth could that be?

Rader proposed the following explanation: Avoidance of dropoffs in human infants is assumed to be partly mediated by an internal "visual-motor program" that is probably specific to crawling. This program supposedly directs infants to shift their weight forward onto their hands only when visual information specifying a solid surface is present. It inhibits the forward weight shift if a dropoff is detected. Rader further assumes that this program is the product of maturation rather than learning, and that it becomes functional at about 6 or 7 months of age on average; like crawling itself and other maturationally governed developments, the exact age would be expected to vary from child to child. If an infant happened to develop the ability to crawl relatively late, after this program had already become functional, the program would tend to prevent her from shifting her weight forward onto the glass covering the deep side of the visual cliff. In other words, if crawling matures after the visual-motor program matures, the program can and will partly control crawling. Consistent with this proposed maturational rather than learning account, Rader et al. (1980) found some late crawlers who avoided the cliff even though they had only had a few days of experience crawling when tested. The program would not necessarily be expected to control other forms of locomotion, such as locomotion via the walker device mentioned earlier. If crawling happens to mature before the visual-motor program does, the infant may come to rely on touch more than vision to guide her crawling: If she feels a solid surface with her hands, she will shift her weight forward and crawl on it; if she feels empty space, she will not shift her weight forward. Since the glass over the deep side feels solid to the touch, the early-crawling infant will tend to crawl onto it. However, the five infants who crawled off the edge of the real cliff in the Rader and Ashley (1983) study were earlier crawlers than the seven who did not, a finding that Rader and Ashley accept as going counter to this hypothesis about the more tactually dominated behavior of early crawlers. If evidence from subsequent studies with larger subject samples also goes counter to this half of Rader's theory, it is not clear to me how viable the other half would be.

Rader's theory is an attempt only to provide a maturational explanation of why (later-crawling) infants tend not to crawl over the edge of a visually perceived abyss. She intends it to be a theory only of the early development of *behavioral avoidance* of depths, not of the later development of either *emotional fear* of depths or *conceptual understanding* of the dangers they present. She joins Campos in thinking that experience may play important roles in these later developments, and even that these later developments may in turn help mediate behavioral avoidance:

> While experience does not determine avoidance behavior at this stage, we would like to stress that it may contribute to the development of the ability to evaluate the consequences of a drop-off and to fear of a drop-off. Such evaluation or fear may be an important part of the response to a cliff at a later stage in development subsequent to crawling. That is, experience locomoting may be necessary for the development of an understanding or a fearfulness of drop-offs, and such understanding or fear may play an important role in mediating avoidance behavior after the first year of life (Rader et al., 1980, p. 67).

The development in humans of the abilities to (1) perceive; (2) avoid; (3) fear; and (4) comprehend the potential dangers of deep dropoffs is clearly a very complicated affair, probably entailing multiple interactions between maturational and experiential-learning processes.

1. The development of depth perception is itself a complex, heterogeneous, and temporally extended process (Banks & Salapatek, 1983) in which both maturation and experience play important roles. For example, maturation is undoubtedly crucial in producing the basic capacity to see that X is "far down," but experience will obviously be needed to produce the capacity to see that X is or is not "too far down for me to drop into without getting hurt."

2. If Rader is right, avoidance of depths is also mediated by biological-maturational as well as by experiential processes. Given the importance of innate, biological determinants of depth avoidance in other animals, it would not be surprising to find similar determinants in our species. However, the fact that so many babies go off so many cliffs suggests that such biological determinants are less early appearing, less powerful and constraining, and less universal (Rader's deprived early crawlers?) in humans than in some other species; they appear to be more like biases and tendencies than like absolute prohibitions or imperatives.

3. Normal fear of deep dropoffs is clearly absent in young babies and undoubtedly develops with the aid of experience (Campos et al., 1978). At the same time, there is currently reason to believe that the very capacity to experience fear may not be present before the third quarter year of life (see Campos et al., 1978, pp. 172–173), and its development may well also have strong maturational components.

4. The acquisition of conceptual understanding (e.g., the ability to evaluate the consequences of falling) probably both mediates normal fear and is mediated by it; moreover, it too may be subject to maturational constraints as well as experiential influences. Finally, as already mentioned, fearfulness and understanding of potential hazards in the face of dangerous dropoffs are virtually certain to reinforce any avoidance tendencies instigated by visual-motor programs or their like. What appears to be a very simple and straightforward developmental phenomenon in some animals turns out to be surprisingly intricate and multifaceted in humans. And, in all likelihood, we do not have the developmental story straight yet.

Relating Information from Different Senses

As mentioned in Chapter 5 (pp. 133–135), objects and events commonly offer information to more than one of our sense modalities. For instance, they not only look a certain way when we glance at them, but they also sound and feel certain ways when we listen to and touch them. Furthermore, we experience these looks, sounds, and feels as related to one another. The most important of these experienced relationships is that of equivalence or common source: We experience that look, that sound, and that feel in a unitary fashion as all originating from one and the same object or event. We experience a single, unitary object or event multimodally; we detect cross-modal or intersensory equivalences and other relationships; in short, we are capable of what is sometimes called *intermodal perception* (e.g., Spelke, in press).

Some perceptual features are modality specific. For example, an object can look red but it cannot feel red. Other features can be specified in more than one sense modality. They are supramodal or amodal, and hence could be considered higher order or more abstract. As two examples, a sight and a sound can be perceived as both occurring simultaneously in time and in the same location in space. Similarly, an object can both look and feel bumpy. Amodal or supramodal features include intensity, rate, duration, spatial location, spatial extent, rhythm, and shape (Lewkowicz & Turkewitz, 1980). Obviously, the ability to detect perceptually such abstract, amodal features is very important in intermodal perception. For instance, if we can detect that a sight and a sound are occurring at the same time and place (amodal features of duration and spatial location) we can perceive them as part of a unitary event—for example, with the sight's possibly causing the sound.

Philosophers and psychologists have presented a variety of views over the centuries concerning the development of intermodal perception abilities (Bower, 1974; Meltzoff, 1981; Spelke, in press). They have seldom disagreed about whether learning and experience play a role in this development. They clearly must play a role. For example, it is obvious that only through experience could a child attain the ability to apprehend, from the sound alone, that the object he dimly sees off there in the fog is an ambulance rather than some other kind of vehicle (Spelke, in press). Likewise, only through experience could he perceive a "singing bird" rather than merely hear a sound and see a small, far-away object simultaneously. Theorists have disagreed, however, on whether, or to what extent, or how, the senses might be related innately—prior to experience—versus being largely or wholly dependent upon experience for their coordination. (If this issue does not have a familiar ring to you, you have been dozing your way through this chapter.) Many theorists, including Piaget, have believed that the major perceptual modalities (visual, auditory, tactile) are entirely uncoordinated at birth and that the young infant consequently has no intermodal perception ability. Piaget believed that only gradually, in the course of months of sensory-motor action and experience, does the infant come to relate information from these different sense modalities. Other theorists, including Gibsonians, believe that we are born with some intermodal perception abilities and/or with aptitudes and predispositions that greatly facilitate the early acquisition of such abilities through experience (Bower, 1974; Gibson & Spelke, 1983; Meltzoff & Moore, 1983a, 1983b; Spelke, in press). Meltzoff and Moore (1983a) state their own (strong) version of this general point of view thusly:

> The critical theoretical point is that we do not follow the view that young infants have perceptual-cognitive constraints that restrict them to utilizing intramodal comparisons. Instead, we postulate that infants can recognize and use inter-modal equivalences from birth onward. In our view, the proclivity to represent actions intermodally is the starting point of infant psychological development, not an end point reached after many months of postnatal development (p. 708).

Let us now examine briefly some of the recent research on infant intermodal perception, keeping in mind this familiar issue of "innate early" versus "learned late." The existing research deals mainly with infants' abilities to relate (1) sights and sounds; (2) sights and feels; and (3) sights and body movements that imitate what is seen. I take them up in that order.

Like adults, infants tend to look for and look at an object that they hear, even if the visual and auditory information about the object do not come from the same location in space (Spelke, in press). This tendency provides the researcher with an experimental window on infants' intermodal perception abilities with respect to sights and sounds (Chapter 5, pp. 133–135). Two visible events can be presented successively or simultaneously and a sound specific to one of them can be played from a neutral (e.g., central) location. If the infants do in fact perceive the sound as related to its sound-specified event, they should look longer or more often at that event than at the other one. How can a sound be "specific to" a sight? One way would be for the two to share some higher-order, amodal property, perhaps a temporal one such as synchrony of occurrence.

Spelke and other investigators have recently tested the abilities of infants (mostly 3 or 4 months of age) to relate sights and sounds on the basis of amodal temporal properties (Gibson & Spelke, 1983; Spelke, in press). In one series of experiments (Spelke, 1979), 4 month olds were presented with films of two toy stuffed animals, a kangaroo and a donkey side by side. Each animal was lifted into the air by puppet strings and dropped to the ground repeatedly, at a steady tempo. Each impact was accompanied by a thump or a gong sound, a different sound for each animal. On any given trial, the child saw both of the moving animals but heard the sound of only one of them coming from a source midway between them (recall the experiments using this method reported in Chapter 5, pp. (133–135). In one experiment, the impacts of one animal were always exactly synchronous and simultaneous with its sounds; for the other animal, its impacts and sounds were temporally unrelated. Spelke found that the infants tended to look for and look at the sound-synchronized object. In another experiment, infants did the same when the impacts and the sounds of one object were related only by common tempo—that is, one following the other after a regular brief interval rather than the two occurring simultaneously. The third experiment showed that simultaneity of object impacts and sounds led infants to associate those sounds with that object, even though the other object's impacts, though not simultaneous with the sounds, also shared a common tempo with them.

These and other experiments clearly show that by 4 months of age babies are sensitive to the simultaneity of impacts seen and sounds heard and seem to link the two together perceptually (Spelke, in press). This perceptual linkage could be largely or wholly the product of associative learning, one might think. As Spelke (in press) points out, the impact of two surfaces is the most common source of any inanimate sound, and we can often see the impact while simultaneously hearing the sound it makes. Perhaps babies of 4 months of age could have learned some primitive version of that fact in the course of 4 months of experience looking at and listening to objects hitting other objects. Perhaps. But some other experimental findings obtained by Spelke and her students (Spelke, in press; Spelke, Born, & Chu, in press) make me wonder if any such learning might not be guided by some inborn intermodal perception biases—some of those "aptitudes and predispositions" mentioned earlier.

Spelke et al. (in press) found that 4 month olds would tend to perceptually relate a sound and an object whenever the sound occurred simultaneously with an abrupt change in the object's movement; moreover, they did so equally strongly whether that abrupt change was or was not an impact. For example, if a puppet animal were raised up by its strings and the sound occurred at the moment that the animal reached its highest point and stopped abruptly (in midair, of course, without touching anything), the babies would relate the sound to that object. They would also do the same if the sound occurred simultaneously with an abrupt change in the object's movement from one direction to another—again, in midair, without contacting any surface. Adults shown these various displays were much less likely to connect the sound to the seen object in the latter two, nonimpact cases than in the case in which the abrupt change of movement resulted from an impact. Perhaps infants are born with the tendency to relate sounds to simultaneously occurring changes in object movement or at least to notice or show an attentional preference for this general class of sight-sound synchronisms. This tendency could, of course, facilitate learning to relate impact sounds to impacting objects because impacts constitute a subclass of this general class of sight-sound synchronisms. The same tendency could help infants notice sight-sound synchronisms between people's speech and the facial movements that accompany speech (cf. Spelke, in press). Recall from Chapter 5 (p. 134) that infants of 4 months of age are in fact sensitive to whether a speaker's facial movements are or are not "in synch" with her speech. As Spelke (in press) notes, however, the case for inborn tendencies to unite perceptually auditory and visual events that are temporally synchronous would be stronger if these tendencies could be shown to exist in infants younger than 3 or 4 months of age—especially in newborns or near-newborns. To my knowledge, the relevant studies on younger infants have not yet been carried out. Although Lewkowicz and Turkewitz (1980) have apparently found a type of auditory-visual intermodal perception in 3 week olds, it is not the type we are concerned with here.

There are two other studies of sight-sound relationships that I cannot resist citing, because their results are so striking and counterintuitive. Kuhl and Meltzoff (1982) found that, in effect, 4½- to 5-month-old babies recognized that a certain, more open mouth movement went with the articulation of the sound /a/ (as in *pop*) rather than the sound /i/ (as in *peep*), and that another, less open mouth movement went with the pronunciation of /i/ rather than

/a/. These results suggest that youngish, clearly prelinguistic babies can actualy *lip-read* some speech sounds, as well as "merely" detect global asynchronisms between speech sounds and speech movements. Wagner, Winner, Cicchetti, and Gardner (1981) report that 11 month olds are sensitive to auditory-visual similarities that are "metaphorical" rather than literal-physical in nature. For example, if first exposed to an ascending tone and then shown two arrows, one pointing upward and the other downward, their infant subjects tended to show a visual preference for the "metaphorically similar" upward arrow. One would like to see such surprising results confirmed by other investigations.

Some startling results have also been reported in the other two areas of intermodal perception mentioned: (2) sights and feels; and (3) sights and imitative bodily movements. In the case of (2), Meltzoff and Borton (1979) found in two experiments that 1 month olds are apparently able to recognize which of two visually perceived shapes matches a shape they previously had explored tactually, in their mouths, but had not previously seen. The experimenter first put special pacifiers in the infants' mouths for 90 seconds: round, smooth ones for half of the infants; round ones with eight hard rubber nubs on them for the other half. The infants then saw two styrofoam spheres (larger than the pacifiers) for 20 seconds, one visually resembling the smooth pacifier and the other resembling the nubbed pacifier. The investigators found that the infants tended to look more at whichever sphere resembled the pacifier they had previously felt in their mouths. Think of what these near-neonates would have had to do to detect a visual-tactile match here:

> (1) tactually discriminate between the shapes presented, (2) visually discriminate between them, (3) store some representation of the tactually perceived shape, and (4) relate a subsequent visual perception to the stored representation of the tactually perceived shape (Meltzoff & Borton, 1979, p. 404).

Gibson and Spelke (1983) report that an unpublished study by Baker, Brown, and Gottfried (1982) failed to replicate these results, but also that a somewhat different experiment by Gibson and Walker (1982)—likewise unpublished— yielded findings consistent with Meltzoff and Borton's. Gunderson (1983) also replicated Meltzoff and Borton's findings using 0- to 1-month-old pigtail macaque monkeys as subjects. Thus, it may be too soon to accept Meltzoff and Borton's dramatic results as gospel truth. If they do prove out, however, they will certainly constitute very strong evidence for an initial, innately given capacity and predisposition for visual-tactual intermodal perception.

In Chapter 2 (p. 25) there is a brief discussion of the ability to imitate actions that one cannot see oneself perform. To illustrate this sort of imitation, suppose that you make a strange face, one that I have never made before, and ask me to make one exactly like it. I can probably manage to produce a passable imitation of that face, despite its novelty for me and—especially important here—despite the fact that I cannot watch myself making it or visually compare my facial appearance to yours when I have finished. It is unclear how I manage this feat. Presumably, I must somehow coordinate and unite within a single, amodal representation the visual information my eyes provide and the proprioceptive (muscle-sensation) information my own facial motor movements provide (Meltzoff & Moore, 1983a, 1983b). In other words, I may have to engage in a form of intermodal perception to do this kind of imitation—namely, that of type (3) mentioned earlier.

Meltzoff and Moore (1977, 1983a, 1983b) have obtained evidence in several studies which suggests that *newborns*, no less, are capable of this sophisticated-looking kind of imitation, and therefore, presumably, of that type of intermodal perception. As might be imagined, the field's responses to these incredible seeming results have included skepticism and experimental attempts to verify them. At this writing, some efforts at verification have been successful and some have not (see references cited in Meltzoff & Moore, 1983a, 1983b). Part of the problem is that it can be difficult to distinguish experimentally between genuine imitation and behavioral reactions that look like it but are not—"imitation imitations," so to speak. My hunch from examining the evidence and arguments pro and con is that Meltzoff and Moore have a better than even chance of being right in their scientific claims. However, as with the Meltzoff and Borton (1979) findings, there is no way at present anyone can be absolutely sure one way or the other. As with the Meltzoff and Borton findings also, valid positive results here would constitute important additional evidence for inborn capacities for intermodal perception. They would also surely mean that the widely accepted Piagetian account of the growth of imitation skills with age during infancy would need considerable revising: Piagetian Stage 1 infants should not be able to engage in Stage 4 imitation (Chapter 2).

You may wonder how anyone could test for this ability in neonates. In their most recently published experiment (1983a), Meltzoff and Moore used the following method: The testing was done in a darkened room. The experimenter's face was illuminated by a spotlight to make it perceptually salient to the baby. The baby was seated semiupright in an infant's seat with its face positioned 25 centimeters (about 10 inches) from the experimenter's. The experimenter would slowly open and close his mouth four times during a 20-second period, then adopt a passive face for 20 seconds, then slowly stick out and withdraw his tongue four times during a 20-second period, then adopt the passive face again for 20 seconds, and so on, for a total of twelve such alternating periods of mouth opening, passive face, and tongue protrusion; pilot work had shown that interspersing a passive face with the facial gestures helped maintain attention and responsivity. The baby's face was videotaped close up with an infrared-sensitive video camera during all these goings-on. The videotapes were later scored for mouth openings and tongue protrusions by an observer who was uninformed about which gesture had been shown to the infant in any given period. Meltzoff and Moore (1983a) found that the neonates opened their mouths significantly more often in response to the experimenter's mouth openings than to his tongue protrusions, and also stuck out their tongues significantly more often in response to his tongue protrusions than to his mouth openings. Quite reasonably, the authors took these findings as evidence that the newborns had selectively imitated each of the two different facial movements.

Postscript on Infant Perception

If Chapters 2 and 5 did not convince you that young infants have better information-processing capabilities than used to be thought, this chapter must surely have done so—quite possibly to the point of tedium. Yet, the message is worth reiterating because it has such far-reaching implications. A clearer picture of what the young baby is like provides a better understanding of what humankind is like—and *that* is surely of interest to everyone, including those who neither know nor care about babies and developmental psychology. Such a picture helps us understand what we begin with in the way of initial processing equipment, what we need to acquire, and how what we begin with might be used to help us acquire it. Thoughtful people have wanted to know such things about human beings from time immemorial.

But, of course, the picture is still not really very clear. Experts continue to disagree vigorously about what is inborn, what matures, what is learned, as well as when the maturing and learning get accomplished. There is currently an almost palpable tension in the field of infant perception and cognition between those who look for and often see much initial competence and those—every bit as experienced and astute as baby watchers—who do not. One feels it when one reads the literature or attends professional meetings. Moreover, what the two camps agree about is often not all that reassuring. As one prominent example, all the experts agree that there are still gaping holes in our factual knowledge of how most perceptual competencies develop, step by step, over long stretches of infancy and perhaps beyond. For instance, we may know something of what the 2 month old and the 10 month old can do in a given area, but not know anything about what the developmental chain of intervening competencies in that area looks like. This is true for competencies at both the sensation and the perception end of the continuum.

No matter: Infant perception is one of the headiest, most exhilarating areas in all of developmental psychology today, and it will surely continue to be for some time to come. It is clearly an area in which genuine novelties of great significance can be discovered, if one is only sufficiently clever and inventive. It is an area that can generate high excitement in people who do not work in it—as witness my own obvious enthusiasm.

CHILDHOOD AND ADOLESCENCE

According to Bower (1974): "During infancy . . . perceptual development is virtually completed" (p. vii). Although that statement is a bit extreme, it does seem to be the case that at least most of the basic perceptual competencies are well in place by the end of infancy. As the child continues to grow past infancy, it becomes harder and harder to think of her cognitive advances as pure instances of "perceptual development," much less of "sensory development." A good deal of what passes for "perceptual development" after infancy might more aptly be described as "perceptual-attentional development"; certainly not all, but a good deal. Attention could be described roughly as the focusing of cognitive activities (thought, memory, or—in the present case—perception) on some content, often in pursuit of some goal:

"Attending" refers to perceiving in relation to a task or goal, internally or exter- nally motivated. To be described as attending, a person must be set to do something, be motivated to perform a task or to achieve some end. . . . At its epitome, attending is the perceptual pickup of information that has optimal utility for the task at hand, resulting in perception that is efficient and economi- cal for performance (Gibson & Rader, 1979, pp. 2–3).

There is a large research literature on perceptual-attentional changes during the postinfancy years. Useful reviews of it can be found in Gibson (1969), Gibson and Spelke (1983), Goodnow (1971), Hagen and Hale (1973), Hale and Lewis (1979), Lane and Pearson (1982), Maccoby (1969), Pick et al. (1975), Pick and Pick (1970), and Rosinski (1977). I do not attempt to survey this work, nor discuss the various theoretical issues and questions that have stimulated much of it (e.g., see Lane & Pearson, 1982). Instead, I try to paint a general, overall picture of how development seems to proceed in this area. This picture has elements of best guess as well as established fact in it, but I think it accords reasonably well with what most researchers in this area believe. There is a good mnemonic for remembering the highlights of child- hood perceptual-attentional development, which is somewhat reminiscent of the one proposed for cognitive motivation in Chapter 2. Imagine what prop- erties a good, adaptive attentional system ought to have, and then assume that the child's system increasingly tends to resemble this ideal as a function of attentional experience and general cognitive growth.

Environmental Influences

Pick et al. (1975) suggest that a rough distinction can be made between environmental contributions to attentional selectivity and those provided by the subject herself. Much of the existing developmental literature deals with environmental contributions, often considered in conjunction with the child's attentional dispositions. For instance, we may be able to guide and control a young child's attention by careful instruction, by perceptually highlighting the stimuli to be attended to, and so on. What she cannot do on her own, the child may be able to do if we structure her perceptual environment for her in such ways. In addition, she is likely to walk into our task situation with her own, preexisting attentional biases and preferences. Some stimulus dimensions (e.g., color, shape, size) are likely to be more noticeable or perceptually salient for her than others; indeed, there may be whole hierarchies of dimen- sional salience (e.g., Odom, 1982; Odom & Guzman, 1972).

In addition, a younger child is likelier than an older one to find the holistic similarity between objects (how similar they are overall, considered globally) more perceptually salient than their identity on some single dimension, such as length (e.g., Smith, 1981). These preexisting attentional dispositions, like the instructions, highlighting, and so on, may be important in influencing what the child processes, learns, and remembers in a task situation. For instance, he is likely to learn more easily that a certain dimension is the "correct" one in a discrimination or concept-learning task, to sort on the basis of it in a classification task, and so on, if that dimension has high perceptual salience for him. Perceptual salience is undoubtedly a factor to be reckoned with at any age, but it seems to be particularly important in affecting the young child's attentional deployment. What stimulus features or dimensions are most salient may also change with age, as well as differ from subject to subject and from task setting to task setting at any given age.

Perhaps more interesting than the foregoing, however, are developmental changes in other attentional abilities and dispositions within the subject. These are the changes for which the previously mentioned mnemonic is most useful.

Control

As children develop, they generally become more capable of deliberately directing and controlling the deployment of their own attention. They become better able to focus their attention in an active, controlled fashion on just those external data which are relevant to their task objectives, while disregarding task-irrelevant data that are also present and equally perceptible. The process of disregarding irrelevant data may vary from a relatively effortless ignoring of nonsalient features to an active and effortful shutting out of unwanted input, as when a person consciously forces himself not to attend to clamorous, distracting, attention-compelling stimuli. One thing that seems to develop, then, is the capacity for controlled selective attention to wanted information coupled with controlled selected inattention to unwanted information. A good attentional system will look where it wants to, discriminate and identify only the wanted portion of what it sees, and give full, cognitive attention (in perception, thought, or memory) only to the wanted portion of what it discriminates and identifies. There is much that we still do not know about how, where, and when these selection or filtering processes operate, and also just what does and what does not develop in these respects (Lane & Pearson, 1982). But almost certainly an overall developmental trend exists towards greater voluntary control over one's perceptual-attentional processes (Hagen & Wilson, 1982).

Adaptability

This increase in attentional control serves as a means to the end of attentional adaptability. An attentional system is adaptive if it can flexibly, efficiently, and economically adjust itself to what the situation requires (Gibson, 1969; Gibson & Rader, 1979; Hagen & Hale, 1973). As the individual matures, he uses his control capability to shape and accommodate his attentional behavior to the idiosyncracies of the task or problem before him. In one study (Hale & Taweel, 1974), for instance, 8 year olds were shown to be more apt than 5 year olds to attend to two features of a stimulus when that was the adaptive (efficient, economical) thing to do and to attend to only one feature when that was the better strategy. The older children spontaneously broadened or narrowed their attentional tuning, depending on what the task seemed to call for. Similarly, sixth graders have been found to be better than second graders at rapidly adapting their attentional strategy to trial-to-trial changes in task demands (Pick & Frankel, 1974). As the authors indicate: "This finding is in accord with the hypothesis of a developmental trend toward greater flexibility and adaptability of strategies of selection or of attention" (p. 1164).

My own mental image of a cognitively mature information processor is that of a conductor who directs her ensemble of musicians (attentional processes and resources)—now calling forth one instrument, now another, now a blended combination of several or all, depending upon the effect desired. I think we do not so much "pay attention" as "play our attentional system"—that is, we intentionally exploit and deploy it in a flexible, situation-contingent, adaptive fashion (cf. Lane, 1979).

Planfulness

"Intentionally exploit and deploy" suggests that mature attending is planful and strategic, and this is indeed often the case. The conductor obviously has a plan in mind as she shapes the behavior of her orchestra (control) to make its musical product accord with the composer's intentions (adaptability). A mature attention system may foresightedly pretune itself to process a specific kind of information efficiently and economically, if it knows beforehand that this information rather than some other kind is coming its way. If second graders and sixth graders are told what to attend to before rather than after a stimulus array is presented, both groups respond more quickly—that is, they benefit from the foreknowledge. More importantly, however, the older children derive relatively more benefit from this foreknowledge than the younger children do (Pick, Christy, & Frankel, 1972).

Similarly, an older child is more apt than a younger one to search for information in a planful, systematic fashion (Brown & DeLoache, 1978). Vurpillot (1968) gave children of different ages the task of comparing pairs of houses to determine whether or not they were identical. Some were, in fact, identical, whereas others showed differences in one or more pairs of corresponding windows. For instance, the top left window of one house might have a different appearance from the top left window of the other. Older children proved likelier than younger ones to approximate the ideal perceptual-attentional strategy for this task: Scan corresponding windows pair by pair in some systematic, planful fashion that ensures that none will be missed—for example, scan column by column. If a difference is detected, stop—the houses are nonidentical. If no difference is detected after all pairs have been compared, stop—the houses are identical. The perceptual search of the young child is often, as here, incomplete (centered versus decentered, in Piaget's terms) and unsystematic in relation to what the task demands. It is, in a real sense, less "intelligent" than that of the older child in its lack of planfulness. In Maccoby's words: "With increasing age, the child's perceptions are more and more dominated by organized search patterns that are related to sustained 'plans' or ongoing behavior patterns of the perceiver" (1969, p. 94).

Not all planful-looking behavior need be accompanied by conscious awareness that a plan is being followed, but this is surely the case sometimes. Older subjects are probably more aware than younger ones of their own ongoing patterns of attentional deployment, as well as those of others (Chapter 5, *Percepts* section). Conscious monitoring and guiding of one's own planful attentional behavior is a form of metacognition (Chapter 4) and, like other forms, is subject to development. In this connection, recent research has shown an increase with age in children's knowledge of what attention is and what variables affect it (Miller & Weiss, 1982; Miller & Zalenski, 1982).

Attention over Time

One of the principal characteristics of attentional behavior in real life is that it is extended in time (Hagen & Wilson, 1982). Everyday attentional deployment does not ordinarily consist of single, isolated acts of noticing and processing this rather than that, as the existing research literature would sometimes lead one to believe. Rather it commonly entails a complex sequencing and interweaving of interrelated attentional acts over whole stretches of time, with feedback from earlier acts affecting the nature and course of subsequent ones. The cognitively mature individual uses his capacity for control, adaptability, and planfulness to impart an integrated and patterned character to his attentional deployment over time. He maintains an attentional strategy if it continues to work but is liable to change it when he discovers that it was— or has now become—inappropriate to his objectives. He avoids hasty perceptual decisions based on an inadequate or incomplete sampling of the pertinent information, as Vurpillot's (1968) study illustrated. He also resamples or rescans stimulus elements already investigated if he believes he may have missed or misinterpreted something. Both illustrate his ability to avoid premature attentional closure. Finally, he is capable of enacting multiple as well as single attentional sets or plans, maintaining and continuously updating several perceptual search enterprises at once over a considerable period of time. Future research in this area would do well to investigate the development of these more complex, extended, multiset patterns of attentional deployment.

SUMMARY

Are our adult perceptual abilities and perceptual knowledge the products of inborn biological *nature* or of postnatal experiential *nurture*? There are two answers to this question. The first is that, here as elsewhere in psychological development, both factors play vital roles. The other is that this ancient question is not precise and differentiated enough for present-day investigators. They would prefer instead to ask this sort of question: How much of exactly what kind of experience during what specific period of ontogeny is necessary and/or sufficient for the acquisition of precisely what perceptual competency? One recent conceptual scheme distinguishes five different roles of experience in perceptual development. In the limiting case of pure *maturation*, specific experience plays virtually no role. In the case of *maintenance*, experience serves only to sustain or stabilize an already fully developed perceptual competency. In *facilitation*, experience hastens the development of the competency but does not affect its final form or level. If, instead, experience modifies the final developmental outcome, its role is said to be that of *attunement*. Finally, in *induction* the fact and form of the development are very heavily dependent on the presence and the specific nature of the experience.

Infant perceptual development is currently one of the "hottest" areas in developmental psychology, thanks largely to the invention of research methods that made it possible to assess the perceptual abilities and dispositions of even very young infants. Babies cannot report their perceptual experiences, of course, but researchers can make inferences about their perception from their nonverbal behaviors (sucking, head turning, blinking, reaching, and, especially, looking) and physiological responses (heart rate, electrical activity of neurons). For example, researchers can measure which of two stimulus patterns an infant tends to look at more. They can also assess whether the infant's visual attention to a pattern *habituates* (wanes) after repeated presentation and *recovers from habituation* or *dishabituates* when a new pattern is presented. Such perceptual "preferences" tell us two important things about the infant's perceptual system: (1) what the system can discriminate perceptually, since a preference implies that a discrimination has been made; (2) what the system is especially sensitive to or selectively attentive to in its perceptual processing.

Although the auditory system appears to be functional at least several weeks before birth, the fetus may not be able to hear significant external sounds (e.g., speech) very well within its rather noisy intrauterine environment. Newborns appear to have almost normal hearing, however. The most interesting evidence on infant auditory perception has to do with speech perception. Unlike the perception of most things, the perception of speech consonants in adults is discontinuous or categorical rather than continuous: A very small change at a certain point on the relevant dimension results in the hearing of an entirely different consonant from the one heard just before the change. Studies have shown that very young infants also perceive consonantal sounds categorically, an innately given capability that should help them learn language. These dramatic findings led to the hypothesis that we are equipped from birth with a highly specialized mode of perception, a "speech mode" designed solely and specifically to help us acquire human natural languages. Contrary to this hypothesis, however, it has recently been found both that other animals also show speech-mode-like auditory perception and that humans also show it when processing certain nonspeech sounds.

The neural systems that subserve visual functioning are not fully developed at birth in humans. Consequently, the newborn's visual functioning is of poorer quality than it will be in late infancy and early childhood, or even than it will be at 2 or 3 months of age. Newborns have some difficulty both in visually fixating a stationary object and in maintaining fixation on a moving one. Both eyes do not always converge on the same visual target and focusing (visual accommodation) errors are common. Two closely related visual capacities that are important in detecting and discriminating patterns are visual acuity and contrast sensitivity. Visual acuity is surprisingly poor at birth—perhaps no better than 20/600 Snellen. Its gradual improvement during infancy appears to be due largely to maturational changes in the visual nervous system. Contrast sensitivity is also quite poor at birth and also improves considerably during the first 6 months of life. Newborns' visual capabilities are certainly sufficient to permit them to see such ecologically significant stimuli as looming, smiling faces. How completely they scan them and how well they see what they fixate is not so certain.

The newborn visual system is clearly more attracted or sensitive to some visual patterns than to others. It has proven very difficult to characterize and explain these systematic visual preferences adequately, however. In general, young infants tend to show a visual preference for patterns with high contour density. As infants learn more about specific objects and events in the environment (e.g., people and their actions), memory and meaning become more important determinants of what they look at than these inborn pattern preferences. Visual scanning and color vision also improve during the first few postnatal months.

Researchers in the Gibsonian tradition study the development of higher-order perceptual processing, including the infant's ability to perceive events, objects, places, and pictures. They are interested in the infant's perceptual pick-up of complex, often temporally extended patterns of sensory stimulation, especially those specifying meaningful, ecologically significant happenings. Gibsonian researchers (Spelke and associates) have shown that infants of 3 or 4 months of age appear to be similar to adults in some ways and different in other ways in their ability to perceive an object as a continuous and unitary entity, distinct from other objects or surfaces that form its background, that touch it, or that partly occlude it. For example, they seem to perceive (correctly) the two visible ends of an object whose center portion is occluded from sight by another object as being parts of a single entity, but only if the two ends are seen to move together behind the occluding object. If the two ends do not move they seem to be perceived (incorrectly) as two separate objects, rather than as one object partly hidden by another. Conversely, two separate objects that touch each other may be incorrectly perceived as constituting a single object. However, like adults, infants of this age can perceive biological motion and can attend selectively to one of two events which are superimposed on the same television screen.

The perception of an optical "loom" pattern as specifying an object about to collide with the observer has been shown to be innate in some species. It also appears to be the outcome of a maturational process in human infants, although experience may play some role in its development as well. Research using a "visual cliff" device has shown that perceptual detection and behavioral avoidance of deep dropoffs are also inborn in some animals. The development of various reactions to dropoffs is more complicated in our species. Before they begin to crawl (circa 7 months), human infants seem to have acquired sufficient depth-perception capabilities to be able to see that a dropoff is indeed deep. Nevertheless, they show no fear of dropoffs until several months later. The tendency to avoid dropoffs once they learn to crawl does not seem to be as dependable as it is in some species and may have maturational as well as learning-experiential determinants.

Theorists have disagreed for centuries about whether the senses are related to one another (*intermodal perception*) innately—prior to experience—or whether they only become intercoordinated as a function of experience. Piaget and many others have believed the latter to be true; other theorists, including Gibsonians, favor the former view. Recent studies have shown that by 3 or 4 months of age, at least, babies tend to perceive sights and sounds as parts of the same event if they are temporally synchronous. There is at least suggestive evidence that 1 month olds may be able to detect equivalences between what something looks like and how it feels in the mouth (visual-tactual intermodal perception). Perhaps even more surprising are recent findings suggesting that newborns may be able to imitate facial movements that they cannot see themselves make. If such research reports of very early intermodal perception continue to accumulate and are verified by other investigators, the Gibsonian position on the origins of intermodal perception will receive strong confirmation.

Much of postinfancy perceptual development might more accurately be characterized as "perceptual-attentional development." A useful way to remember the highlights of this development is to imagine what properties an effective perceptual-attentional system ought to have and then assume that the growing child's system becomes progressively more similar to this ideal. One such developing property is the ability to *control* the deployment of one's attention deliberately, especially to attend selectively to wanted information in the sensory input while disregarding or "tuning out" unwanted information. Acquiring this ability to control their attention voluntarily allows children to make their attentional deployment more flexible, more *adaptive* to the situation they are in. For example, they become able to deploy their attention more broadly so as to pick up several stimulus features at a time, if the situation should call for that strategy; and they can also tune it narrowly to a single feature, if the situation seems to demand that approach. A third developmental trend is towards greater *planfulness* in attentional behavior. A fourth outcome of development in this area is the ability to use these acquired capacities for control, adaptability, and planfulness to monitor, guide, and modify *attention over time*, even to the extent of managing several, temporally extended attentional enterprises simultaneously.

Memory

Suppose I were to read aloud to you a random sequence of numbers at the rate of one per second. Your task is to reproduce the sequence exactly, just as soon as I stop reciting it. I might begin, for instance, with "3-5-4-9," and you immediately respond "3549." I then try a five-digit series, then a six-digit one, and continue making them longer and longer until you reach your limit, sometimes referred to as your *memory span* for this kind of input. Simple memory problems such as this *digit-span* task have been included in intelligence-test batteries for over half a century. They correlate moderately well with other measures of intelligence, and performance on such tasks definitely improves with chronological age. A 4 year old is likely to have a digit span of about three or four, a 12 year old one of about six or seven.

It is only a slight exaggeration to say that, prior to the past 20 years or so, our knowledge of memory development consisted of little more than a few descriptive facts of that sort. We knew, in effect, that if we fed younger and older memory machines the same amount of information, the older machines could usually give more of it back to us than the younger ones could.

But *why* could they? Possibly because the older ones were thinking and doing something different or better than the younger ones were in the period between the beginning of our learning input to them and the conclusion of their memory output to us. We were, in retrospect, surprisingly late in asking this question and in formulating that sort of possible answer. The study of memory development began to quicken when researchers started inquiring into age differences in the kinds of cognitive processes and knowledge that might underlie and account for these more superficial age differences in sheer memory output. Memory development is currently one of the more active research areas in the field of developmental psychology, and this redirection of attention from overt memory products to the cognitive activities that generate them is largely responsible. Good secondary sources on memory development include Brown (1978), Brown et al. (1983), Chi (1983), Cohen and Gelber (1975), Kail (1979), Kail and Hagen (1977), Kail and Spear (1984), Liben (1982), Moscovitch (1984), Olson (1976), Olson and Sherman (1983), Ornstein (1978), Perlmutter (1980), Piaget and Inhelder (1973), and Wagner (1981).

SOME CONCEPTS AND DISTINCTIONS

Let us begin with some concepts and distinctions that are useful in thinking about memory and its development. Consider first the following three assertions: (1) I remember seeing a particular object fall off my kitchen table yesterday; (2) I remember that that object and all others of the same sort are called "cups"; (3) I remember that cups and all other objects normally continue to exist when I stop looking at them (Piaget's object permanence) and continue to weigh the same when broken into pieces (Piaget's conservation of weight). You are likely to feel an increasing urge to substitute the word "know" for the word "remember" as you progress from assertions (1) to (2) to (3). Yet the retention and recovery of knowledge acquired in the past is somehow involved in all three cases, and hence "memory" is somehow implicated in all three cases. In fact, it is difficult to make a clear-cut demarcation between what is ordinarily meant by "memory" and what is ordinarily meant by "knowledge" (including cognitive concepts, operations, skills, and the like). Moreover, as we shall see, the two interact with one another in important ways.

Piaget and Inhelder (1973) had something like this memory-knowledge contrast in mind when they distinguished between *memory in the strict sense* and *memory in the wider sense*. Memory in the strict sense essentially means the remembering of a specific event, accompanied by the definite feeling on the rememberer's part that this event occurred at a particular time and place in the past and that he or she personally experienced it. Assertion (1) illustrates this ordinary-usage, conventional meaning of "memory." Essentially, memory in the wider sense means the retention of all the products and achievements of one's cognitive development to date. The two cognitive-developmental attainments mentioned in (3) would certainly be good, Piagetian examples of memory in this wider, less-conventional sense. As Piaget and Inhelder (1973) put it, the subject "conserves" in memory her previously acquired cognitive "schemes."

Tulving (1972) has a somewhat similar dimension in mind when he contrasts *episodic* and *semantic* memory (see also Nelson & Brown, 1978). Assertion (1) would exemplify the first, assertion (2)—and perhaps (3)—the second. Assertions (2) and (3) illustrate that, at the knowing versus remembering end of the dimension, what is retained in memory can be as specific and unremarkable-looking as an isolated vocabulary item (cups are called "cups"), or as general and conceptually momentous as a Piagetian developmental milestone (object permanence, conservation of weight). How we remember or activate any sort of stored knowledge whatever, important or unimportant, is a question of great interest to contemporary students of human memory. Furthermore, it is becoming clear that the nature and development of "memory" even in the narrower, episodic sense simply cannot be understood without taking the structure and content of the rememberer's entire knowledge system into account.

Students of memory also distinguish between *storage* and *retrieval* activities. As their names suggest, storage activities put information into memory while retrieval activities recover information from memory. Storage means attending to, encoding, memorizing, studying, and the like: "Learning" is sometimes a good synonym. Retrieval means recognizing, recalling, reconstructing—the "remembering" of what had previously been stored. It would seem to be unnaturally constraining and restrictive to consider only those storage and retrieval activities that transpire between the subject's ears (Flavell & Wellman, 1977; Kreutzer, Leonard, & Flavell, 1975). If you want to store information for later retrieval you will, of course, often do nothing else but memorize it mentally and later recall it from your internal memory store. But you may also opt to take notes on it (tape record it, store it in a computer) or ask others to help you remember it. People use external storage and retrieval resources all the time in real-life mnemonic undertakings, and it would be foolish for psychologists not to study the nature and development of such intelligent behavior on the grounds that it is not "memory" (or not "*real* memory"). Such a claim would generally be untrue as well as irrelevant, since most mnemonic scenarios of this kind involve a sequential, back-and-forth movement between internal and external memory stores. For example, you remember (internal) that you made a note on your calendar and so you go look at it; it explicitly spells out (external) certain information, which in turn reminds you (internal) of yet other information not contained in the note.

There are a few other concepts to mention on the retrieval side of memory. Something that reminds you of something else is called a *retrieval cue* in the trade, since it leads to or "cues" the retrieval from memory of that something else. Two kinds of retrieval are commonly distinguished: *recognition* and *recall*. You may recognize as familiar something which is presently perceived or thought about—that is, you may identify it as identical to, similar to, or reminiscent of something previously experienced. There must be some sort of enduring representation of the previously experienced something in memory that is somehow contacted in the course of your experiencing the present something, and this contact somehow gives rise to the feeling of recognition. In recall, on the other hand, the familiar something is not initially present in conscious thought or perception. Rather, *recall* is the term we use for the very process of retrieving a representation of it from memory. In recognition, the thing that is recognized is already there to serve as its own retrieval cue, in effect. In recall, the subject has to do more of the retrieval job on his own (but not all of it, because it is usually assumed that there must be some sort of retrieval cue present to lend a hand). Recall-like processes are often involved in recognition activities and recognition-like processes are often involved in recall activities. For example, after recognizing something as familiar we commonly go on to recall additional information about it, such as where we were and who we were with when we first encountered it. Similarly, when trying to recall someone's name, for instance, we will test for recognition any name that comes to mind—that is, we see if we can recognize it as being the name we are after. Storage and retrieval are also more closely interdependent in practice than the foregoing description may suggest. For instance, how information is organized when initially stored in memory determines in what manner (e.g., via what retrieval cues) and how successfully it will be retrieved subsequently. For more information about these and other memory processes, see any recent textbook on the topic (e.g., Zechmeister & Nyberg, 1982).

Four categories of phenomena are useful to distinguish in analyzing memory development (Flavell & Wellman, 1977). The first, *basic processes*, includes the most fundamental operations and capacities of the memory system—for example, the processes by which an object is instantly and automatically recognized as familiar. The second, *knowledge*, refers to the more or less automatic effects of what you have come to know on what you will store and retrieve—roughly, the effects of memory in the wider sense on memory in the strict sense. The third is a special class of storage and retrieval activities which are called memory *strategies*. Deliberately rehearsing someone's name in order to memorize it would be an example of a memory strategy. The fourth category is called *metamemory*, and it refers to an individual's knowledge or cognition about anything pertaining to memory (e.g., that certain kinds of information are harder to learn and remember than others). Metamemory is metacognition (Chapter 4) concerning anything having to do with memory. The nature and course of memory development are summarized by considering each of these four categories in turn.

BASIC PROCESSES

Not surprisingly, the interesting developmental questions about basic memory processes center on the infancy period. The first one to ask is whether babies have any sort of memory capability. Both logical considerations and a great deal of research evidence clearly indicate that they do (Cohen & Gelber, 1975; Mandler, 1984; Moscovitch, 1984; Olson, 1976; Olson & Sherman, 1983; Olson & Strauss, 1984; Sophian, 1980; Strauss & Carter, 1984). Infants do many things that logically imply the existence of a memory system. Following are a few examples. As indicated in Chapter 6, habituation of attention presupposes some sort of recognition-type memory ability. If the baby could not somehow retain the fact that the repeatedly presented stimulus has been experienced previously, the baby could not habituate to it—that is, treat it as "old" or familiar. Infants also come to recognize familiar people, objects, and events (e.g., daily routines). It is clear that an organism with no memory capability could not develop social attachments (Chapter 5). Imitation and search for hidden objects (object permanence) likewise require memory for previous events. Young infants also show classical- and operant-conditioning behaviors. Because conditioning is a form of learning and because learning presupposes memory, these behaviors constitute additional evidence for an infant mnemonic system. In fact, experiments have shown that infants have quite good information-retention abilities. In an experiment by Fagan (1973), 5 month olds exposed to a photograph of a face for only a couple of minutes gave evidence of recognizing it as long as 2 weeks later. Sullivan, Rovee-Collier, and Tynes (1979) operantly conditioned 3 month olds to kick their feet when they saw a mobile. Some of the infants retained this learned association between the sight of the mobile and the kicking response for a period of 2 weeks. We can safely assume that everyday stimulus patterns and stimulus-response associations, with which the infant has much more experience than these, must be retained in memory for periods considerably longer than 2 weeks. Sullivan et al. (1979) nicely state the case for the necessary existence of memory abilities during infancy:

> When one considers the vast amount of learning which infants demonstrate in the first year of life, it becomes apparent that they must have an efficient means by which to code and retrieve information. Without this, early experiences which are hypothesized to play such a critical role in development would have little lasting import (p. 160; see also Rovee-Collier & Sullivan, 1980).

Are there developmental changes in basic memory processes during infancy? Do young children possess memory abilities that young infants lack? Piaget thought so (Piaget, 1968; Piaget & Inhelder, 1973). He made the interesting proposal that the infant is capable of recognition memory but not of recall memory, because recall requires symbolic-representational abilities that the infant lacks. In the following passage, Piaget (1968) used the term "evocation" where we would say "recall":

> Recognition can rely on perception and sensori-motor "schemes" alone, while evocation requires mental imagery or language, that is, some form of the symbolic function, some form of operational or preoperational representation. For this reason, there is no evocative memory in children before the age of 1½ or 2 years, while recognition memory is present during the first few months of life (p. 11).

The development of memory during infancy currently appears to be more complicated than is suggested by Piaget's account (e.g., Mandler, 1984; Nelson, 1984). Consider first recognition memory. An act of recognition in an older infant or young child undoubtedly includes processes not found in the young baby. Older individuals are likely to be conscious and explicitly aware of the fact that the object or event they have recognized is familiar and has been experienced before, at some past time. Furthermore, recognizing it may stimulate additional retrieval activity. This activity could even include, in older children, deliberate and effortful attempts to recall further information concerning the recognized stimulus. In contrast, recognition in the neonate is probably of the unelaborated, "bare-bones" variety that we associate with recognition processes in lower organisms (Mandler, 1984; Piaget, 1968). The very young infant may respond differently to familiar stimuli than to unfamiliar stimuli, but probably has no "I-have-seen-that-before" type feelings or cognitions, and perhaps also no additional retrieval activity, even of a passive, nondeliberate sort. It has even been suggested recently (Dannemiller & Banks, 1983) that what appears to be habituation (and thus, recognition) in very young infants may actually be a form of sensory adaptation rather than a higher-level, cognitive process.

Thus, recognition memory appears to have developmentally advanced as well as developmentally primitive forms. Conversely, recall seems to have primitive as well as advanced forms. Recall or recall-like memory processes appear to be operative much earlier in ontogenesis than Piaget thought. In particular, conditioning and expectancy learning seem to require more recall of stored information than does primitive recognition, although occurring just as early in infancy (Mandler, 1984). In Sullivan et al.'s (1979) operant conditioning study, for instance, the 3-month-old subjects both recognized the mobile and "recalled" that kicking their feet was the appropriate response to it. The successful subject in their study "not only recognizes a visual target but also recalls what to do with it" (Sullivan et al., 1979, p. 161). In Chapter 6 I described Meltzoff and Moore's (1977, 1983a, 1983b) surprising finding that newborns can imitate movements (mouth openings and tongue protrusions) that they cannot see themselves make. In one of their experiments (Meltzoff & Moore, 1977), the infants had pacifiers in their mouths while the to-be-imitated movement was being produced, and they were thereby prevented from imitating the movement until after it was no longer perceptually present. The imitations observed were therefore similar to Piaget's older infants' "deferred imitations" (Chapter 2), except that the delay between offset of the modeled behavior and onset of its imitation was much briefer in the neonates' case. Piaget quite reasonably considered deferred imitations to be instances of recall memory (Piaget & Inhelder, 1973, p. 394) because they reproduce a previous event that is no longer perceptually present. One could argue on the same grounds that the imitations Meltzoff and Moore (1977) observed in newborns were also mediated by some sort of recall or recall-like memorial process, despite the extreme developmental immaturity of the subjects doing the imitating.

However, in recall as in recognition, what happens early on in infancy undoubtedly differs from what happens later on—although, as Olson and Sherman wryly observe, "It's difficult to pin down what the difference is" (Olson & Sherman, 1983, p. 1052). As with recognition, whatever recall-like processes occur in young infants may well not be accompanied by any conscious awareness of the information that these processes retrieve from memory (Mandler, 1984; Olson & Sherman, 1983). When might infants first become capable of conscious recall, roughly defined as having any sort of conscious representation "or mental image" of something that is not presently perceptible? We really do not know yet, but there is some evidence to suggest that this capability emerges earlier than Piaget believed—perhaps even as early as 8 or 9 months of age (Brody, 1981; Mandler, 1984). Ashmead and Perlmutter (1980) collected parents' observations of their 7- to 11-month-old infants' memories; the observations suggested that the infants had at least some capacity for conscious recall. For example, the heroine of the following vignette was only 7 months old:

> Trying to change Anne's diaper and dress in a.m. on changing table. She immediately turns over and crawls to top edge of table and reaches over edge several times. Today I had picked up the pink lotion so it wasn't where she expected it to be. Anne paused, looked back and forth and looked at me puzzled. Her eyes brightened when she saw the bottle—immediately took it from me (Ashmead & Perlmutter, 1980, p. 11).

In Chapter 2 (pp. 42-44) I argued from the research evidence that infants can represent the continued existence of an absent object by about 9 months of age, and possibly even earlier. Although that was an argument for the presence of object permanence at this early age, it also constitutes a good argument for the presence of a capacity for conscious recall at the same age.

There is undoubtedly more that develops in the domain of recall processes than the capacity for conscious recall, although that capacity is certainly a developmental milestone (Mandler, 1984). As with recognition, one would think that children must eventually become aware not only of the specific item recalled, but also of other related matters. For example, they must eventually become aware that the item was a specific one-time happening in the past (an episodic memory), rather than a daily event or something planned for the future, and aware that they are in the process of recalling the item—that is, awareness that they *are* recollecting or reminiscing (Nelson, 1984). Similarly, the capacity to engage in deliberate, intentional efforts at recall surely develops later than the capacity for unintentional, automatic, incidental recall, passively instigated by an external or internal retrieval cue (Mandler, 1984). It is also likely that deliberate recall efforts spontaneously initiated by the self emerge later in ontogenesis than those set in motion by another person's request that one try to remember something. Nelson (1984) has further speculated that recall can be triggered by external cues earlier than it can be triggered by purely internal ones. It seems likely that most of the recall-like phenomena seen in early infancy are set in motion by external rather than internal cues—for example, the sight of the mobile cueing the "recall" of the conditioned kicking response (Sullivan et al., 1979).

Two other, closely interrelated developments have massive beneficial effects on infants' abilities to attend to, store, and retrieve information from their environments. The first is their ever-expanding store of organized knowledge about the world. The second is their ability to categorize incoming information and form concepts concerning it, both before and after they acquire the capacity to use symbols and learn language (Chapter 2). For good discussions of these and other influences on infant memory abilities, see Mandler (1984), Olson and Sherman (1983), and Olson and Strauss (1984).

The pace of research and writing about infant memory has increased dramatically in the past few years. As illustration, the previous edition of this book (Flavell, 1977) contained only two pages on the subject. The idea of a whole book on it (Moscovitch, 1984) would have seemed absurd when those two pages were written, so little research evidence was available. It should be apparent from the tentative and speculative tone of this section that we still really do not know much about memory development during infancy and very early childhood. However, if the present pace continues—and it probably will—we will know a good bit more about it before long.

KNOWLEDGE

A person's acquired knowledge, or his "memory in the wider sense" (Piaget & Inhelder, 1973), powerfully influences what he stores and what he retrieves from storage, or his "memory in the strict sense." As an example, master chess players and amateurs show an interesting pattern of similarities and differences in their ability to reconstruct from memory the positions of chess pieces on a chessboard (Chase & Simon, 1973). If the pieces are arranged randomly, both groups perform equally poorly. If the arrangement of pieces is one that could legitimately occur in an actual chess game, the masters' abilities to remember the positions are far better than the amateurs'. A further illustration is that one item of information can hardly serve as a retrieval cue for another if the two are unrelated in a particular rememberer's system of knowledge. Similarly, inputs that have little meaning for the individual—that do not fit readily into his acquired knowledge structure, that cannot easily be assimilated into his existing cognitive schemes, and so on—tend to be hard to store and retrieve.

Thus, what the head knows has an enormous effect on what the head learns and remembers. But, of course, what the head knows changes enormously in the course of development, and these changes consequently make for changes in memory behavior. The point is a simple but very important one:

> Older individuals will presumably store, retain, and retrieve a great many inputs better or differently than younger ones, for example, simply because developmental advances in the content and structure of their semantic or conceptual

systems render these inputs more familiar, meaningful, conceptually inter-related, subject to gap-filling, or otherwise more memorable for them (Flavell & Wellman, 1977, p. 4).

This line of reasoning suggests an interesting hypothesis: Children might actually be able to perform *better* than adults on a memory task if, in contrast to the usual case, they were more knowledgeable than the adults about the content to be remembered. Chi (1978) did a clever experiment to test this hypothesis. She tested good and poor chess players on their abilities to remember legitimate chessboard arrangements and found, as Chase and Simon (1973) had, that the good players remembered them better. No surprise so far. In Chi's experiment, however, the poor players were adults and the good players were children (mean age = 10.5 years), recruited from a local chess tournament (see also Chi & Koeske, 1983). Other studies have also confirmed this hypothesis. For example, Lindberg (1980) found that third graders outperformed college students on a free-recall test that contained items which were highly salient and familiar to the third graders (e.g., cartoon characters).

Research on Constructive Memory

This research is animated by a view of memory and its development very similar to Piaget's (Paris & Lindauer, 1977). It stresses the essential role that the subject's general knowledge and cognitive activities play in specific acts of memory. Students of constructive memory share with the Piagetians and others the view that memory is "applied cognition" (Flavell, 1971b, p. 273)—that is, the application to mnemonic problems of whatever intellectual weaponry the individual has so far developed.

Most of the things we remember in everyday life, say the proponents of constructive memory, are meaningful, organized events or bodies of structured information. They are not the isolated, largely meaningless "items" of the classical laboratory study of rote learning. Pairs of nonsense syllables, random sequences of digits, or lists of unrelated words are not usually the objects of everyday, extralaboratory learning and remembering. Moreover, these meaningful, structured inputs are not just copied or printed into memory at storage time and equally literally and faithfully recopied or reproduced at retrieval time. Rather, the act of comprehending and encoding into memory is a Piagetian assimilation-type process of *construction* of an internal conceptual representation of the input (hence, "constructive memory"). What is usually constructed and stored in memory could variously be described as a sensible (to the subject) interpretation of what he has perceived, an integrated rendering of it, or an organized representation of its gist. The mnemonic construction disregards some features of the input, highlights others, integrates or reorganizes still others, and even adds information not actually present in the input.

Similarly, retrieval is conceptualized as an equally active and assimilatory process of *reconstruction*, rather than as a passive, unedited copying out of what is stored in memory. It is somewhat akin to the archaeological reconstruction of an ancient civilization based upon building fragments, bits of pottery, and other artifacts, plus a lot of logical inference, conceptual integration, and just plain guessing on the archaeologist's part. These constructions and reconstructions which are so ubiquitous in everyday, meaningful memory are usually more automatic, involuntary, and unconscious than I have made them sound here, although they certainly can be, and sometimes are, very conscious and intentional (very "strategic," very "metamnemonic"). The point is that, automatic or deliberate, the memory machine is nothing at all like a tape recorder or camera. We most emphatically do *not* simply take mental photographs of inputs at storage and then simply develop them at retrieval.

It is time for an example. The following story certainly qualifies as a meaningful input to memory:

> Linda was playing with her new doll in front of her big red house. Suddenly she heard a strange sound coming from under the porch. It was the flapping of wings. Linda wanted to help so much, but she did not know what to do. She ran inside the house and grabbed a shoe box from the closet. Then Linda looked inside her desk until she found eight sheets of yellow paper. She cut up the paper into little pieces and put them in the bottom of the box. Linda gently picked up the helpless creature and took it with her. Her teacher knew what to do (Paris, 1975b).

A person could not really understand Linda's adventure, let alone recall it, without doing a lot more than simply copying its constituent sentences into memory. Consider the eight memory questions Paris (1975b) asked his subjects after reading them the story:

1. Was Linda's doll new?
2. Did Linda grab a match box?
3. Was the strange sound coming from under the porch?
4. Was Linda playing behind her house?
5. Did Linda like to take care of animals?
6. Did Linda take what she found to the police station?
7. Did Linda find a frog?
8. Did Linda use a pair of scissors?

You may have noticed a difference between questions 1 to 4 and questions 5 to 8. The first four could be answered by a tape-recorder-type of memory machine, since the answers are literally "there" in the surface structure of the story. In sharp contrast, questions 5 to 8 can only be answered by a human type of memory machine, since they require the subject to draw inferences from what is on the surface. The ability to make those inferences clearly depends, in turn, upon Piagetian memory in the wider sense, including stored knowledge about the world (e.g., that birds have wings but frogs do not) and reasoning abilities (e.g., a person who would do what Linda did probably likes to take care of animals).

The constructivist's argument is that we are constantly making spontaneous inferences and interpretations of this sort in processing, storing, and retrieving information. Such additions and elaborations are the rule rather than the exception, and they are believed to be of the very essence of cognition and memory. The argument is buttressed by the fact that we may not even be able to distinguish on a later memory test what we have constructed or elaborated from what had actually been initially presented (Bransford & Franks, 1971). For instance, after hearing sentences like "The box is to the right of the tree." and "The chair is on top of the box." the subject may falsely believe that "The chair is to the right of the tree." was one of the presented sentences, because it is semantically consistent with the mental representation of the input she has constructed (Paris & Mahoney, 1974). A similar but nonconsistent sentence like "The chair is to the left of the tree." will likely be identified as nonpresented, on the other hand. Under some circumstances, the subject actually may be even *more* confident that she remembers hearing a semantically consistent but never-presented proposition than one that was presented (e.g., Bransford & Franks, 1971).

We have so far said quite a lot about constructive memory but nothing about its relation to children. Do children construct and reconstruct in this fashion when they store and retrieve information? Are there developmental changes in constructive memory?

The answer to the first question is an unequivocal "yes." Studies by Paris and others (Paris, 1975b; Paris & Mahoney, 1974; see Paris & Lindauer, 1977) have found that grade school children show the sorts of constructive-memory phenomena just described. They are apt to believe that Linda found a bird, used scissors, and so on. Similarly, they are likely to think they previously had heard semantically consistent but nonpresented sentences, while correctly denying that they had heard nonpresented sentences that were not consistent with their semantic integration of the input. As Hagen, Jongeward, and Kail (1975) point out, children could scarcely carry on everyday conversations if they could not make the kinds of spontaneous inference, integrations, elaborations, and reorganizations we have been talking about. A great deal has to be assumed, presupposed, or otherwise added by a listener in understanding and remembering what a speaker says; a surprising amount of what gets said in an ordinary conversation is inexplicit and elliptical.

The first few developmental studies of constructive memory failed to find clear-cut age differences, but some solid evidence for developmental changes has now emerged (Paris, 1975a; Paris & Lindauer, 1977). As children grow older, they generally seem more prone and able to make the sorts of inferences that allow for a full, integrated, and meaningful memory representation of what they experience. During the middle-childhood years, at least, "the ability to spontaneously apply inferential processes to discourse increases with age" (Paris, 1975a, p. 9). However, probably more significant than any such developmental changes in the disposition and ability to make inferences is the acquisition of "sense 1 representations" or general structures of knowledge of the sorts described in Chapter 3. As children acquire story and scene schemas, scripts for everyday routines, category knowledge, and innumerable other "mental templates" (Chapter 3), they automatically use these templates to constructively process inputs at storage and to reconstruct them at retrieval (Liben, 1982; Nelson, Fivush, Hudson, & Lucariello, 1983). Thus, the most important developmental changes in constructive memory are changes in what knowledge structures the child has with which to constructively remember. To repeat an important point made earlier, what the head knows has an enormous effect on what the head learns and remembers, and what the head knows changes enormously in the course of development.

STRATEGIES

I am the experimenter and you are the subject. I show you a card with these twelve words printed on it, arranged as shown here:

pork	bicycle	house	bear
beef	lion	apartment	tiger
chicken	car	hotel	bus

Your task is to memorize them well enough to be able to recall them all, in any order, when I remove the card. What might you do to prepare yourself for this free-recall test? Some one or combination of the following activities, most likely: Rehearse the list by saying the words over and over to yourself. Organize the list by studying together words that are closely related semantically. This means mentally rearranging it so that, for instance, "lion" is moved over with the other two animals and "bus" with the other two vehicles. Elaborate the list by creating meaningful connections among the words; for instance, by making up a story or imaging a scene that includes these objects. Test yourself for readiness to recall all the words before you let me test you. And when I do test you, check to be sure you have recalled all three objects from each of the four categories (meat, vehicles, dwellings, animals) before you say you are finished. All of these activities are memory strategies.

The category of memory strategies encompasses the large and diverse range of potentially conscious activities a person may voluntarily carry out as means to various mnemonic ends. Verbally rehearsing a telephone number during the brief interval between looking it up in the phone book and going to the phone to dial it is an everyday, nonlaboratory example of a mnemonic strategy. Others include: (1) taking notes in class; (2) underlining key expressions in a textbook; (3) noting tomorrow's dentist appointment on your calendar; (4) trying to reconstruct your day's events step-by-step in hopes of recalling where you may have left that missing watch; and (5) attempting to remember someone's name by trying to recall people and events associated with that person.

Strategies are most clearly distinguishable from the two preceding categories when they are highly conscious, deliberate, and planful. Brown (1975) spoke of the previous category as involving "knowing," and of this one as "knowing how to know." In its purest form, a memory strategy is a voluntary, purposeful move a person decides to make in an effort to enhance some desired mnemonic outcome.

The distinction between the first two and the last two of our four categories may be more apparent if we consider memory in animals (Flavell & Wellman, 1977). An adult horse surely has basic memory processes—for example, mechanisms of recognition memory. It has also certainly acquired much practical knowledge of its world from years of experience that enormously influences what it will learn and remember (knowledge category). I doubt, however, if many psychologists would want to argue for the existence of intentional and planful equine memory strategies, let alone equine metamemory.

The childhood acquisition of memory strategies has been the subject of a great deal of research. In fact, it was mainly the discovery of memory strategies as fruitful objects of developmental investigation in the 1960s that launched memory development as a popular area of scientific inquiry. Naturally, there is no shortage of useful secondary sources on this topic. These are only a few of them: Brown (1975, 1978), Brown et al. (1983), Hagen et al. (1975), Kail (1979), Kail and Hagen (1977), Naus and Ornstein (1983), Ornstein (1978), and Waters and Andreassen (1983).

Rehearsal

There is an ill-defined group of memory strategies collectively referred to as "rehearsal." As we see, rehearsal is by no means the most effective mnemonic strategy available to a sophisticated and resourceful information processor. It does, however, make a good concrete example or vehicle within which to present some general conclusions about the development of memory strategies in children. Let us begin by examining two early studies of the development of verbal rehearsal as a mnemonic strategy.

Flavell, Beach, and Chinsky (1966) administered the following task to kindergarten, second-grade, and fifth-grade children (ages 5, 7, and 10, roughly). On each of several trials, seven pictures of common objects were displayed and an experimenter slowly pointed in turn to, say, three of them. The child understood that his task would subsequently be to point to those same three pictures in exactly the same serial order that the experimenter had. In the experimental condition of most interest here, the delay interval between the experimenter's pointing and the subject's recall was 15 seconds. The child wore a toy space helmet with a translucent visor. The visor was pulled down over the child's eyes during the delay interval, so the child could see neither pictures nor experimenters. One of the experimenters had been trained to lip-read semicovert verbalization of these particular object names and carefully recorded whatever spontaneous verbal rehearsal he could detect. Of the twenty subjects at each age level, two kindergarteners, twelve second graders, and seventeen fifth graders showed detectable verbal rehearsal on one or more trials. Thus, the study showed a clear increase with age in the spontaneous use of verbal rehearsal as a mnemonic strategy.

A subsequent experiment (Keeney, Cannizzo, & Flavell, 1967) used the same procedure with a group of first graders, a transitional age at which some children would be expected to have developed a tendency to rehearse and some would not. There were four major findings. First, children who spontaneously rehearsed the picture names, according to our lip-reading evidence, recalled the sequences of pictures better than those who did not. Second, the nonrehearsers were quite capable of rehearsing and could be gotten to do so with only minimal instruction and demonstration by the experimenter. Third, once induced to rehearse, their recall rose to the level of that of the spontaneous rehearsers. Fourth, when subsequently given the option on later trials of rehearsing or not rehearsing, more than half of them abandoned the strategy, thereby reverting to their original, preexperimental status as non-rehearsers.

These studies typify the research literature on memory-strategy development in two respects. First, they dealt primarily with strategies that are initiated during the storage rather than the retrieval phase of a memory problem. Rehearsal is something you start doing now, at storage, in hopes that starting it now will facilitate performance later, at retrieval. You know in advance you will have to remember something later, so you try to prepare for the recall test by rehearsing.

Suppose you did not know beforehand that you would later need to remember something, as in the earlier-mentioned examples of trying to recall a person's name or the location of your missing watch. In such instances, where the need to retrieve was unanticipated and came as a surprise, psychologists speak of *incidental* as opposed to *intentional* memory problems. The only strategies possible for solving incidental memory problems are of the retrieval versus storage variety. To be sure, the distinction between storage and retrieval strategies is not as clear as I am making it out to be. For instance, a storage strategy like rehearsal is likely to extend into the retrieval period and function as a retrieval strategy, and a retrieval strategy may involve trying to reconstruct and exploit the way the sought-for information was originally stored. The present point is that most developmental investigations to date have concentrated on storage strategies in intentional-memory task settings. As we see, however, some interesting work has also been done on the equally important question of how retrieval strategies develop.

These two studies are also typical of the field in a second way. The task materials used were discrete, rote-type "items," as contrasted with the highly meaningful, connected discourse often used as memory input in research on knowledge-memory relationships (the knowledge category). Similarly, they presented the children with traditional, in-the-head storage and retrieval problems. In neither study could the children use the strategy of writing down the object names, for example, or of asking someone else to help them remember the names. In short, the tasks were definitely of the traditional laboratory-memory-experiment genre and, as such, were not wholly representative of the information storage and retrieval enterprises that children and adults undertake in the real world.

Table 7-1 presents a simplified overview of how memory strategies such as verbal rehearsal usually seem to develop (cf. Brown et al., 1983, p. 87; Flavell, 1970b). Initially (left column), the component skills and skill integrations which make up an act of verbal rehearsal are largely or wholly absent from the child's repertoire. These components might include: the ability to recognize and subvocalize stimulus names quickly and accurately; the ability to repeat (rehearse) words or word sequences to yourself in a fluent, rapid, well-controlled fashion; and the ability to keep constant track of where you have been and where you are going in the execution of your rehearsal plan. When you stop to think about it, it is apparent that verbal rehearsal entails a rather complex coordination and integration of skills. Needless to say, if a child is unable to rehearse at all, it follows that she will show no spontaneous rehearsal in a memory-task context. We also assume, to simplify matters, that no significant amount of mnemonically useful rehearsal can be elicited from

TABLE 7-1 Typical Course of Development of a Memory Strategy

	MAJOR PERIODS IN STRATEGY DEVELOPMENT		
	Strategy Not Available	*Production Deficiency*	*Mature Strategy Use*
Basic ability to execute strategy	Absent to poor	Fair to good	Good to excellent
Spontaneous strategy use	Absent	Absent	Present
Attempts to elicit strategy use	Ineffective	Effective	Unnecessary
Effects of strategy use of retrieval	—	Positive	Positive

the child in this earliest period, even with strenuous efforts at rehearsal training.

The second period in Table 7-1 (middle column) is much more interesting. As Hagen et al. (1975, p. 73) indicate: "Some of our most important insights have resulted from experiments that have focused on this transitional period." The experiment by Keeney et al. (1967) described previously is only one of a number that testify to the existence of this curious transitional stage (Brown et al., 1983, p. 87). Recall that some of their first-grade subjects did little or no spontaneous, deliberate rehearsing in that particular memory-task setting. Nevertheless, these children proved to have good ability to rehearse, rehearsal was easily elicited by the experimenter, and its elicitation did have positive effects on their subsequent retrieval. A distinction frequently is made in memory-development research between a *production deficiency* and a *mediational deficiency* (Flavell, 1970b). A child is said to have a production deficiency for a particular strategy if she fails to produce it on her own for reasons other than the sheer lack of ability or skill to enact it properly. A child is said to have a mediational deficiency if his execution of the strategy, whether spontaneous or elicited, does not facilitate his recall. The transitional pattern usually observed in research studies is the one shown in Keeney et al. (1967) and in Table 7-1—namely, a marked production deficiency coupled with no apparent mediational deficiency.

Why would a child exhibit a production deficiency? If he is equipped to carry out the strategy and if its production would benefit his memory performance, why on earth would he fail to produce it spontaneously? To say that he does not produce it because it does not occur to him to produce it sounds like a gross evasion of the question. Nevertheless, thinking about production deficiencies this way may point us towards some deeper explanations.

There are several possible reasons why it might not occur to him to produce it. One possibility is that he does not yet fully grasp the implicit demands of this or perhaps any storage-memorization task (Bem, 1970). It may not be as obvious to him as it would be to you that he ought to do *something* special with those pictures now in order to enhance his memory of them later. He may not achieve or maintain, at storage time, a clear image of what is going to happen later, at retrieval time. In short, he may be insufficiently planful, foresighted, or goal oriented, at least in this particular memory-task situation (Paris, 1978a).

Another possibility is that he cannot spontaneously invoke and use th.> particular strategy—for example, verbal rehearsal specifically—again, either in this particular task situation or more generally. One reason for this might be that the task situation tends to call forth some other mnemonic strategy instead. Another strategy might win out over rehearsal because it has been in the child's repertoire longer, is less difficult and effortful to execute, or for some other psychologically sensible reason. Such a strategy would, therefore, generally be an earlier-developing, more elementary-looking one than rehearsal. Examples from the Flavell et al. (1966) task might be simple one-time naming, or careful visual inspection, of each object as the experimenter points to it, but without any appreciable cognitive processing of the items during the 15-second delay period that follows. Such a child may be behaving more or less planfully and strategically with respect to the eventual mnemonic goal, unlike the possibility described in the previous paragraph, but the plan or strategy he has selected happens not to be rehearsal.

There may be yet other reasons why it "happens not to be rehearsal," however. A rather banal one is that this child simply has not yet learned that rehearsal can benefit recall (and indeed, there are circumstances in which some kinds of rehearsal probably do not). In fact, many studies have shown that young children are likelier to use a memory strategy spontaneously once they have learned that using it aids their recall (e.g., Borkowski, Levers, & Gruenenfelder, 1976; Fabricius & Hagen, in press; Kennedy & Miller, 1976; Lodico, Ghatala, Levin, Pressley, & Bell, 1983; Ringel & Springer, 1980).

A less banal reason has been proposed by several Russian investigators (e.g., Smirnov & Zinchenko, 1969). They suggest that a skill must be fairly well developed in its own right before it can be effectively deployed as a strategic means to a memory goal:

> Before a cognitive operation . . . can become a means of remembering, it must be comparatively well formed. The initial use of a cognitive process for mnemonic ends becomes possible only when the individual can exercise a certain degree of freedom in operating with it (Smirnov & Zinchenko, 1969, p. 469).

If a behavior pattern like verbal rehearsal is still rather effortful, challenging, and attention demanding as an act in itself, the child may have trouble incorporating it as a subroutine within a larger cognitive program such as a memorization problem. Her trouble could take the form of not readily thinking to use it that way in the first place, or of failing to maintain and continue its use without outside prompting. Recall that Keeney et al.'s (1967) first-grade nonrehearsers showed both kinds of trouble. Needless to say, such problems are likely to be more severe as we move leftward in Table 7-1—that is, as the child we are considering has a fair rather than good or a poor rather than fair ability to execute the strategy. The child's production deficiency may be then coupled with a marked *production inefficiency*—that is, an actual inability to carry out the strategy skillfully and efficiently (Flavell, 1970b). In summary, then, there are many reasons why a child might exhibit a production deficiency for a given strategy.

The rightmost column of Table 7-1 is almost self-explanatory. Production of the strategy can now occur spontaneously, without the experimenter's assistance. As already suggested, this spontaneity may be explainable partly by the child's increased ease and fluency in executing the strategy. There may now be enough space in his cognitive operating room to rehearse efficiently, *and* to monitor the progress of his memorization, *and* to keep the upcoming retrieval task firmly in mind—*and* perhaps even to worry about how well he will perform on it. With all that space available for strategy use, the likeliest reason for a failure to rehearse is the judicious selection of some better mnemonic strategy.

The course of strategy development shown in Table 7-1 is often illustrated experimentally by what is called an *age by treatment interaction*. Subjects of, say, three age levels are divided into two groups. One group at each age level is simply given the memory task. The second group is additionally provided with some sort of aid in using a certain strategy—for example, instruction or training in using it, or task conditions that favor its employment. Then the experiment may show that providing such aid greatly increases strategy use, but only in the intermediate (production-deficient) age group. It does not significantly increase strategy use in either the youngest or the oldest groups because the former is unable to profit from it and the latter is already using the strategy spontaneously. The effects of the treatment vary with (statistically interact with) the age of its recipients; hence, the age by treatment interaction effect.

As always, I have made things seem more straightforward than they really are. For example, the concept of production deficiency, while useful, is flawed by our inability to define "spontaneous production" unambiguously. People "spontaneously" rehearse only in the context of some memory-task environment. But this environment always contains stronger or weaker cues, more or less subtle prompts, as possible facilitators or elicitors of rehearsal activity (Naus & Ornstein, 1983). The specifics of the task and task setting play an important but as yet poorly understood role in determining whether a subject will or will not "spontaneously" think to rehearse. An important implication of this is that one cannot speak of *the* age when the child changes from being production deficient to spontaneously productive for a particular strategy because that age is likely to vary considerably within a single individual as a function of the exact task conditions in which strategy use-nonuse is assessed. When—or even whether—a particular memory strategy comes to be used spontaneously in a particular task setting also depends on other factors, such as culture, schooling, and intelligence (Cole & Scribner, 1977; Kail, 1979; Rogoff, 1981; Wagner, 1981).

Ages of transition are also relative rather than absolute in other ways. In the first place, many possible types and patterns of rehearsal or rehearsal-like activity exist (Flavell et al., 1970), and there is reason to believe that each may have its own developmental time table. Suppose, for example, you are to memorize a list of words. I present them to you by successively exposing the words on a screen, only one at a time but for several seconds each. One rehearsal strategy would be to say each word over and over again during its presentation period. A different rehearsal strategy would be to repeat several words rather than just one—for example, to rehearse the first, second, and third words rather than just the third word alone during the third word's presentation interval. The second strategy appears to yield better recall than the first; in addition, the first is more likely to be elected by younger subjects, the second by older subjects (Cuvo, 1975; Naus & Ornstein, 1983; Ornstein, Naus, & Liberty, 1975). A related finding alluded to earlier is that children tend to verbalize stimulus names only while the stimuli are present perceptually before they develop the strategy of continuing to verbalize them after they are no longer present—for example, during a Flavell et al. (1966) type prerecall delay period (Flavell et al., 1970; Garrity, 1975; Hagen et al., 1975).

Research by a number of investigators has shown that enormous variety exists in when, what, and how people rehearse in memory tasks (e.g., Butterfield, Wambold, & Belmont, 1973; Flavell, 1970b), and that rehearsal strategies vary greatly in complexity and sophistication (Naus & Ornstein, 1983). Clearly, to ask when "rehearsal" develops as "a" mnemonic strategy is to ask a meaningless question.

Waters and Andreassen (1983) and Brown et al. (1983) have recently described the general course of memory-strategy development in ways that are consistent with, but supplement, the account just given (see also Naus & Ornstein, 1983). Waters and Andreassen (1983) propose three developmental principles of strategy use and strategy generalization: (1) memory strategies first appear under task conditions that encourage optimal processing of the material to be remembered (e.g., that allow more time to study the materials); (2) memory strategies first appear with materials that encourage their use (e.g., in the case of organizational strategies, semantically related materials that are easy for young children to organize and interrelate conceptually); (3) as children become older and more experienced, they become more active in initiating strategy use in a variety of situations, including those that do not so strongly encourage optimal processing or strategy use—that is, they show strategy generalization. Similarly, Brown et al. (1983) conclude that:

> the young child's use of a primitive rehearsal strategy is unreliable; he fails to refine it to conform with changing task demands, and he often fails to use it in a variety of situations where it would be applicable. Strategy use in mature users is characterized by its robust nature, its internal coherence, and its transitational flexibility. There are, of course, limits to this transitational flexibility. Everyone's knowledge is context-bound to a certain degree . . . and this is true of strategy utilization (p. 95).

Just as there are many rehearsal strategies, so also are there many memory strategies besides rehearsal. Their ages of acquisition are similarly relative—similarly variable between and within strategies.

Other Memory Strategies

Even though it can be quite complex and sophisticated, rehearsal is fundamentally a rather prosaic memory strategy. It is, after all, only a form of imitation or mimicry. Items are presented and the rehearser simply parrots them over and over, quite possibly adding little or nothing conceptual to the process. In particular, he may not be trying, as he rehearses, to discover or create meaningful relationships among the items that might cause groups of items to clump together at retrieval. Other memory strategies do go beyond the bare bones of the input by adding relationships (Pressley, 1982).

ORGANIZATION. One of the most frequently studied of these strategies is semantic grouping or categorization. The generic term often used is *organization*. The memorizer might automatically notice that the list of items contains a few articles of clothing and some things to eat. With a little more active search for interitem semantic connections, she might also discover that three other items could be construed as school-related objects—for example, bus, desk, and book. Then she might think of the same-category items together during item presentation, and perhaps even rehearse them by category. If she did all these things her subsequent recall would tend to be strongly *clustered* by category, with most or all of the foods reported out together, as a string, and the same for the clothing and school-related items. Such clustering need not be and often would not be complete, and there are ways of measuring the amount or degree of clustering present in the subject's item-recall sequence. The following recall sequence, for instance, is partially but not completely clustered, in terms of the categories just mentioned: desk, bus, bread, ice cream, book, apple, hat, shoes, dress.

The mere presence of clustering in a subject's recall does not prove that she had consciously and intentionally used a grouping strategy when storing and retrieving those items (Lange, 1978). To illustrate, Goldberg, Perlmutter, and Myers (1974) found that recall of one item can cue the recall of a semantically related item even in 2 year olds. Two year olds may have some impressive mnemonic talents (DeLoache, in press) but conscious, intentional use of a grouping strategy is surely not one of them (Myers & Perlmutter, 1978). Nevertheless, there is a developmental trend towards such deliberate use. If allowed to manipulate a randomly arranged but potentially categorizable set of object pictures during a study period, for instance, older subjects are likelier than younger ones to adopt the strategy of physically segregating the pictures into groups by category and then studying same-category items together (Moely, Olson, Halwes, & Flavell, 1969; Neimark, Slotnick, & Ulrich, 1971). Moreover, younger subjects exhibit the same kind of transitional production-deficiency pattern with respect to this strategy as they do in the case of rehearsal (see Table 7-1):

(a) Except when assisted to do so by hints or instruction, they tended not to rearrange the pictures into spatial groups by class membership during the study periods, a study tactic which the oldest subjects tended to adopt spontaneously; (b) given such assistance, however, the resulting increase in study period manual clustering was accompanied by a decided increase in subsequent recall (Moely et al., 1969, p. 26).

ELABORATION. Another, closely related type of strategy is called *elaboration* (e.g., Rohwer, 1973). It involves the identification of a common referent or a shared meaning between two or more things to be remembered. Elaboration strategies are usually studied in the context of a paired-associate learning task. In such tasks, the subject has to learn pairs of stimulus and response items (commonly words) so that when the stimulus (e.g., "elephant") is presented, she can recall the response (e.g., "pin"). You would be using an elaboration strategy here if you deliberately generated an absurd or otherwise memorable visual image linking the two members of the pair. You might, for example, create an image of an elephant delicately balanced on the head of a pin, demurely acknowledging the applause of the audience. Another elaboration strategy would be to think of a sentence that describes an event involving the two—for example, "The elephant picked up the pin with his trunk." A lot of research shows that elaboration can be a very effective method of cementing items together in memory. Just try forgetting what object was paired with "elephant" in the preceding example. As a real-world example, the use of elaboration techniques can be helpful in learning the meaning of new words in one's own or a foreign language (Pressley, Levin, & Bryant, 1983).

As with organization and rehearsal, the older the subject, the less outside help she is liable to need in order to use elaboration strategies (Rohwer, 1973). This should not be taken to imply that deliberate organizing and elaborating are employed universally by adults in all memory problems in which these strategies would be useful. As with most cognitive skills (Chapter 4), their use or nonuse will surely depend upon who the adult is and what the task situation is (Pressley, 1982). It is true, however, that both organization and elaboration are later-developing strategies than at least the simpler forms of rehearsal (Pressley et al., 1983; Schneider, in press). It is also probably true that most forms of conscious and deliberate elaboration are apt to appear later in ontogenesis—and less certainly, less universally—than most forms of conscious and deliberate organization (Pressley, 1982; Schneider, in press).

The acme of development here, however, is not the mere ability to invoke this or that strategy spontaneously. Rather, it is the ability to select the most effective strategy or strategies for the memory problem at hand, and then to modify or replace those strategies appropriately as the mnemonic situation changes—for example, as one's learning progresses, or when changes appear in the nature of the information that has to be memorized (Brown et al., 1983; Butterfield & Belmont, 1977; Lodico et al.,1983).

RETRIEVAL STRATEGIES. So far, I have discussed only storage strategies— that is, the kinds of mnemonically oriented data processing an individual does now because he knows he will have to retrieve those data later. As indicated earlier, retrieval strategies refer to the resourceful moves an individual may make when actually trying to recover things from memory storage, whether he had previously known he would now be doing that (intentional memory) or not (incidental memory). Like storage strategies, retrieval strategies vary greatly in complexity and sophistication. A less sophisticated one is not to give up your memory search immediately just because the sought-for item does not come to mind immediately (Flavell, 1978d). Sticking with the problem a little longer does not always pay off, of course, but it certainly qualifies as an elementary retrieval strategy. More sophisticated, later-developing strategies often involve a complex interplay between specific memory fragments, general knowledge of the world, and reasoning or inference: "I remember hearing the sound of waves outside (memory fragment), so it probably happened near an ocean (inference, general knowledge); but I've only been to the ocean once, in 1969 (memory fragment), so it must have been that summer, during vacation (inference)." At their most sophisticated levels:

> The individual's retrieval strategies have something of the quality of a Sherlock Holmes tour de force. . . . When he realizes that X [the retrieval target] probably will not come to mind by just sitting and waiting . . . he deliberately searches his memory for related data, in hopes that something recalled will bring him closer to X. In the most elaborate cases of this sort of intelligent, highly indirect and circumlocutious retrieving, the process is virtually one of rational reconstruction of "what must have been," in the light of remembered data, general knowledge, and logical reasoning (Flavell & Wellman, 1977, p. 20).

A study by Keniston and Flavell (1979) illustrates some of the developmental changes that have been observed in this area (see also Kobasigawa, 1977). Subjects of grades one, three, seven, and college were given an incidental memory problem. The experimenter named a letter of the alphabet, the subject wrote it on a small card, the experimenter removed the card and named another letter, the subject wrote that letter on a new small card, and so on, until a random sequence of twenty different letters had been written. The subjects were then given a surprise memory test: to write down on a big piece of paper all (and only) the letters they had just previously written on the cards. A very effective retrieval strategy in such a situation is to go through the entire alphabet in your mind and write down each letter that you recognize as having just recently been seen and written out. This strategy deftly transforms a very difficult free-recall task into a very easy recognition task. It is easy for the experimenter to tell when a subject has used this strategy: The target letters are retrieved in alphabetical order. The younger subjects in the Keniston and Flavell (1979) study could use the recognition strategy both skillfully and effectively (i.e., it improved their recall) when merely *told* to use it; no training or practice was needed. If not told to use the strategy, however, it did not occur to most of them to use it, and their recall suffered accordingly. Thus, they showed the familiar production-deficiency pattern of being quite capable of using the strategy effectively when told to use it but of not being able to think of it on their own. In contrast, the older subjects were able to: (1) think of the strategy and propose its use prior to actually attempting to retrieve the letters; (2) use it spontaneously (i.e., without instruction to do so) during retrieval; (3) after retrieval, report accurately and completely the retrieval methods they had used during retrieval.

Based on the results of this and other studies (Flavell, 1978d; Kobasigawa, 1974, 1977; Salatas & Flavell, 1976; Williams & Hollan, 1981), Keniston and Flavell (1979) proposed that, with age and experience, children gradually acquire at least two important pieces of strategy knowledge about how to retrieve information effectively:

1. The knowledge that a systematic, exhaustive search through an entire "memory space" (e.g., the alphabet) is often an appropriate strategy. It is especially appropriate in retrieval problems such as Keniston and Flavell's, for which you do not

know at the outset exactly how many targets the space contains but for which there exists an effective method for searching it exhaustively.

2. Closely related to 1, the knowledge that in some retrieval problems it is good strategy to make a deliberate effort to retrieve items that you know beforehand may not prove to be targets at all—thus, an indirect, circumlocutious retrieval strategy. The reason is that, if recalled and thought about, some items may trigger recall of other, target items (i.e., may prove to be good retrieval cues) and some items may themselves be recognized as targets. In the latter case, you have spontaneously converted what was ostensibly a recall problem (recall as many targets—but only targets—as you can) into a recognition problem (recall as many items in the memory space as possible, and try to recognize the targets among them). The recognition problem should be easier than the original recall problem to the extent that, as in the case of the alphabet, the space can be searched systematically and exhaustively. The use of such indirect, circumlocutious retrieval strategies may partly depend on previously acquired knowledge that one thing can remind us of another (Beal, 1983; Gordon & Flavell, 1977) and that a recognition task is generally easier than a recall task (Speer & Flavell, 1979).

Similarly, researchers have found that young children tend to be less efficient (Ackerman, 1982; Kobasigawa, 1974, 1977) and less flexible (Ceci & Howe, 1978) than older ones in their exploitation of available retrieval cues. As an example of inefficient cue use, Kobasigawa (1974, 1977) showed that young children will search a three-item category in a recall task when suitably prompted and cued, but will often fail to search it completely; they are likely instead to retrieve only one of the three items, and then skip on to the next category. More generally, the research evidence indicates that young children have much to learn about what retrieval cues are and about how to use them effectively (Beal, 1983; Fabricius & Wellman, 1983; Flavell, 1978d; Gordon & Flavell, 1977; Kreutzer et al., 1975; Ritter, 1978).

A deliberate effort to retrieve something from memory involves a search through the internal world. "Trying to remember something" and "searching one's memory for something" are roughly synonymous. Accordingly, as we have seen, much of what develops in the area of memory retrieval consists of the ability and propensity to search the internal world intelligently: efficiently, flexibly, systematically, exhaustively, selectively, indirectly—whatever the retrieval problem at hand demands (Flavell, 1978d; Keniston & Flavell, 1979). The available evidence indicates that this ability develops relatively late in ontogenesis—during middle childhood and adolescence rather than during infancy and early childhood.

In marked contrast, recent research by Wellman and Somerville (1982) shows that there is considerable growth during infancy and early childhood in the ability to search the *external* world. Even infants show some ability to search the external world when they seek and find hidden objects in Piaget's object-permanence tasks (Chapter 2). By 3 or 4 years of age, young children are quite accomplished searchers. If, from available evidence, a hidden object could logically be in any one of the hiding places present, children of this age will conduct a systematic, exhaustive search of all these places— analogous to what older subjects do in the internal world when faced with certain memory-retrieval tasks (Keniston & Flavell, 1979). Contrariwise, if the evidence indicates that the missing object must be located in a particular subset of the available hiding places—that logically it could not be in other available hiding places—then they will selectively focus their search on this logically possible subset. A study by Haake, Somerville, and Wellman (1980) showed this quite clearly. In this study, an experimenter took each preschool subject's picture with a camera at locations 1, 2, 3 of an itinerary that included stops at eight locations. When experimenter and child reached location 7 they discovered that the camera was missing. Thus, location 3 was the locus of last-known possession of the camera and location 7 was the locus of first-known nonpossession, making locations 4 to 6 the critical subset. Much as a grown-up would do, these young children tended to concentrate their search at locations 4, 5, and 6, and—impressively—to avoid searching at 1, 2, and 3, the only locations that had actually been associated with the camera in their experience. Older individuals are similarly selective in their search of the internal world, often concentrating their search in areas of remembered past experience that are likely to contain the retrieval target (Keniston & Flavell, 1979; Williams & Hollan, 1981).

It is interesting to speculate about possible developmental relationships between outer-world search skills and inner-world (memory) search skills. Perhaps the principles of intelligent, task-adaptive external search that are gradually worked out during late infancy and early childhood (Wellman & Somerville, 1982) subsequently become generalized and applied to formally similar problems of internal search. As argued earlier in this chapter, mnemonic scenarios in everyday life frequently entail a sequential, back-and-forth movement between internal and external memory stores. Similarly, we often search our memory stores to aid us in finding things in the external world and often search the external world for retrieval cues that will jog our memories. We often search memory to help ourselves find lost objects, and we often search the environment to help ourselves remember things. It would be surprising if such formally similar and functionally interconnected skills were not also developmentally related.

STRATEGIES FOR LEARNING AND REMEMBERING COMPLEX MATERIAL. I mentioned earlier that most studies of strategy development have used, as the material to be remembered, discrete, rote-type "items" (words, depicted objects) rather than semantically rich information structures. However, it is both feasible and adaptive to apply voluntary, deliberate strategies to the understanding, storage, and retrieval of complex, meaningful, and organized information as well as simple word lists and paired associates (Brown, 1975; Brown et al., 1983). Learning to study effectively in school settings is a familiar and very important example of developing planful storage strategies for comprehending and retaining constructive-memory-type, meaningful information. Just idly reading a passage about the complex and interrelated causes of World War II probably will yield some understanding and memory. But reading it very actively and "intelligently," taking really good notes, deliberately searching for relationships which are only implicit in the text—these are strategies that can yield much better understanding and memory (Chapter 4). For this kind of material, the best memory strategy is, ultimately, to strive for a really rich and deep understanding. The same is true on the retrieval side. The previously mentioned sophisticated retrieval strategies, which interweave specific memories, general knowledge, and inferences, are equally applicable to highly meaningful material—to semantic as well as episodic memory. They can be used to reconstruct the causes of World War II as well as to reconstruct that single, isolated experience by the ocean mentioned earlier. It is obvious that a better understanding of the nature and development of these types of storage and retrieval strategies, and especially about how they might be solidly and permanently instilled through systematic training and instruction, would have considerable educational significance (Baker & Brown, 1984; Brown et al., 1983).

Ann Brown and other developmental psychologists have recently been studying the developmental acquisition of a variety of such strategies. Strategies investigated include identifying, selectively attending to, underlining, and summarizing the main ideas in a segment of meaningful text; asking oneself questions about the text and other methods of fostering and monitoring one's comprehension and memory of it; and judicious, task-adaptive allocation of study effort and retrieval effort (Brown et al., 1983; Wellman, 1983). A study by Brown, Smiley, and Lawton (1978) will serve to illustrate this "new wave" of strategy development research. Students from grades five to twelve and college students first read a story and then selected those idea units from it that they would prefer to have by them if they were asked to remember the story. In effect, their task was to select the most useful retrieval cues for recalling a body of organized, meaningful information. Half of each group (naive students) selected idea units before they were given practice studying and recalling the passage; the other half (experienced students) selected them after having had this study and recall experience. Naive students at all ages tended to select as their retrieval cues the most important, central ideas of the story. So did the experienced students—except for the college students, who selected idea units of intermediate importance. Why? The college students said they realized from their recent recall experience that they would probably remember the main ideas without further effort on the next trial, whereas those of intermediate importance had been and probably still would be harder to remember; ergo, to maximize overall recall, select the latter rather than the former as retrieval aids next time. As Brown, Smiley, and Lawton (1978) make clear, this memory strategy is a rather high level, complex one—so much so that even their high school seniors did not discover it.

Although strategies for learning and remembering complex meaningful material tend to be acquired later than some of the rote-recall ones considered earlier (e.g., rehearsal), their developmental course seems to be quite similar:

> In many senses, the qualitative developmental pattern found between grades 6 and 12 on reading and writing tasks is very similar to that found between grades 1 to 6 on simple rote-recall tasks. First, there is the early sporadic emergence of an appropriate activity, followed by increasing stability and transitational application with repeated use. These activities gradually become systematized and consolidated into a robust, reliable pattern of attacking reading and writing tasks. Production deficiencies and inefficiencies (Flavell, 1970b) occur along the way and these are related to performance decrements exactly as they are in young children undertaking simpler list-learning tasks (Brown et al., 1983, p. 90).

METAMEMORY

The subjects of one investigation, an extensive interview study of children's metamemory, or knowledge about memory (Kreutzer et al., 1975), were kindergarteners, first graders, third graders, and fifth graders. In one of the interview items, the experimenter said to each child:

> Jim and Bill are in grade _____ (S's own grade). The teacher wanted them to learn the names of all the kinds of birds they might find in their city. Jim had learned them last year and then forgot them. Bill had never learned them before. Do you think one of these boys would find it easier to learn the names of all the birds? Which one? Why? (Kreutzer et al., 1975, p. 8).

It is obvious that this task does not fit neatly under the *Basic Processes* or *Knowledge* headings of this chapter. It does not fit neatly under *Strategies* either, because the subject's method of learning bird names was not being studied. Rather it was meant to probe the child's intuitions about a specific memory phenomenon—namely, the advantage or "savings" involved in relearning something previously learned versus learning something for the first time. In short, it was intended to assess knowledge of memory, or metamemory.

Many of Kreutzer et al.'s subjects, even at the kindergarten and first-grade levels, did, in fact, seem to intuit that the relearner would have the advantage. Moreover, a number of them gave reasonable justifications for their choice—for example, "Because as soon as he heard the names, they would probably all come back to him" (an allusion to the process of recognition memory). That answer clearly testifies to some metamemory. This third grader's answer clearly testifies to even more: The new learner would actually do better than the relearner, the subject said, "because the kid who learned them might think he knew them, and then he would get them wrong, but the kid who didn't learn them last year might study more than the kid who *thought* he knew them" (Kreutzer et all., 1975, p. 9).

In Chapter 4 metacognition was defined as any knowledge or cognitive activity that takes as its object, or regulates, any aspect of any cognitive enterprise. When the enterprise is a mnemonic one, the knowledge or cognitive activity bearing on it is commonly called metamemory. The nature and development of metamemory has been a very popular scientific topic during the past decade. Useful reviews and critiques of this work include: Borkowski (in press), Brown et al. (1983), Cavanaugh and Perlmutter (1982), Chi (1984), Flavell (1978d), Flavell and Wellman (1977), Forrest-Pressley, MacKinnon, and Waller (in press), Kail (1979), Pressley, Borkowski, and O'Sullivan (in press), Schneider (in press), Wellman (1983, in press), Yussen (in press), and Zechmeister and Nyberg (1982). Following the conceptualization given in Chapter 4, we can roughly distinguish between *metacognitive knowledge concerning memory* and *metacognitive experiences concerning memory*, with the former further divisible into knowledge about mnemonic *persons*, *tasks*, and *strategies*. Before discussing metamemory development, however, a quick test of *your* metamemory: Can you recall everything I said about metacognition in Chapter 4? If you cannot (and my own knowledge about memory assures me that you couldn't possibly), I suggest that you review it before reading on. (I also recognize—my social cognition?—that readers often hate to have textbook writers try to direct their reading, so feel free to ignore this [extremely valuable, well-intended] suggestion!)

Metacognitive Knowledge Concerning Memory

PERSONS. This category refers to what children could come to know about themselves and others as mnemonic beings. Probably the most basic acquisition in this category is the ability to recognize and identify experiences of remembering and forgetting when they occur, conceptually differentiating these experiences from such others as thinking, dreaming, and perceiving. There is recent evidence that primitive concepts of remembering and forgetting begin to be formed during the early preschool years, as part of the development of the child's implicit "theory of mind" (Bretherton et al., 1981; Johnson & Wellman, 1980; Shatz, Wellman & Silber, 1983; Wellman, in press; see also Chapter 4). Once the child has acquired some sense of what it is to remember and forget:

> There is . . . much to learn about the capacities, limitations, and idiosyncracies of the human memory system. The growing person could discover that immediate memory is of small span and limited duration, and that additional processing may be needed to optimize subsequent retrieval. He could also induce from experience the related, sad fact that one cannot always count on retrieving later what was stored earlier, plus the happy fact that what cannot be remembered right now will often be remembered eventually. There is the further knowledge that the memory system can be untrustworthy as well as porous: It is possible to remember what did not happen and to misremember what did, in addition to outright forgetting (Flavell & Wellman, 1977, p. 11).

As regards the first of Flavell and Wellman's proposed "acquirables," there is evidence that older children tend to have a more realistic and accurate picture of their own memory abilities and limitations than younger ones do, at least on tasks of the following kind (Flavell & Wellman, 1977; Schneider, in press; Wellman, in press): The experimenter briefly exposes a horizontal strip of two pictures of common objects and asks the subject if she could correctly name the objects in left-to-right serial order after the experimenter covers them up again. Subjects of all ages make the realistic judgment that they would. The subject is then asked the same question about a briefly exposed strip of three pictures, then four, and so on. The process stops either when the subject says the series has now gotten too long for her to recall accurately or when a strip of ten pictures has been presented (a series much too long for any subject to remember under these task conditions). The subject is then tested for her actual, as opposed to the foregoing predicted, memory span on this task. Younger children tend to overestimate their memory ability here—that is, their predicted memory span exceeds their actual memory span, often by a considerable amount. With increasing age the two come closer together; the predicted span realistically decreases to meet an increasing actual span. However, when the span-prediction task is presented in a context that is more familiar and meaningful to them (a board game, a simulated shopping situation), young children's span estimations tend to be more realistic (Schneider, in press); here as elsewhere in the assessment of children's competencies, the specifics of the task and testing context have an important influence on age of task mastery.

When discussing retrieval strategies in the previous section I mentioned that young children have much to learn about the nature and use of memory-retrieval cues. Gordon and Flavell (1977) and Beal (1983) have proposed that the core acquisition here is the concept of *cognitive cueing*. Cognitive cueing refers to the fact that thinking about one thing can lead you to think about another thing—that one mental event tends to trigger or cue others. It can be argued that this "obvious" fact about how our minds work is an exceptionally important piece of person metamemory for children to acquire, a key component of their developing "theory of mind" or "naive cognitive psychology." For the arguments, see Beal (1983) and Gordon and Flavell (1977). What little developmental evidence we have on children's awareness of the cognitive cueing process suggests that it may emerge somewhere around the beginning of middle childhood, or perhaps even earlier (Gordon & Flavell, 1977).

Tasks. There is a great deal for the developing child to learn about what makes some memory tasks more difficult than others. First, a memory task can be harder or easier because of the amount and kind of information to be learned and remembered. Second, for any given amount and kind of stored information, some retrieval demands or requirements are more severe and taxing than others. As already mentioned, for example, the requirement merely to recognize, as previously encountered, something experienced earlier is usually much easier than the requirement to recall it from memory—that is, without its being perceptually present. Therefore, task difficulty is a joint function of two things: what has to be stored and the nature of subsequent retrieval demands.

Certain memory-relevant properties of what is stored have to do with individual items of information, rather than with relationships among items. Some of Kreutzer et al.'s (1975) kindergarten and first-grade subjects seemed to believe that an individual item that was familiar or perceptually salient would be especially easy to learn and remember. Practically all of them knew that increasing the sheer number of individual items to be remembered made a memory task harder (see also Wellman, 1977; Yussen & Bird, 1979).

As implied in the earlier discussion of organization and elaboration strategies, items also become easier to remember if the learner discovers or creates meaningful connections among them. Several studies have documented the growing child's increasing awareness of the mnemonic value of various kinds of interitem relationships (Flavell, 1978b; Flavell & Wellman, 1977; Schneider, in press). For example, Moynahan (1973) found that third and fifth graders were more likely than first graders to predict that a list of categorizable items (food items, items of clothing, etc.) would be easier to remember than a comparable list of unrelated items. Similarly, when asked to think of three words that would be very easy to remember along with the word "blue," say, older elementary school children are much likelier than younger ones to think of three more color words (Tenney, 1975). Tenney's younger subjects could readily generate other words of the same category as the initial word (here, color) if explicitly asked to, but they did not spontaneously think of doing this under the just-described, "easy-to-remember" instruction. Kreutzer et al. (1975) also found developmental trends across the elementary grades in the child's knowledge that paired associates composed of verbal opposites (e.g., "hard"–"soft") and a list of words that are meaningfully linked together by a story are easier to remember than pairs and lists without strong interitem relationships.

Kreutzer et al. (1975) found the same age trends with respect to two insights concerning retrieval demands. First, their older subjects sensed that it may become harder to recall one set of words if, before the recall test, you also have to learn a second set of words that is easily confused with the first set; as you may know, students of memory call this phenomenon *retroactive interference*. Second, Kreutzer et al.'s (1975) older subjects knew that it is easier to retell a story in your own words than in the exact words it was told to you—that is, memory for the semantic gist of a story is better than memory for its exact linguistic form (see also Myers & Paris, 1978). Finally, even first graders understand that it is easier merely to recognize things than to recall them outright, according to one study (Speer & Flavell, 1979).

STRATEGIES. Since this topic has been discussed at length in the previous section, I only mention a few examples in which the metamemory component is expecially prominent—that is, in which the emphasis is on verbalizable knowledge about strategies as distinguished from actual "on-line" strategy use in memory situations. In several of Kreutzer et al.'s (1975) interview items, the subjects were presented with hypothetical storage (preparation for future retrieval) and retrieval problems and asked how they would solve them. In one storage problem, for instance, the child was asked how many things he could think of to do to make sure he would not forget to take his ice skates to school with him the next morning. The older subjects were able to think of more different things to do than the younger ones, and generally they seemed more strategic and planful in their approach to this real-world type memory problem. Nonetheless, a number of kindergarten and first-grade subjects were able to describe appropriate strategies. Interestingly, for them as for the third and fifth graders, the most commonly mentioned strategies were not of the familiar, in-the-head variety, such as thinking again and again about bringing the skates (rehearsal). Rather, they involved external actions and the use of outside memory stores, such as putting the skates where you are sure to see them the next morning, asking your mother to remind you, and writing yourself a note. The fact that they could not write failed to deter a number of the younger subjects from proposing the note-writing strategy. This tendency to think of external versus internal mnemonic aids was also noted in children's responses to other interview items in the same study (see also Neisser, 1982, Part VI).

Some of Kreutzer et al.'s (1975) subjects gave strategy descriptions that attested to some unexpectedly sophisticated intuitions about the nature of memory. The following is my favorite example. The question was: "What do you do when you want to remember a phone number?" A third-grade girl replied:

> Say the number is 633–8854. Then what I'd do is—say that my number is 633, so I won't have to remember that, really. And then I would think now I've got to

remember 88. Now I'm 8 years old, so I can remember, say, my age two times. Then I say how old my brother is, and how old he was last year. And that's how I'd usually remember that phone number. [Is that how you would most often remember a phone number?] Well, usually I write it down (Kreutzer et al., 1975, p. 11).

In actual memory situations, how well you remember is influenced by the interactive effects of a number of person, task, or strategy variables rather than by the workings of just a single variable (Chapter 4). Wellman has shown that 10 year olds are likelier than 5 year olds to take account of such interactions in their predictions of memory performance (Wellman, 1978), but also that even 5 year olds can recognize the joint influences of two variables under some task circumstances (Wellman, Collins, & Glieberman, 1981).

Metacognitive Experiences
Concerning Memory

Many of these experiences consist of judgments or feelings about the ease or difficulty of remembering something. Adults have learned how to monitor these experiences carefully and how to use the information these experiences provide to regulate their memory efforts and strategies (Chapter 4). Flavell and Wellman (1977) have described some of what needs to be acquired in the area of memory monitoring and regulation:

> The growing child may gradually learn how to read his own memory states and statuses with fair accuracy and also to understand the behavioral implications of being in this as opposed to that state. As he becomes more attuned to internal "mnemonic sensations" he might intuit that one datum was never stored and another is in memory somewhere, but absolutely unrecoverable right now. The behavioral implication in both cases is to forego or abandon efforts at retrieval. In contrast, a third datum might be experienced as right on the threshold of recall (the "tip of the tongue" feeling), and the child could have learned to be more optimistic when he senses his memory to be in that particular state. He may also have discovered that when learning something, the clear implication of a feeling of poor or uncertain retrievability is to keep on studying until some more satisfactory state of recall readiness is experienced (Flavell & Wellman, 1977, p. 11).

Many of these "mnemonic sensations" bear on material that is or may already be in memory, as in the examples just cited. Others bear on material that will eventually need to be remembered but has not yet been stored. For instance, as you skim through next week's reading assignment you may get the buoyant feeling that the material will be very easy to remember—or the sinking feeling that it will be almost impossible to remember (e.g., because you just cannot understand it). You then react accordingly: Study lightly in the former case; study hard, get help from others, or give up in despair in the latter case.

Your reactions to external or internal memory materials and to your own metacognitive experiences regarding them may often be automatic or reflex-like. Through years of experience as a rememberer (and forgetter), you have learned to recognize and respond adaptively to numerous "patterns"

(Chapter 4) of memory-relevant material and feelings—and to do so quickly and automatically, with little or no conscious reflection. A person who has acquired a great deal of knowledge about memory could be thought of as an excellent pattern recognizer in mnemonic situations, much as the physicist and the chess expert are excellent pattern recognizers in their domains of expertise (Chapter 4; cf. Chi, 1984).

What are the patterns of internal feelings and external data that such a person detects so automatically and reacts to so appropriately? We have already described a number of them. Examples are that tantalizing "tip-of-the-tongue" experience, the feeling that X is (or is not) stored in memory, and lengthy, hard-to-comprehend memory material. Seasoned rememberers recognize automatically and respond appropriately to such "stimuli." Other examples are included in what Henry Wellman and I have termed the child's developing "sensitivity" to the objective need for efforts at (a) present retrieval and (b) present storage for purposes of future retrieval (Flavell, 1977; Flavell & Wellman, 1977). We argued that one of the things the child presumably develops is a sense of attunement for when the situation calls for storage or retrieval efforts. This sense or attunement, too, can be conceptualized as an ability to recognize automatically and respond appropriately to complex classes of input patterns. You recognize these zillion situations as situations in which you should try to store the material well, because you will surely need to retrieve it later. Someone's telling you the address of a future rendez-vous is an instance of this class of situations; you respond automatically, without thinking, by trying to store that address effectively. In contrast, you recognize these zillion other situations as ones in which you should deliberately search memory, because they call for sustained retrieval efforts. For instance, you suddenly discover that you have lost your keys, and automatically respond by trying to remember where they might be. Furthermore, you readily discriminate these two zillion situations from zillions of others, some of them quite similar to these, in which neither preparation-for-retrieval nor retrieval efforts are needed.

Flavell (1977, 1978d), Flavell and Wellman (1977), Schneider (in press), and Wellman (1983) have reviewed most of what little we have learned so far about the development of these sorts of metamemory competencies. Following are some sample findings: As mentioned in Chapter 4, Flavell et al. (1970) found that elementary school children were better able than preschoolers to sense when a set of items had been memorized sufficiently to ensure perfect recall. Likewise, younger children may be less skilled than older ones at detecting and responding appropriately to at least some of the situations ("patterns") that implicitly call for deliberate storage efforts. For example, older children have been shown to be more aware than younger ones that items they have just failed to recall on a test are more in need of further study than ones they have just succeeded in recalling (Masur, McIntyre, & Flavell, 1973). Similarly, older children appear more sensitive than younger ones to the usefulness of keeping written records of past solution attempts in a problem-solving task, so as to avoid skipping possible solution moves or repeating previous ones (Siegler & Liebert, 1975).

On the other hand, young children have been found to possess some important competencies of this genre. For example, kindergarteners are likelier to keep trying to recall items they feel they once knew than items they feel they never knew (Wellman, 1983); "items that feel known" may have become for them a recognized "pattern" that automatically triggers further retrieval efforts. In fact, Cultice, Somerville, and Wellman (1983) have recently shown that even preschoolers give evidence of some basic memory-monitoring skills. Furthermore, although young children may not always detect and react appropriately to patterns that implicitly call for deliberate storage or retrieval efforts, they usually will do so if the call is explicit rather than implicit. If you ask them to recall something (explicit call for deliberate retrieval), even very young children will try to oblige (DeLoache, 1983; Todd & Perlmutter, 1980). More surprisingly, the same appears to be true when you ask them to remember something (explicit call for deliberate storage, or preparation for future retrieval). For instance, 2 to 3 year olds will sometimes act as if they are deliberately, intentionally trying to keep in mind the location of a hidden object during a delay period, as if to ease the task of finding it later (DeLoache, in press; Wellman, Ritter, & Flavell, 1975). In other words, they will sometimes show what looks like deliberate memory strategies, something that the literature on strategy development would not lead us to expect to find in children so young.

CURRENT ISSUES IN MEMORY DEVELOPMENT

What issues, questions, and research problems most preoccupy students of memory development these days? One that certainly preoccupies them has already been discussed in Chapter 4: Is there really a maturation-based increase during childhood in structural, "hard-wired" working memory capacity— a postinfancy change in a "basic process"? Or, alternatively, can improvements with age in memory performance always be fully accounted for by changes with age in the "knowledge," "strategies," or "metamemory" categories? As I said in Chapter 4, we simply cannot decide this important issue on present evidence.

You know from other chapters in this book that there is currently great interest in unearthing the earliest possible competencies or "protocompetencies" in all areas of cognitive development. The area of memory functioning is no exception. The recent surge of interest in infant memory is one symptom. The recent search for evidence of memory strategies and metamemory in the early postinfancy years is another (e.g., DeLoache, in press; various chapters in Perlmutter, 1980).

The possible influences on memory functioning and memory development of the growth of knowledge constitute another topic of recent and growing interest (Chapter 4; Brown et al., 1983; Chi, 1978, 1983, 1984; Chi & Koeske, 1983; Flavell & Wellman, 1977; Liben, 1982; Naus & Ornstein, 1983; Nelson et al., 1983; Ornstein & Naus, in press). Some of the more obvious ways that knowledge acquisition can benefit memory have already been described in the section on *Knowledge* in this chapter and in Chapter 4. Less obvious, perhaps, is the strong possibility that becoming more knowledgeable in an area can also improve memory strategy use and metamemory in that area (cf. Chi, 1984; Naus & Ornstein, 1983; Ornstein & Naus, in press). To illustrate how this might work, my "expertise" in the area of cognitive development should help me to select or construct highly efficient, specific-content-adapted ("custom-tailored") strategies for storing and retrieving information about cognitive development. For instance, like any professional in any area, I know a lot of fancy, roundabout ways to search memory (and external information sources) for needed facts and ideas here. For metamemory, similarly, I know a lot about what I will find easy and hard to remember, I am quite good at monitoring and regulating my memory activities (recognizing and reacting appropriately to all sorts of those "patterns"), and the like. Such benefits seem only to be expected, given how familiar I am by now with the content and structure of information in this area and how many years of practice I have had in storing and retrieving such information. Investigating the possible effects of knowledge acquisition on memory strategy use and metamemory seems well worth doing, but it has scarcely been tried at this writing (Ornstein & Naus, in press).

There are a number of currently very controversial issues regarding metamemory (and, more generally, metacognition). Discussions of these issues can be found in the sources cited previously, at the beginning of the *Metamemory* section. Many of the issues flow from the basic question of how best (most insightfully, most usefully) to define and conceptualize metamemory. That this is a real, knotty issue is attested to by the definitional and conceptual finessing I have done on previous pages of this chapter. For instance, how and to what extent do the processes or phenomena subsumable under "strategies" and "metamemory" really differ? You may have noticed that I did not tell you that. And if they can or should be differentiated, how should we conceive of the functional and developmental connections between them? Should we suppose, for instance, that the child first acquires the verbalizable declarative knowledge that using a particular memory strategy in a specific class of memory situations benefits memory performance, and from then on repeatedly employs this conscious knowledge to impel or mediate the regular use of that strategy in those situations? That sounds like simplistic, wrong-headed psychological theorizing to me. Or should we suppose, instead, that some strategy use (however instigated) leads to some dim knowledge of the strategy's usefulness, which in turn mediates more strategy use, which then leads to more or better knowledge of its usefulness, and so on, in this reciprocally mediative fashion through developmental time? That sounds more plausible, given how we think cognitive development normally proceeds. Or perhaps "strategy use" and "strategy metamemory" should not be differentiated in this way at all (cf. Chapter 4). Perhaps the path to scientific progress here would be to suppose that "knowing to" use a strategy appropriately—thus, knowledge of a more procedural than declarative character—is *itself* part of what we ought to mean by "knowledge about memory" or "metamemory" (cf. Chi, 1984). "Knowing to" use a strategy might then be reconceptualized as recognizing and responding appropriately to those "patterns" of memory-relevant stimulation described earlier.

The foregoing is but a small sample of the mare's nest of unresolved issues and problems concerning the nature, development, and uses of metamemory. However, I would not like to leave you with the impression that all is perplexity and pessimism in the areas (area?) of strategy and metamemory development. On the contrary, these issues are stimulating some interesting new ideas and research directions. As an example, Michael Pressley, John Borkowski, and their colleagues have recently begun to study the effects of training children in the use of what they call *metamemory acquisition procedures* (Borkowski & Pressley, 1983; Lodico et al., 1983; Pressley et al., in press). These are general procedures that children can employ on their own to monitor and evaluate the mnemonic efficacy of various memory strategies. The new knowledge about strategy effectiveness that may be gained by using these memory-monitoring procedures qualifies as new metamemory, of course—hence the designation "metamemory acquisition procedures." According to this approach, then, children might learn or be taught not only specific strategies and metamemory, but also general strategies ("metastrategies," really) for acquiring new metamemory about specific strategies. As the authors rightly point out, this approach has potential educational as well as developmental implications.

SUMMARY

Memory development became a popular field of inquiry when researchers turned their attention from the overt products of the child's memory to the underlying cognitive processes that generate these products. Several concepts are useful in analyzing memory development. *Memory in the strict sense* and *episodic memory* refer to memories for specific, personally experienced, past happenings—for example, remembering that you saw a cup fall and break yesterday. *Memory in the wider sense* and *semantic memory* refer to acquired knowledge of all sorts—for example, that cups are called "cups" in English and that cups exhibit Piagetian object permanence. Getting things into memory is called *storage*; getting them out again, *retrieval*. Retrieval may consist of: *recognition* of something that is already present in perception or thought; *recall* of something that is not present (often with the help of reminders or *retrieval cues*); blends and mixtures of the two.

It is convenient to discuss memory development under four major headings: *basic processes, knowledge, strategies, and metamemory. Basic processes* refer to the human memory system's most fundamental operations and capabilities—for example, those which permit us to store, recognize, and recall information. The interesting developmental questions about basic processes mainly concern the period of infancy. First, do infants show any sort of memory capability? Clearly they do, as evidenced by such memory-mediated processes as habituation of attention, recognition of familiar people, objects, and events, imitation, search for hidden objects, and classical and operant conditioning. Second, are there developmental changes in basic memory processes during infancy? Again, the answer is yes, although we still have much to learn about the exact nature of these changes. At least some primitive form of recognition memory appears to be operative very early on. In later infancy and early childhood, however, acts of recognition are probably accompanied by the conscious awareness that one is encountering something previously experienced and by spontaneous or deliberate acts of recall. Likewise, the presence of conditioning and imitation capabilities suggests the presence of some sort of recall or recall-like processes in early infancy. Towards the end of the first year, however, recall appears to become a more conscious experience, one in which some kind of mental representation of the past object or event is present in focal awareness. Other developments may include the ability to make self-initiated and deliberate efforts at recall and (see Chapter 4) a possible maturation-based increase with age in structural working memory capacity.

In the *Knowledge* section, the argument was made that what people know (memory in the wider sense) greatly influences what they learn and remember (memory in the strict sense). Consequently, developmental changes in the knowledge structures should lead to developmental changes in what is stored and retrieved. For example, people who are very knowledgeable about chess can remember chessboard arrangements better than those who are less knowledgeable. This result holds even when the more knowledgeable chess players are children and the less knowledgeable ones are adults. This reversal of the usual adult-over-child advantage in memory performance dramatically illustrates the potent role of knowledge acquisition in memory development.

Most students of memory share Piaget's view that storage is *construction* and retrieval is *reconstruction*. According to this view, we do not simply make a copy of information presented at storage and then simply reprint that copy when we retrieve. Rather, both storage and retrieval involve a great deal of active conceptual organization and reorganization, much gap filling and inference, as the individual tries to achieve a meaningful representation of the information. There is considerable evidence that children as well as adults use constructive and reconstructive processes when they remember. There is also evidence that older children may be more spontaneously inferential, and perhaps use more complex and difficult inferences, in their mnemonic constructions and reconstructions than is true of younger children. Probably even more significant for memory development than these changes, however, is the acquisition of the knowledge structures or "mental templates" (schemas, scripts, etc.) described in Chapter 3.

Strategies are potentially conscious activities that a person may use to facilitate memory. *Rehearsal* constitutes one frequently studied class of storage strategies. Table 7-1 shows what may be the typical course of development of rehearsal and other memory strategies. Initially, the child is unable to execute the potentially strategic activity at all, even under experimenter instruction or tuition. Subsequently, the child is likely to exhibit a pattern of *production deficiency* with respect to the strategy. That is, he can and will use it if explicitly directed to do so, and using it benefits his memory in the expected fashion, but he does not use the strategy spontaneously, on his own initiative. The causes of production deficiencies are not well understood, but some possible ones were suggested: (1) The child may not have the foresight to use any special cognitive activity now, in order to facilitate retrieval later. (2) The task situation may trigger the use of some other, better-developed strategy than the one under study. (3) The target strategy may not yet be well-enough mastered—qua cognitive activity, as an end in itself—to be brought into service as a means to a mnemonic goal. In the final period shown in Table 7-1, such obstacles are no longer in force, and the child employs the strategy spontaneously. Factors that complicate this simple picture of strategy development are also presented in this section.

There are other storage strategies that are more sophisticated and mnemonically effective than rehearsal. The learner would be using an *organization* strategy if she studied conceptually related items together, in groups by category membership, and then tended to *cluster* same-category items together in recall. *Elaboration* strategies also add meaning to what is presented. An example of elaboration would be the construction of a vivid visual image linking together two normally unrelated objects that are supposed to be remembered together, as in a paired-associate learning task. The ontogenetic pattern shown in Table 7-1 also appears to apply to these two types of strategies.

The developing child acquires retrieval strategies as well as storage strategies. Development here consists largely of an increasing ability and propensity to search memory intelligently: efficiently, flexibly, systematically, exhaustively, selectively, indirectly—in whatever manner the specific retrieval problem at hand requires. In some problems, for example, the best retrieval strategy is to make a systematic and exhaustive search through an entire "memory space," recognizing as retrieval targets some of the items encountered during the search and using other encountered items as retrieval cues for targets that are not encountered. There is research evidence that older rememberers are likelier than younger ones to think of using such indirect retrieval methods, methods that may nicely transform a difficult recall task into a much less difficult recognition test. It was speculated that strategies for searching for and finding memory targets in the internal world might be generalizations of early-developed strategies for searching for and finding objects in the external world.

Investigators have recently begun to study the development of effective strategies for storing and retrieving complex, meaningful, organized material—for example, the sorts of strategies that would be useful in studying for and subsequently taking an essay exam in a history course. Although these strategies are acquired later than some of the rote-recall ones already discussed (e.g., rehearsal), the course of their acquisition appears to be quite similar.

Metamemory means knowledge or cognitive activity bearing on anything mnemonic; it is, therefore, metacognition (Chapter 4) that takes memory enterprises as its object. Two major categories of metamemory were distinguished: *metacognitive knowledge concerning memory* and *metacognitive experiences concerning memory*. The former is further divisible into knowledge about mnemonic *persons*, *tasks*, and *strategies*. In the *person* case, children learn, among other things, to identify as such experiences of remembering and forgetting and to distinguish them from other mental experiences; come to recognize the capacities, limitations, and idiosyncracies of the human memory system; and acquire the concept of cognitive cueing and knowledge about the nature and use of retrieval cues.

Evidence also exists that children come to learn a great deal about what makes some memory *tasks* easier than others. They discover that a set of items will be easier to recall if the items are few in number, familiar, and meaningfully related to one another—for example, categorizable. Similarly, they come to appreciate the fact that some retrieval-test requirements are more taxing than others. As an example, it is a more demanding test of memory to repeat a story word for word than to retell it in your own words.

Children also become better able to think of and articulate plausible storage and retrieval *strategies* in response to hypothetical memory problems. Younger and older children alike tend to favor the use of external memory aids over unaided internal memory. They think that written notes and other people make useful reminders, for example.

The other major category of metamemory, *metacognitive experiences concerning memory*, includes judgments or feelings ("mnemonic sensations") about how difficult or time-consuming something will likely be to store or retrieve, about whether the present situation is one that tacitly calls for storage or retrieval efforts, and the like. It is likely that years of experience in remembering and forgetting have made most adults sensitive to innumerable "patterns" of internal and external stimulation that have implications for the conduct and probable success/failure of their memory enterprises. They detect and respond appropriately to these patterns, often automatically and unconsciously. Not much is known about the ontogenesis of these pattern-recognition or memory-monitoring skills, but recent studies suggest that some of them are already in evidence during the early-childhood years.

A number of issues, questions, and research problems currently preoccupy students of memory development. What memory-relevant competencies do the infant and very young child possess? Does the growth of knowledge in an area benefit memory strategy use and metamemory in that area, and if so, how? What is the most scientifically fruitful way to conceptualize metamemory and its relationship to strategy use? Although this and other difficult questions about strategy use and metamemory remain unresolved, they are stimulating some interesting new ideas and research directions.

eight

Language

Father, making up a story to help his little girl settle down for the night: ". . . and then Trina (the canine heroine of his impromptu narrative) was chased by another dog. I wonder what happened next." Girl: "I know—the dog catched her!"

What tacit knowledge about language can we reasonably attribute to this little girl on the basis of this brief interchange? First, she has clearly acquired a lot of expertise in both producing and understanding the speech sounds of English. Thanks to her considerable *phonological* development, she effortlessly segmented and interpreted her father's rapid and unbroken burst of sound ("anthentrinawuz . . . ," roughly) as the English word string ". . . and-then-Trina-was . . . " Imagine what it would have sounded like to a person who knew no English; he would likely not even be able to make out the individual vowels and consonants, let alone know where one word ended and the next began. Similarly, the "accentless," native-speaker-like word pronunciation and intonation pattern of her reply would be the envy and despair of most adults trying to learn English as a second language. A little probing would undoubtedly also show that her knowledge of English phonology is a productive, generative, rule-governed affair, like the rest of her linguistic knowledge. For instance, "Trina" undoubtedly sounds like a proper word to her, although she has never heard it before. In contrast, "Zdrina"—which does not follow English phonological rules for word construction—would probably just not sound right.

Second, there is also evidence of substantial *semantic* development, or acquisition of linguistic meaning. She knows how a great many concepts and relationships among concepts can be expressed in English words and word combinations (phrases, sentences). She probably knows by now which creatures are called "dogs" and which are not almost as well as her father does. She has also acquired more subtle semantic knowledge: She knows that "chase" implies more than just "run" but is not synonymous with "catch." And she knows that the "I" her father utters does not refer to the same person as the "I" she utters. She also knows how semantic relations like agent-action-object (e.g., one animal chasing another) can be expressed in English—that is, by the left-to-right order of words.

Third, her tacit knowledge of English *grammar* (*syntax* and *morphology*) is likewise noteworthy. She knows how word order (syntax) and word formation, such as the addition of inflections (morphology), are used as clues to sentence meaning. For instance, she tacitly knows that "another dog" is the logical subject and "Trina" is the logical object of the verb "chase" in her father's passive sentence. A younger, less grammatically advanced child would not have learned to interpret sequences like "was-verb-ed-by" as clues that the normal subject-object order is reversed; in fact, the younger child would undoubtedly interpret the sentence as a declarative and think that it was Trina rather than the other dog that did the chasing. Even the childish expression "catched" attests to an important grammatical attainment. Her addition of the inflection or grammatical morpheme "-ed" to "catch" proves that she has productive, generative command of the grammatical rule for forming the simple past tense in English. What she has not yet learned is the much more trivial fact that the past tense of a few common verbs (irregular verbs like "catch") is not generated by this rule.

Finally, the little girl has learned much about the *pragmatic* or *communicative* side of language. She knows how to produce and comprehend *speech acts*, such as assertions, requests, and questions, and to engage in linguistic discourse with others. For example, she knows that her father's second utterance is not the simple assertion a purely syntactical analysis of it would indicate. Rather, it is really an indirect question or request that invites the child to participate in the story-construction process. That is the kind of speech act the father intended to produce and that is the kind of speech act the child interpreted it to be. Similarly, the child seems to have acquired the rule of discourse according to which (roughly stated) one first refers to something by an indefinite article (*a* dog, *a*nother dog) and only subsequently by the definite article (*the* dog). It is a good bet that she would have used "a" rather than "the" if the unnamed chaser of Trina had not already been introduced into the story when she referred to it.

This interchange hints at the many and diverse sorts of accomplishments which mark the miraculous-seeming accomplishment that is human language acquisition. The field of language development has undergone a striking metamorphosis in the past two decades. For those of us who are old enough to remember, it used to be a dull field. What facts we had seemed colorless and pedestrian. The main reason they seemed so was that there were no interesting theoretical perspectives to organize and enliven them. We lacked an adequate, theoretically informed conception of all the many and marvelous things a person knows and can do when she has acquired a native language. Since we had an impoverished vision of what people end up having inside their heads when language has been fully acquired, we had a correspondingly impoverished vision of the developmental steps, sequences, and processes or mechanisms that describe and explain the course of that acquisition.

Thanks to the work of Noam Chomsky, George Miller, Roger Brown, and many other scientists, both visions are far richer now. As a consequence, language development has become one of the most stimulating and challenging areas in all of developmental psychology. It also has the frustrating property of being more stimulating and challenging the more one knows about it. Frustrating, because that means an introductory chapter like this just cannot communicate all the excitement that is really there. For instance, it may be necessary to know a fair amount of linguistic theory to fully appreciate the staggering amount of complexly organized grammatical knowledge a native speaker of any language tacitly has. The excitement comes from trying to imagine how on earth she could possibly have acquired all that as a young child.

PREVERBAL DEVELOPMENTS

Important developments in infancy help prepare the child to acquire his first words. Phonological skills, both innate and acquired, help him discriminate and produce the speech sounds that compose these words. Cognitive acquisitions enable him to construe words as symbols and provide him with the meanings and intentions he will try to express in words. Communicative skills allow him to exchange these linguistically expressed meanings and intentions with other people through discourse.

Phonological Development

PERCEPTION OF SPEECH SOUNDS. As already indicated (Chapter 5), human infants seem to be biologically pretuned and predisposed to process human speech sounds (Gibson & Spelke, 1983). De Villiers and de Villiers (1979) summarize some of the evidence for this conclusion:

> Within a matter of days after birth, they are highly responsive to speech or other sounds of similar pitch to the human voice. In fact, speech seems to be rewarding to the infant in a way that other sounds are not. Newborns will learn to suck on an artificial nipple hooked to a switch that turns on a brief portion of recorded speech or vocal music, but they will not suck as readily in order to hear instrumental music or other rhythmical sound. In the first few months of life, speech elicits greater electrical activity in the left half of the child's brain and music elicits greater activity in the right half of the brain, as is the case with adults. This suggests that at a very early age the two hemispheres of the brain are already specialized for dealing with the different kinds of sound. So from the beginning of infancy children are able to discriminate speech from nonspeech, and they seem to pay particular attention to speech (p. 16).

Recall (Chapter 6) that young infants have also been shown to possess an astonishing ability to hear the difference between certain consonant sounds that are physically and acoustically almost identical (Eimas, 1975; Jusczyk, 1979; see Aslin et al., 1983). This remarkable innately given perceptual skill, called *categorical speech perception,* may later help the young child "crack the phonological code" of the language he is trying to learn.

But why not now, in early infancy, rather than "later"? Why could not young infants use these perceptual sensitivities and capabilities to learn the meanings of spoken words? Why could not young infants at least learn to comprehend words, even though not yet capable of producing them? One important reason, as we shall see, may be that they have not yet acquired crucial cognitive prerequisites for language, such as the ability to make use of symbols.

PRODUCTION OF SPEECH SOUNDS. Between 3 and 6 months of age, roughly, infants begin to *babble*—that is, to make vocalizations that sound quite speech-like. Vintage babbling, complete with complex intonation patterns, sounds for all the world like fluent speech in a language you do not happen to know. Infants will usually continue to do some babbling even after they start producing words, at about 1 to 1½ years. There are good reasons to believe that at least the onset and early course of babbling are largely controlled by maturational factors rather than inputs from the external environment (cf. de Villiers & de Villiers, 1978). First, babies the world over begin to babble at about the same age, and their initial babbling sounds much alike from one speech community to another. Second, Lenneberg, Rebelsky, and Nichols (1965) have shown that infants doggedly begin to make the usual babbling sounds at the usual age even if those around them cannot hear and respond (deaf parents), and even if they cannot hear themselves babble (deaf infants). Finally, there seems to be no evidence that one can change the kinds of sounds young babblers produce by modeling or selective reinforcement (de Villiers and de Villiers, 1978, pp. 36–37).

The period of babbling certainly seems like it ought to constitute a crucial first step in language development. For instance, it might be a preparatory period in which infants perfect the ability to produce the speech sounds they will need to make when, at a later period, they become developmentally ready to produce words. However, the existing evidence for any such clear-cut and straightforward developmental continuity between babbling and genuine speech is surprisingly thin (e.g., Clark & Clark, 1977; de Villiers & de Villiers, 1978; Maratsos, 1976).

Some scientists used to believe, for example, that infants begin by babbling all the different speech sounds found in all human languages. Later on, through differential social reinforcement or some similar mechanism, they gradually stop producing those speech sounds they do not hear in their speech communities and continue to practice and perfect those they do hear. But the research evidence now suggests that infants do not come even close to babbling all the world's speech sounds. This naturally implies that there will normally be a good number of speech sounds in whatever specific language they do learn that they will never have practiced during the babbling period, and the research evidence supports this implication. Interestingly, the converse also turns out to be true: Young children may later prove incapable of producing, when deliberately trying to utter a particular word, a speech sound that they have frequently (but probably nondeliberately) produced in their idle babbling. Some children may even stop babbling altogether just before starting to produce words, "as though to mark the discontinuity" (Maratsos, 1976, p. 8). Finally, there are some odd differences between the developmental courses of babbling and word production. For instance, back-of-the-mouth consonants like "k" and "g" tend to be produced earlier in the babbling period than front ones like "t" and "b," whereas the opposite is true in the case of word production.

Nonetheless, it is hard to imagine why ever there should exist a universal and extended period of babbling if it did not serve *some* vital role in the development of speech-production ability. However, perhaps we should rest content with Clark and Clark's (1977) moderate conclusion on the matter, at least until such time as there may be clear evidence for a stronger, more direct and specific developmental relation:

> Neither continuity nor discontinuity fully accounts for the facts. The relation between babbling and speech is probably an indirect one. For example, experience with babbling could be a necessary preliminary to gaining articulatory control of certain organs in the mouth and vocal tract. Babbling would give children practice in producing sequences of sounds and in adding a melodic contour—intonation—to those sequences. If babbling simply provided exercise for the vocal apparatus, there would be little reason to expect any connection between the sounds produced in babbling and those produced later on (but see Oller et al., 1976). Still there is at least some discontinuity. Mastery of some phonetic segments only begins when children start to use their first words (pp. 390–391).

The story of phonological development from the one-word-utterance period on is a fascinating one, but too complex and detailed to recount here.

Like other aspects of language development, it appears to involve an active search by the child for dependable rules and regularities (Clark & Clark, 1977; de Villiers & de Villiers, 1978). The child often acts as if she were testing and revising hypotheses or hunches about how various types of words should be pronounced. She also acts as if she were using various simplifying principles or strategies for getting as close to her articulatory target as her available articulatory programs permit. For example, consonant clusters like the "st" in "step" are at first consistently simplified to reasonable but more phonologically manageable approximations, like "tep."

Cognitive Development

COGNITIVE PREREQUISITES FOR LANGUAGE ACQUISITION. It seems very likely that some cognitive acquisitions serve as developmental underpinnings for some language acquisitions (Brown, 1973; Clark, 1983; Dale, 1976; de Villiers & de Villiers, 1978; Slobin, 1979; see also Chapter 2). Perhaps the most important cognitive prerequisite for language acquisition is Piaget's semiotic or symbolic function—that is, the acquired ability to use one thing to refer to and mean something else. Piaget believed that this capacity for symbolic representation is expressed in such late-infancy phenomena as object permanence, deferred imitation, and symbolic play (Chapter 2). This same capacity should also make possible the use of words and sentences to express meanings and make reference—especially regarding nonpresent objects and experiences. Another important part of linguistic competence is the ability to use language instrumentally—that is, to get others to do what you want them to by making verbal requests or demands. An acquired conception of human beings as possible causal intermediaries, means, or "tools" for achieving desired goals may undergird this competence (Bates, 1976).

It is also necessary to have acquired knowledge before one can express that knowledge in language. In Dale's (1976) words, "the child can talk about only what he knows" (p. 154). Clark (1983) argues that young children acquire knowledge of *objects* (things and substances), *situations* (states, processes, and events), and *properties* (shape, size, position, etc.) and subsequently learn how to express much of this knowledge in their native languages. Similarly, in view of what children have learned during the sensory-motor period: "It does not seem surprising that the child's earliest sentences are about agents, the actions they perform, the objects on which they act, and the locations of persons and objects" (Dale, 1976, p. 154).

Hypothetical statements represent a particularly compelling instance of how language acquisitions may await and depend upon cognition advances (de Villiers & de Villiers, 1978, pp. 224–225). Sentences like "If you hit me I'm gonna hit you back." tend to appear later in the child's speech than their purely grammatical complexity would lead us to expect (Cromer, 1974). In Russian, similarly, hypotheticals are very simple grammatically but appear late (Slobin, 1966). The probable reason is that they await the development of the intellectual ability to think of two future events, with one represented as causally dependent on the occurrence of the other—not surprisingly, a rather late-emerging ability.

PROBLEMS IN IDENTIFYING PREREQUISITES FOR LANGUAGE ACQUISITION. The identification of prerequisites for language development is not as straight-forward and uncontroversial a matter as I have made it seem, however. For an excellent discussion of its complexities and perplexities, see Harris (1983). A comparison between children and chimpanzees illustrates some of these difficulties.

Chimps appear to possess the sorts of cognitive skills and knowledge described previously, including considerable symbolic capacity (e.g., Premack & Woodruff, 1978). Moreover, it is now well known that they are capable of some language-like acquisitions (e.g., Slobin, 1979). However, they have not yet been shown capable of acquiring the specific kinds of rich and complex grammatical systems that all human languages possess—and that all normal human children spontaneously acquire. Moreover, learning and using even rudimentary languages is obviously not what chimps were born to do. One has to train them long and carefully to engender any language learning and then continually reinforce them with material rewards to main-tain language use (Slobin, 1979). In dramatic contrast, draconian measures would be needed to *prevent* most children from learning to talk and from continually expressing the language they have learned in incessant chatter.

What accounts for the difference? Do children have and chimpanzees lack some propensity and capacity that is exclusively and specifically human-natural-language-like in nature? Is it something more cognitive and social than linguistic, such as an abiding thirst to learn about the world and an irrepressi-ble need to articulate and communicate that knowledge to ourselves and others (cf. Slobin, 1979, pp. 141–142)? My guess is that both kinds of posses-sions undergird and impel language development of the human kind, but it can only be a guess in our present state of knowledge. There is a great deal we still do not know about the prerequisites and instigators of human language development (see the later section *Explaining Grammatical Development*).

LANGUAGE ASSISTANCE IN COGNITIVE GROWTH. Linguistic abilities and experiences also facilitate cognitive acquisitions—a very large and complex topic I do not venture into here. To cite only one example, Clark and Clark (1977) describe how the acquisition of a well-differentiated specialized vocabulary can assist the learning of a complex subject matter. They cite (Clark & Clark, 1977) as an example the role of acquiring anatomical terms in the acquisition of surgical knowledge and suggest a parallel in the child's development:

> The education of the surgeon may be compared to the education of children as they develop into adults. The "highly specialized" language they hear is really a distillation of generations of human experience, and this knowledge is most effectively transmitted to children through this "adult jargon." The process is cumulative. Learning new words enables children to conquer new areas of knowledge, and these new areas enable them to learn new words, and so on. Thus, a well-differentiated vocabulary may be a crucial aid to children in becoming "experts"—adults (p. 555).

Communicative Development

EARLY COMMUNICATION SKILLS. Children have already acquired some communicative skills by the time they start learning to talk, and these skills continue to serve them when their interchanges with others become linguistic (e.g., Bates, 1976; Bruner, 1975; Clark & Clark, 1977; Shatz, 1983). These same communicative (pragmatic, discourse) competencies may also help children learn the grammatical structures of their languages, although this possibility is currently in dispute (Cromer, 1980; Stevenson, 1980).

Preverbal infants learn how to attract and maintain other people's attention to themselves and to physically present objects or events. One way they do this unintentionally is simply by looking, either at the people or at the objects. The people can then "read" their gaze directions and attend accordingly, either to them or to the objects to which they are attending. Children can terminate interactions by averting their gazes from the people, as well as initiate them by making eye contact with them. They can similarly engage and direct other people's attention by vocal and manual actions, such as cries and points. Conversely, they become able to respond appropriately to other people's attention-directing actions—that is, they gradually acquire the abilities to look where they are looking or pointing, rather than merely staring at their eyes or fingers (e.g., Butterworth & Jarret, 1980; Lempers et al., 1977).

Infants also become capable of more than just directing and reading others' attention. They also seem to acquire early, preverbal forms of two basic speech acts: *requesting* and *asserting* (Bates, 1976; Bates, Camaioni, & Volterra, 1975; Bruner, 1975). Requests for objects that are out of reach may be made by urgent and insistent open-handed reaching out towards the objects, often accompanied by heart-rending calls or whines and beseeching looks at their would-be adult "tools." If you have ever been the recipient of this communicative package you know that it has "REQUEST!" written all over it.

The nonverbal precursors of verbal assertions look quite different. Infants see objects that interest them and they touch them, hold them up and show them, or point to them. In the clearest, easiest-to-interpret cases, the touching is a one-finger pointing-like affair that is not followed by picking up, the object showing is not followed by object giving, and the pointing is done with hand closed and index finger extended, not at all like the open-handed request. In addition, the manual gestures are accompanied by looks at the other people, perhaps to make sure that they also see the interesting objects. However, these gestures do not usually shout "ASSERTION!" the way the other ones shout "REQUEST!" The cognition underlying a pointing gesture may indeed be an assertion (something roughly like "That's an X." or "There goes something."). But it may also or instead be a question ("What's that?") or even a request ("Look at that!"). It may not even have any communicative intent at all—that is, the child may not know or care whether others attend to her pointing gesture. There is always the danger of reading more into the child's communicative act than is there, or even of misreading it entirely. As is shown later, the same problem arises at all levels of language acquisition: Should our interpretations of the child's language competence be "lean" or "rich" (Brown, 1973, pp. 63–64)? For example, should we interpret the young child's one-word utterances as having the force and meaning of full sentences? Similarly, are we justified in reading grammatical structure, and hence acquired grammatical knowledge, into the child's two-word utterances? As Clark and Clark (1977, p. 314) have pointed out, however, the hypothesis that preverbal gestures request and (perhaps) assert is also supported by the fact that children later accompany their verbal requests and assertions with these same reaching and pointing gestures. And even without any accompanying words, nonverbal communicative intentions are sometimes as clear as can be. For instance, an infant I know wanted his father to turn on a light switch that was too high for him to reach. He requested the action with one hand (rapid opening and closing of fingers) while simultaneously asserting the identity and location of the object of this requested action with the other (index finger outstretched and immobile, pointed directly at the switch).

Finally, in addition to knowing how to send and receive isolated nonverbal messages, young children know something about how to behave in a continuing nonverbal dialogue, involving an alternating sequence of communicative sending and receiving. For example, they are likely to have learned how to take turns in peek-a-boo games or other ritualized interactional routines. This skill will serve them well later, when they begin to engage in verbal conversations.

ONE-WORD UTTERANCES

Children usually begin to produce their first words sometime around 10 to 13 months of age. Then, as later, they may understand words that they do not yet produce themselves. Although the number of words they know of course increases during subsequent months, their utterances continue for some time to consist of only single words—hence the title of a book about this developmental period, *One Word at a Time* (Bloom, 1973). Children's first words often refer to things that the children themselves can act on (Dale, 1976, pp. 8–9), and more generally, to objects and events that are salient, familiar, and important to them in their everyday lives. In our society, at least, first words often denote family members (e.g., "Mama"), animals ("dog"), vehicles ("car"), toys ("ball"), edibles ("juice"), salient body parts ("eye"), items of clothing ("hat"), and household implements ("cup"); there may also be a greeting word ("hi") and a few action or other terms ("up," "more," "that") (Clark, 1983). Objects and events tend to be named at those levels of abstraction or generality that are most functionally useful for children, usually intermediate levels (Anglin, 1977; Brown, 1958). For example, "dog" will be learned before "spaniel" (less general) and "animal" (more general) because it is more useful for children to distinguish dogs from other animals than spaniels from other dogs or animals from nonanimals.

ONE-WORD SENTENCES? There has been considerable debate about what mental content the young child might be trying to convey in her single-word utterances—that is, about exactly what meanings she might be trying to express linguistically when she produces these utterances (e.g., Bloom, 1973; Brown, 1973; Dale, 1976; de Villiers & de Villiers, 1978; Greenfield & Smith,

1976). One interpretation—the "rich" one mentioned in the previous section—is that she has something very like a full sentence in mind but uses a single word to express it. This mental, unspoken sentence might contain an additional word or two beyond the one uttered or it might not. However, the child cannot produce an utterance longer than one word because of cognitive and/or linguistic immaturities. According to this interpretation, then, many of the child's one-word utterances are really one-word sentences (sometimes called *holophrases*). To illustrate, suppose the child points to her father's pipe and says "Daddy." If "Daddy" is interpreted as a holophrase, the underlying mental sentence it expresses might be "That is Daddy's pipe."

It would take more pages than I can spare to elaborate the arguments and evidence for and against existing variations of this interpretation. Indeed, even the precise meaning and implications of one-word-sentence positions are elusive; as Dale (1976) says, "It is very difficult to be more precise about this notion" (pp. 13–14). It should be said, however, that the child in the foregoing example could have meant less than "That is Daddy's pipe." The pipe might have simply called Daddy to mind, with this mental event then automatically calling "Daddy" to mouth. An older child who could actually say this whole sentence has probably acquired the concepts of "possessor" and "possessed." Such a child has probably also acquired the specifically linguistic knowledge that the semantic relation between possessors and the things they possess can be unambiguously conveyed in language by such grammatical devices as inflections ("Daddy's"), intonation (stress on "Daddy" rather than "pipe"), and word order ("Daddy" said before "pipe"). Saying only "Daddy," therefore, does not prove that one has a *sentence* in mind, under any reasonable linguistic definition of that term.

Does the child mean *anything* more than the lonely word she says aloud? Quite likely, and perhaps increasingly so as she nears the end of the one-word-utterance period (Gardner, 1978, pp. 166–167; Greenfield & Smith, 1976). An excessively lean and stingy interpretation of the young child's expressive powers should be avoided as much as an excessively rich one. The boy who pushes his empty glass in your face and shouts "Milk!" is surely doing more than just associating a word with a familiar liquid. De Villiers and de Villiers (1978) semilean position seems about right until we learn more:

> It would seem prudent, until further evidence is forthcoming, to conclude that while the child *does* know more than the single words he speaks, this knowledge has no clear linguistic manifestation beyond the word uttered. We do not gain by saying that the single word stands for a whole sentence. However, the child at this stage can use his single words in combination with gestures and possibly intonation to serve a variety of pragmatic goals. In this way he communicates his desire for an object, makes queries or demands, and labels objects and events (Dore, 1974) (de Villiers & de Villiers, 1978, p. 52).

THE MEANINGS OF CHILDREN'S FIRST WORDS. When first learning a new word, the child may not use it to refer to exactly the same objects or events an adult would (e.g., Clark, 1983; de Villiers & de Villiers, 1978; Harris, 1983). A common and easily observed referential error is *overextension*. For example, a child might initially overextend "cat" by applying it not only to cats, but to other animals as well. Words are often overextended to objects that are perceptually similar to the words' correct referents, and sometimes also to objects that are functionally similar—for example, those that can be acted on in the same way by the child (Clark, 1983). Clark (1973) formulated an interesting theory to account for the appearance and subsequent correction of such errors. According to this theory, for adults a word's meaning is made up of a set of component features or properties that serve to distinguish its meaning from those of other words. For instance, the meaning components of "cat" might comprise the features "animate," "four legs," "soft fur," "whiskers," "meows," and so on. When a child first starts trying to learn how to apply this word, he is apt to notice only a small subset of the adult set of features. For example, he may only notice that it applies to animates with four legs, and hence he overextends it to other animals besides cats. With subsequent experience, he adds the missing features and thereby achieves the adult meaning of the term.

As often happens with clearly formulated, testable theories, Clark's theory stimulated a lot of good research which told us important new things about semantic development—and largely discredited the theory *en passant*. (Clark herself currently advocates a quite different theory of semantic development—see Clark, 1983.) The research showed that young children make other types of referential errors that Clark's original theory would not predict.

They sometimes *underextend* word meanings instead of overextending them. For instance, a child may initially apply "cat" only to cats seen out the window, rather than to all cats, let alone all animals. That child's problem is to get rid of an unneeded semantic feature ("seen out the window") rather than, as the theory would have it, to accumulate needed ones.

Also troublesome for the theory are unstable, *complexive* word meanings (Bowerman, 1977). Here, the child seems to shift from one feature or set of features to another when using the same word in different situations, with there being no single feature that all objects named by that word have in common. As a striking example (de Villiers & de Villiers, 1979), the de Villiers' son Nicholas successively applied the family dog's name to other dogs, to all animals and birds, to various other furry or cuddly objects, and even to a salad with black and shiny pitted olives reminiscent of the dog's nose! In fact, the correct referents of most words we use do not share tight, exclusive bundles of features or properties (Rosch & Mervis, 1975). For example, try to think of a set of properties that everything we would call a "chair" has and that everything we would not call a "chair" does not have. (How about a bean bag "chair" versus a stuffed "footstool," for openers?) In this respect, the child's complexes somewhat resemble adult word meanings.

Another problem for Clark's (1973) theory is that the early overextensions it was designed to explain are much less evident in young children's comprehension of words spoken by others than in their own production of words. This is part of a general tendency for children's language comprehension to be more advanced than their language production. Thus, the same child who calls many round objects "ball" is likely to have no trouble at all correctly picking out a ball from an array of round objects when asked to "find the *ball*." If the child knows the word as well as this informal comprehension test suggests, why does she overextend it in production (Clark, 1983; Harris,

1983)? She may have learned that this round object is called "apple" but, unable to recall that word on a particular occasion (perhaps it is not yet well learned), she produces a word that the apple's shape does call to mind: "ball." Alternatively, she may not yet have learned "apple" at all; however, trying to find some name to apply to this interesting object, she comes up with the most appropriate name she can think of: again, "ball." Both possibilities suggest a way that initial overextensions might diminish (see Harris, 1983): The child learns and uses other (correct) words for those objects and events that were originally mislabeled via overextension, and the use of these new labels automatically prevents the old, overextended words from occurring. A new word becomes king of the hill, so to speak, and takes up all the space on the summit.

TWO-WORD UTTERANCES

Around 18 months of age, children's single-word utterances begin to be joined by two-word and sometimes even longer expressions. Parents start to hear the likes of "put book," "mommy sock," and "more milk." Just before genuine two-word utterances appear, parents may hear two one-word utterances produced close together in time—for instance, "mommy" (pause) "sock" (Bloom, 1973). The utterances of young children the world over have a "telegraphic speech" quality (Brown, 1973). Much like telegrams, they tend to omit the small and communicatively less essential words, such as articles (e.g., "the"), conjunctions ("and"), auxiliary verbs ("can," "will"), and prepositions ("on"). Two-word utterances also seldom contain any morphological inflections (e.g., progressive "-ing," as in "going," plural "-s").

Moreover, there appears to be considerable universality in the meanings young children try to express in their two-word utterances. The research evidence presently available suggests that these meanings are likely to be very similar in different languages the world over: "If you ignore word order and read through transcriptions of two word utterances in the various languages we have studied, the utterances read like direct translations of one another" (Slobin, 1970, p. 177).

What are these early meanings? Brown (1973) carefully reviewed developmental data from a number of languages and suggested that the majority of two-word utterances seem to express any of eight semantic relations: *agent-action* (e.g., "mommy kiss"); *action-object* ("hit ball"); *agent-object* ("mommy doll," when the child wants her mother to do something with the doll); *action-locative* ("sit chair"); *entity-locative* ("cup table"); *possessor-possession* ("daddy car"); *entity-attributive* ("big car"); and *demonstrative-entity* ("that car"). Two-word utterances also seem to express meanings like *recurrence* ("more milk") and *nonexistence* ("allgone milk"). It is now clearer than it was in the one-word-utterance period that the child must be expressing meaning relations in her speech.

Two things remain unclear, however (cf. Braine, 1976; Clark & Clark, 1977, pp. 307–310; de Villiers & de Villiers, 1978, pp. 75–82; Maratsos, 1983). First, do abstract and highly general expressions like *possessor-possessed* accurately capture what the young child knows and is trying to convey in his two-word utterances? His knowledge might be much more concrete, narrow, and context-specific than such categorizations suggest. Perhaps all he really knows is that the big person he calls "daddy" is frequently seen inside the interesting object he calls "car." Or perhaps he has the somewhat more advanced notion that he and his older sister both have things they will not let others take away from them ("*my* doll!"). Or perhaps one utterance classified as expressing a *possessor-possessed* meaning is actually expressing mere association, another a primitive concept of "*mine!*", another something else— and none of them anything very close to the abstract and general adult concept of "possession." *Possessor-possessed* may be too rich an interpretation of what the child knows and is trying to express in language.

It is also unclear to what extent children in this period should be credited with grammatical knowledge. If a child consistently said "pat daddy" when she was patting her father and "daddy pat" when he was doing the patting, and did the same for all other action-object and actor-action expressions, we could credit her with some grammatical knowledge: She would be exploiting the purely grammatical device of differential word ordering (syntax) to signal differences in intended meaning. The words are the same in both utterances; only the word order discriminates them. Some young children do seem to make use of this syntactical device in their two-word utterances. Likewise, in this period children can often use word order as a clue to meaning when listening to the speech of others (de Villiers & de Villiers, 1973b). For some children, however, evidence for the systematic use of word order to signal differences in meaning is less compelling. And there is no good evidence that children in this period have any kind of grasp of such abstract, purely grammatical categories as "subject of the sentence" and "direct object of the main verb" (Braine, 1976; de Villiers & de Villiers, 1978, pp. 78–81; Maratsos, 1983).

LATER DEVELOPMENTS

Grammatical Development

As the child's sentences become longer, morphological inflections are added to words and the syntactic use of word order to specify sentence meaning becomes unmistakable. The child's sentences also begin to exhibit the hierarchical grammatical structure so characteristic of human language. In the four-word child sentence "Big dog run home," for instance, "Big dog" is one main sentence constituent (called a *noun phrase*), "run home" is another (*verb phrase*), and the syntax of English demands that the two be produced in that order. However, each of these main constituents also has lower-level constituents nested within it (hence, "hierarchical") that must also be produced in the order given: "Big" before "dog," "run" before "home." As in the passage from one-word utterances to two-word ones, transitional forms are sometimes seen. For instance, the child might say "Go nursery" and then immediately afterwards crank it up to "Lucy go nursery" (Maratsos, 1976, p. 9).

THE ORDERED DEVELOPMENT OF GRAMMATICAL MORPHEMES. The acquisition of what Brown (1973) calls "*grammatical morphemes*" makes an interesting developmental story. These morphemes consist of the little function words and inflections that "tune" or "modulate" (Brown, 1973, p. 253) the meanings associated with the major content words like nouns, verbs, and adjectives. For example, adding the grammatical morpheme "-ed" on the end of "push" to make "pushed" modulates or qualifies the verb's meaning by indicating that the pushing action (the main meaning expressed) occurred in the past (modulation of that main meaning). The presence of these morphemes in the child's sentence makes the sentences seem more adult-like, less telegraphic. Brown (1973) made an intensive developmental study of fourteen grammatical morphemes. They included three "-s" inflections: the plural ("dogs"), the possessive ("dog's"), and the third-person singular verb ending ("runs"). They also included the present progressive ("-ing") and past ("-ed") inflections, the prepositions "in" and "on," the articles "the" and "a," various forms of "be," both when used as an auxiliary verb ("I *was* going home") and as a main verb ("I *was* home"), plus several other morphemes. The reason the developmental story here is interesting is the remarkable finding (Brown, 1973; de Villiers & de Villiers, 1973a) that all young children tend to master these fourteen morphemes in the same fixed sequence. For example, although the three "-s" inflections are identical phonologically, children almost always acquire the plural earliest, the possessive later, and the verb inflection later still.

Why a constant order of development, and why the particular constant order found? Perhaps how often children hear these morphemes in their parents' speech explains the order of their acquisition. Morphemes frequently modeled by parents offer more learning opportunities for the child and therefore might be acquired first. Although this explanation seems reasonable, the available evidence suggests that it is wrong: The frequency of occurrence of these morphemes in parental speech to children and their order of appearance in children's speech seem to be essentially uncorrelated (Brown, 1973). The favored explanation at this writing is that one or another type of cognitive-processing complexity determines the acquisitional sequence (Brown, 1973; Tolbert, 1980). An example involving semantic complexity shows how this explanation works (de Villiers & de Villiers, 1978). To use "was" correctly the child has to take into account the person of the subject ("I" and "he/she" can precede "was" but "you" cannot), the number of the subject (e.g., singular "I" but not plural "we"), and when the event happened (in the past rather than in the present or future). In contrast, to use the verb ending "-ed" correctly the child has to take into account only one of these three factors—when the event happened. The correct use of "was" can therefore be interpreted as a more complex cognitive achievement than the correct use of "-ed," because the user must not only keep track of time of occurrence, but also person and number. Accordingly, "-ed" should be mastered before "was" and other forms of "be," and it is. Similar analyses of complexity lead to correct developmental-order predictions of the other grammatical morphemes. How well such analyses of the differing information-processing requirements of different linguistic acts can explain other acquisitional sequences in language development remains to be seen.

THE CHILD AS HYPOTHESIS TESTER AND RULE LEARNER—THE ACQUISITION OF INFLECTIONS. The past-tense inflection "-ed" is one of innumerable illustrations of the important fact that to master the grammatical structure of one's native language is to acquire a rich network of implicit, functional rules. Adding "-ed" to verbs to indicate past occurrence is a simple but very general rule of English that we have all acquired. There is a big dictionary next to me as I write these words. A moment ago I opened it at random and found a verb I never heard of before—"hackle"—which has the somewhat chilling meaning "to mangle while hacking." If I wanted to talk about the mangling while hacking I did yesterday I would of course say "hackled," as would you. "Hackled" was generated by our internalized system of grammatical rules; it was obviously not a new, rote-learned linguistic item for us, unlike the root verb "hackle" itself.

It is, therefore, a striking fact about human languages that they are strongly rule governed. What is even more striking, however, is that young children seem to expect them to be strongly rule governed. They are constantly on the qui vive for rules and regularities in every corner of language—in grammar, phonology, semantics, and pragmatics or communication. They act as if they are constantly forming and testing hypotheses about the lawful and systematic properties of their language. They learn by rote when they must, but learn by rule when they can. More than that, they often resist learning by rote when they must—that is, they try to apply rules to irregular, nonrule-governed forms in the language.

Young children's deep-seated and abiding penchant for finding order in language—even when there is not any—is nowhere more striking than in the acquisition of inflections (e.g., Ervin, 1964; Kuczaj, 1977). For instance, the child may begin by using the irregular plural form "feet" as a rote-learned vocabulary item. Then, having discovered the plural "-s" rule and using it to make "dogs," "boys," and so on, she may start alternating "foots" or even "feets" with "feet." Later, having learned the likes of "kisses" and "horses," she may even try "footses" for a while before finally reinstating "feet" as the only plural of "foot." Another developmental sequence that makes the same point is first "went," then "goed" or "went," and finally "went" again.

> Their exuberance in applying these rules even leads sometimes to the production of forms like *footses, broked, breakded,* or *thoughted* (as in *I thoughted you eated mine*), where the forms are marked and then marked once more for good measure (Maratsos, 1976, p. 10).

It is obvious that these strange forms could not possibly be rote parrotings of adult utterances. What adult ever said "breakded" to his child? Rather, they are reasonable—creative, actually—overgeneralizations of grammatical rules that are in process of acquisition. Such overgeneralizations are not limited to young learners of English. Children the world over exhibit the same predilection for hypothesis testing and rule discovery in their grammatical acquisition. And, as indicated earlier, the search for systematicity is not limited to grammar. In the area of semantic development, for instance, children may invent "tomorrow day" and "yesternight" in analogy with "tomorrow night" and "yesterday," respectively (Maratsos, 1976).

NEGATION AND QUESTIONS. Other grammatical acquisitions may also proceed according to a fixed and sensible-looking sequence of developmental steps (e.g., Clark & Clark, 1977, Chapter 9; de Villiers & de Villiers, 1978, Chapter 4). For example, children usually begin to express negation by shaking their heads or saying "no." Next, they simply attach "no" or "not" to whatever utterance they want to negate—for example, "No mitten" or "Wear mitten no." This primitive syntactic rule of merely attaching a negative marker to whatever is to be negated is also an initial developmental step in languages in which the full negation system differs appreciably from that of English. Perhaps it is a near-universal first step because its cognitive processing demands are so low. The next developmental step for young English speakers is to insert the negative word inside the sentence, in front of the verb it negates. "No I go" now gives way to "I no go" or "I not go." Then, as the child gradually learns how to use auxiliary verbs correctly (a complicated enterprise in English), grammatically correct negative sentences like "He won't bite me." and "Mary isn't coming." become more frequent. However, the more subtle and tricky aspects of negation in English may continue to give children trouble for some time, resulting in sentences like "No one didn't come in." and "I didn't see something" (Clark & Clark, 1977, pp. 350–351).

The developmental sequence is somewhat similar for so-called *wh* questions—those beginning with "where," "what," "why," and so on. At first, the question word is simply tacked onto the front end of an unmodified affirmative, as in early negations. One hears "What Mommy doing?" and later, when auxiliary verbs are used, "What Mommy is doing?" Still later, the child correctly inverts subject and auxiliary verb to produce "What is Mommy doing?"; "Where are we going?"; and so on. However, more complicated interrogatives still present difficulties. When asking negative questions, for instance, the child may fail to invert subject and auxiliary and thus produce questions like "Why you aren't going?"

OTHER GRAMMATICAL ACQUISITIONS. Needless to say, children acquire a functional command of many other grammatical rules and rule systems during the early- and middle-childhood years. For example, they learn how to relate sentences and clauses to one another to form more intricate sentences, just as they earlier learned how to relate individual words to one another to make simple sentences (Dale, 1976, p. 112; de Villiers & de Villiers, 1979, pp. 72–76). They become able to coordinate two sentences or sentence parts and embed one within another. Following are some examples, with one of the two related sentence parts italicized: "Billy ran *and so did I.*" "If you hit me *I'll hit you back.*" "The man *who fixed the fence* went home." "I don't want *you to use my bike.*" and "I asked him *what to do.*" In fact, the whole foregoing sentence itself represents an extremely complex case in point. If you tried to write a system of rules of sentence production that would always generate grammatically correct English sentences of these complicated types and never generate any grammatically incorrect ones, you would better appreciate what a prodigious, almost unbelievable cognitive accomplishment the child's acquisition of grammar is. Those who try to do it for their living tend to be downright awestruck when they contemplate human grammatical development (see the later section *Explaining Grammatical Development*).

Semantic Development

Considerable research has been done on the acquisition of word meanings beyond the earliest stages of language development (e.g., Clark, 1983; Clark & Clark, 1977; Dale, 1976; de Villiers & de Villiers, 1978). Most of it has focused on relational words that are semantically linked to one another to form contrasting pairs or larger semantic systems. Some examples are spatial and temporal opposites like "big" and "little," "here" and "there," "before" and "after"; kinship terms like "brother," "mother," "grandmother," and so on; and verbs of possession and transfer, such as "give," "trade," and "sell." The hope has been that we will learn something about processes of semantic development by finding interpretable regularities in the order in which the members of a semantic system are mastered, and by finding revealing errors of comprehension prior to mastery.

A study by Gentner (1975) illustrates this strategy. Gentner divided verbs of possession and transfer into three groups based on their semantic complexity. The semantic analysis of these verbs given here is oversimplified, but it is faithful to the spirit of Gentner's analysis. "Give" and "take" include the meaning of the transfer of an object from one individual to another. "Pay" and "trade" include this meaning plus that of an obligation involving money ("pay") or of a mutual contract for the exchange of goods ("trade"). "Buy," "sell," and "spend" include all three of these meanings: transfer of possession, an obligation involving money, and a mutual contract (to exchange an object for money). Notice that we have here an inclusion relation based on cognitive complexity similar to that said to obtain among Brown's (1973) grammatical morphemes; for instance, "give" includes meaning component X, "pay" includes X plus Y, and "buy" includes X plus Y plus Z. Children of 3 to 8 years of age were asked to make two dolls act out sentences containing these terms—for example, "Make Bert sell a car to Ernie." Gentner (1975) predicted and found that the developmental order of mastery of these terms nicely paralleled their order of semantic complexity. Moreover, the children's comprehension errors indicated that they often processed more complex terms as if they were simpler ones. For instance, they would act out "buy" as if it meant "take," and "sell" as if it meant "give." It is, of course, possible that children's relative inexperience with buying and selling transactions (as opposed to giving and taking) is responsible for the obtained order of mastery. A number of other studies also suggest that semantic complexity may be an important determinant of the order in which word meanings are acquired. There appear to be other important determinants of the what, when, and how of word-meaning acquisitions, but their story is too lengthy and controversial to go into here (e.g., see Anglin, 1977; Carey, 1978; Clark, 1983; de Villiers & de Villiers, 1978, Chapter 5; Richards, 1979).

Communicative Development

COMMUNICATION SKILLS. As their cognitive and linguistic development progress, children acquire a wealth of knowledge and skill in the social-communicative uses of language (e.g., Asher, 1979; Clark & Clark, 1977; de Villiers & de Villiers, 1978; Dickson, 1981; Shatz, 1983). They learn how to converse as well as to talk—that is, how to maintain focus on a single topic during an extended verbal interchange with another person. They gradually become able to go beyond the here, the now, and the real in what they converse about. They gain command of new and cognitively more advanced types of speech acts (Clark & Clark, 1977, pp. 364–367). For instance, they eventually find out that language can be used not only to assert, request, and question, but also to express psychological states ("I'm sorry"), to commit oneself to future actions ("I promise I'll come"), and even to bring about new states of affairs by verbal declarations ("I quit").

Children learn that what is really meant by an utterance often goes beyond or even differs from what is literally said. They become able to infer what is implied and presupposed but not stated explicitly, an absolutely essential skill for comprehending ordinary discourse. For example, they learn that a statement such as "That's not a cat." does more than explicitly deny that some creature is a feline; it also implicitly presupposes that someone thought or said it *was* a cat. One does not normally deny what nobody has asserted. Similarly, they discover that an utterance that sounds like one kind of speech act may really be another in disguise. For instance, children early discover that the assertion "My, it is noisy in here." and the question "Why are we so noisy today?" are really adult euphemisms for the request "Please be quieter."

Children also learn to adapt their speech production and comprehension to numerous properties of the speakers, the listeners, and the social settings in which the speech occurs. They discover that the referents of certain words depend upon who is speaking them—for example, "I" and "you," "my" and "your," "here" and "there," "this" and "that." "My cup" means the child's cup if the child says it, but her mother's cup if the mother says it. Likewise, recall that the correct use of the indefinite article "a" and definite article "the" requires keeping in mind what the listener knows. If the listener has not yet heard about some dog you have in mind, you should introduce it to her as "a dog." Once introduced in this way, you can and should refer to it thereafter as "the dog," and she will know exactly which dog you mean. Studies have shown that, whereas subjects of all ages correctly employ "the" once the referent has been introduced, young children will sometimes disregard the listener's lack of knowledge and use "the" rather than "a" when first mentioning the referent (e.g., Maratsos, 1974).

Children learn how to adapt the form and content of their speech to different listeners and different social situations. For instance, the child learns that he should usually be more polite and formal when his interlocutor is an adult rather than a peer, or a stranger rather than a friend or family member. We used to believe with Piaget that the young child communicates in an egocentric fashion, without adapting or tailoring his speech to the communication-relevant properties of his listener (Flavell et al., 1968; Glucksberg, Krauss, & Higgins, 1975). However, more recent developmental research in this and other areas of cognitive functioning suggests that we had underestimated the young child's capacity for nonegocentric thinking (e.g., Gelman, 1978). In the communication area, there have been several impressive demonstrations of nonegocentric-looking adaptation of young children's speech to listener characteristics and needs (e.g., Maratsos, 1973; Menig-Peterson, 1975; Shatz & Gelman, 1973). When a 4 year old tells a 2 year old rather than a peer or an adult about a toy, he is likely to "talk down" to his young listener—for example, use shorter utterances (Shatz & Gelman, 1973). Adult *A* and a preschooler are in room *X* (Menig-Peterson, 1975). Adult *A* "accidentally" spills a cup of juice on a tablecloth. The two discuss how best to clean it up and eventually do so. A week later the preschooler returns to room *X* with either adult *A* or supposedly naive adult *B*. The empty cup is present and the adult asks, "I wonder what that cup is doing there." and similar queries (if adult *B*), or "Look at that cup. Do you remember what happened when we were here before?" (if adult *A*). Menig-Peterson (1975) found that her preschool subjects appropriately varied their recounting of the spilling incident as a function of which adult was the listener. Other investigations have shown that even 2 year olds communicate with one another quite effectively (e.g., Wellman & Lempers, 1977).

METACOMMUNICATION. On the other hand, a number of recent studies have turned up some unexpected, even startling shortcomings in young children's thought and behavior in communication situations (Asher, 1979; Baker & Brown, 1984; Dickson, 1981; Flavell, 1981a; Flavell, Speer, Green, & August, 1981; Markman, 1977, 1981a; Patterson & Kister, 1981; Robinson, 1981a, 1981b; Robinson & Robinson, 1981; Whitehurst & Sonnenschein, 1981). Most of these studies bear on the child's knowledge and cognitive actions concerning communications—thus, on a type of metacognition or cognition-about-cognition (Brown, 1978; Flavell, 1979) sometimes referred to as *metacommunication* (Flavell, 1976).

The researchers have frequently used variations of the referential-communication task developed by Glucksberg and Krauss (Glucksberg et al., 1975). In one version of this task, the speaker and the listener cannot see one another but both know they have identical sets of objects in front of them. The speaker's task is to describe one of her objects specifically enough for her listener to identify its duplicate in his own set. Many of the young child's meta-communicative problems can be illustrated using this simple task situation.

Suppose the speaker's message is referentially ambiguous. For instance, suppose she says "Pick the red block" but there are two red blocks, one square and one round, in each person's set of objects. The research evidence suggests that a young child listener—age 5, say—would be less likely than an older one to show even minimal signs of detecting the ambiguity. He would be more apt than an older child to listen to the message, focus his attention on only one of the red blocks in front of him, and unhesitatingly pick that block. He should feel that he does not know which red block she means, one would think, but he does not appear to. Young children turn out to be surprisingly poor monitors of their own comprehension. They do not understand something but are often not aware that they do not understand it. A study by Markman (1977) dramatically illustrates young children's undeveloped comprehension monitoring skills. Six through 8 year olds were asked to evaluate the communicative adequacy of orally presented instructions for playing a game and performing a magic trick. Their task was to let the experimenter know of any omissions, unclarities, or suggested improvements in these instructions. Markman's instructions were blatantly inadequate—really atrocious. Nevertheless, the younger subjects, especially, were astonishingly poor at detecting these problems prior to actually trying to carry out the instructions. Thanks to such studies, the development of the disposition and ability to monitor one's own comprehension while listening or reading is currently emerging as an educationally significant research topic (e.g., Baker & Brown, 1984; Flavell, 1979).

Markman (1977, 1981a) suggests that one reason young children may not realize that they do not understand is that they do not process incoming information deeply and thoroughly enough to detect whatever comprehension problems the information may present. In the previously mentioned referential-communication task, similarly, they may not systematically inspect and compare all the objects in their set and therefore may not even notice that each of two objects could fit the speaker's description equally well.

Other metacommunicative immaturities may become apparent even if the young child does notice that two objects fit the speaker's description. If he does notice it, we may see him look properly uncertain and hesitant before settling on one of the two red blocks. However, this feeling of uncertainty is likely not to have the same meaning, importance, and implications for him that it would for an older child or adult. Thus, he probably will not ask the speaker to be more specific, even though he knows he may ask her questions at any time. Also, if asked if he is sure the block he chose is identical to the one the speaker had in mind, he is apt to say that he is sure it is. And finally, if asked whether the speaker or the speaker's message did a good or a poor job of telling him exactly which block to pick, he is very likely to say she or it did a good job (Beal & Flavell, 1982; Flavell et al., 1981).

Suppose it then becomes evident that the listener chose a different block than the speaker did; the child sees that the task outcome is a communication failure. Who is responsible? The Robinsons found that older children correctly blame the speaker and her inadequate message, whereas younger ones are likely to blame the listener and his incorrect block selection (e.g., Robinson & Robinson, 1981). Moreover, they are about equally likely to blame the listener no matter who is playing the listener role—for example, a doll or the experimenter rather than them. Moreover, children who blame the listener in this situation are less clear than children who blame the speaker about how to deliberately make the communicative quality of a message better or worse (Robinson, 1981b). They also are likelier to accept a disambiguated description of the block they have chosen (e.g., "Pick the red *square* block.") as being what the speaker had actually said, when what she actually had said was "Pick the red block" (Robinson, 1981b). Lastly, many studies have shown that young children are apt to produce ambiguous messages when in the speaker role (e.g., Asher, 1979), as well as respond to them in the curious ways just described when in the listener role.

Why do they respond in these curious ways? Here are some possible reasons, based on current thinking in the field (e.g., Flavell, 1976; Flavell et al., 1981; Patterson & Kister, 1981; Robinson, 1981b; Whitehurst & Sonnenschein, 1981). The most general reason may be that they are just not much given to thinking about and critically analyzing such intangible mental products as spoken messages. In this area as in others, the development of metacognitive dispositions and skills is simply not very far advanced. As a corollary, they tend not to understand as clearly as older children the seemingly obvious fact that the quality of a message affects communicative success. The listener's incorrect choice is a salient and recent event that the child may easily interpret as the cause of a communication failure; in contrast, the speaker's inadequate message may be generally less salient for young children, as already argued, and is also more temporally distant from the outcome. Finally, ambiguous, insufficiently specific messages may be particularly hard for young children to evaluate accurately. They may have learned that a speaker's message should refer to whatever the speaker has in mind, but may not have also learned that the message should refer to that *alone*—in other words, that it should not be referentially ambiguous. Consistent with this interpretation, Robinson and Robinson (1981) have found that if the young child sees that the message does not refer to what the speaker seems to have in mind (e.g., the speaker points to one block but "carelessly" names another), the child is in fact likely to judge it to be an inadequate message. In contrast, he may maintain that an ambiguous message is an adequate message even when its ambiguity has been made very apparent to him (Beal & Flavell, 1982; Singer & Flavell, 1981).

According to this account, then, the young child lacks crucial information and know-how regarding the nature of the communicative process (see Robinson, 1981a, 1981b; Robinson & Robinson, 1981). The Robinsons suggest that the young child may lack this knowledge because his everyday communicative experience may not provide it. Adults and peers may usually understand what he means to say well enough to permit the interaction to continue. And when other people do signal a communication problem, they may not do it explicitly enough to make it clear to the child that the cause of the problem lies in his utterance—if, indeed, any sense of "problem" is conveyed at all. "You didn't say which of the two red blocks you mean." explicitly calls attention to the child's message, whereas "Which block?" does not. However, the child undoubtedly receives the latter kind of inexplicit feedback much more often than the former kind. There is even a little evidence suggesting that parents who occasionally provide this sort of explicit feedback at home are likelier than those who do not to have children who, at age 6, correctly blame the speaker rather than the listener for communication failures caused by ambiguous messages (Robinson & Robinson, 1981). Providing such explicit feedback in laboratory settings has also proved effective in helping children better understand the communicative process (Robinson & Robinson, 1981). Similarly, the young child may seldom have experiences in the listener role that compel her to attend to and evaluate the communicative quality of messages. The message may induce feelings of uncertainty or lead to incorrect behavioral responses. However, the young child may either fail to construe these feelings or responses as problem indicators (they may in fact seldom be followed by negative consequences at this age), or else fail to locate their causal source in the message.

Perhaps experiences associated with formal schooling help children learn about the nature and management of communicative enterprises (Flavell et al., 1981). In school they may encounter more frequent and explicit demands to communicate clearly to others and to monitor the clarity and comprehensibility of the communications they receive. Experience in reading and writing may facilitate the development of metacommunication; unlike evanescent spoken messages, written ones "stay put" and remain accessible to the recipient for critical evaluation (cf. Donaldson, 1976; Olson, 1972). Nevertheless, school and other life experiences do not advance the child's metacognitive development as fast or as far as might be desirable, and there is a growing feeling that we should try to find ways to teach it more directly and systematically (e.g., Baker & Brown, 1984; Collins & Smith, 1982; Flavell, 1979, 1981a; Markman, 1981a; Robinson, 1981b). Obviously, the communicative and metacommunicative skills of most adults leave much to be desired.

EXPLAINING GRAMMATICAL DEVELOPMENT

We would naturally like to be able to explain development as well as describe it, and attempts have therefore been made to account for various types of acquisitions within the broad field of language and communication. Clark's (1973) proposed explanation of the acquisition of word meanings is an example cited earlier in this chapter. It is grammatical development that most of the field has been obsessed with explaining, however. If a Nobel Prize could be given in the field—only one, and only once—many developmental psycholinguists would want to save it for the genius who finally succeeds in explaining grammatical development. Why the great interest in how grammatical acquisition is accomplished? If you know something about the work of another genius, Noam Chomsky (e.g., 1972), you may already know the answer. Chomsky showed that to "know" a language as an adult native speaker does is to have a functional command of an exceedingly rich and intricate system of grammatical categories and rules. If our grammatical knowledge were a very simple, impoverished system, clearly evident in the speech we hear, then explaining its acquisition would not present much of a problem. However, almost everyone in the field today agrees with Chomsky's claim that the system is in fact incredibly vast and complex. Many also agree that clues to the underlying grammatical structure of sentences are often not present in the surface structure or external form of these sentences. These facts make the task of explaining grammatical development more intriguing— and much more difficult. Useful secondary sources on this topic include Clark and Clark (1977), Dale (1976), de Villiers and de Villiers (1978, 1979), Maratsos (1976, 1983), and Slobin (1979).

There are three key questions involved. First, what do children do to master the grammatical structures of their native languages? What specific cognitive operations do they carry out on language or language-relevant data, many times a day and year after year, such that they end up with adult commands of the systems? Second, what assistance in acquiring the systems do they get from the external environment? How much and what kind of help is provided by what other people do and say in their company? Finally, how much and what kind of innately given, biologically evolved, species-wide knowledge, skills, and dispositions must we assume they have when they begin the process of grammatical acquisition? What must they have and be like such that they are capable of doing what they do with the relevant input, and by doing it, eventually acquire the systems? The answers to these questions are interdependent. For instance, if it turned out that the environment provided a great deal of highly specific effective assistance, we would probably infer less, and less specific, innate equipment, and also different cognitive operations to do the learning.

The Role of the Environment

Let us first examine possible roles of the external environment, especially of what other people do and say. We can immediately reject the extreme—and absurd—possibility that the external environment plays no role whatever. For example, although all normal children are obviously capable of acquiring as a native language any human language to which they are exposed—witness the many, many different languages in the world—they just as obviously have to be exposed to that one to learn it. But is mere exposure enough? It seems not. There is some evidence to suggest that children will not acquire either a first or a second language merely from observing adults use it on television (Clark & Clark, 1977, pp. 329-340; de Villiers & de Villiers, 1979, pp. 103-106). It seems likely that children at least need some concrete social and linguistic interchanges with older children or adults to acquire language. However, exactly how much interaction they need, and of what kind and quality, is still unknown.

How about the other extreme? Perhaps very specific kinds of interactions are necessary for the acquisition of grammar. For example, maybe the child learns to speak like adults because his caretakers model grammatically correct sentences in their speech, he imitates these sentences, and his caretakers selectively reinforce for grammaticality these imitations and his other, spontaneous utterances. This view seems plausible on its face, and versions of it have been proposed in the past as theoretical explanations of grammatical acquisition. Nonetheless, the available evidence goes strongly counter to this extreme view, too. I mainly just list the objections; details and supporting evidence can be found in the previously mentioned secondary sources.

IMITATION. The evidence clearly shows that a great deal of grammatical learning can and does go on without benefit of sentence imitation. Some children hardly ever imitate adult sentences. Most children rarely imitate adult sentences after the early phases of grammatical acquisition, although of course they still continue to acquire many new grammatical rules. Children tend to show evidence of comprehending new grammatical forms before they produce them in their own speech—again, grammatical acquisition without benefit of imitation. The ultimate case of comprehension preceding production, and thus of imitationless grammatical acquisition, was an otherwise normal boy who was physically incapable of producing speech (Lenneberg, 1962). Even though he could never have imitated even a single English sentence, this boy achieved a good receptive command of English grammatical structure. Many childish expressions that appear to reflect the ongoing acquisition of grammatical rules are manifestly not literal imitations of anything their elders said. My favorite example is "I'm magic, amn't I?" Finally, just as grammatical learning can take place when imitation does not, so too can imitation occur when grammatical learning does not. That is, imitations often appear to reflect grammatical knowledge that has already been achieved by other means, rather than to mediate the acquisition of new grammatical knowledge. Altogether, the correlation between imitative activity and grammatical learning activity seems very low. And although correlation does not prove causation, lack of correlation certainly suggests lack of causation.

REINFORCEMENT. Selective reinforcement of grammatical versus ungrammatical utterances also does not seem to be a necessary or even an important shaper of grammatical development. It certainly did not shape that of Lenneberg's (1962) speechless boy. Even in normal children, parents tend to reinforce and correct on the basis of the truth value rather than the grammatical quality of their children's utterances. A mother who is curling her child's hair responds "That's right" to the child's ungrammatical "Her curling my hair." However, the grammatical but factually incorrect sentence "There's the animal farmhouse." gets a "No, that's *not* the animal farmhouse" (Brown & Hanlon, 1970; see Maratsos, 1976, p. 12). I love Brown, Cazden, and Bellugi's wry comment on this rather surprising finding: "Which renders mildly paradoxical the fact that the usual product of such a training schedule is an adult whose speech is highly grammatical but not notably truthful" (1969, p. 71). What about other possible reinforcements for speaking grammatically? For instance, perhaps happiness is being understood and getting what you want by learning to speak more grammatically. But Brown and Hanlon (1970) found that children's ungrammatical sentences seemed to be about as well understood and otherwise positively reinforced by their parents as their grammatical sentences were. It appears that "Her curl my hair." will bring as much parental understanding—and child happiness—as "She curls my hair."

OTHER POSSIBILITIES. Imitation and reinforcement are not the only possible forms of environmental assistance, however. Studies have shown that adults talk to young children in ways that look like they could aid the children's grammatical acquisition. They tend to use simple, short, grammatically correct sentences that refer to present objects and events, exaggerated sentence intonation and stress, pauses between sentences, and partial or complete repetitions of sentences said earlier in the interaction by child or adult (e.g., de Villiers & de Villiers, 1979, p. 99). Such talk has been dubbed "motherese," but mothers are not its only practitioners: As indicated earlier, even 4 year olds will "talk down" to 2 year olds (Shatz & Gelman, 1973). In addition, others may prompt or partly echo the child's speech through such follow-up questions as "You're going where?" They may also expand or recast what the child says. For example, they may expand a child's ungrammatical "Throw daddy." to the grammatical "Throw it to daddy." Or they might occasionally recast the grammatical "He's going home." into a semantically similar expression that adds new but related grammatical information, such as "He is going home, isn't he?" or "Is that where he's going?" Or they may both expand and recast an ungrammatical utterance, or elaborate on what the child says in some other way.

How helpful, in fact, are these helpful-looking behaviors? Are they essential to the grammatical-acquisition process? If not essential, are they at least facilitative? As you can imagine, it is very hard to obtain decisive research answers to such questions. What evidence there is provides a mixed and inconclusive picture (Dale, 1976; de Villiers & de Villiers, 1978). To illustrate, many parents (in some cultures and subcultures, at least) do often expand their young children's ungrammatical utterances. However, the available research evidence does not indicate that such expansions aid grammatical development. In contrast, there is some evidence that recasting can aid it, but recasting does not appear to be used very often by parents. My guess is that *some* adaptation of others' speech to the young child's cognitive and linguistic level must at least be very helpful and is probably necessary. It was probably necessary for Lenneberg's (1962) speechless boy and it is probably necessary for the homeless and parentless street children who haunt so many of the world's cities. In fact—and happily—it seems virtually impossible to talk with a young child without some such adaptation. The stereotypic doting parent will automatically adapt, but so will the older sibling or whoever it is that keeps the young street child alive. And I would bet that the young street child will also gradually pick up the ambient language, grammatical structure and all. On the other hand, it is hard for me to believe that careful, finely tuned "grammar lessons" of the expansion and recasting variety could be necessary for grammatical acquisition; once again, there is Lenneberg's boy to consider. They might make it a bit easier or speed it up somewhat, but we cannot be sure of even that on present evidence. The earlier conclusion remains my working hypothesis: Some genuine interchanges with people who can speak the language are probably essential, but we do not know how much, and of what kind and quality.

The Role of the Child

The available evidence suggests, then, that grammatical structure is not gradually impressed on a passive young mind by a pedagogically intrusive and directive interpersonal environment. Grammatical development is just not that sort of process at all. The evidence suggests, rather, that it is the child who is the active, directive one in the learning process; as indicated earlier, the child is a rule learner and hypothesis tester. The child acquires the system largely on her own initiative and at her own pace, through the repeated activation of very powerful, if still poorly understood, learning equipment. The specific nature of this equipment and this process is the legacy of our biosocial evolution as a species, and grammatical acquisition has a strongly biological-maturational flavor to it. Several interrelated considerations favor this general view of grammatical development (e.g., Chomsky, 1972; Lenneberg, 1967; Slobin, 1979).

BIOLOGY. We are biologically constructed to learn and use oral language of the human type. The human brain and articulatory apparatus are specialized for producing rapid and extended streams of human speech sounds. There is also some left-hemisphere specialization in the brain for the analysis of language-like input. As indicated earlier, we are biologically programmed to attend to and analyze the speech sounds we hear. We seem to be biologically prepared for language learning in rather the same way we are biologically prepared for perceptual and motor-skill learning. We are strongly disposed to do all three and are born with powerful, specialized tools for doing them. That is, evolution has provided us with an indispensable head start or leg up for such learning.

UNIVERSALITY. Human language is species-wide or universal. All societies have rich, grammatically complex languages. Language of the human type is also species-specific. Other species have systems of communication, some quite intricate, but none of them closely resembles human language. Of particular relevance to the present argument, none has a grammar of the type and complexity found in all human natural languages.

MATURATION. Language development obviously involves learning through experience. However, it also has properties that suggest the workings of an endogenous, maturation-like process. Children the world over go through roughly the same major stages of language acquisition, in the same order, and at approximately the same ages. Recall, for example, that even deaf children begin babbling at about the same age that hearing children do. Studies by Goldin-Meadow and her co-workers (Goldin-Meadow, 1979) have shown something else about deaf children that seems even more remarkable. These researchers observed six young deaf children whose parents had normal hearing and did not know the sign-language system used by the deaf. Thus, these children did not receive input from any complex linguistic system, oral or manual, and consequently had no opportunity even to learn what human language systems are like. But biology was not to be denied in this instance: These children nevertheless proceeded to develop their own gestural sign language, and in the normal human sequence—first one-sign utterances, then two-sign ones, then longer ones. Moreover, their multisign utterances made use of sign order to specify meaning, a very common grammatical device (syntax) in human languages, as you know. For example, the children would consistently produce the sign for the recipient of an object after the sign for the object received, analogous to "book Mother," when the book was to be given to Mother. It is hard to disagree with Goldin-Meadow's (1979) conclusions that "Even under adverse circumstances, the human child has the natural inclination and the capacity to develop a structured communication system" (p. 186), and that "It may not be unreasonable to suppose that the child, hearing or deaf, brings to the language learning situation certain predispositions which narrow down the field of potential languages to be acquired" (p. 186). Thus, children seem to have a strong, internally given push to develop a language of the human type, and to develop it in the human sequence (see also Newport, 1981).

PREADAPTATION. It has been suggested that there is a biologically evolved fit or preadaptation between specific properties of human beings and specific properties of human languages. For example, Slobin (1979, Chapters 3, 7) argues that there are competing pressures on the structure of human languages to be clear, humanly processible in ongoing time, quick and easy to use, and semantically and rhetorically expressive. These conflicting pressures obviously arise from the cognitive capacities and limitations and the communicative needs and wants of human beings. Languages that meet these diverse needs tolerably well are languages that people can acquire fairly easily and use fairly effectively. Although this argument sounds suspiciously circular, it does have a testable implication: All human languages should have a substantial number of important properties in common, properties that many imaginable but nonexistent languages do not have. There is good evidence that this is true; there are a number of "linguistic universals," as these important common properties are called (Chomsky, 1972; Clark & Clark, 1977, Chapter 14).

NATIVISM. Finally, there is the Chomskyian nativist or innatist argument, briefly alluded to at the beginning of this section. The following rough and simplified version of it has three parts:

1. The grammatical structure of any human language is extremely complex.
2. Clear clues to this complex structure are surprisingly lacking in the utterances children hear. In consequence, an infinite number of different grammars could be induced or inferred from these utterances by a grammar-learning device that was not specifically designed by nature to look for only certain kinds—namely, those found in human languages.
3. Since children do succeed in acquiring the correct grammar in a few short years, they must have such specific design features. They must bring to their learning task the functional equivalent of specific, innately given ideas and expectations about the general kinds of grammatical rules and structures they will find.

The idea that evolution has provided us with language-learning equipment *that* powerful and specific seemed highly implausible to most of us when Chomsky first proposed it, and still seems farfetched to many. However, my view is that the various alternatives which have been put forward also seem implausible when examined carefully, and that something like Chomsky's innatist position may well prove to be close to the truth. In any case, it is one thing to favor Chomsky's or some other general stance on the issue and quite another to formulate a detailed and specific theory of grammatical acquisition. To return to the first of the three key questions posed earlier: What do children actually *do* with the utterances they hear such that progress in grammatical acquisition results? Interesting theories about what they might do are beginning to appear (e.g., Anderson, 1977; Maratsos, 1983; Pinker, 1982; see also Morgan and Newport, 1981). Although they are still incompletely developed and have not yet been adequately tested empirically, such theories represent a promising start. And they certainly have their work cut out for them. How little children actually acquire grammar is still, to borrow from Winston Churchill, "a riddle wrapped in a mystery inside an enigma."

SUMMARY

Thanks to the work of Chomsky and others, we now recognize that the native speaker of any human language commands astonishingly rich systems of knowledge and skills. Our picture of the childhood acquisition of these systems is also becoming correspondingly rich, and the field of language development is currently one of the most exciting areas in developmental psychology.

The developmental story begins before the advent of language. A number of phonological, cognitive, and communicative acquisitions precede and prepare the way for the acquisition of language. Human babies appear to be biologically primed to attend to and discriminate human speech sounds. The onset and early course of prelinguistic *babbling* (speech-like vocalizing) are also governed by biological-maturational factors. Exactly what contribution practice in babbling makes to later phonological development is still uncertain, however. A number of late-infancy cognitive achievements are probably prerequisites for language acquisition, although there is controversy and uncertainty here as well. Likely prerequisites include Piaget's semiotic function—that is, the capacity to use one thing as a symbol for another; the ability to use other people as causal intermediaries or "tools"; and some knowledge of mundane objects, situations, and properties. Conversely, linguistic acquisitions can also assist cognitive acquisitions. Prelinguistic communication achievements include the ability to direct and "read" another person's attention, to produce preverbal forms of two *speech acts* (requests and assertions), and to take turns in nonverbal "conversations."

Children usually begin to produce recognizable words sometime around their first birthdays. Although the child in this period may well be trying to express more meaning than her single-word utterances suggest, it seems misleading to think of these utterances as one-word "sentences." When first learning a new word, its meaning for the child may differ from the standard meaning. *Overextensions* (e.g., "dog" used to refer to all animals) are common, especially in production versus comprehension. *Underextensions* (e.g., "dog" refers only to the family dog) and *complexive* (unstable, shifting) word meanings have also been noted. There is at present no satisfactory comprehensive theory of how word meanings are acquired and modified over time.

Two-word utterances often begin to appear around 18 months of age. These telegram-like expressions ("more milk," "mommy kiss," etc.) are remarkably similar in form and meaning the world over. Nonetheless, questions remain as to exactly how much and what kind of *semantic* (linguistic meaning) and *grammatical* (*syntax* and *morphology*) knowledge we should attribute to the child in this period.

Important grammatical advances are made subsequent to this period. The child develops *grammatical morphemes* (function words like "in," *inflections* like the past-tense "-ed" ending on verb stems) in a systematic order that is probably determined by their cognitive-processing complexity. The child's acquisition of inflections illustrates her active propensity for testing hypotheses and searching for rules when learning language. For example, we may see developmental sequences like: irregular "feet" alone–regular, rule-governed "foots" alternating with "feet"–"feet" alone again. Other grammatical acquisitions cited concern negative, *wh* questions, and methods of combining simple sentences to make more complicated ones.

Semantic development beyond the early periods was only briefly discussed. As with the earlier grammatical morphemes, the order of acquisition of some semantically related words (e.g., "give"–"pay"–"buy") may also reflect their cognitive-processing complexity.

Later communicative development was discussed at greater length. Communication skills that develop during the preschool years include the ability to sustain a conversation on a single topic, to discuss the nonpresent and nonreal, to infer what is presupposed and implied from what is explicitly said, and to adapt one's speech production and comprehension to numerous properties of speakers, listeners, and social settings. Impressive as these skills are, however, recent work on *metacommunication* (knowledge and cognition concerning communications) suggests that children of kindergarten age and older still have some important communicative development ahead of them. They need to learn to monitor their own comprehension and to recognize the meaning and implications of feelings of uncertainty or lack of understanding. They need to learn that the communicative quality of a message affects its communicative success, and that referentially ambiguous messages are in many situations communicatively inadequate. Some metacommunicative knowledge and skill may be the incidental byproduct of formal schooling. However, it might also be possible, as well as desirable, to teach these and other useful metacognitive competencies directly.

Explaining the acquisition of grammar has been the primary theoretical goal in the area of language development. The role of the environment in grammatical acquisition does not appear to be as direct and specific as previously believed. The child obviously needs to hear his native language spoken to acquire its grammatical infrastructure. Moreover, he very likely needs to hear it spoken to him, and adapted to some extent to his cognitive and linguistic level. On the other hand, he very likely does not acquire it through imitation, reinforcement, or combinations of the two. Expansions of ungrammatical utterances and other adult elaborations of the child's speech are probably not necessary either, although they might be helpful.

In contrast, the role of the child in his own grammatical development appears to be an extremely active, powerful, and specific one. He is biologically well equipped to acquire language of the human type; he will encounter one with rich and complex grammatical structure in any human society he is born into; and he will acquire it in an inexorable, age- and stage-related fashion that looks strongly maturational. Although not all students of language development would agree, I believe that a good case can be made for some version of Chomsky's innatist position on grammatical development. Whatever one's general position on the matter, however, it is heartening to see some beginning theoretical attempts to specify in detail what young children actually do with the linguistic input they receive to convert it into grammatical knowledge.

nine

Questions and Problems

Most textbooks fail to give the reader an insider's view of the field they cover. A field looks very different to an insider—a "pro"—than it does to an outsider. The insider continually lives with its numerous questions, problems, ambiguities, and uncertainities. She becomes used to, although never unconcerned about, its untidy, open-ended, no-problem-ever-seems-to-get-solved character. She knows how incredibly difficult it is even to think up a research study that will tell us something we really want to know.

Experiences like the following bring home the reality of this insider-outsider distinction. When I read in the popular press about some new medical claim or discovery, I nod approvingly at this Latest Advance in Our Understanding of Nature. When the claim or discovery is in the area of cognitive development, on the other hand, I usually have two reactions. The first is that, as always, the reporter has partly misunderstood what the developmental psychologist was trying to tell him. The second is that the developmental psychologist who told it to him is just old Bleatworthy, peddling *that* view again, and that Bleatworthy herself is probably just as conscious as I am of all the unresolved questions and problems that shroud it.

The aim of this chapter is to present some of the questions and problems you would live with if you were an insider in the field of cognitive growth. By implication, the aim is also to make you feel more insecure and skeptical about everything you have read in previous chapters. I can imagine two reactions that different readers might have to the content of this chapter, depending upon their backgrounds and interests. One is that finally, at long last, we are getting into the *real* issues. The author has finished describing all the different ways that kids get smarter as they grow older and will now get into more substantive matters. As the section headings indicate, he now talks about how to assess or diagnose the child's cognitive level, how cognitive growth may be explained rather than just described, and the sorts of systematic patterns (stages, sequences) it exhibits. He, in short, is trying to tie it all together, provide an overview and perspective, show us What It All Means. The other reaction is that things have suddenly gotten very abstract and hard to follow. The child's cognitive development is now populated with false positives, underlying processes, cognitive entities, structures, concurrences, qualitative changes, and other intangibles. Where did the child go?

Both reactions are perfectly understandable and reasonable. To those who have the first reaction I would suggest only that even the purely descriptive aspects of cognitive development are scientifically important, and also that—the insider's plight once again—those real issues and substantive matters are going to look very messy, very far from being resolved. To those with the second reaction, I would suggest that you either skip this chapter altogether (if that option is open to you) or else read it in a special way. The special way is to let it wash over you, trying only to get the main points. Above all, try to get a sense or feeling for how cognitive growth might proceed—or more accurately, for the *alternative* conceptions among which the insiders are struggling to decide of how cognitive growth might proceed. Try, in other words, to get some sort of wide-angle view of the cognitive-developmental panorama, including the outstanding questions and problems concerning it. Regardless of which of the two reactions you may have, if either, providing you with such a view is one of the main objectives of this chapter.

DIAGNOSIS

What problems and issues do psychologists face in trying to diagnose or analyze children's developing knowledge and abilities? They are many, varied, and very, very troublesome. Discussions of these problems and issues can be found in, for example, Bortner and Birch (1970), Brainerd (1977, 1983), Cole and Bruner (1971), Flavell (1970a, pp. 1032–1034; 1971c, pp. 429–435), Flavell and Wohlwill (1969), Miller (1976), Smedslund (1969), and Zimiles (1971).

What is involved in cognitive-developmental diagnosis can best be communicated with reference to a specific example. Transitive inference is a concrete-operational acquisition within Piaget's theoretical system. As mentioned in Chapter 4 (*Improving Existing Competencies* section), one form of it is conceived by Piaget as consisting of this type of reasoning process: if $A > B$ (e.g., A is longer than B) and $B > C$, then it has to be true that $A > C$—no measurement is necessary. Developmental psychologists may ask two sorts of questions about this or any other cognitive acquisition. They both involve "diagnosis," but in somewhat different senses. One has to do with our *conceptualization* of the acquisition itself, the other with its *assessment* in children.

Conceptualization questions ask what this ability or behavior we call "transitive inference" consists of, in psychological terms. What are the cognitive processes that actually underlie or comprise acts of so-called transitive inference? What, exactly, happens inside the individual's head when, given $A > B$, $B > C$, and $A ? C$, she responds $A > C$? In short, *what* develops when transitive inference develops?

There are several kinds of assessment questions. Some are more concrete and practical; others are more abstract and theoretical; all are related to one another and to the conceptualization questions. Following are some concrete and practical ones: Suppose we provisionally accept someone's (e.g., Piaget's) characterization of what "transitive inference" is—that is, we accept as a point of departure *some* answer to the conceptualization question. The practical assessment question then arises. How can we determine (diagnose) whether a given child has or has not acquired transitive inference? What assessment procedures should we use to test for its presence in the child's cognitive repertoire? These procedures should neither overestimate nor underestimate the child's capacity for transitive inference. Overestimation would lead to diagnostic errors of the *false-positive* variety: The child does not really have transitive inference, but your testing procedure wrongly leads you to conclude that he does. Underestimation would produce *false-negative* errors: The child does really have it, but your testing procedure wrongly leads you to conclude that he does not—your procedure is too insensitive. How do we find a method of diagnostic testing that decreases the likelihood of both kinds of errors? In order to find such a method, we would obviously have to know what could cause a child to appear to have transitive inference but not really have it (false positive), and vice versa (false negative).

We cannot work on these concrete and practical assessment problems very long without being confronted with certain more abstract and theoretical questions. What, exactly, do we really mean to say about a child when we say she "has" or "does not have" transitive inference? Let us assume (contrary to actual fact) that we possess a completely valid test of transitive-inference behavior, one that will always be right when it says that a child did or did not engage in transitive inference in any appropriate task situation. Suppose further that we discover that every child we test does one or the other of two things: (1) engages in transitive inference in all and only those situations in which transitive inference can legitimately be made; (2) never engages in it. If every child did either 1 or 2, then "having" versus "not having" transitive inference would possess reasonably clear meanings. The child who does 1 definitely "has" it. The child who does 2 "does not have" it, but less definitely so. (It is theoretically possible that some capacity for it exists, but the capacity is too underdeveloped to be expressed even in the "easiest," most "child-friendly" transitive inference task we have yet been able to devise.)

Suppose instead that, in addition to finding these two types of children, we also find some (3) who engage in transitive inference in only a few, very easy task situations; others (4) who do the same in all but a few, very difficult task situations; and (5) many children in between. I am sure you will not be surprised to learn that this additional supposition is well-founded in reality. We definitely do find a whole gamut of 3's, 4's, and 5's between the two extremes of 1 and 2—not just in the case of transitive inference, but apparently for all sorts of Piagetian and non-Piagetian cognitive achievements.

What theoretical sense can we make of this untidy state of affairs? Will we need to distinguish several, or even many, different kinds or degrees of "having transitive inference"? If so, how should such distinctions be drawn? Perhaps the several or many we distinguish will line up nicely to form an orderly developmental sequence or progression. That is, we might theoretically define a "beginning" kind (degree? amount?) of capability for transitive inference, followed by a "more advanced" one (in what way?), and so on, until a "completely mature" (in what sense?) capability is achieved. But if we think of transitive inference as more like a developmental succession of different things than like a unitary, unchanging cognitive entity, we find ourselves confronting the conceptualization form of the diagnosis question once again. The conceptualization question, you will recall, asks what cognitive processes actually make up or underlie "transitive inferences." However, if "transitive inference" changes with age, then those cognitive processes must also change with age.

To recapitulate, we begin with a preliminary, working notion of what transitive inference is (conceptualization questions). We then try to find ways to accurately diagnose its presence/absence in the child's task performance (concrete and practical assessment questions). The best available diagnostic procedures suggest that, for many children, it is present sometimes and absent sometimes, depending upon the specifics of the task situation and perhaps other factors. Then, we try to make developmental sense out of this lack of consistency (abstract and theoretical assessment questions), perhaps by hypothesizing an ontogenetic progression of different forms (degrees, or whatever) of transitive-inference-related capabilities. The existence of such a progression implies that these capabilities must change in some way from one point in that progression to another, and therefore, so also must the nature and/or organization of the cognitive processes underlying them (back to conceptualization problems again). Let us now examine this diagnostic cycle in more detail, beginning with the more concrete and practical sorts of assessment questions.

Assessment Questions

CONCRETE AND PRACTICAL ASPECTS. We begin with the simplifying assumption that a child either does or does not possess the ability to make a transitive inference—with no gradations in between—and that our diagnostic goal is to find out which is the case for an individual child. Suppose the child really does possess this ability but gives no evidence of it in her performance on some test of transitive inference, leading us to make a false-negative diagnostic error. This could happen for a number of reasons. The child might fail to understand the task instructions, fail to attend to or comprehend the premises of the inference (i.e., the fact that $A > B$ and $B > C$), or forget either the instructions or the premises at the moment when the inference normally would be made (Smedslund, 1969). Also, as with production deficiencies for particular memory strategies (Chapter 7), for some reason the task may elicit from the child a problem-solving approach or strategy that is incompatible with transitive inference. For instance, having just learned through perception rather than inference that $A > B$ and $B > C$, he may assume that A ? C must also be solved by perception rather than inference.

His true ability can also be masked by motivational and emotional factors, such as disinterest in your "game," or apprehension about you as an adult stranger. Some cognitive tasks require the child to generate a complex verbal response (e.g., an explanation) in order to demonstrate the cognitive ability in which the examiner is interested; the child may be incapable of generating the verbal response and yet possess the cognitive ability. Every task demands from the child knowledge and skills other than, and in addition to, the target concept or ability it was designed to tap. If the child does not or cannot meet any of these additional, nontarget demands, a false-negative diagnostic error can result. It is small wonder that Bortner and Birch (1970) say that "performance levels under particular conditions are but fragmentary indicators of capacity" (p. 735).

The chances of underestimating the child's capacity become especially great if his experiences and expectancies concerning cognitive tasks are markedly different from the examiner's—for example, because he belongs to a different culture or subculture (Cole & Bruner, 1971; Cole & Scribner, 1974). Psychologists who attempt to do cross-cultural studies of cognitive growth have a particularly difficult problem avoiding false-negative errors of diagnosis.

False-positive diagnostic errors can also stem from several causes. Under certain task conditions, the child may get the right answer by guessing, by direct perception of $A > C$, or by using some irrelevant (i.e., nontransitive-inference) solution strategy which happens to yield the $A > C$ conclusion (Smedslund, 1969). One such strategy that has been identified stems from the young child's frequent tendency to think in absolute (e.g., "A is *long*") rather than relative or comparative terms (e.g., "A is *longer than B*"). He may code the premises $A > B$ and $B > C$ as something like "A is long, B isn't," and "B is long, C isn't," respectively. Since in this coding, A has been thought of as "long" once but C never has, for this reason the child may tend to choose A when asked which is "longer." The answer is, of course, correct, but it was not generated by transitive inference.

Researchers have thought of some clever ways to reduce the likelihood of such false-positive, nontransitive but correct solutions (Smedslund, 1969; Trabasso, 1975). It is possible, for instance, to show sticks A and C on a background of Müller-Lyer arrows, which creates the visual illusion that C is longer than A rather than vice versa. We have already seen how transitivity of weight can appear to be violated by a rigged-scale balance (Miller's studies in Chapter 4, *Improving Existing Competencies* section). In both cases, the child is actually given false perceptual information about the A-C relation, which, of course, greatly reduces his chances of getting the right answer by processes other than transitive inference. Similarly, suppose we give the child this transitive-inference problem: Given that $A > B$, $B > C$, $C > D$, $D > E$, what is the length relation between B and D? Since both B and D have been shown to be longer than one thing and shorter than another in this problem, the child cannot get the right answer by using the just-mentioned strategy of coding relative terms as absolutes; both B and D have had a chance to be coded as "long." Also, we can reduce markedly the chances of making a false-positive diagnostic error by requiring the child to explain or justify his $A > C$ conclusion. An answer like, "*A has* to be longer than C because it is longer than B, and even B is longer than C," could hardly emanate from a child who had no understanding of the transitivity rule.

But the reduction of false positives is very likely to result in an increase in false negatives. It is not hard to conceive of a child who would not fare at all well on these more stringent tests, while yet possessing at least some genuine capability for transitive inference. In the illusion condition, a young child might simply think that his direct perception of $C > A$ is a more trustworthy guide to decision making than logical inference. Give me a logical inference as novel and complex for me as transitive inference may be for the young child, and I might feel the same way. The child may also not entertain the possibility that the adult experimenter could be deceiving him, although this is, of course, exactly what that authority figure is doing in using those Müller-Lyer arrows. You might not entertain it either, if the Pope or George Washington were testing you. The illusion could even lead him to misinterpret the problem altogether as one of determining which stick *looks* longer, rather than which one *really is* longer (cf. Chapter 3, *The Appearance-Reality Distinction* section). The added complexity of five terms rather than three in the $A > B$ . . . $D > E$ task could overload the child's attention and memory capabilities, decreasing the likelihood that $B > C$ and $C > D$ will be front and center in his consciousness when B ? D has to be decided. Finally, of course it is possible that the child could have just solved the problem by transitive inference and yet lack the wherewithal—conceptual, linguistic, emotional, motivational—to generate a satisfactory verbal justification of his choice.

It should be apparent by now that the concrete and practical task of assessing transitive inference or any other cognitive acquisition is fraught with difficulties. As Smedslund (1959) put it: "The relationship between any set of behavioral indices and a mental process, therefore, is an uncertain one, and a diagnosis will always have the status of a working hypothesis" (p. 247). This does not mean that diagnosis of a child's cognitive-developmental status is inherently impossible, incapable of being improved, or just generally not worth trying. "Uncertain" does not mean "unknown" or "unknowable," and "working hypotheses" are necessary and useful in all fields.

ABSTRACT AND THEORETICAL ASPECTS. It does mean, however, that we need to stand back a bit from our measurement efforts and examine the whole assessment enterprise in a more abstract and theoretical way. In particular, we have to ask what range and diversity of cognitive phenomena we may be tapping when we try to measure "transitive inference" in children of different cognitive-developmental levels. What *are* the different possible meanings and manners of "having," of "possessing," something like transitive inference? Does the growing child first "have" it in manner *A*, and later in manner *B*, and still later in manner *C*? The following is one way to think about these questions (Flavell, 1971c; Flavell & Wohlwill, 1969); see also Chapter 4, *Improving Existing Competencies* section; Greeno, Riley, and Gelman (1984), and Wilkinson (1984). It is not the only way, and it will not necessarily prove to be the best way. It is hard to overstress how unconfident most of us feel about these matters at the present time.

Let us suppose that one child may "have" transitive inference in a more advanced fashion than another child, in the specific sense of being able to call it into play more easily and being able to apply it successfully in more task situations. According to this view of how development might proceed, transitive inference is "in there somewhere" in both cases, but it is more readily and more generally available for use in the one case than in the other. What could cause this difference in availability? We have already mentioned a number of specific causes in our discussion of how false-negative diagnostic errors may arise, and there are no doubt many, many more. In some instances, the child may not use transitive inference because she does not think to. The task situation, for example, may evoke some other, competing solution strategy instead. In other instances, the task may evoke a transitive-inference strategy, but the inferential problem is so complex the child cannot successfully execute the strategy. In the first case, the problem is one of strategy *evocation*; in the second, it is one of strategy *utilization* (Flavell, 1971c, p. 429).

When the child begins to acquire transitive inference, first "has" it in some rudimentary sense, it may be both difficult to evoke, and if evoked, difficult to execute or utilize. We might have to evoke it directly—for example, by actually instructing him to use it, and then we might also have to assist him a bit in its step-by-step utilization. If a great deal of such instruction and assistance were required, we might prefer to conclude instead that the child, in fact, did not "have" transitive inference in even the most rudimentary sense, prior to our intervention. We might conclude instead that we had simply taught it to him outright—built it in from the ground up. Yet, as we saw in Chapter 4, it seems plausible to think that a newly developed cognitive form could be so fragile and unstable that a good deal of environmental support would be needed for its successful evocation and utilization. A cognitive training study might therefore be done for a somewhat unusual purpose—namely, to diagnose whether and how a child "has" transitive inference, based on his responsiveness to our training efforts (Gelman & Gallistel, 1978, Chapter 2). How much he can do as a function of how much training he is given may give us ideas as to what he "had" prior to training (Flavell, 1970a, p. 1043).

According to this scheme as so far presented, transitive inference itself, once in the repertoire at all, remains the same basic entity from then on; what changes with subsequent development is its evocability and utilizability. It is quite conceivable, however, that transitive inference itself may also change, and even that its own modifications are partly responsible for its increased evocability and utilizability (Larsen, 1977). For instance, the child might think initially that, given $A > B$ and $B > C$, $A > C$ is only probable rather than certain—a good guess rather than a sure bet. There is at first, perhaps, no sense that A "has to be" longer than C, and hence no great confidence in the child's $A > C$ answer. Moreover, he may experience his $A > C$ response only as a tentative intuition of unknown origin. He may literally have no idea at all why $A > C$ should be concluded from $A > B$ and $B > C$; that conclusion just "feels right" to him on trial after trial. It is plausible to suppose that this kind of "transitive inference" could be highly vulnerable to all manner of countervailing factors. A child who "had" it that way would likely show it in one situation but not in another, when in this state of mind but not when in that, and so on.

Conceptualization Questions

We now see why cognitive-developmental diagnosis is such a nettlesome venture. In addition to shortcomings in our diagnostic procedures, the very thing we are trying to diagnose undergoes changes as the child matures. We have just hypothesized that these changes may be of two interacting types. First, the target acquisition becomes more readily evoked and more effectively utilized over an ever-widening range of appropriate, applicable situations. It acquires good delivery services, so to speak. Second, it may itself undergo important alterations with age, some of which may also cause it to become more evocable and utilizable.

Suppose that cognitive capacities like transitive inference typically show this sort of developmental course. What more would we want to know? A great deal, actually, because we have not yet discovered what "transitive inference"—at any point in this developmental course—really is. We need to move on to what Smedslund (1969, p. 244) called "higher order inferences": "An even more complex diagnostic task is to determine the exact content and sequencing of the mental processes involved in solving a given task" (p. 244). What actually happens, in cognitive-process terms, between problem presentation and the subject's response? When confronted with the problem, he presumably assembles and executes cognitive processes of some sort, processes that are integrated and sequenced in some fashion. What are those processes and how are they organized—for example, in the case of transitive inference? Also, why is some one particular structured set of processes assembled, rather than some other? What abilities, limitations, biases, task representations, and so on, within the child lead him to generate that particular set? Finally, how might the answers to these two questions—the what and the why of the child's process organization—change as the manner in which he "has" transitive inference changes with development?

Unfortunately, we possess little certain knowledge about the actual process organizations underlying transitive inference, or any other interesting cognitive acquisition, for that matter. However, research by Trabasso and his coworkers (Trabasso, 1975, 1977) constituted an important beginning in the case of transitive inference. They obtained evidence that people often—perhaps even typically—solve transitivity problems in the following way: The subject is repeatedly shown the adjacent pairs of a series of different length sticks, $A > B$, $B > C$, $C > D$, $D > E$, each stick identifiable by its color. Their data suggested that, during these presentations, the subject gradually constructs an internal, possibly image-like representation of the entire ordered array $A > B > C > D > E$. Essentially, the process is one of constructive memory, as described in the *Knowledge* section of Chapter 7.

When then asked to compare a pair of lengths he has never seen together before—for example, B and D—the subject does not, as we had always thought, work out the answer through a step-by-step process of logical inference. Rather, he simply "reads" $B > D$ off his internal representation, much as though the five sticks were all lined up in order of length before his eyes. If logical inference were the solution process, questions about the relative lengths of widely separated pairs that had never been experienced—for example, $B ? D$ or $B ? E$—should certainly take longer to answer than questions about pairs that are adjacent and had been previously experienced—for example, $A ? B$ or $C ? D$. But if the solution process were akin to comparing lengths perceptually, the opposite should be true since, for example, A and D are more different in length and are farther apart in the subject's internal $A \dots E$ linear representation than are, say B and C. Trabasso (1975, 1977) found that the opposite is, in fact, true: The farther away one length is from another in the $A \dots E$ series, the shorter the solution time. It is harder to achieve this sort of quasispatial internal representation in preschool children than in older subjects—for example, more presentations of the adjacent pairs are required. Once achieved, however, preschool children can solve transitive-inference problems, and they appear to solve them in this very same, essentially noninferential fashion. Previously, most investigators had not found that children this young could solve transitive-inference problems.

Trabasso has not shown that people never use inferential rather than quasiperceptual processes when dealing with transitivity problems, or that older children do not know anything about transitive inference that younger ones do not. On the contrary, the nature and development of transitive reasoning in children continues to be a controversial and actively researched topic (Brainerd & Kingma, 1984; Breslow, 1981; Halford, 1982, 1984; Thayer & Collyer, 1978). Nevertheless, I believe that Trabasso's work has irrevocably changed the way we must think about the nature and development of transitive inference. By identifying some plausible underlying processes, he has helped us understand what "transitive inference" might really refer to psychologically. Such a process-level understanding will ultimately be essential if we are ever to diagnose accurately and chart developmentally the important cognitive acquisitions of human childhood.

The Importance of Diagnosis

Let Y stand for any of these acquisitions—transitive inference or any other. We have said that the objectives of diagnosis include: (1) determining Y's psychological nature, or underlying process organization; (2) determining its typical developmental course, including sequential changes in its psychological nature, its evocability, and its utilizability; (3) determining what a particular child "has," or where she stands developmentally, with respect to (1) and (2). The successful achievement of all three diagnostic objectives is crucially important for several reasons.

One reason is that we cannot determine the relationship of Y to other cognitive acquisitions—for example, X and Z—without accurate diagnosis. Suppose, for example, we hypothesize (erroneously) the existence of an invariant developmental sequence X-Y-Z, such that the acquisition of X makes possible and helps produce the subsequent development of Y, and Y does the same in relation to Z. There are at least two ways that inaccurate diagnosis could have led us to propose that erroneous hypothesis, and subsequent improvements in diagnosis lead us to abandon it. First, better diagnosis might show that the true temporal order of acquisition is not X-Y-Z but, say, Y-X-Z. More sensitive and valid assessment procedures might reveal that Y really emerges considerably earlier in childhood than we had previously thought, thus making it logically impossible on purely temporal-sequential grounds for X to be its developmental progenitor. As Miller (1976) put it, "we cannot postulate mediating mechanisms that postdate the development that they supposedly explain" (p. 406). Second, a better analysis of the processes composing Y might make it clear that Y is an entirely different kind of cognitive creature than we had believed. Y might now appear to be utterly unrelated and unrelatable to X and Z either conceptually or logically, so much so that we just cannot conceive of how it could possibly be X's descendant and Z's ancestor. It would be like trying to imagine how hailstones could come from halberds and subsequently produce highbrows.

We might instead hypothesize (again contrary to fact, let us suppose) that X, Y, and Z emerge together, synchronously or concurrently rather than sequentially or successively. X, Y, and Z might all be conceived as belonging to a common developmental stage, perhaps as integral parts of a common cognitive structure. We might believe, for instance, that they are three closely linked Piagetian concrete-operational acquisitions, and therefore they should develop together. It is easy to see that the same two points about diagnosis apply to stages and structures as apply to sequences. Better methods of assessment may show us that our developmental timetable was wrong: X, Y, and Z really emerge at rather different ages rather than at roughly the same age. The greater the difference among their ages of emergence, the harder it would be to think of them as belonging to a common structure and stage (Miller, 1976). Similarly, drastic reconceptualizations of X, Y, and/or Z, based upon deeper, process-oriented analyses, may make them look so conceptually unrelated to one another that we would again be unable to see how they could plausibly form part of the same cognitive-structural whole or be meaningfully assigned to the same cognitive-developmental stage. Trabasso's (1975, 1977) research might be a straw in the wind here. It suggests that transitive-inference tasks are solved earlier, and by different cognitive processes, than we had believed. Such results may eventually force Piagetians and others to revise their ideas about any hypothesized sequences, structures, and stages containing transitive inference as a Y.

Other reasons why accurate diagnosis is important have to do with Y itself, considered more or less in isolation from other major acquisitions (cf. Miller, 1976). Educators as well as developmental psychologists may want to know when Y first emerges in rudimentary form and what its subsequent developmental course is likely to be. They may have reasons to want to help the child to acquire Y earlier or more adequately than he would without special training, or to teach him other things for which Y is an educational prerequisite. Accurate developmental diagnosis could help guide the nature and timing of their educational interventions. Among other things, a good diagnosis can help to define educational "readiness."

Some interventions are introduced more for theoretical-developmental than for practical-educational reasons. They are called "training studies" in the literature on cognitive development, and a great many of them have been done with reference to Piagetian acquisitions. The investigator theorizes that experience A may be important in the real-life acquisition of some Piagetian Y. She does a training study to test her theory. In skeletal form (omitting consideration of control groups, transfer tasks, delayed posttests, etc.), a training study consists of an assessment of the child's initial, preexperimental grasp of Y, the introduction of the experience A, and a subsequent reassessment of his grasp of Y. (The educator may, of course, use a similar design to measure the effects of his more pedagogically motivated intervention.) It is obvious that inaccurate pre- and postintervention assessment of Y could yield quite erroneous conclusions about the role of A in the ontogenesis of Y.

Finally, diagnosis is central to all psychological study, cognitive developmental or other. In the case of cognitive development, we absolutely must somehow penetrate to the processual heart of the acquisitions we call "transitive inference," "conservation," and so on, and also we must be able to assess with precision where individual children stand in relation to these acquisitions. Good process analyses of cognitive functioning are exceedingly difficult to do, especially with child subjects. However, we are beginning to realize that they are indispensable if we are ever to make real progress in describing and explaining cognitive growth. As Klahr (1984) recently put it: "Unambiguous theories of knowledge states are a prerequisite for theories of transition, for a transition theory can be no better than a theory of what it is that is undergoing transition" (p. 104).

EXPLANATIONS

How is cognitive growth accomplished? What factors or variables play what roles in influencing the nature, rate of growth, and ultimate adult level of various forms of knowledge and cognitive ability? Possible variables here include: hereditary and maturational factors; diverse forms of social and nonsocial experience; developmental principles, processes, or mechanisms, such as differentiation, coordination, integration, and equilibrium. What do we really mean when we speak of "explaining" cognitive development, of finding its "causes"? How would human cognitive growth appear if viewed from a biological-evolutionary perspective? Would viewing it from such a perspective help us understand the meaning of developmental "explanations" and "causes"? Experience is obviously very important in the child's cognitive development, but how shall we conceptualize experience and its developmental effects? Are there a number of different types of experience, for instance? More generally, how shall we think about the "processes" of cognitive growth, those events taking place in the child's mind which cause her mind to exhibit developmental changes? How shall we model the process of cognitive development? In sum, how and to what extent can we *explain* the various changes we may have *diagnosed*?

Not surprisingly, accounting for cognitive growth is at least as problematic as diagnosing or describing it. Also predictable is that uncertainties and questions concerning diagnosis make for uncertainties and questions concerning explanation, and vice versa. Useful references on this topic include Beilin (1971), Cole and Scribner (1974), Flavell (1970a, pp. 1040–1043), Kuhn (1974), Scarr-Salapatek (1976), Wohlwill (1973a), and especially Sternberg (1984) and Wohlwill (1973b, Chapters 2 and 11). Accounts of Piaget's revised equilibration theory (his conception of how children make cognitive-developmental progress) can be found in Furth (1981, Chapter 15) and Piaget (1977).

Perspectives on the Explanation Problem

Why does the child develop cognitively at all? Although this question is obviously fundamental, it is surprising how seldom it is raised and discussed in the literature in cognitive growth. Wohlwill's (1973b) thoughtful treatment is one of the few exceptions. Wohlwill takes an interesting if somewhat extreme position on the problem of explaining psychological development. His arguments bear on noncognitive as well as cognitive aspects of ontogenesis, but I present them as if he were talking only about cognitive growth.

We currently know nothing about the physiological events and processes underlying cognitive development. If we knew a great deal about these, it is conceivable—although not certain—that we could explain the basic fact that children's cognitive systems undergo important changes as they grow older. Limited as we presently are to the psychological plane, however, we might be better off conceptualizing this basic fact in the following way: Childhood cognitive growth is essentially inevitable, and it should be regarded as a given rather than as something to be explained. This growth is a process of change that human young, like those of other species, are simply destined and designed to undergo. Cognitive development has a sturdy, relentless, inexorable quality to it. Although Wohlwill does not say this, a sense of this intrinsic momentum towards growth becomes especially strong if we try to imagine what we would have to do to *prevent* a child from making any cognitive progress between the ages of 0 and 15 years. During the period of childhood, a human being is best construed as a device that is programmed to undergo marked changes over time. It is built to develop, and develop it will, if given any reasonable opportunity to do so.

This sounds like a conception of cognitive growth that assigns no formative role at all to environmental and experiential factors, but Wohlwill's (1973b) position is not that extreme. He speaks of such factors as "variables which modulate or modify the course or character of those [inevitable developmental] changes" (p. 24), and thinks of them as "superimposed on an ongoing developmental process" (p. 318).Wohlwill believes that experience fuels and feeds this developmental process, and may also influence its direction and acquired content to an extent (to what extent is not made clear). If I understand him rightly, however, he does not believe that experiential variables can actually generate, cause, or otherwise serve to explain the fundamental process of cognitive growth itself.

I think that Wohlwill's conception of cognitive development somewhat underestimates the contributions of environment and experience. His views deserve a hearing, nevertheless, because they serve to counterbalance the many developmental accounts which seem either tacitly or explicitly to overestimate the contributions of external factors. Wohlwill makes an important point when he says that there is an impetus to childhood cognitive growth that is not ultimately explainable by this environmental push or that experiential shove. The latter are indeed essential to development—there is no denying that. However, they operate within the context of a preexisting disposition towards growth and an ongoing developmental movement. They do not create that disposition and they do not generate that movement.

Some highly interesting speculations about sensory-motor development by Scarr-Salapatek (1976) also provide a useful perspective on the explanation problem. A specialist in behavior genetics and human development, Scarr-Salapatek approaches this problem from an unusual point of view—that of evolutionary theory. As is not true of later cognitive acquisitions, Scarr-Salapatek notes, normal human beings everywhere are virtually certain to complete Piagetian sensory-motor development. As she puts it: "Do you know anyone who didn't make it to preoperational thought" (p. 185)? She speculates that the sensory-motor ontogenetic pattern evolved earlier in our primate past than those that follow it in childhood cognitive development—for example, concrete-operational thought.

The evolutionary selection pressures that led to the establishment of sensory-motor development ensured its species-wide universality in two ways: They acted on the infant *and* they acted on his environment, including the behavior of his caretakers. This important point needs elaboration.

On the infant's side, selection pressures are hypothesized to have produced an organism genetically predisposed or "canalized" towards the sequential acquisition of Piagetian sensory-motor schemes rather than other imaginable cognitive attainments. This organism's evolutionary history has powerfully biased it to develop in that direction, and we would presumably have to rear it in a highly deviant, "nonhuman" way to prevent that development or deflect its basic course. Language development is similarly canalized (see Chapter 8).

So far, the emphasis is similar to Wohlwill's (1973b), except that the inexorable and constrained character of the child's developmental movement is given an evolutionary and genetic justification. What Scarr-Salapatek's account adds, however, is the idea that evolutionary selection pressures also have produced a species-typical, characteristically "human" rearing environment for this genetically specialized organism. Moreover, it is just the sort of environment needed to promote sensory-motor development in this particular organism. Naturally, human environments differ in many ways, and these differences undeniably contribute to individual differences in cognition, especially in later childhood and adulthood. There are also some basic commonalities across human environments, however, and these are believed to constitute the essential psychological nutriments for the acquisition of sensory-motor intelligence. Despite their diversity within and between cultures, infant worlds are "functionally equivalent," as Scarr-Salapatek puts it, in their capacities to support this particular process of acquisition. They all provide social and nonsocial objects, events, and experiential opportunities of the kinds needed to allow a properly designed organism to develop sensory-motor cognitive structures.

Notice that this view in no way denies the vital role of environment and experience in the process of cognitive growth. Environmental elements do not become any less essential to a particular form of development just because they are virtually certain to be available for its use. Their near-universality may make it difficult for us to detect them, but they are no less indispensable because of their low visibility. Scarr-Salapatek (1976) summarizes her position on these matters as follows:

> The ontogeny of infant intelligence has a distinctive pattern and timing. The species pattern, I would argue, is not an unfolding of some genetic program, but a dynamic interplay of genetic preadaptations and developmental adaptations to features of the caretaking environment. Individual variation is limited by canalization, on the other hand, and by common human environments, on the other (p. 166).

> I would argue that the genetic preadaptation in sensorimotor intelligence is a strong bias toward learning the typical schemes of infancy and toward combining them in innovative, flexible ways. What human environments do is to provide the materials and opportunities to learn. For the development of sensorimotor skills, nearly any natural, human environment will suffice to produce criterion level performance (p. 186).

Let us now examine more closely the environmental, experiential side of this organism-milieu developmental interaction. In what ways can environments or experiences differ in the amount and kind of contribution they make to cognitive development?

Environmental-Experiential Contributions to Cognitive Development

The concepts of *necessary* and *sufficient* contributions to development are useful in answering this question (cf. Wohlwill, 1973b, Chapter 11). A type of experience or environmental input A could contribute to the development of cognitive knowledge or ability X at any one of four levels. First, X will develop if, and only if, A has occurred; A is both necessary and sufficient for X's development. Second, A must occur if X is to develop, but so must other things; A is a necessary but not a sufficient precondition for X. Third, A alone can mediate the development of X, but other things can also do so in its stead; it is sufficient but not necessary. Finally, A need not occur for X to develop and cannot generate it unaided if it does occur. It can, however, assist the development of X in concert with other developmental factors; it can therefore be helpful and contributory, but it is neither necessary nor sufficient in itself.

We can make inferences about A's level of contribution to X by seeing how X fares in children who have been provided with A versus those who have not. Such investigations are often called *enrichment* and *deprivation* studies, respectively. Piagetian training studies are enrichment studies; see Beilin (1971), Brainerd (1974), Halford (1982), and Kuhn (1974) for more information on this extensive body of research. An investigator interested in explaining Piagetian acquisitions might hypothesize that a certain A is the usual developmental bridge to a certain X in everyday human ontogenesis. That is, children normally acquire X via A. She might believe, for example, that children gradually acquire conservation of number in the natural environment by gradually learning, through practice coupled with informational feedback, to attend to number-relevant information and disregard number-irrelevant information, such as length of row. She then does a training study to test her hypothesis. Children who do not yet conserve number are provided with such practice and feedback to see if it leads them to give conservation instead of nonconservation responses. In effect, the investigator attempts to simulate or mimic development in the laboratory in order to explain how it proceeds in everyday life, much as other psychologists try to simulate human problem solving on the computer in hopes of explaining how it proceeds in human minds.

In neither case, however, is it possible for the researcher to conclude that nature has been faithfully imitated—that what happened in the training experience or in the computer is the same as what normally happens in real-life conservation development or problem solving. The same outcomes or products may have been achieved in both nature and its attempted simulation (although it is sometimes hard to be sure even of this). This is no guarantee, however, that the same processes were responsible for those outcomes or products. In the developmental case, it is unfortunately true that enrichment studies are just logically incapable of proving that a certain kind of experiential or milieu factor is a *necessary* contributor to any development. In real life, some or all children may acquire conservation of number with the aid of a wholly different factor, via some entirely different "developmental route." The investigator's enrichment study cannot rule out this possibility, no matter how effective her training regimen proved to be in that study.

Could her study at least prove that the A in question is *sufficient* to engender the development of X? Many developmental psychologists would argue that it could. Wohlwill (1973b, p. 319) argues that it could not, however. The reason is that, as already indicated, he conceives of all such factors as developmental modulators or "superimpositions," rather than as outright manufacturers of the developmental process. Therefore, he would probably interpret them as instances of the fourth type of contribution mentioned earlier, rather than of the third: A successful enrichment study may show that

A can be an "assistant mediator" of *X*, but it cannot show that *A* is a necessary or even sufficient contributor to its achievement in everyday, extralaboratory development. Wohlwill (1973b) states his position this way:

> Once we grant the existence of "normal developmental processes," that is, acting independently of particularly specifiable external agents or conditions, there follows a much more far-reaching consequence. That is that we can only hope to isolate necessary rather than sufficient causes, i.e., those without which we can assert development does not take place, rather than those *thanks to which* it does take place. This would suggest, in other words, that the basic tool in the experimental study of development is the deprivation study, rather than the enrichment or special experience study (p. 319).

Even if one does not take quite this dim a view of enrichment studies, it is clear that their use in "explaining development" is inherently limited. At most, they can suggest how the development of something *could* proceed, and therefore how it *might* actually proceed in the real world of growing children. Knowing even this much is sometimes useful, to be sure. It is wholly incapable, however, of proving how this development *does* normally proceed in that world, and the latter is what we would most like to know. Enrichment studies, of course, are very valuable in educationally oriented research. It is also only fair to add that many developmentalists have a higher opinion of their value for cognitive-developmental inquiry than is expressed here.

What of the deprivation study Wohlwill mentioned? Unlike the case with enrichment experiments, it would be highly unethical to do a deprivation experiment on children. One can, however, study the effects of deprivations that occur naturally. But there are problems in interpreting deprivation studies. It may be difficult, for example, to determine precisely of what the child in question has and has not been deprived. Deprivation studies can nevertheless be very useful, as Wohlwill points out.

What they have mainly shown us, in my opinion, is how well guaranteed or "canalized" (Scarr-Salapatek, 1976) many of our fundamental cognitive acquisitions are. Alternatively put, they show how many environmental inputs and experiences seem developmentally helpful or sufficient and how few seem developmentally necessary. As indicated in Chapter 2 (*More on the Semiotic Function* section), research by Furth (1971) and others on deaf children has shown that cognitive growth can progress surprisingly well in human beings who have little or no command of any sort of linguistic system. Similarly, case reports by Jordan (1972) and Kopp and Shaperman (1973) suggest that the ability to manipulate objects with hands or feet is not a necessary condition for normal cognitive development.

Jordan's "case" was a middle-aged woman, living in an institution, who had never had any functional use of her limbs. Despite this handicap: "She was one of the most popular and intelligent of the patients, serving as a regular discussion leader, and being of great help to both the other patients and the staff in filling out income tax returns" (Jordan, 1972, p. 380). As one who stands in awe of income-tax consultants, I would be more than willing to credit her with full formal-operational competence.

What is significant here, as Jordan points out, is that she could never have had the motor half of ordinary, Piagetian sensory-motor experience and development. According to Piaget's theory, sensory-motor intelligence is constructed out of numerous sensory-motor interactions with the environment, and serves as an essential foundation for subsequent cognitive growth. Jordan believed that this woman's developmental history contradicts Piaget's theory; Piaget disagreed (Jordan, 1972, p. 380). I think Jordan was right (Flavell, 1970a, p. 1041), but that is not the major point here. Whatever its implications for Piaget's theory, this case clearly shows that a lot of normal, significant-looking infant experience may be helpful or even sufficient for a lot of important cognitive acquisitions, but yet not necessary or essential for them. To be sure, this woman's massive handicap could have caused her to develop more slowly intellectually than she otherwise would have, even though it did not prevent her from reaching a normal (at least) adult level eventually. Experiential deficiencies and other adverse environmental circumstances sometimes can affect the *rate* at which something develops without necessarily affecting its *final level* of development (Scarr-Salapatek, 1976; Wohlwill, 1973b; see also Chapter 6, *Possible Roles of Experience in Perceptual Development* section).

I believe that cases like Jordan's (1972) suggest an hypothesis about cognitive development and its explanation, one echoing ideas of Scarr-Salapatek (1976) and Wohlwill (1973b) described earlier. The hypothesis is that, when it comes to acquiring certain major kinds of cognition, human beings are amazing *versatile*. They can often make do with whatever acquisitional machinery they possess and with whatever environmental content comes their way. If the usual, typical developmental route is blocked, children may find an unusual, atypical one that somehow gets them to at least approximately the same cognitive destination.

Kagan and Klein (1973) report a case study which suggests that the growing child may also be *resilient*, as they term it, as well as versatile. An extremely nonstimulating, cognitively impoverished early environment can, not surprisingly, seriously retard a young child's intellectual growth. If the child is then removed from that barren environment and subsequently reared in a more developmentally hospitable one, however, the child may show accelerated, "catch-up" cognitive growth and even achieve a normal or near-normal final level.

There is a problem with these optimistic, Rousseauesque notions of developmental versatility and resiliency, however. The problem is that children do not always prove versatile and resilient in the face of organismic or environmental handicaps. Many writers of books on cognitive growth would emphasize and document this fact more than I have. What we need to know, and do not yet know, is what combinations of the relevant variables result in favorable versus unfavorable developmental outcomes: what kinds of children, what kinds of handicaps, when these handicaps are incurred and when removed, and what kind of cognitive acquisitions we are talking about. The importance of this last variable is sometimes overlooked. The ability to read and write and the ability to speak and understand oral language are both enormously significant cognitive accomplishments. The development of the latter seems much more "biological-evolutionary" than the former, however, and is much more certain to result from exposure to a normal human environment (see Chapter 8). Some forms of cognitive development clearly exhibit much more versatility and resiliency than others.

Processes or Principles
of Cognitive Development

One approach to the problem of explaining cognitive development is to attempt to identify processes or principles that seem to be operative in many or all cases in which cognitive growth occurs (Flavell, 1982b, 1984; Sternberg, 1984). Two major classes of these processes or principles seem to be distinguishable. One class generates distinctions within cognitive entities. The other relates one cognitive entity to one or more others. The first class of processes is almost always called *differentiation* or *discrimination*. There is no satisfactory generic name for the second, because more than one kind of relationship among entities can be postulated. For example, the terms used to characterize various kinds of relationships among cognitive entities include *integration, hierarchic integration, subordination, coordination, intercoordination, compounding, regulation, conflict,* and *equilibration*.

E. J. Gibson (1969) uses the principle of differentiation in her theory of perceptual development (Gibson, 1969; Gibson & Spelke, 1983). In another developmental theory which has not been described in this book (Werner, 1948, 1957), cognitive entities are also progressively differentiated as the child grows. Werner's theory further asserts that the products of this differentiation process—that is, the new entities which result from it—become related to one another by a process of hierarchic integration. Differentiated entities or products that are lower in the hierarchy are said to stand in a subordinate or subordination relationship to those higher in the hierarchy. For example, thought, perception, motor action, and emotion are said to be relatively undifferentiated in the young child's experience. They become increasingly experienced as distinct and different from one another as the child grows older, and also mutually relatable in a hierarchically integrated fashion—for example, such that thought may direct or subordinate perception, emotion, or motor action in certain situations.

As indicated in Chapter 2, Piaget describes the progressive differentiation, coordination, and integration of sensory-motor schemes during infant development. For example, the hallmark of Stage 4 is the coordination or integration of two schemes into a means-end whole, with the means scheme becoming subordinated to the end or goal scheme. (Werner also uses the case of means-goal organization to illustrate his developmental principles.) In addition, Piaget has argued that a relationship of conflict or discrepancy between two cognitive entities leads to cognitive progress, and that cognitive development proceeds by coordination, self-regulation, and equilibration (e.g., Flavell, 1963, pp. 237–249; Furth, 1981, Chapter 15; Piaget, 1970a, pp. 722–726, 1977). Piaget's "equilibration model," as it is called, is quite influential in current thinking about the process of cognitive growth, and has stimulated a considerable amount of research (Beilin, 1971; Brainerd, 1974;

Cantor, 1983; Kuhn, 1974; Murray, 1983; Zimmerman & Blom, 1983a, 1983b). As such, it warrants a brief summary and critical examination.

Piaget would use his equilibration model to explain the development of conservation of liquid quantity, for example, in roughly the following manner: Recall from Chapter 3 that the nonconserver usually focuses his attention only on the greater height of the liquid column in the taller, thinner glass, and therefore concludes that it has more liquid than the standard. His thinking about this problem is said to be in equilibrium, albeit at an immature, nonconservation level.

Suppose, however, that at some point he also notices that the new column is thinner, a fact that by itself would incline him to conclude that the new glass contains less liquid than the standard. If he finds both of these opposing conclusions plausible at the same psychological moment, his cognitive system has moved from a state of equilibrium to one of disequilibrium or cognitive conflict with respect to this problem. According to Piaget, states of cognitive conflict and disequilibrium impel the child to make cognitive progress. In this case, the child achieves a new, more intellectually advanced equilibrium state by conceptualizing both the height increase and the width decrease as predictable, mutually compensatory changes in a process of physical transformation that leaves liquid quantity unchanged. A developmental advance has been made by means of a process of equilibration composed of these major steps: (1) cognitive equilibrium at a lower developmental level; (2) cognitive disequilibrium or conflict, induced by awareness of contradictory, discrepant, "nonassimilable" data not previously attended to; (3) cognitive equilibrium (or reequilibration) at a higher developmental level, caused by reconceptualizing the problem in such a way as to harmonize what had earlier been seen as conflicting. Piaget argues that all significant cognitive-developmental advances are made through this kind of equilibration or self-regulation process. Notice that this process is an elaboration of the one described in Chapter 1 (*Assimilation-Accommodation as a Model of Cognitive Development* section).

There appear to be problems with Piaget's equilibration model (cf. Flavell, 1971a; Murray, 1983; Zimmerman & Bloom, 1983a). In order for equilibration to take place the child would seem to need the ability or disposition to do these four things in sequence: (1) attend to or notice both of the apparently conflicting elements in the situation; (2) interpret and appreciate them *as* conflicting and, therefore, problematic—something one cannot assume a young child would automatically do; (3) respond to the sensed conflict by progressing rather than regressing—for example, by trying to explain it rather than by clinging defensively to his initial belief or refusing to have anything more to do with the problem; (4) come up with a better conceptualization of the situation that can resolve the apparent conflict and thereby "reequilibrate" his mental structure at a higher developmental level. It is not apparent how the emergence and subsequent development of these abilities and dispositions can themselves be accounted for by equilibration processes. Rather, the successful running off of an equilibration process is itself in need of explanation, and these abilities and dispositions would presumably figure importantly in that explanation.

Since a given child could lack one or more of these four prerequisites in relation to some specific cognitive problem, it is obvious that he may not be able to complete, or possibly even begin, a Piagetian process of equilibration with respect to it. In addition, however, it is hard to see how certain cognitive achievements could develop via an equilibration process at all, regardless of what the child possessed. Is it likely that many people hit on, say, systematic formal-operational methods for finding all possible combinations or permutations of a set of elements through cognitive conflict or disequilibrium? Similarly, I find it hard to believe that children master seriation and certain other concrete-operational concepts through such a process. A final problem with Piaget's revised equilibration model (Furth, 1981, Chapter 15; Piaget, 1977) is its apparent lack of clarity and specificity as a theory. It is hard for the reader (or at least this reader) to figure out exactly what the model's theoretical claims are and how they might be tested scientifically.

In sum, I believe the equilibration process itself needs explaining when and where it does occur, and also that it does not occur in all instances of cognitive development. I think it likely, in fact, that there is no single, overarching process or principle sufficient to describe how all cognitive-developmental advances are made (Flavell, 1982b, 1984). Different sets of processes may typically be involved in different kinds of cognitive acquisitions. Equilibration is probably one such process, and it may be a very important one, especially for certain kinds of acquisitions. It is worth noting in this connection that other process-oriented approaches to various aspects of cognitive development are now appearing in the literature (Sternberg, 1984). For example, Klahr (1984) has proposed a very interesting account of how children might acquire knowledge about quantity.

Finally, it remains to point out how matters of explanation ultimately hinge on matters of diagnosis. As indicated in the section on Diagnosis, a process analysis may change our ideas about what has actually developed when we say that X has developed. This reconceptualization of what X is then may suggest or force a reinterpretation of X's probable developmental history. As an example, Wohlwill (1973b, pp. 331–332) has suggested that the Piagetian conservations may not be acquired as such at all—at least not in the same sense one would say a specific vocabulary item or a specific motor skill has been acquired (see also Aebli, 1963). Rather, the child may acquire a variety of information and skills concerning quantitative dimensions, measurement, and the like, in the course of many and diverse everyday experiences. When confronted with a conservation task, these acquisitions are brought out of the cognitive stock room, so to speak, and used to assemble a conservation judgment. Unlike the case of the vocabulary item and the motor skill, the child had not actually formed or formulated a "conservation concept" per se before serving as an experimental subject, and probably never would if he steered clear of Piaget's conservation tasks. Does this way of conceptualizing what has developed when "conservation" has developed make sense? I'm not wholly sure it does. But if it does, Piaget's equilibration-process account of development in this area may also be awry. If the child does not really acquire what you thought he did, he probably also does not develop whatever he does acquire instead in the way you had originally hypothesized.

PATTERNS

A number of cognitive-developmental products or entities (concepts, skills, etc.) emerge during an individual's childhood. How and to what extent might these entities be related to one another in ontogenetic time? What patterns might be discernible in the developmental mosaic? Perhaps, during a certain period of childhood, a whole group of similar or related entities emerges synchronously or concurrently. Such an ensemble of concurrent, tightly knit developments would probably be referred to as a major *stage* of cognitive growth. Thus, a stage would constitute one important type of developmental pattern.

A close look at the developmental mosaic might show that one stage regularly precedes another or, even if no major stages were evident, that one individual cognitive entity regularly develops prior to another. The pattern in this case is one of systematic asynchrony rather than systematic synchrony of acquisitions. The developments in question are temporally ordered rather than temporally concurrent, and the pattern thus is one of *sequence* rather than stage.

Stages

There are a number of unresolved issues concerning the meaning and possible existence of stage-like patterns in cognitive development. Useful sources on this topic include Brainerd (1978a, 1978b, plus commentaries by others on 1978b), Case (1985), Colby, Kohlberg, Gibbs, and Lieberman (1983), Damon (1983), Ennis (1975), Feldman (1980), Feldman and Toulmin (1976), Fischer (1980), Flavell (1963, 1970a, 1971c, 1982a, 1982b), Flavell and Wohlwill (1969), Gelman and Baillargeon (1983), Halford (1982), Osherson (1974), Pinard and Laurendeau (1969), Rest (1979), Selman (1980), Siegler (1979a), Turiel (1983), and Wohlwill (1973b). It is useful to focus on Piaget's stage of concrete operations when discussing this topic, since it has been the subject of more theoretical and experimental attention than any other. Our tentative conclusions about stages extend beyond that particular one, however. Most of what needs discussing in this area falls under the headings of *structures, qualitative change, abruptness*, and, above all, *concurrence* (cf. Flavell, 1971c).

STRUCTURES. Piaget argued that what we actually acquire when we acquire, say, concrete operations is a unified set of cognitive *structures*, not just an accumulation of mutually isolated and independent, psychologically unconnected cognitive entities. In fact, the presence of such unified structures—*structures d'ensemble* he called them—was one of Piaget's major criteria for asserting that a given set of developments constitutes a stage.

We can ask two questions concerning cognitive-developmental structures. First, when a given body of knowledge, cognitive skills, and so on, has been acquired, might cognitive structures of any sort have been acquired? Do at least some of the products of cognitive growth become interrelated in our heads, get linked together into organized functional wholes, or do they tend to remain unorganized, unintegrated, and unconnected? There are good reasons to think that they do become interrelated (Flavell, 1971c, pp. 443–450), both in the area of concrete-operational thinking and elsewhere. I doubt if a serious case could be made that the various processes and concepts inhabiting our cognitive systems do not interact with or otherwise link up with one another— do not exhibit "structure" (Flavell, 1982b).

Piaget did not just assert that concrete-operational thinking is structured. Rather, he argued that it possesses a definite, specific type of structure or organization. As mentioned in Chapter 4 (*Concrete and Formal Operations* section), Piaget proposed a logical-mathematical model of how cognition is structured in that stage. It was also suggested in that section that Piagetian structural models are coming under heavy critical attack these days. It seems reasonable, then, to conclude that, in fact, there is considerable mental organization in the area of concrete-operational thinking, as there undoubtedly is in other areas, but that the specific formal structures Piaget proposed may not capture it very well (Flavell, 1982a, 1982b).

QUALITATIVE CHANGE. One is not tempted to talk about developmental stages in the case of age changes that are purely quantitative in nature. Consider the digit-span memory test mentioned at the beginning of Chapter 7. It would sound silly to say that Mary was in the "three-digit stage" last year but has now entered the "four-digit stage." A stage-type characterization perhaps would not sound so silly if she had used a rehearsal strategy to memorize things last year but then switched over to a wholly different strategy this year—for example, elaboration. A quantitative change from little apples to big apples is never called a stage change; a qualitative change from apples to oranges might be. If there were no qualitative changes in cognitive development, there could be no "stages" of cognitive development in any meaningful sense.

Are there any such qualitative changes? The answer depends on what one means by "qualitative" and on one's level of analysis or universe of discourse (Werner, 1957). I personally find it easy to think of the substitution of one memory strategy for another, or a switch from a perceptually based nonconservation answer to a conceptually based conservation one, as qualitative developmental changes; they seem like apples-to-oranges-type transformations to me. On the other hand, the developmental processes—whatever they are—that underlie these behavioral changes may not exhibit any real qualitative transformations, any significant discontinuities. What looks like a qualitative change at one level of analysis may not at another.

ABRUPTNESS. Cognitive development would look very stage-like if the transition from one cognitive level to another were abrupt rather than gradual. Consider as an example conservation of weight, a concrete-operational acquisition. Suppose that acquisition typically occurred very abruptly. One day, the child shows no signs of weight conservation. The next day, it is present in fully mature form: The child can adequately explain her conservation judgment, the experimenter cannot extinguish it by rigging the scale balance, and so on. If the emergence of weight conservation and other concrete-operational accomplishments occurred in such an abrupt, metamorphosis-like fashion, it would seem wholly natural to speak of stages. Indeed, even that abrupt a *quantitative* change would seem somewhat stage-like.

The truth of the matter, however, is that most important cognitive developments appear to proceed slowly and gradually rather than abruptly (Flavell, 1971c, pp. 425–435). As indicated in Chapter 4 (*Improving Existing Competencies* section), conservation of weight may continue to mature, in the sense of becoming further consolidated and solidified, well after the end of the concrete-operational period. Once again, there are more and less mature ways of "having" weight conservation and other cognitive-developmental products. Research evidence suggests that the period in the child's life between initial, minimal possession and fully mature, maximal command of many of these products can be a matter of years.

Such evidence changes the meaning of "stage" in an interesting way. For a major stage like concrete operations, we might have expected a very brief period of change and transition, during which concrete operations emerge and mature, followed by several years of relative stasis and quiescence, during which the child is more or less stably and unchangeably concrete-operational in his thinking. If, instead, the child actually continues to perfect, generalize, and solidify his grasp of weight conservation throughout most of middle childhood and perhaps also well into adolescence, the stage of concrete operations is all change and transition, with little or no stasis and stability. Thus, the stage itself, and not the transition to it, becomes the period of continuous growth and change. Because of this continuous growth and change, one cannot predict the child's responses to concrete-operational tasks merely from the knowledge that he is in the concrete-operational stage, as one could have if being in that stage meant continuing to have essentially the same mental structure for a period of years. This loss of predictability reduces the scientific value of the stage concept, but I do not think it makes it valueless. Suppose that all concrete-operational skills developed concurrently in an interdependent, mutually facilitative fashion. The fact that all these synchronous, closely interacting developments took a long rather than a short time to be completed would not mean that the term "stage" could not be applied meaningfully and usefully to this developmental pattern. We would simply have a more dynamic concept of stage, one that refers to an extended process of concurrent, interdependent developmental changes. Wohlwill thinks the concept of stage is theoretically useful, and the sort of stage he has in mind is of this dynamic sort (Wohlwill, 1973b, Chapter 9).

CONCURRENCE. In fact, most developmental psychologists believe that just this kind of tightly interlocked, concurrent growth must obtain in an area of cognitive development if the term "stage" is to be usefully applied to that area. If concrete-operational entities do not really develop concurrently, for instance, they would say that the concept "concrete-operational stage" is theoretically vacuous. (For a dissenting view on this point, however, see Wohlwill, 1973b, Chapter 9.) The following excerpt from an experimental study of the concrete-operational stage probably expresses the majority opinion on this point:

The structuring or *structure d'ensemble* criterion, one of Piaget's defining characteristics of the stage construct, postulates that mutual connections and reciprocal interdependencies exist between the logical operations, and that it is these interrelationships which create the unified system of the logical structures that characterize a given period of development. . . . Two important consequences that follow from this postulate are: (a) that the acquisition or development of a family of related concepts should be expected to occur at about the same time, and consequently (b) that solutions to tasks of related logical structure should be expected to be of equivalent difficulty (Toussaint, 1974, p. 992).

Unfortunately, it is very difficult to determine whether two or more cognitive entities do or do not develop concurrently and interdependently (Flavell, 1971c, pp. 435–443). As indicated earlier in this chapter, much of the difficulty stems from diagnostic uncertainties. Suppose that, without our knowing it, our test x for development X had extraneous but very taxing performance demands not present in our test y for development Y. That is, test x is harder and less sensitive than test y because of heavy information-processing requirements or other task factors that have nothing intrinsically to do with the cognitive acquisition the test was designed to measure. Accordingly, test x will underestimate the child's level of development of X much more than y will with respect to Y, since it will yield more false-negative type misdiagnoses. This difference in the sensitivities of the two tests could cause developments X and Y to look concurrent when X actually occurs earlier in ontogenesis than Y; conversely, it could make a true developmental concurrence look sequential, with Y seeming to emerge before X.

A number of investigators have tried to find out if concrete-operational attainments develop concurrently. Some of them have attempted to equate their developmental measures for information-processing demands and related sources of differential test sensitivity (e.g., Brainerd, 1972; Dagenais, 1973; Smedslund, 1964; Toussaint, 1974; Weinreb & Brainerd, 1975). Some of these attempts appear to have been more successful than others. I say "appear" because there really is no way one can be sure that two tests have equivalent sensitivities in this respect, and therefore no way to be absolutely sure that the concurrence hypothesis is receiving a valid assessment.

Despite these problems, I think it is possible to make an educated guess about concurrence-nonconcurrence, based on the general drift of the existing evidence. My guess is that nonconcurrence is the rule and concurrence the exception. Two types of relationships among concrete-operational entities are perhaps most commonly "seen" (albeit through a murky diagnostic lens). In one type, a pair of these entities may develop at roughly the same age, on the average, but their levels of development are not highly correlated with one another within individuals. One may be developmentally more advanced than the other in this child; the opposite may be true in that child. There is little evidence, in other words, that their developments are interdependent or mutually facilitative in any way. In the other type, one entity regularly develops prior to another in most or all individuals tested, suggesting that the earlier one might play some facilitative role in the genesis of the later one. In this latter case, the investigator looked for synchronous development, which would suggest a stage, and found instead systematically asynchronous development, which suggests a fixed sequence. Neither of these two types of relationships testifies to the psychological reality of a concrete-operational "stage," as the term is generally taken to mean.

CONCLUSIONS ABOUT STAGES. As noted in Chapter 4 (*Problems in Demonstrating Fundamental Developmental Changes in the Human Cognitive System During the Postinfancy Years* section), developmental psychologists have become increasingly skeptical in recent years about the theoretical utility of the construct of "cognitive-developmental stage." In particular, Piaget's concrete-operational and formal-operational "stages" have been sharply criticized. The structures used to model concrete- and formal-operational thinking appear inadequate; the stage-to-stage developmental changes not quite so exclusively qualitative if you look at underlying processes; the within-stage changes more gradual, important, and extended in time than originally believed; and the same-stage developments less concurrent than Piagetian theory seemed to require. This is not to say that "stages" or their close kin no longer have able advocates. Case (1981, 1985), Damon (1983), Feldman (1980), Halford (1982), Kohlberg (e.g., Colby et al., 1983), Pascual-Leone (1970), Selman (1980), Turiel (1983), Wohlwill (1973b), and others have proposed weaker or stronger versions of stage-like or level-by-level developmental models. These theorists are, of course, aware of the problems cited earlier and attempt to deal with them in various ways. Whether the concept of stage will continue to figure importantly in scientific work on cognitive growth in decades to come is difficult to predict. Some think it might or will, others do not, and still others are undecided to the point of public self-contradiction:

> . . . human cognitive growth is generally *not* very "stage-like" (Flavell, 1982b, p. 17).

> Maybe there really is something general-stage-like about the child's cognitive development, if only we knew where and how to look (Flavell, 1982a, p. 9).

Sequences

The following discussion of cognitive-developmental sequences is largely based on Flavell (1972, 1982b). Other useful sources include Fischer (1980), Gagné (1968a, 1968b), Glaser and Resnick (1972, pp. 210–213), Resnick (1970), Van den Daele (1969), and Wohlwill (1973b, Chapters 4, 8, and especially 6).

As we have already seen, diagnostic problems may make it difficult to be sure that two cognitive entities, X and Y, really develop in the sequence X–Y. In addition, sequences are interesting to us only if X and Y seem to be importantly related to one another. For instance, the fact that sensory-motor secondary circular reactions (X) always develop before concrete-operational weight conservation (Y) is not very interesting, because we cannot imagine how the former could figure directly and importantly in the ontogenesis of the latter. Suppose, however, that we could be sure that X and Y usually do or always do emerge in the sequence X–Y and can also imagine an interesting developmental relationship between the two. What might that relationship be? I have previously (Flavell, 1972) suggested that there are five major types or categories of such relationships: *addition, substitution, modification, inclusion,* and *mediation.*

ADDITION. In most addition sequences, *X* and *Y* are alternative cognitive means to the same goal. *Y* does not replace *X* once it develops; it is simply added to the active repertoire of routes to that goal. For example (Chapter 7), children learn to use simple rehearsal strategies (*X*) before acquiring organizational ones (*Y*) in memory situations, but the former continue to be used in many of these situations after the latter are developed.

SUBSTITUTION. *X* and *Y* again represent possible alternatives, but here *Y* more or less completely replaces or substitutes for *X* once it is acquired. Younger children respond to number-conservation problems by comparing row lengths and concluding that the longer row has more. When they get older they will abandon that strategy completely, substituting for it an inferential approach that will yield a conservation conclusion.

MODIFICATION. In addition and substitution sequences, *X* and *Y* are clearly two different cognitive entities. Here, as the name suggests, there is instead some sort of developmentally progressive modification of a single entity. *Y* is clearly continuous with and derived from *X*, as woman from girl or man from boy. Three types of modifications are distinguished: *differentiation, generalization, and stabilization.* Initially, a child may rehearse items to be remembered in only one way, for example, but in subsequent years she may differentiate several different rehearsal patterns. Likewise, any given way of rehearsing may with development become progressively generalized to more and more different memory problems. Finally, as any rehearsal pattern continues to be practiced, it stabilizes as a skill—becomes more readily initiated in appropriate circumstances, more skillfully and effortlessly carried out, and so on. As an additional example, sensory-motor schemes differentiate, generalize, and stabilize during infancy.

INCLUSION. At some point in *X*'s development, *X* becomes interconnected or coordinated with one or more other cognitive entities to form part of (become included in) a larger cognitive unit *Y*. The processes or principles of hierarchic integration, subordination, and coordination described earlier in this chapter generate inclusion sequences—for example, the progressive coordination of two sensory-motor schemes to form a means-end whole. In the area of memory development, the earlier-developing ability to name objects becomes integrated into a later-developing rehearsal strategy.

MEDIATION. In these sequences, *X* serves as a bridge, facilitator, or mediator with respect to the subsequent development of *Y* Unlike inclusion sequences, however, *X* does not become an actual part or component of *Y*; once developed with the help of (mediation by) *X*, *Y* functions independently of *X*. The inversion and compensation forms of concrete-operational reversible thinking (Chapter 4, *Irreversibility versus reversibility* section) could conceivably help the child achieve conservation solutions to various conservation problems. These forms of thinking do not become integral parts of conservation concepts as, say, a means scheme becomes an integral part of a means-end whole. If I present an adult with a liquid-quantity conservation problem, she surely does not need to go through a whole train of reasoning about how height changes might compensate for width changes in order to reach a conservation conclusion.

Each of these five types of sequences illustrates something about how cognitive growth occurs. The cognitive repertoire is enriched by addition sequences: The child used to have only one approach (X) to a problem but now has two (X and Y). Substitution sequences serve to replace less (X) with more (Y) mature cognitive approaches to problems. A cognitive entity (X) develops to a higher, more mature level (Y) via a modification sequence. Inclusion sequences illustrate that developmental change often occurs neither by modifying old cognitive entities nor by adding or substituting new ones, but by coordinating or integrating existing ones to form larger wholes. Finally, mediation sequences show that the development of one cognitive entity can substantially assist the development of another, distinct and independent entity. It should also be mentioned that the sequencing of cognitive acquisitions is a topic of great interest to educational theorists and researchers (e.g., Gagné, 1968a, 1968b; Glaser & Resnick, 1972; Resnick, 1970; Wang, Resnick, & Boozer, 1971) as well as to developmental psychologists (see Flavell, 1982b).

AN IMAGE OF COGNITIVE DEVELOPMENT. When I doff my parent/layperson hat and don my developmental psychologist hat, I sometimes try to understand the child and his cognitive growth by means of images. One of these images depicts the child as an arena in which a large number of sequential changes of these diverse types are all taking place at once. There are psychological interdependencies among some of the developments going on in the arena: within individual sequences, certainly; between sequences, sometimes. There is also probably bidirectional or reciprocal as well as unidirectional mediation (Flavell, 1972, pp. 336–344): X may not only facilitate the development of Y, but Y may also, once partly developed, facilitate the further evolution of X.

As indicated earlier, there may not prove to be enough developmental interdependence and coherence across sequences to warrant a Piagetian-style stage-by-stage account of what happens in the arena over ontogenetic time. The present evidence suggests that something more like a three-ring circus than like a chamber-music trio is performing in that arena. There appears to be some psychological interdependencies within each ring, binding successive portions of that ring's act together, but not much across rings. Perhaps what the field needs is another genius like Piaget to show us how, and to what extent, all those cognitive-developmental strands within the growing child are really knotted together (Flavell, 1982a, 1982b).

SUMMARY

Psychologists who work in the area of cognitive development see it as replete with difficult questions and problems. Many of these can be subsumed under the headings of *diagnosis, explanations,* and *patterns.*

There are three closely related types of questions and problems in the area of diagnosis—namely, those concerning (1) *concrete and practical aspects of assessment,* (2) *abstract and theoretical aspects of assessment,* and (3) *conceptualization.* A useful cognitive-developmental acquisition to illustrate these is transitive inference concerning length relations—for example, if $A > B$ and $B > C$, then $A > C$ can be inferred.

A concrete and practical type of assessment problem is to find ways to minimize *false-negative* and *false-positive* diagnostic errors. A false-negative error consists of falsely concluding, based on one's testing results, that a particular child has not yet acquired a capability for, say, transitive inference. Even though the child does really possess this capability, he or she fails to show it in test performance because of information-processing, linguistic, motivational, emotional, or other problems. All tasks demand more from the child than the target cognitive entity the experimenter is interested in assessing. If the child fails to respond appropriately to any of these nontarget demands, a false-negative diagnostic error can result. Conversely, a false-positive error consists in falsely concluding, based on test performance, that a child does possess the target capability. For example, the child may conclude that $A > C$ simply because A had been called "longer than" something else (i.e., B) whereas C had not; the child therefore reaches the correct conclusion, but not by means of transitive inference. It is often possible to design a cognitive task in such a way that the probability of making a false-positive diagnostic error is greatly reduced. Unfortunately, these very same changes may increase the risk of false-negative errors.

Such facts suggest that there may be developmental changes in how the child "has" cognitive entities like transitive reasoning, and this possibility leads us to examine the diagnosis problem in a more abstract and theoretical fashion. A younger child may exhibit such reasoning only under the most favorable and facilitative task conditions, whereas an older one may exhibit it in almost all appropriate task situations. How can we characterize the difference in the way these two children "have" transitive inference? One possibility is that the older child may be better than the younger one in recognizing those task situations that call for a transitive-inference solution strategy; more task situations appropriately evoke an attempt to use that strategy (*evocation*). The older child may also be better at utilizing or executing the strategy successfully when it is evoked (*utilization*). An additional possibility is that the psychological nature of transitive inference itself may change as the child matures, and that this change may be partially responsible for its increased evocability and utilizability.

Consideration of these possibilities in turn raises the fundamental question of how cognitive entities like transitive inference are to be conceptualized. What is the nature and organization of the cognitive processes involved in an act of transitive inference? What psychological events are actually taking place in the child's head as the child solves a transitive-inference problem?

Recent process-oriented studies suggest that the underlying processes here may be quite different from those previously assumed.

Good diagnosis is essential for determining which cognitive entities regularly emerge in sequence, and which ones regularly develop synchronously or concurrently. Adequate conceptualizations of the process organizations which compose these entities are also needed to tell us whether these entities could plausibly be developmentally interdependent. Finally, diagnosis plays a crucial role in all intervention studies.

How is cognitive growth to be explained? Not entirely by environmental factors, according to two recent writings summarized in this chapter. The first stresses the essentially inevitable, inexorable quality of human cognitive growth. Although environmental factors certainly modulate and modify its course, they do not generate it and cannot explain the basic fact that growth occurs. The second argues that selection pressures during the evolutionary history of our species have contributed two things which virtually guarantee that children the world over will acquire sensory-motor intelligence. One contribution is an organism (the human infant) which is strongly biased, genetically, to acquire sensory-motor schemes. The other is a normal human caretaking environment which supplies just the kinds of inputs and experiential opportunities that an organism of that design needs to acquire sensory-motor schemes.

Environments or experiences differ in the amount and kind of contribution they could potentially make to cognitive development. A particular type of experience could conceivably be both *necessary* and *sufficient* for a particular type of development, necessary but not sufficient, sufficient but not necessary, or helpful without being either necessary or sufficient. The results of *enrichment* and *deprivation* studies are often used to make inferences about environmental-experiential contributions. Piagetian training experiments are instances of enrichment studies, whereas investigations of individuals born with sensory or motor handicaps, or reared in psychologically impoverished circumstances, would be examples of deprivation studies. An enrichment study can show that experience A is capable of facilitating the development of cognitive skill X, but it cannot show that A is necessary to X's acquisition, nor even that it normally plays a formative role in the real-world, extralaboratory ontogenesis of X. In contrast, a deprivation study is potentially capable of showing that A is or is not necessary to X's real-world ontogenesis. Several deprivation studies illustrate how *versatile* and *resilient* a developing child can be: If the usual development route is blocked, he may find an unusual route to the same destination (versatility); if his cognitive growth is initially arrested because he has been reared in an abnormal environment, there may be pronounced "catch-up" growth if he is subsequently reared in a normal environment (resilience). Developmental versatility and resilience are not always in evidence, however, and we still know very little about the circumstances under which a child will and will not exhibit them.

Some theorists have proposed general processes or principles to explain the course of cognitive development. For example, Werner argued that development always proceeds by means of *differentiation* and *hierarchic integration*. Piaget's *equilibration model* of cognitive growth has been especially interesting to contemporary researchers. The process of development via equilibration takes place in three basic steps. Initially, the child's cognitive system with respect to some problem or conceptual domain is in equilibrium at a lower developmental level. Subsequently, the child detects something that conflicts or is discrepant with his present system, something that the system cannot assimilate or accommodate to, and therefore something which puts it in a state of disequilibrium. Finally, equilibrium is reestablished at a higher developmental level by modifying the cognitive system so that what was formerly perceived as discordant is now readily assimilable. There appear to be at least two difficulties with Piaget's equilibration model: (1) certain prerequisite skills seem to be needed in order to develop via an equilibration process, and the theory does not explain how the child develops these prerequisites; (2) not all major cognitive acquisitions look like they would have developed through a process of equilibration.

Two possible types of cognitive-developmental patterns are *stages* and *sequences*. The concepts of *structures, qualitative change, abruptness*, and especially, *concurrence* are relevant to the question of whether cognitive growth is stage-like. Tentative conclusions were made about each: Cognitive structures develop, but Piaget's structural models may not accurately characterize them. Many of the major cognitive-developmental changes appear to be qualitative rather than quantitative, at least at some level of analysis. Cognitive growth is gradual—perhaps very gradual—rather than abrupt. Same-stage cognitive acquisitions (e.g., concrete-operational ones) ought to develop in a closely interdependent, temporally concurrent fashion, according to most interpretations, if Piaget's concept of stage-by-stage development is to have any real meaning or validity. Although diagnostic problems make it difficult to tell for sure, it does not appear that they do normally develop in this tightly knit, concurrent fashion. The existing evidence suggests that cognitive growth is not as strongly and clearly a stage-like process as Piaget's theory claims it is. It should be added, however, that a number of developmental psychologists still advocate some form of stage theory of cognitive development.

Five types of X–Y developmental sequences can be distinguished, where X and Y represent cognitive entities: Y develops after X and constitutes an additional, alternative cognitive means to the same goal (*addition* sequence). Later-developing Y replaces earlier-developing X as an approach to a given problem (*substitution*). Y is derived from X by *differentiation, generalization*, or *stabilization* (*modification*). X becomes a component part of a larger cognitive unit Y (*inclusion*). X serves as a developmental facilitator of, or bridge to, Y (*mediation*).

References

ABRAHAMS, B. A. (1979). *An integrative approach to the study of the development of perspective-taking abilities.* Unpublished doctoral dissertation, Stanford University.

ACKERMAN, B. P. (1982). Retrieval variability: The inefficient use of retrieval cues by young children. *Journal of Experimental Child Psychology, 33,* 413–428.

ACREDELO, C. (1982). Conservation/nonconservation: Alternative explanations. In C. J. Brainerd (Ed.), *Progress in cognitive development* (Vol. 1). New York: Springer-Verlag.

ACREDELO, L. P. (1979). Laboratory versus home: The effect of environment on the 9-month-old infant's choice of spatial reference system. *Developmental Psychology, 14,* 666–667.

AEBLI, H. (1963). *Über die geistige Entwicklung des Kindes.* Stuttgart: Klett.

ALLOWAY, T., PLINE, P., & KRAMES, L. (Eds.). (1977). *Advances in the study of communication and affect: Attachment behavior* (Vol. 3). New York: Plenum Press.

ANDERSON, J. R. (1977). Induction of augmented transition networks. *Cognitive Science, 1,* 125–157.

ANDERSON, J. R. (1980). *Cognitive psychology and its implications.* San Francisco: W. H. Freeman.

ANDERSON, N. H., & CUNEO, D. O. (1978). The height + width rule in children's judgments of quantity. *Journal of Experimental Psychology: General, 107,* 335–378.

ANGLIN, J. M. (1977). *Word, object, and conceptual development.* New York: Norton.

ASHER, S. R. (1979). Referential communication. In G. J. Whitehurst & B. J. Zimmerman (Eds.), *The functions of language and cognition.* New York: Academic Press.

ASHER, S. R., & RENSHAW, P. D. (1981). Children without friends: Social knowledge and social skill training. In S. R. Asher & J. M. Gottman (Eds.), *The development of children's friendships.* New York: Cambridge University Press.

ASHMEAD, D. H., & PERLMUTTER, M. (1980). Infant memory in everyday life. In M. Perlmutter (Ed.), *New directions for child development: Children's memory* (No. 10). San Francisco: Jossey-Bass.

ASLIN, R. N. (1981). Experiential influences and sensitive periods in perceptual development: A unified model. In R. N. Aslin, J. R. Alberts, & M. R. Peterson (Eds.), *Development of perception: Psychobiological perspectives. Vol. 2: The visual system.* New York: Academic Press.

ASLIN, R. N., ALBERTS, J. R., & PETERSON, M. R. (Eds.). (1981). *Development of perception: Psychobiological perspectives.* New York: Academic Press.

ASLIN, R. N., PISONI, D. P., & JUSCZYK, P. W. (1983). Auditory development and speech perception in infancy. In M. M. Haith & J. J. Campos (Eds.), *Handbook of child psychology: Infancy and developmental psychobiology* (Vol. 2). New York: Wiley. (P. H. Mussen, General Editor)

ATKINSON, J., & BRADDICK, O. (1981). Acuity, contrast sensitivity, and accommodation in infancy. In R. N. Aslin, J. R. Alberts, & M. R. Peterson (Eds.), *Development of perception: Psychobiological perspectives.* Vol. 1. *The visual system.* New York: Academic Press.

BADDELEY, A. D., & HITCH, G. (1974). Working memory. In G. Bower (Ed.), *The psychology of learning and motivation* (Vol. 8). New York: Academic Press.

BAHRICK, L. E., WALKER, A. S., & NEISSER, U. (1981). Selective looking by infants. *Cognitive Psychology, 13,* 377–390.

BAKER, L. (1982). An evaluation of the role of metacognitive deficits in learning disabilities. *Topics in Learning and Learning Disabilities, 2,* 27–35.

BAKER, L., & BROWN, A. L. (1984). Metacognition and the reading process. In P.D. Pearson (Ed.), *A handbook of reading research.* New York: Longman.

BAKER, R. A., BROWN, K. W., & GOTTFRIED, A. W. (1982, March). *Ontogeny of tactile-visual cross-modal transfer.* Paper presented at the meeting of the International Conference on Infant Studies, Austin, Texas.

BANKS, M. S., & SALAPATEK, P. (1981). Infant pattern vision: A new approach based on the contrast sensitivity function. *Journal of Experimental Child Psychology, 31,* 1–45.

BANKS, M. S., & SALAPATEK, P. (1983). Infant visual perception. In M. M. Haith & J. J. Campos (Eds.), *Handbook of child psychology: Infancy and developmental biology* (Vol. 2). New York: Wiley. (P. H. Mussen, General Editor)

BARENBOIM, C. (1977). Developmental changes in the interpersonal cognitive system from middle childhood to adolescence. *Child Development, 48,* 1467–1474.

BARENBOIM, C. (1978). Development of recursive and nonrecursive thinking about persons. *Developmental Psychology, 14,* 419–420.

BARENBOIM, C. (1981). The development of person perception in childhood and adolescence: From behavioral comparisons to psychological constructs to psychological comparisons. *Child Development, 52,* 129–144.

BATES, E. (1976). *Language and context: The acquisition of pragmatics.* New York: Academic Press.

BATES, E., CAMAIONI, L., & VOLTERRA, V. (1975). The acquisition of performatives prior to speech. *Merrill-Palmer Quarterly, 21,* 205–226.

BEAL, C. R. (1983). *The development of knowledge about cognitive cueing.* Unpublished doctoral dissertation, Stanford University.

BEAL, C. R., & FLAVELL, J. H. (1982). The effect of increasing the salience of message ambiguities on kindergartners' evaluations of communicative success and message adequacy. *Developmental Psychology, 18,* 43–48.

BEARISON, D. J. (1969). Role of measurement operations in the acquisition of conservation. *Developmental Psychology, 1,* 653–660.

BEILIN, H. (1971). The training and acquisition of logical operations. In M. F. Rosskopf, L. P. Steffe, & S. Taback (Eds.), *Piagetian cognitive-development research and mathematical education.* Washington, D.C.: National Council of Teachers of Mathematics.

BEM, S. (1970). The role of comprehension in children's problem-solving. *Developmental Psychology, 2,* 351–358.

BERNDT, T. J. (1981). Relations between social cognition, nonsocial cognition, and social behavior: The case of friendship. In J. H. Flavell & L. Ross (Eds.), *Social cognitive development: Frontiers and possible futures.* New York: Cambridge University Press.

BERNDT, T., & BERNDT, E. G. (1975). Children's use of motives and intentionality in person perception and moral judgment. *Child Development, 46,* 904–912.

BERNDT, T., & HELLER, K. (in press). Predictions of future behavior, trait ratings, and responses to open-ended questions as measures of children's personality attributions. In S. R. Yussen (Ed.), *The growth of reflection.* New York: Academic Press.

BIGELOW, B. J. (1977). Children's friendship expectations: A cognitive-developmental study. *Child Development, 48,* 246–253.

BLOOM, L. M. (1973). *One word at a time: The use of single word utterances before syntax.* The Hague: Mouton.

BORKE, H. (1971). Interpersonal perception of young children: Egocentrism or empathy? *Developmental Psychology, 5,* 263–269.

BORKE, H. (1973). The development of empathy in Chinese and American children between three and six years of age: A cross-culture study. *Developmental Psychology, 9,* 102–108.

BORKOWSKI, J. G. (in press). Signs of intelligence: Strategy generalization and metacognition. In S. R. Yussen (Ed.), *The growth of reflection.* New York: Academic Press.

BORKOWSKI, J. G., LEVERS, S., & GRUENENFELDER, T. M. (1976). Transfer of mediational strategies in children: The role of activity and awareness during strategy acquisition. *Child Development, 47,* 779–786.

BORKOWSKI, J. G., & PRESSLEY, M. (1983). *Children's metamemory: Cognitive interventions and prior knowledge states.* Unpublished paper.

BORTNER, M., & BIRCH, H. G. (1970). Cognitive capacity and cognitive competence. *American Journal of Mental Deficiency, 74,* 735–744.

BOWER, T. G. R. (1974). *Development in infancy.* San Francisco: W. H. Freeman.

BOWER, T. G. R. (1977). Comment on Yonas et al., "The development of sensitivity to information for impending collision." *Perception and Psychophysics, 21,* 281–282.

BOWER, T. G. R., & PATTERSON, J. G. (1972). Stages in the development of the object concept. *Cognition, 1,* 47–55.

BOWERMAN, M. F. (1977). The acquisition of word meaning: An investigation of some current conflicts. In N. Waterson & C. Snow (Eds.), *Proceedings of the Third International Child Language Symposium.* New York: Wiley.

BOWLBY, J. (1969). *Attachment and loss* (Vol. I): *Attachment.* New York: Basic Books.

BRAINE, M. D. S. (1976). Children's first word combinations. *Monographs of the Society for Research in Child Development, 40*(1, Serial No. 164).

BRAINE, M. D. S., & RUMAIN, B. (1983). Logical reasoning. In J. H. Flavell & E. M. Markman (Eds.), *Handbook of child psychology: Cognitive development* (Vol. 3). New York: Wiley. (P. H. Mussen, General Editor)

BRAINE, M. D. S., & SHANKS, B. L. (1965a). The conservation of a shape property and a proposal about the origin of the conservations. *Canadian Journal of Psychology, 19,* 197–207.

BRAINE, M. D. S., & SHANKS, B. L. (1965b). The development of conservation of size. *Journal of Verbal Learning and Verbal Behavior, 4,* 227–242.

BRAINERD, C. J. (1972, March–April) *Structures of thought in middle-childhood: Recent research on Piaget's concrete-operational groupements.* Paper presented at the Third Interdisciplinary Meeting on Structural Learning, Philadelphia.

BRAINERD, C. J. (1974). Neo-Piagetian training experiments revisited: Is there any support for the cognitive-developmental stage hypothesis? *Cognition, 2,* 349–370.

BRAINERD, C. J. (1977). Response criteria in concept development research. *Child Development, 48,* 360–366.

BRAINERD, C. J. (1978a). *Piaget's theory of intelligence.* Englewood Cliffs, N.J.: Prentice-Hall.

BRAINERD, C. J. (1978b). The stage question in cognitive-developmental theory. *Behavioral and Brain Sciences, 2,* 173–213.

BRAINERD, C. J. (1979). *The origins of the number concept.* New York: Praeger.

BRAINERD, C. J. (1983). Working memory systems and cognitive development. In C. J. Brainerd (Ed.), *Recent advances in cognitive-development theory: Progress in cognitive developmental research.* New York: Springer-Verlag.

BRAINERD, C. J., & KINGMA, J. (1984). Do children have to remember to reason? A fuzzy-trace theory of transitivity development. *Developmental Review.*

BRANDT, M. M. (1978). Relations between cognitive role-taking performance and age, task presentation, and response requirements. *Developmental Psychology, 14,* 206–213.

BRANSFORD, J. D., & FRANKS, J. J. (1971). The abstraction of linguistic ideas. *Cognitive Psychology, 2,* 331–350.

BRESLOW, L. (1981). Reevaluation of the literature on the development of transitive inferences. *Psychological Bulletin, 89,* 325–351.

BRETHERTON, I., MCNEW, S., & BEEGHLY-SMITH, M. (1981). Early person knowledge as expressed in gestural and verbal communication: When do infants acquire a "theory of mind"? In M. E. Lamb & L. R. Sherrod (Eds.), *Infant social cognition.* Hillsdale, N.J.: Lawrence Erlbaum Associates.

BRODY, L. R. (1981). Visual short-term cued recall memory in infancy. *Child Development, 52,* 242–250.

BRONSON, G. (1974). The postnatal growth of visual capacity. *Child Development, 45,* 873–890.

BRONSON, W. A. (1971). The growth of competence: Issues of conceptualization and measurement. In H. R. Schaffer (Ed.), *The origins of human social relations.* New York: Academic Press.

BROUGHTON, J. (1978). Development of concepts of self, mind, reality, and knowledge. *New Directions for Child Development, 1,* 75–100.

BROWN, A. L. (1975). The development of memory: Knowing, knowing about knowing, and knowing how to know. In H. W. Reese (Ed.), *Advances in child development and behavior* (Vol. 10). New York: Academic Press.

BROWN, A. L. (1978). Knowing when, where, and how to remember: A problem of metacognition. In R. Glaser (Ed.), *Advances in instructional psychology* (Vol. 1). Hillsdale, N.J.: Lawrence Erlbaum Associates.

BROWN, A. L. (1979, March). *Reflections on metacognition: Discussant's comments.* Paper presented at the meeting of the Society for Research in Child Development, San Francisco.

BROWN, A. L., BRANSFORD, J. D., FERRARA, R. A., & CAMPIONE, J. C. (1983). Learning, remembering, and understanding. In J. H. Flavell & E. M. Markman (Eds.), *Handbook of child psychology: Cognitive development* (Vol. 3). New York: Wiley. (P. H. Mussen, General Editor)

BROWN, A. L., & DELOACHE, J. S. (1978). Skills, plans, and self-regulation. In R. S. Siegler (Ed.), *Children's thinking: What develops?* Hillsdale, N.J.: Lawrence Erlbaum Associates.

BROWN, A. L., SMILEY, S. S., & LAWTON, S. Q. C. (1978). The effects of experience on the selection of suitable retrieval cues for studying texts. *Child Development, 49,* 829–835.

BROWN, G., & DESFORGES, C. (1979). *Piaget's theory: A psychological critique.* London: Routledge and Kegan Paul.

BROWN, R. (1958). How shall a thing be called? *Psychological Review, 65,* 14–21.

BROWN, R. (1973). *A first language: The early stages.* Cambridge, Mass.: Harvard University Press.

BROWN, R., CAZDEN, C. B., & BELLUGI, U. (1969). The child's grammar from I to III. In J. P. Hill (Ed.), *Minnesota symposium on child psychology* (Vol. 2). Minneapolis: University of Minnesota Press.

BROWN, R., & HANLON, C. (1970). Derivational complexity and order of acquisition. In J. R. Hayes (Ed.), *Cognition and the development of language.* New York: Wiley.

BRUNER, J. S. (1967, September). *Origins of mind in infancy.* Paper presented at the meeting of Division 8 of the American Psychological Association, Washington, D.C.

BRUNER, J. S. (1975). The ontogenesis of speech acts. *Journal of Child Language, 2,* 1–19.

BRYANT, P. E., & KOPYTYNSKA, H. (1976). Spontaneous measurement by young children. *Nature, 260,* 773.

BULLOCK, M., & GELMAN, R. (1979). Preschool children's assumptions about cause and effect: Temporal ordering. *Child Development, 50,* 89–96.

BULLOCK, M., GELMAN, R., & BAILLARGEON, R. (1982). The development of causal reasoning. In W. Friedman (Ed.), *The developmental psychology of time.* New York: Academic Press.

BUTTERFIELD, E. C., & BELMONT, J. M. (1977). Assessing and improving the executive cognitive functions of mentally retarded people. In I. Bialer & M. Sternlicht (Eds.), *Psychological issues in mental retardation.* Chicago: Aldine-Atherton.

BUTTERFIELD, E. C., & SIPERSTEIN, G. N. (1972). Influence of contingent auditory stimulation upon non-nutritional suckle. In J. Bosma (Ed.), *Third symposium on oral sensation and perception: The mouth of the infant.* Springfield, Ill.: Charles C Thomas.

BUTTERFIELD, E. C., WAMBOLD, C., & BELMONT, J. M. (1973). On the theory and practice of improving short-term memory. *American Journal of Mental Deficiency, 77,* 654–669.

BUTTERWORTH, G. (1977). Object disappearance and error in Piaget's Stage IV task. *Journal of Experimental Child Psychology, 23,* 391–401.

BUTTERWORTH, G. (1982). A brief account of the conflict between the individual and the social in models of cognitive growth. In G. Butterworth & P. Light (Eds.), *Social cognition: Studies of the development of social understanding.* Chicago: University of Chicago Press.

BUTTERWORTH, G., & JARRET, N. (1980, September). *The geometry of pre-verbal communication.* Paper presented at the meeting of the British Psychological Society, Developmental Psychology Section, Edinburgh.

BUTTERWORTH, G., & LIGHT, P. (Eds.). (1982). *Social cognition: Studies of the development of understanding.* Chicago: University of Chicago Press.

CAMPOS, J. J., HIATT, S., RAMSAY, D., HENDERSON, C., & SVEJDA, M. (1978). The emergence of fear on the visual cliff. In M. Lewis & L. A. Rosenblum (Eds.), *The origins of affect.* New York: Plenum.

CAMPOS, J. J., & STENBERG, C. R. (1981). Perception, appraisal and emotion: The onset of social referencing. In M. E. Lamb & L. R. Sherrod (Eds.), *Infant social cognition: Empirical and theoretical considerations.* Hillsdale, N.J.: Lawrence Erlbaum Associates.

CAMPOS, J. J., SVEJDA, M., BERTENTHAL, B., BENSON, N., & SCHMID, D. (1981, April). *Self-produced locomotion and wariness of heights: New evidence from training studies.* Paper presented at the meeting of the Society for Research in Child Development, Boston.

CANTOR, G. N. (1983). Conflict, learning, and Piaget; Comments on Zimmerman and Blom's "Toward an empirical test of the role of cognitive conflict in learning." *Developmental Review, 3,* 39–53.

CAPLOVITZ, K. S., & CAMPOS, J. J. (1983, April). *Wariness of heights: An outcome of locomotor experience or age?* Paper presented at the meeting of the Society for Research in Child Development, Detroit.

CAREY, S. (1978). The child as word learner. In M. Halle, J. Bresnan, & G. A. Miller (Eds.), *Linguistic theory and psychological reality.* Cambridge, Mass.: MIT Press.

CAREY, S. (1982). *Are children fundamentally different kinds of thinkers and learners than adults?* Unpublished paper.

CARON, A. J., & CARON, R. F. (1982). Cognitive development in early infancy. In T. Field (Ed.), *Review of human development.* New York: Wiley.

CARON, A. J., CARON, R. F., & CARLSON, V. R. (1979). Infant perception of the invariant shape of objects differing in slant. *Child Development, 50,* 716–721.

CARROLL, J. J., & GIBSON, E. J. (1981, April). *Differentiation of an aperture from an obstacle under conditions of motion by three-month-old infants.* Paper presented at the meeting of the Society for Research in Child Development, Boston.

CASE, R. S. (1978). Intellectual development from birth to adulthood: A neo-Piagetian interpretation. In R. W. Siegler (Ed.), *Children's thinking: What develops?* Hillsdale, N.J.: Lawrence Erlbaum Associates.

CASE, R. (1981, April). *The search for horizontal structure in children's development.* Paper presented at the meeting of the Society for Research in Child Development, Boston.

CASE, R. (1985). *Intellectual development: A systematic reinterpretation.* New York: Academic Press.

CASE, R., KURLAND, D. M., & GOLDBERG, J. (1982). Operational efficiency and the growth of short-term memory span. *Journal of Experimental Child Psychology, 33,* 386–404.

CAVANAUGH, J. C., & PERLMUTTER, M. (1982). Metamemory: A critical examination. *Child Development, 53,* 11–28.

CECI, S. J., & HOWE, M. J. A. (1978). Age-related differences in free recall as a function of retrieval flexibility. *Journal of Experimental Child Psychology, 26,* 432–442.

CHANDLER, M. J. (1977). Social cognition: A selective review of current research. In W. F. Overton & J. M. Gallagher (Eds.), *Knowledge and development* (Vol. 1). New York: Plenum Press.

CHARLESWORTH, W. R. (1966, September). *Development of the object concept: A methodological study.* Paper presented at the meeting of the American Psychological Association, New York.

CHASE, W. G., & SIMON, H. A. (1973). Perception in chess. *Cognitive Psychology, 4,* 55–81.

CHI, M. T. H. (1976). Short-term memory limitations in children: Capacity or processing deficits? *Memory and Cognition, 4*(5), 559–572.

CHI, M. T. H. (1978). Knowledge structures and memory development. In R. S. Siegler (Ed.), *Children's thinking: What develops?* Hillsdale, N.J.: Lawrence Erlbaum Associates.

CHI, M. T. H. (Ed.). (1983). *Trends in memory development research.* Basel, Switzerland: Karger.

CHI, M. T. H. (1984). Representing knowledge and metaknowledge: Implications for interpreting metamemory research. In F. E. Weinert and R. H. Kluwe (Eds.), Metakognition, motivation und lernen. Stuttgart: Kohlhammer.

CHI, M. T. H., FELTOVICH, P. J., & GLASER, R. (1981). Categorization and representation of physics problems by experts and novices. *Cognitive Science, 5,* 121–152.

CHI, M. T. H., & GALLAGHER, J. D. (in press). Speed of processing: A developmental source of limitation. *Topics in Learning and Learning Disabilities.*

CHI, M. T. H., & GLASER, R. (1980). The measurement of expertise: Analysis of the development of knowledge and skill as a basis for assessing achievement. In E. L. Baker & E. S. Quellmalz (Eds.), *Educational testing and evaluation: Design, analysis and policy.* Beverly Hills, Calif.: Sage Publications.

CHI, M. T. H., GLASER, R., & REES, E. (1982). Expertise in problem solving. In R. J. Sternberg (Ed.), *Advances in the psychology of human intelligence* (Vol. 1). Hillsdale, N.J.: Lawrence Erlbaum Associates.

CHI, M. T. H., & KOESKE, R. D. (1983). Network representation of a child's dinosaur knowledge. *Developmental Psychology, 19,* 29–39.

CHI, M. T. H., & REES, E. T. (1983). A learning framework for development. In M. T. H. Chi (Ed.), *Trends in memory development.* Basel, Switzerland: Karger.

CHOMSKY, N. (1972). *Language and mind* (enlarged ed.). San Diego, Calif.: Harcourt Brace Jovanovich.

CHURCHER, J., & SCAIFE, M. (1982). How infants see the point. In G. Butterworth & P. Light (Eds.), *Social cognition: Studies of the development of understanding.* Chicago: University of Chicago Press.

CLARK, E. V. (1973). What's in a word? On the child's acquisition of semantics in his first language. In T. Moore (Ed.), *Cognitive development and the acquisition of language.* New York: Academic Press.

CLARK, E. V. (1983). Meanings and concepts. In J. H. Flavell & E. M. Markman (Eds.), *Handbook of child psychology: Cognitive development* (Vol. 3). New York: Wiley.

CLARK, H. H., & CLARK, E. V. (1977). *Psychology and language: An introduction to psycholinguistics.* San Diego, Calif.: Harcourt Brace Jovanovich.

CLARK, H. H., & MARSHALL, C. (1978). Reference diaries. In D. L. Waltz (Ed.), *Theoretical issues in natural language processing-2.* New York: Association for Computing Machinery.

COHEN, L. B., DELOACHE, J. S., & STRAUSS, M. S. (1979). Infant visual perception. In J. D. Osofsky (Ed.), *Handbook of infant development.* New York: Wiley.

COHEN, L. B., & GELBER, E. R. (1975). Infant visual memory. In L. B. Cohen & P. Salapatek (Eds.), *Infant perception: From sensation to cognition.* New York: Academic Press.

COHEN, L. B. & STRAUSS, M. S. (1979). Concept acquisition in the human infant. *Child Development, 50,* 419–424.

COIE, J. D., COSTANZO, P. R., & FARNILL, D. (1973). Specific transitions in the development of spatial perspective-taking ability. *Developmental Psychology, 9,* 167–177.

COLBY, A., KOHLBERG, L., GIBBS, J., & LIEBERMAN, M. (1983). A longitudinal study of moral judgment. *Monographs of the Society for Research in Child Development, 48,* (1–2, Serial No. 200).

COLE, M., & BRUNER, J. S. (1971). Cultural differences and inferences about psychological processes. *American Psychologist, 26,* 867–876.

COLE, M., & SCRIBNER, S. (1974). *Culture and thought: A psychological introduction.* New York: Wiley.

COLE, M., & SCRIBNER, S. (1977). Cross-cultural studies of memory and cognition. In R. V. Kail & J. W. Hagen (Eds.), *Perspectives on the development of memory and cognition.* Hillsdale, N.J.: Lawrence Erlbaum Associates.

COLLINS, A., & SMITH, E. E. (1982). Teaching the process of reading comprehension. In D. K. Detterman & R. J. Sternberg (Eds.), *How and how much can intelligence be raised?* Norwood N.J.: Ablex.

COLLINS, W. A. (Ed.). (1980). *Minnesota symposia on child psychology (Vol. 13): Development of cognition, affect, and social relations.* Hillsdale, N.J.: Lawrence Erlbaum Associates.

CROMER, R. F. (1974). The development of language and cognition: The cognition hypothesis. In B. Foss (Ed.), *New perspectives in child development.* Harmondsworth, Eng.: Penguin Books.

CROMER, R. F. (1980, September). *Language acquisition reconsidered.* Paper presented at the meeting of the British Psychological Society, Developmental Psychology Section, Edinburgh.

CULTICE, J. C., SOMERVILLE, S. C., & WELLMAN, H. M. (1983). Preschoolers' memory monitoring: Feeling of knowing judgments. *Child Development, 54,* 1480–1486.

CUVO, A. J. (1975). Developmental differences in rehearsal and free recall. *Journal of Experimental Child Psychology, 19,* 265–278.

DAGENAIS, Y. (1973). *Analyse de la cohérence opératoire entre les groupements d'addition des classes, de multiplication des classes et d'addition des relations asymétriques.* Unpublished doctoral dissertation, Université de Montréal.

DALE, P. S. (1976). *Language development* (2nd ed.). New York: Holt, Rinehart & Winston.

DAMON, W. (1977). *The social world of the child.* San Francisco: Jossey-Bass.

DAMON, W. (Ed.). (1978). *New directions for child development* (Vol. 1): *Social cognition.* San Francisco: Jossey-Bass.

DAMON, W. (1981). Exploring children's social cognition on two fronts. In J. H. Flavell & L. Ross (Eds.), *Social cognitive development: Frontiers and possible futures.* New York: Cambridge University Press.

DAMON, W. (1983). The nature of social-cognitive change in the developing child. In W. F. Overton (Ed.), *The relationship between social and cognitive development.* Hillsdale, N.J.: Lawrence Erlbaum Associates.

DAMON, W., & HART, D. (1982). The development of self-understanding from infancy through adolescence. *Child Development, 53,* 841–864.

DANNEMILLER, J. L., & BANKS, M. S. (1983). Can selective adaptation account for early infant habituation? *Merrill-Palmer Quarterly, 29,* 151–158.

DASEN, P. R. (Ed.). (1977). *Piagetian psychology: Cross-cultural contributions.* New York: Gardner.

DAY, R. H., & McKENZIE, B. E. (1977). Constancies in the perceptual world of the infant. In W. Epstein (Ed.), *Stability and constancy in visual perception: Mechanisms and processes.* New York: Wiley.

DECASPER, A. J., & FIFER, W. P. (1980). Of human bonding: Newborns prefer their mother's voice. *Science, 208,* 1174–1176.

DELOACHE, J. S. (1983, April). *Joint picture book reading as memory training for toddlers.* Paper presented at the meeting of the Society for Research in Child Development, Detroit.

DELOACHE, J. S. (in press). Oh where, oh where: Memory-based searching by very young children. In C. Sophian (Ed.), *Origins of cognitive skills.* Hillsdale, N.J.: Lawrence Erlbaum Associates.

DEMPSTER, F. N. (1981). Memory span: Sources of individual and developmental differences. *Psychological Bulletin, 89,* 63–100.

DE VILLIERS, J. G., & DE VILLIERS, P. A. (1973a). A cross-sectional study of the acquisition of grammatical morphemes. *Journal of Psycholinguistic Research, 2,* 267–278.

DE VILLIERS, J. G., & DE VILLIERS, P. A.(1973b). Development of the use of word order in comprehension. *Journal of Psycholinguistic Research, 2,* 331–341.

DE VILLIERS, P. A., & DE VILLIERS, J. G. (1978). *Language acquisition.* Cambridge, Mass.: Harvard University Press.

DE VILLIERS, P. A., & DE VILLIERS, J. G. (1979). *Early language.* Cambridge, Mass.: Harvard University Press.

DICKSON, W. P. (Ed.). (1981). *Children's oral communication skills.* New York: Academic Press.

DODD, B. (1979). Lip reading in infants: Attention to speech presented in- and out-of synchrony. *Cognitive Psychology, 11,* 478–484.

DONALDSON, M. (1976). Development of conceptualization. In V. Hamilton & M. D. Vernon (Eds.), *The development of cognitive processes.* London: Academic Press.

DONALDSON, M. (1978). *Children's minds.* New York: Norton.

DORE, J. (1974). A pragmatic description of early language development. *Journal of Psycholinguistic Research, 3,* 343–350.

DWECK, C. S. (1981). Social-cognitive processes in children's friendships. In S. R. Asher & J. M. Gottman (Eds.), *The development of children's friendships.* New York: Cambridge University Press.

EIMAS, P. D. (1975). Developmental studies of speech perception. In L. B. Cohen & P. Salapatek (Eds.), *Infant perception: From sensation to perception* (Vol. 7). New York: Academic Press.

EIMAS, P. D., SIQUELAND, E. R., JUSCZYK, P., & VIGORITO, J. (1971). Speech perception in infants. *Science, 171,* 303–306.

ELDER, J. L., & PEDERSON, D. R. (1978). Preschool children's use of objects in symbolic play. *Child Development, 49,* 500–504.

ELKIND, D. (1967). Egocentrism in adolescence. *Child Development, 38,* 1025–1034.

ENNIS, R. H. (1975). Children's ability to handle Piaget's propositional logic: A conceptual critique. *Review of Educational Research, 45,* 1–41.

ERVIN, S. M. (1964). Imitation and structural change in children's language. In E. H. Lenneberg (Ed.), *New directions in the study of language.* Cambridge, Mass.: MIT Press.

EVANS, W. F., & GRATCH, G. (1972). The stage IV error in Piaget's theory of object concept development: Difficulties in object conceptualization or spatial localization? *Child Development, 43,* 682–688.

FABRICIUS, W. V., & HAGEN, J. W. (in press). The use of causal attributions about recall performance to assess metamemory and predict strategic memory behavior in young children. *Child Development.*

FABRICIUS, W. V., & WELLMAN, H. M. (1983). Children's understanding of retrieval cue utilization. *Developmental Psychology, 19,* 15–21.

FAGAN, J. F. (1973). Infants' delayed recognition memory and forgetting. *Journal of Experimental Child Psychology, 16,* 424-450.

FANTZ, R. L., FAGAN, J. F., & MIRANDA, S. B. (1975). Early visual selectivity. In L. B. Cohen & P. Salapatek (Eds.), *Infant perception: From sensation to cognition* (Vol. 1). New York: Academic Press.

FEIN, G. G. (1975). A transformational analysis of pretending. *Developmental Psychology, 11,* 291-296.

FEIN, G. G. (1979). Play and the acquisition of symbols. In L. Katz (Ed.), *Current topics in early childhood education.* Norwood, N.J.: Ablex.

FEIN, G. G. (1981). Pretend play: New perspectives. In E. M. Hetherington & R. D. Parke (Eds.), *Contemporary readings in child psychology* (2nd ed.). New York: McGraw-Hill.

FELDMAN C. F., & TOULMIN, S. (1976). Logic and theory of mind. *Nebraska Symposium on Motivation, 23,* 409-476.

FELDMAN, D. H. (1980). *Beyond universals in cognitive development.* Norwood, N.J.: Ablex.

FESHBACH, N. D. (1973, August). *Empathy: An interpersonal process.* Paper presented at the meeting of the American Psychological Association, Montreal.

FISCHER, K. W. (1980). A theory of cognitive development: The control and construction of hierarchies of skills. *Psychological Reviews, 87,* 477-531.

FISCHER, K. W., & BULLOCK, D. (1981). Patterns of data: Sequence, synchrony, and constraint in cognitive development. In K. W. Fischer (Ed.), *Cognitive development.* San Francisco: Jossey-Bass.

FLAPAN, D. (1968). *Children's understanding of social interaction.* New York: Teachers College Press.

FLAVELL, J. H. (1963). *The developmental psychology of Jean Piaget.* Princeton, N.J.: Van Nostrand.

FLAVELL, J. H. (1970a). Concept development. In P. H. Mussen (Ed.), *Carmichael's manual of child psychology* (Vol. 1). New York: Wiley.

FLAVELL, J. H. (1970b). Developmental studies of mediated memory. In H. W. Reese & L. P. Lipsitt (Eds.), *Advances in child development and behavior* (Vol. 5). New York: Academic Press.

FLAVELL, J. H. (1971a). Comments on Beilin's "The development of physical concepts." In T. Mischel (Ed.), *Cognitive development and epistemology.* New York: Academic Press.

FLAVELL, J. H. (1971b). First discussant's comments: What is memory development the development of? *Human Development, 14,* 272-278.

FLAVELL, J. H. (1971c). Stage-related properties of cognitive development. *Cognitive Psychology, 2,* 421-453.

FLAVELL, J. H. (1972). An analysis of cognitive-developmental sequences. *Genetic Psychology Monographs, 86,* 279-350.

FLAVELL, J. H. (1974). The development of inferences about others. In T. Mischel (Ed.), *Understanding other persons.* Oxford, Eng.: Blackwell, Basil, and Mott.

FLAVELL, J. H. (1976, July). *The development of metacommunication.* Paper presented at the Twenty-First International Congress of Psychology, Paris.

FLAVELL, J. H. (1977). *Cognitive development* (1st ed.). Englewood Cliffs, N.J.: Prentice-Hall.

FLAVELL, J. H. (1978a). Comments. In R. S. Siegler (Ed.), *Children's thinking: What develops?* Hillsdale, N.J.: Lawrence Erlbaum Associates.

FLAVELL, J. H. (1978b). The development of knowledge about visual perception. In C. B. Keasey (Ed.), *Nebraska symposium on motivation* (Vol. 25). Lincoln: University of Nebraska Press.

FLAVELL, J. H. (1978c, August). *Metacognition.* Paper presented at the meeting of the American Psychological Association, Toronto.

FLAVELL, J. H. (1978d). Metacognitive development. In J. M. Scandura & C. J. Brainerd (Eds.), *Structural/process theories of complex human behavior.* Alphen a. d. Rijn, The Netherlands: Sijthoff and Noordhoff.

FLAVELL, J. H. (1979). Metacognition and cognitive monitoring: A new area of cognitive-developmental inquiry. *American Psychologist, 34,* 906-911.

FLAVELL, J. H. (1981a). Cognitive monitoring. In W. P. Dickson (Ed.), *Children's oral communication skills.* New York: Academic Press.

FLAVELL, J. H. (1981b). Monitoring social cognitive enterprises: Something else that may develop in the area of social cognition. In J. H. Flavell & L. Ross (Eds.), *Social cognitive development: Frontiers and possible futures.* New York: Cambridge University Press.

FLAVELL, J. H. (1982a). On cognitive development. *Child Development, 53,* 1–10.

FLAVELL, J. H. (1982b). Structures, stages, and sequences in cognitive development. In W. A. Collins (Ed.), *Minnesota symposia on child psychology* (Vol. 15). Hillsdale, N.J.: Lawrence Erlbaum Associates.

FLAVELL, J. H. (1984a). Discussion. In R. J. Sternberg (Ed.), *Mechanisms of cognitive development.* New York: W. H. Freeman.

FLAVELL, J. H. (1984b). Speculations about the nature and development of metacognition. In F. E. Weinert & R. H. Kluwe (Eds.), *Metakognition, motivation und lernen.* Stuttgart: Kohlhammer.

FLAVELL, J. H., BEACH, D. H., & CHINSKY, J. M. (1966). Spontaneous verbal rehearsal in a memory task as a function of age. *Child Development, 37,* 283–299.

FLAVELL, J. H., BOTKIN, P. T., FRY, C. L., WRIGHT, J. W., & JARVIS, P. E. (1968). *The development of role-taking and communication skills in children.* New York: Wiley. (Reprinted by Robert E. Krieger Publishing Company, Huntington, New York, 1975.)

FLAVELL, J. H., EVERETT, B. A., CROFT, K., & FLAVELL, E. R. (1981). Young children's knowledge about visual perception: Further evidence for the Level 1-Level 2 distinction. *Developmental Psychology, 17,* 99–103.

FLAVELL, J. H., FLAVELL, E. R., & GREEN, F. L. (1983). Development of the appearance-reality distinction. *Cognitive Psychology, 15,* 95–120.

FLAVELL, J. H., FRIEDRICHS, A. G., & HOYT, J. D. (1970). Developmental changes in memorization processes. *Cognitive Psychology, 1,* 324–340.

FLAVELL, J. H., & MARKMAN, E. M. (Eds.). (1983). *Handbook of child psychology: Cognitive development* (Vol. 3). New York: Wiley. (P. H. Mussen, General Editor)

FLAVELL, J. H., OMANSON, R. C., & LATHAM, C. (1978). Solving spatial perspective-taking problems by rule versus computation: A developmental study. *Developmental Psychology, 14,* 462–473.

FLAVELL, J. H., & ROSS, L. (1981a). Concluding remarks. In J. H. Flavell & L. Ross (Eds.), *Social cognitive development: Frontiers and possible futures.* New York: Cambridge University Press.

FLAVELL, J. H., & ROSS, L. (Eds.). (1981b). *Social cognitive development: Frontiers and possible futures.* New York: Cambridge University Press.

FLAVELL, J. H., SHIPSTEAD, S. G., & CROFT, K. (1978) Young children's knowledge about visual perception: Hiding objects from others. *Child Development, 49,* 1208–1211.

FLAVELL, J. H., SHIPSTEAD, S. G., & CROFT, K. (1980). What young children think you see when their eyes are closed. *Cognition, 8,* 369–387.

FLAVELL, J. H., SPEER, J. R., GREEN, F. L., & AUGUST, D. L. (1981). The development of comprehension monitoring and knowledge about communication. *Monographs of the Society for Research in Child Development, 46,* (5, Serial No. 192).

FLAVELL, J. H., & WELLMAN, H. M. (1977). Metamemory. In R. V. Kail & J. W. Hagen (Eds.), *Perspectives on the development of memory and cognition.* Hillsdale, N.J.: Lawrence Erlbaum Associates.

FLAVELL, J. H., & WOHLWILL, J. F. (1969). Formal and functional aspects of cognitive development. In D. Elkind & J. H. Flavell (Eds.), *Studies in cognitive development: Essays in honor of Jean Piaget.* New York: Oxford University Press.

FORREST-PRESSLEY, D. L., MACKINNON, E., & WALLER, T.G. (Eds.). (in press). *Metacognition, cognition, and human performance.* New York: Academic Press.

FORREST, D. L., & WALLER, T. G. (1979, March). *Cognitive and metacognitive aspects of reading.* Paper presented at the meeting of the Society for Research in Child Development, San Francisco.

FOX, R., & MCDANIEL, C. (1982). The perception of biological motion by human infants. *Science, 218,* 486–487.

FRANCIS, D. (1978). *Trial run.* New York: Harper & Row.

FREEMAN, N. H. (1980). *Strategies of representation in children: Analysis of spatial skills and drawing processes.* London: Academic Press.

FRIJDA, N. H. (1972). Simulation of human long-term memory. *Psychological Bulletin, 77,* 1–31.

FURTH, H. G. (1970). On language and knowing in Piaget's developmental theory. *Human Development, 13,* 241–57.

FURTH, H. G. (1971). Linguistic deficiency and thinking: Research with deaf subjects 1964–1969. *Psychological Bulletin, 76,* 58–72.

Furth, H. G. (1981). *Piaget and knowledge: Theoretical foundations* (2nd ed.). Chicago: University of Chicago Press.

Gagné, R. M. (1968a). Contributions of learning to human development. *Psychological Review, 75,* 177–191.

Gagné, R. M. (1968b, November). Learning hierarchies. *Educational Psychologist.*

Gallup, G. G. (1977). Self-recognition in primates: A comparative approach to the bidirectional properties of consciousness. *American Psychologist, 32,* 329–338.

Gardner, H. (1973). *The arts and human development.* New York: Wiley.

Gardner, H. (1978). *Developmental psychology: An introduction* (1st ed.). Boston: Little, Brown.

Gardner, H. (1982). *Developmental psychology: An introduction* (2nd ed.). Boston: Little, Brown.

Garner, R., & Haynes, J. (1982). *Acquisition of text lookback expertise.* Unpublished paper, University of Maryland.

Garner, R., & Reis, R. (1981). Monitoring and resolving comprehension obstacles: An investigation of spontaneous text lookbacks among upper-grade good and poor comprehenders. *Reading Research Quarterly, 16,* 569–582.

Garrity, L. I. (1975). An electromyographical study of subvocal speech and recall in preschool children. *Developmental Psychology, 11,* 274–281.

Gelman, R. (1972a). Logical capacity of very young children: Number invariance rules. *Child Development, 43,* 75–90.

Gelman, R. (1972b). The nature and development of early number concepts. In H. W. Reese (Ed.), *Advances in child development and behavior* (Vol. 7). New York: Academic Press.

Gelman, R. (1978). Cognitive development. *Annual Review of Psychology, 29,* 297–332.

Gelman, R. (1979). Preschool thought. *American Psychologist, 34,* 900–905.

Gelman, R. (1980). What young children know about numbers. *Educational Psychologist, 15,* 54–68.

Gelman, R. (1982). Basic numerical abilities. In R. J. Sternberg (Ed.), *Advances in the psychology of human intelligence* (Vol. 1). Hillsdale, N.J.: Lawrence Erlbaum Associates.

Gelman, R., & Baillargeon, R. (1983). A review of Piagetian concepts. In J. H. Flavell & E. M. Markman (Eds.), *Handbook of child psychology: Cognitive development* (Vol. 3). New York: Wiley. (P. H. Mussen, General Editor)

Gelman, R., & Gallistel, C. R. (1978). *The child's understanding of number.* Cambridge, Mass.: Harvard University Press.

Gelman, R., & Spelke, E. (1981). The development of thoughts about animate and inanimate objects: Implications for research on social cognition. In J. H. Flavell & L. Ross (Eds.), *Social cognitive development: Frontiers and possible futures.* New York: Cambridge University Press.

Gelman, R., & Weinberg, D. H. (1972). The relationship between liquid conservation and compensation. *Child Development, 43,* 371–383.

Gentner, D. (1975). Evidence for the psychological reality of semantic components: The verbs of possession. In D. A. Norman, D. E. Rumelhart, & the LNR Research Group, *Explorations in cognition.* San Francisco: W. H. Freeman.

Gibson, E. J. (1969). *Principles of perceptual learning and development.* New York: Appleton-Century-Crofts.

Gibson, E. J. (1982). The concept of affordances in development: The renascence of functionalism. In W. A. Collins (Ed.), *Minnesota symposia on child psychology* (Vol. 15). Hillsdale, N.J.: Lawrence Erlbaum Associates.

Gibson, E. J., & Rader, N. (1979). Attention: The perceiver as performer. In G. A. Hale & M. Lewis (Eds.), *Attention and cognitive development.* New York: Plenum.

Gibson, E. J., & Spelke, E. S. (1983). The development of perception. In J. H. Flavell & E. M. Markman (Eds.), *Handbook of child psychology: Cognitive development* (Vol. 3). New York: Wiley. (P. H. Mussen, General Editor)

Gibson, E. J., & Walk, R. D. (1960). The "visual cliff." *Scientific American, 202,* 64–71.

Gibson, E. J., & Walker, A. (1982, March). *Intermodal perception of substance.* Paper presented at the meeting of the International Conference on Infant Studies, Austin, Texas.

Gibson, J. J. (1966). *The senses considered as perceptual systems.* Boston: Houghton-Mifflin.

Ginsburg, H. (1977). *Children's arithmetic: The learning process.* New York: Van Nostrand.

GINSBURG, H., & OPPER, S. (1979). *Piaget's theory of intellectual development: An introduction* (2nd ed.). Englewood Cliffs, N.J.: Prentice-Hall.

GLASER, R., & RESNICK, L. B. (1972). Instructional psychology. *Annual Review of Psychology, 23,* 207–276.

GLICK, J. (1978). Cognition and social cognition: An introduction. In J. Glick & K. A. Clarke-Stewart (Eds.), *The development of social understanding.* New York: Gardner Press.

GLICK, J., & CLARKE-STEWART, K. A. (Eds.). (1978). *The development of social understanding.* New York: Gardner Press.

GLUCKSBERG, S., KRAUSS, R. M., & HIGGINS, E. T. (1975). The development of communication skills in children. In F. Horowitz (Ed.), *Review of child development research* (Vol. 4). Chicago: University of Chicago Press.

GOLDBERG, S., PERLMUTTER, M., & MYERS, N. (1974). Recall of related and unrelated lists by 2-year-olds. *Journal of Experimental Child Psychology, 18,* 1–8.

GOLDEN, M., MONTARE, A., & BRIDGER, W. (1977). Verbal control of delay behavior in two-year-old boys as a function of social class. *Child Development, 48,* 1107–1111.

GOLDIN-MEADOW, S. (1979). Structure in a manual communication system developed without a conventional language model: Language without a helping hand. In H. Whitaker & H. A. Whitaker (Eds.), *Studies in neurolinguistics* (Vol. 4). New York: Academic Press.

GOLOMB, C., & CORNELIUS, C. B. (1977). Symbolic play and its cognitive significance. *Developmental Psychology, 13,* 246–252.

GOODNOW, J. J. (1971). The role of modalities in perceptual and cognitive development. In J. P. Hill (Ed.), *Minnesota symposia on child psychology* (Vol. 5). Minneapolis: University of Minnesota Press.

GORDON, F. R., & FLAVELL, J. H. (1977). The development of intuitions about cognitive cueing. *Child Development, 48,* 1027–1033.

GOTTLIEB, G. (1976). Conceptions of prenatal development: Behavioral embryology. *Psychological Review, 83,* 215–234.

GOTTLIEB, G. (1981). Roles of early experience in species-specific perceptual development. In R. N. Aslin, J. R. Alberts, & M. R. Peterson (Eds.), *Development of perception: Psychobiological perspectives.* Vol. 1: *Audition, somatic perception, and the chemical senses.* New York: Academic Press.

GOVE, F. L., & KEATING, D. P. (1979). Empathic role-taking precursors. *Developmental Psychology, 15,* 594–600.

GRATCH, G. (1972). A study of the relative dominance of vision and touch in six-month-old infants. *Child Development, 43,* 615–623.

GRATCH, G. (1975). Recent studies based on Piaget's view of object concept development. In L. B. Cohen & P. Salapatek (Eds.), *Infant perception: From sensation to cognition.* New York: Academic Press.

GRATCH, G., & LANDERS, W. F. (1971). Stage IV of Piaget's theory of infants' object concepts: A longitudinal study. *Child Development, 42,* 359–372.

GREENFIELD, P.M., & SMITH, J. H. (1976). *The structure of communication in early language development.* New York: Academic Press.

GREENO, J. G., RILEY, M. S., & GELMAN, R. (1984). Conceptual competence and children's counting. *Cognitive Psychology, 16,* 94–143.

GRUBER, H. E., GIRGUS, J. S., & BANUAZIZI, A. (1971). The development of object permanence in the cat. *Developmental Psychology, 4,* 9–15.

GUNDERSON, V. M. (1983). Development of cross-modal recognition in infant pigtail monkeys (*Macaca nemestrina*). *Developmental Psychology, 19,* 398–404.

HAAKE, R. J., SOMERVILLE, S. C., & WELLMAN, H. M. (1980). Logical ability of young children in searching a large-scale environment. *Child Development, 51,* 1299–1302.

HAGEN, J. W., & HALE, G. A. (1973). The development of attention in children. In A. D. Pick (Ed.), *Minnesota symposia on child psychology* (Vol. 7). Minneapolis: University of Minnesota Press.

HAGEN, J. W., JONGEWARD, R. H., & KAIL, R. V. (1975). Cognitive perspectives on the development of memory. In H. W. Reese (Ed.), *Advances in child development and behavior* (Vol. 10). New York: Academic Press.

HAGEN, J. W., & WILSON, K. P. (1982). Some selected thoughts on attention: A reply to Lane and Pearson. *Merrill-Palmer Quarterly, 28,* 529–532.

HAITH, M. M., & CAMPOS, J. J. (1977). Human infancy. *Annual Review of Psychology, 28*, 251–293.

HAITH, M. M., & CAMPOS, J. J. (Eds.). (1983). *Handbook of child psychology: Infancy and developmental psychobiology* (Vol. 2). New York: Wiley. (P. H. Mussen, General Editor)

HAKES, D. T. (1980). *The development of metalinguistic abilities in children.* Berlin: Springer-Verlag.

HALE, G. A., & LEWIS, M. (Eds.). (1979). *Attention and cognitive development.* New York: Plenum Press.

HALE, G. A., & TAWEEL, S. S. (1974). Age differences in children's performance on measures of component selection and incidental learning. *Journal of Experimental Child Psychology, 18*, 107–116.

HALFORD, G. S. (1982). *The development of thought.* Hillsdale, N.J.: Lawrence Erlbaum Associates.

HALFORD, G. S. (1984). Can young children integrate premises in transitivity and serial order tasks? *Cognitive Psychology, 16*, 65–93.

HALFORD, G. S., & WILSON, W. H. (1980). A category theory approach to cognitive development. *Cognitive Psychology, 12*, 356–411.

HARRIS, P. L. (1974). Perseverative search at a visibly empty place by young infants. *Journal of Experimental Child Psychology, 18*, 535–542.

HARRIS, P. L. (1975). Development of search and object permanence during infancy. *Psychological Bulletin, 82*, 332–344.

HARRIS, P. L. (1983). Infant cognition. In M. M. Haith & J. J. Campos (Eds.), *Handbook of child psychology: Infancy and developmental psychobiology* (Vol. 2). New York: Wiley. (P. H. Mussen, General Editor)

HARRIS, P. L., & OLTHOF, T. (1982). The child's concept of emotion. In G. Butterworth & P. Light (Eds.), *Social cognition: Studies of the development of understanding.* Chicago: University of Chicago Press.

HARRIS, P. L., OLTHOF, T., & MEERUM TERWOGT, M. (1981). Children's knowledge of emotion. *Journal of Child Psychology and Psychiatry, 22*, 247–261.

HIGGINS, E. T. (1981). Role taking and social judgment: Alternative developmental perspectives and processes. In J. H. Flavell & L. Ross (Eds.), *Social cognitive development: Frontiers and possible futures.* New York: Cambridge University Press.

HIGGINS, E. T., RUBLE, D. N., & HARTUP, W. W. (Eds.). (1983). *Social cognition and social development: A sociocultural perspective.* New York: Cambridge University Press.

HILL, J. P., & PALMQUIST, W. J. (1978). Social cognition and social relations in early adolescence. *International Journal of Behavioral Development, 1*, 1–36.

HOCHBERG, J. E. (1962). Nativism and empiricism in perception. In L. Postman (Ed.), *Psychology in the making.* New York: Knopf.

HOFFMAN, M. L. (1972, May). *Toward a developmental theory of prosocial motivation.* Paper presented at the National Institute of Child Health and Human Development Workshop, "The Development of Motivation in Childhood," Elkridge, Maryland.

HOFFMAN, M. L. (1978). Empathy: Its developmental and prosocial implications. In C. B. Keasey (Ed.), *Nebraska symposium on motivation* (Vol. 25). Lincoln: University of Nebraska Press.

HOFFMAN, M. L. (1981). Perspectives on the difference between understanding people and understanding things. The role of affect. In J. H. Flavell & L. Ross (Eds.), *Social cognitive development: Frontiers and possible futures.* New York: Cambridge University Press.

HOROWITZ, F. D. (Ed.). (1974). Visual attention, auditory stimulation, and language discrimination in young infants. *Monographs of the Society for Research in Child Development, 39* (5, Serial No. 158).

HORTON, M. S. (1981). *The conceptual knowledge and organization of young children.* Unpublished doctoral dissertation, Stanford University.

HUGHES, M. (1975). *Egocentrism in preschool children.* Unpublished doctoral dissertation, University of Edinburgh.

HUGHES, M., & DONALDSON, M. (1979). The use of hiding games for studying the coordination of viewpoints. *Educational Review, 31*, 133–140.

HUGHES, R., TINGLE, B. A., & SAWIN, D. B. (1981). Development of empathic understanding in children. *Child Development, 52*, 122–128.

HUNT, E. (1978). Mechanics of verbal ability. *Psychological Review, 85*, 109–130.

HUNT, J. McV. (1969). The impact and limitations of the giant of developmental psychology. In D. Elkind & J. H. Flavell (Eds.), *Studies in cognitive development: Essays in honor of Jean Piaget.* New York: Oxford University Press.

HUTTENLOCHER, J. (1974). The origins of language comprehension. In R. L. Solso (Ed.), *Theories in cognitive psychology: The Loyola Symposium.* Hillsdale, N.J.: Lawrence Erlbaum Associates.

HUTTENLOCHER, J., & HIGGINS, E. T. (1978). Issues in the study of symbolic development. In W. A. Collins (Ed.), *Minnesota symposia on child psychology* (Vol. 11). Hillsdale, N.J.: Lawrence Erlbaum Associates.

INHELDER, B., & PIAGET, J. (1958). *The growth of logical thinking from childhood to adolescence.* New York: Basic Books.

INHELDER, B., & PIAGET, J. (1964). *The early growth of logic in the child.* New York: Harper & Row.

JACKOWITZ, E. R., & WATSON, M. W. (1980). Development of object transformations in early pretend play. *Developmental Psychology, 16,* 543–549.

JOHNSON, C. N., & WELLMAN, H. M. (1980). Children's developing understanding of mental verbs: Remember, know, and guess. *Child Development, 51,* 1095–1102.

JORDAN, N. (1972). Is there an Achilles heel in Piaget's theorizing? *Human Development, 15,* 379–382.

JUSCZYK, P. W. (1979). Infant speech perception: A critical appraisal. In P. D. Eimas & J. L. Miller (Eds.), *Perspectives on the study of speech.* Hillsdale, N.J.: Lawrence Erlbaum Associates.

KAGAN, J. (1970). The determinants of attention in the infant. *American Scientist, 58,* 298–306.

KAGAN, J. (1976). Emergent themes in human development. *American Scientist, 64,* 186–196.

KAGAN, J., KEARSLEY, R. B., & ZELAZO, P. R. (1978). *Infancy: Its place in human development.* Cambridge, Mass.: Harvard University Press.

KAGAN, J., & KLEIN, R. E. (1973). Cross-cultural perspectives on early development. *American Psychologist, 28,* 947–961.

KAIL, R. (1979). *The development of memory in children.* San Francisco: W. H. Freeman.

KAIL, R. V., & HAGEN, J. W. (Eds.). (1977). *Perspectives on the development of memory and cognition.* Hillsdale, N.J.: Lawrence Erlbaum Associates.

KAIL, R., & SPEAR, N. E. (Eds.). (1984). *Comparative perspectives on the development of memory.* Hillsdale, N.J.: Lawrence Erlbaum Associates.

KARMEL, B. Z. (1969). The effect of age, complexity, and amount of control density on pattern preferences in human infants. *Journal of Experimental Child Psychology, 7,* 339–354.

KARNIOL, R. (1978). Children's use of intention cues in evaluating behavior. *Psychological Bulletin, 85,* 76–85.

KATZ, P., & ZIGLER, E. (1967). Self-image disparity: A developmental approach. *Journal of Personality and Social Psychology, 5,* 186–195.

KEASEY, C. B. (1978a). Children's developing awareness and usage of intentionality and motives. In C. B. Keasey (Ed.), *Nebraska symposium on motivation* (Vol. 25). Lincoln: University of Nebraska Press.

KEASEY, C. B. (Ed.). (1978b). *Nebraska symposium on motivation, 1977: Social cognitive development.* Lincoln: University of Nebraska Press.

KEATING, D. P. (1980). Thinking processes in adolescence. In J. Adelson (Ed.), *Handbook of adolescent psychology.* New York: Wiley.

KEATING, D. P., & BOBBITT, B. L. (1978). Individual and developmental differences in cognitive-processing components of mental ability. *Child Development, 49,* 155–167.

KEATS, J. A., COLLIS, K. F., & HALFORD, G. S. (Eds.). (1978). *Cognitive development: Research based on a neo-Piagetian approach.* New York: Wiley.

KEENEY, T. J., CANNIZZO, S. R., & FLAVELL, J. H. (1967). Spontaneous and induced verbal rehearsal in a recall task. *Child Development, 38,* 953–966.

KEIL, F. C. (1981a). Constraints on knowledge and cognitive development. *Psychological Review, 88,* 197–227.

KEIL, F. C. (1981b). *Semantic and conceptual development.* Cambridge, Mass.: Harvard University Press.

KENISTON, A. H., & FLAVELL, J. H. (1979). A developmental study of intelligent retrieval. *Child Development, 50,* 1144–1152.

KENNEDY, B. A., & MILLER, D. (1976). Persistent use of verbal rehearsal as a function of information about its value. *Child Development, 47,* 566–569.

KING, M. (1971). The development of some intention concepts in young children. *Child Development, 42,* 1145–1152.

KLAHR, D. (1984). Transition processes in quantitative development. In R. J. Sternberg (Ed.), *Mechanisms of cognitive development.* New York: W. H. Freeman.

KLAHR, D., & ROBINSON, M. (1981). Formal assessment of problem-solving ability in preschool children. *Cognitive Psychology, 13,* 113–148.

KLAHR, D., & WALLACE, J. G. (1976). *Cognitive development: An information-processing view.* Hillsdale, N.J.: Lawrence Erlbaum Associates.

KLINNERT, M. D., CAMPOS, J. J., SORCE, J. F., EMDE, R. N., & SVEJDA, M. (1983). Emotions as behavior regulators: Social referencing in infancy. In R. Plutchik & H. Kellerman (Eds.), *Emotions in early development* (Vol. 2). New York: Academic Press.

KLUWE, R. H. (1984). The development of metacognitive processes and performance. In F. E. Weinert & R. H. Kluwe (Eds.), *Metakognition, motivation, und lernen.* Stuttgart: Kohlhammer.

KOBASIGAWA, A. (1974). Utilization of retrieval cues by children in recall. *Child Development, 45,* 127–134.

KOBASIGAWA, A. (1977). Retrieval strategies in the development of memory. In R. V. Kail & J. W. Hagen (Eds.), *Perspectives on the development of memory and cognition.* Hillsdale, N.J.: Lawrence Erlbaum Associates.

KOHLBERG, L. (1976). Moral stages and moralization: The cognitive-developmental approach. In T. Lickona (Ed.), *Moral development and behavior: Theory, research, and social issues.* New York: Holt, Rinehart & Winston.

KOPP, C. B. (1982). The antecedents of self-regulation: A developmental perspective. *Developmental Psychology, 18,* 199–214.

KOPP, C. B., & SHAPERMAN, J. (1973). Cognitive development in the absence of object manipulation during infancy. *Developmental Psychology, 9,* 430.

KREUTZER, M. A., & CHARLESWORTH, W. R. (1973, March). *Infants' reactions to different expressions of emotion.* Paper presented at the meeting of the Society for Research in Child Development, Philadelphia.

KREUTZER, M. A., LEONARD, C., & FLAVELL, J. H. (1975). An interview study of children's knowledge about memory. *Monographs of the Society for Research in Child Development, 40* (1, Serial No. 159).

KUCZAJ, S. A., II. (1977). The acquisition of regular and irregular past tense forms. *Journal of Verbal Learning and Verbal Behavior, 16,* 589–600.

KUHL, P. K., & MELTZOFF, A. N. (1982). The bimodal perception of speech in infancy. *Science, 218,* 1138–1141.

KUHL, P. K., & MILLER, J. D. (1975). Speech perception by the chinchilla: Voiced-voiceless distinction in alveolar plosive consonants. *Science, 190,* 69–72.

KUHL, P. K., & PADDEN, D. M. (in press). Speech discrimination by macaques: Auditory constraints on the evolution of language. *Perception and Psychophysics.*

KUHN, D. (1974). Inducing development experimentally: Comments on a research paradigm. *Developmental Psychology, 10,* 590–600.

KUHN, D. (Ed.). (1979). *Intellectual development beyond childhood (New directions for child development,* Vol. 5). San Francisco: Jossey-Bass.

LAMB, M. E., & SHERROD, L. R. (Eds.). (1981). *Infant social cognition: Empirical and theoretical considerations.* Hillsdale, N.J.: Lawrence Erlbaum Associates.

LANDRY, M. O., & LYONS-RUTH, K. (1980). Recursive structure in cognitive perspective taking. *Child Development, 51,* 386–394.

LANE, D. M. (1979). Developmental changes in attention-deployment skills. *Journal of Experimental Child Psychology, 28,* 16–29.

LANE, D. M., & PEARSON, D. A. (1982). The development of selective attention. *Merrill-Palmer Quarterly, 28,* 317–337.

LANGE, G. (1978). Organization-related processes in children's recall. In P. A. Ornstein (Ed.), *Memory development in children.* Hillsdale, N.J.: Lawrence Erlbaum Associates.

LANGER, J. (1980). *The origins of logic: Six to twelve months.* New York: Academic Press.

LARKIN, J. H. (1979). Processing information for effective problem solving. *Engineering Education, 70*(3), 285–288.

LARKIN, J. H. (1981). Enriching formal knowledge: A model for learning to solve textbook physics problems. In J. R. Anderson (Ed.), *Cognitive skills and their acquisition*. Hillsdale, N.J.: Lawrence Erlbaum Associates.

LARKIN, J. H., McDERMOTT, J., SIMON, D. P., & SIMON, H. A. (1980). Expert and novice performance in solving physics problems. *Science, 208*, 1335–1342.

LARSEN, G. Y. (1977). Methodology in developmental psychology: An examination of research on Piagetian theory. *Child Development, 48*, 1160–1166.

LeCOMPTE, G. K., & GRATCH, G. (1972). Violation of a rule as a method of diagnosing infants' levels of object concept. *Child Development, 43*, 385–396.

LEE, T. R., & ARONSON, E. (1974). Visual proprioceptive control of standing in human infants. *Perception and Psychophysics, 15*, 529–532.

LEMPERS, J. D., FLAVELL, E. R., & FLAVELL, J. H. (1977). The development in very young children of tacit knowledge concerning visual perception. *Genetic Psychology Monographs, 95*, 3–53.

LENNEBERG, E. H. (1962). Understanding language without ability to speak: A case report. *Journal of Abnormal and Social Psychology, 65*, 419–425.

LENNEBERG, E. H. (1967). *The biological foundations of language*. New York: Wiley.

LENNEBERG, E. H., REBELSKY, F. G., & NICHOLS, I. A. (1965). The vocalizations of infants born to deaf and hearing parents. *Human Development, 8*, 23–37.

LEWIS, M. (1981). Self-knowledge: A social cognitive perspective on gender identity and sex-role development. In M. E. Lamb & L. R. Sherrod (Eds.), *Infant social cognition: Empirical and theoretical considerations*. Hillsdale, N.J.: Lawrence Erlbaum Associates.

LEWIS, M., & BROOKS-GUNN, J. (1979). *Social cognition and the acquisition of self*. New York: Plenum Press.

LEWKOWICZ, D. J., & TURKEWITZ, G. (1980). Cross-modal equivalence in early infancy: Auditory visual intensity matching. *Developmental Psychology, 16*, 597–607.

LIBEN, L. S. (1982). The developmental study of children's memory. In T. M. Field et al. (Eds.), *Review of human development*. New York: Wiley.

LIBEN, L. S., & BELNAP, B. (1981). Intellectual realism: Implications for investigations of perceptual perspective-taking in young children. *Child Development, 52*, 921–924.

LINDBERG, M. A. (1980). Is knowledge base development a necessary and sufficient condition for memory development? *Journal of Experimental Child Psychology, 30*, 401–410.

LISHMAN, T. R., & LEE, D. N. (1975). The autonomy of visual kinesthesis. *Perception, 2*, 287–294.

LIVESLEY, W. J., & BROMLEY, D. B. (1973). *Person perception in childhood and adolescence*. London: Wiley.

LODICO, M. G., GHATALA, E. S., LEVIN, J. R., PRESSLEY, M., & BELL, J. A. (1983). The effects of strategy-monitoring training on children's selection of effective memory strategies. *Journal of Experimental Child Psychology, 35*, 263–277.

LURIA, A. R. (1959). The directive function of speech in development and dissolution. *Word, 15*, 341–352.

LURIA, A. R. (1961). *The role of speech in the regulation of normal and abnormal behavior*. New York: Pergamon Press.

MACCOBY, E. E. (1969). The development of stimulus selection. In J. P. Hill (Ed.), *Minnesota symposia on child psychology* (Vol. 3). Minneapolis: University of Minnesota Press.

MACCOBY, E. E. (1980). *Social development: Psychological growth and the parent-child relationship*. San Diego, Calif.: Harcourt Brace Jovanovich.

MACCOBY, E. E., & MASTERS, J. C. (1970). Attachment and dependency. In P. H. Mussen (Ed.), *Carmichael's manual of child psychology* (Vol. 2). New York: Wiley.

MACNAMARA, J. (1972). Cognitive basis of language learning in infants. *Psychological Review, 79*, 1–13.

MANDLER, J. M. (1983). Representation. In J. H. Flavell & E. M. Markman (Eds.), *Handbook of child psychology: Cognitive development* (Vol. 3). New York: Wiley. (P. H. Mussen, General Editor)

MANDLER, J. M. (1984). Representation and recall in infancy. In M. Moscovitch (Ed.), *Infant memory*. New York: Plenum Press.

MANDLER, J. M., & DeFOREST, M. (1979). Is there more than one way to recall a story? *Child Development, 50*, 886–889.

MARATSOS, M. P. (1973). Nonegocentric communication abilities in preschool children. *Child Development, 44*, 697–700.

MARATSOS, M. P. (1974). Preschool children's use of definite and indefinite articles. *Child Development, 45,* 446–455.

MARATSOS, M. P. (1976). *Language development: The acquisition of language structure.* Morristown, N.J.: General Learning Press.

MARATSOS, M. P. (1982). The establishment and evolution of grammatical categories in children. In L. R. Gleitman & E. Wanner (Eds.), *Language acquisition: The state of the art.* Cambridge, Eng.: Cambridge University Press.

MARATSOS, M. P. (1983). Some current issues in the study of the acquisition of grammar. In J. H. Flavell & E. M. Markman (Eds.), *Handbook of child psychology: Cognitive development* (Vol. 3). New York: Wiley. (P. H. Mussen, General Editor)

MARKMAN, E. M. (1977). Realizing that you don't understand: A preliminary investigation. *Child Development, 48,* 986–992.

MARKMAN, E. M. (1978). Empirical versus logical solutions to part-whole comparison problems concerning classes and collections. *Child Development, 49,* 168–177.

MARKMAN, E. M. (1979). Review of Siegler's *Children's thinking: What develops?* *Contemporary Psychology, 24,* 963–964.

MARKMAN, E. M. (1981a). Comprehension monitoring. In W. P. Dickson (Ed.), *Children's oral communication skills.* New York: Academic Press.

MARKMAN, E. M. (1981b). Two different principles of conceptual organization. In M. E. Lamb & A. L. Brown (Eds.), *Advances in developmental psychology.* Hillsdale, N.J.: Lawrence Erlbaum Associates.

MASANGKAY, Z. S., MCCLUSKEY, K. A., MCINTYRE, C. W., SIMS-KNIGHT, J., VAUGHN, B. E., & FLAVELL, J. H. (1974). The early development of inferences about the visual percepts of others. *Child Development, 45,* 357–366.

MASTERS, J. C. (1981). Developmental psychology. *Annual Review of Psychology, 32,* 117–151.

MASUR, E. F., MCINTYRE, C. W., & FLAVELL, J. H. (1973). Developmental changes in apportionment of study time among items in a multitrial free recall test. *Journal of Experimental Child Psychology, 15,* 237–246.

MCCALL, R. B., & MCGHEE, P. E. (1977). The discrepancy hypothesis of attention and affect in infants. In F. Weizmann & I. C. Uzgiris (Eds.), *The structuring of experience.* New York: Plenum Press.

MCCALL, R. B., PARKE, R. D., & KAVANAUGH, R. D. (1977). Imitation of live and televised models by children one to three years of age. *Monographs of the Society for Research in Child Development, 42*(5, Serial No. 173).

MCGURK, H., & LEWIS, M. (1974). Space perception in early infancy: Perception within a common auditory-visual space? *Science, 186,* 649–650.

MCKENZIE, B. E., TOOTELL, H. E., & DAY, R. H. (1980). Development of visual size constancy during the 1st year of human infancy. *Developmental Psychology, 16,* 163–174.

MCLAUGHLIN, G. H. (1963). Psycho-logic: A possible alternative to Piaget's formulation. *British Journal of Educational Psychology, 33,* 61–67.

MEHLER, J., BERTONCINI, J., BARRIÈRE, M., & JASSIK-GERSCHENFELD, D. (1978). Infant recognition of mother's voice. *Perception, 7,* 492–497.

MEICHENBAUM, D., & ASARNOW, J. (1979). Cognitive-behavior modification and metacognitive development: Implications for the classroom. In P. Kendall & S. Hollon (Eds.), *Cognitive-behavioral interventions: Theory, research and procedures.* New York: Academic Press.

MELTZOFF, A. N. (1981). Imitation, intermodal coordination and representation in early infancy. In G. Butterworth (Ed.), *Infancy and epistemology.* Brighton, Eng.: Harvester Press.

MELTZOFF, A. N., & BORTON, R. W. (1979). Intermodal matching by human neonates. *Nature, 282,* 403–404.

MELTZOFF, A. N., & MOORE, M. K. (1977). Imitation of facial and manual gestures by human neonates. *Science, 198,* 75–78.

MELTZOFF, A. N., & MOORE, M. K. (1983a). Newborn infants imitate adult facial gestures. *Child Development, 54,* 702–709.

MELTZOFF, A. N., & MOORE, M. K. (1983b). The origins of imitation in infancy: Paradigm, phenomena, and theories. In L. P. Lipsitt & C. Rovee-Collier (Eds.), *Advances in infancy research* (Vol. 2). Norwood, N.J.: Ablex.

MENDELSON, M. J. (1979). Acoustic-optical correspondences and auditory-visual coordination in infancy. *Canadian Journal of Psychology, 33,* 334–346.

MENIG-PETERSON, C. L. (1975). The modification of communicative behavior in preschool-aged children as a function of the listener's perspective. *Child Development, 46,* 1015-1018.

MILLER, D. J., COHEN, L. B., & HILL, K. T. (1970). A methodological investigation of Piaget's theory of object concept development in the sensory-motor period. *Journal of Experimental Child Psychology, 9,* 59-85.

MILLER, G. A., & CANTOR, N. (1982). Review of R. Nisbett and L. Ross. *Human inference: Strategies and shortcomings of social judgment. Social Cognition, 1,* 83-93.

MILLER, P. H., KESSEL, F. S., & FLAVELL, J. H. (1970). Thinking about people thinking about people thinking about . . . : A study of social cognitive development. *Child Development, 41,* 613-623.

MILLER, P. H., & WEISS, M. G. (1982). Children's and adults' knowledge about what variables affect selective attention. *Child Development, 53,* 543-549.

MILLER, P. H., & ZALENSKI, R. (1982). Preschoolers' knowledge about attention. *Developmental Psychology, 18,* 871-875.

MILLER, S. A. (1973). Contradiction, surprise, and cognitive change: The effects of disconfirmation of belief on conservers and nonconservers. *Journal of Experimental Child Psychology, 15,* 47-62.

MILLER, S. A. (1976). Nonverbal assessment of Piagetian concepts. *Psychological Bulletin, 83,* 405-430.

MILLER, S. A., & LIPPS, L. (1973). Extinction of conservation and transitivity of weight. *Journal of Experimental Child Psychology, 16,* 388-402.

MILLER, S. A., SCHWARTZ, L. C., & STEWART, C. (1973). An attempt to extinguish conservation of weight in college students. *Developmental Psychology, 8,* 316.

MISCHEL, W. (1958). Preference for delayed reinforcement: An experimental study of a cultural observation. *Journal of Abnormal and Social Psychology, 56,* 57-61.

MISCHEL, W. (1973). Toward a cognitive social learning reconceptualization of personality. *Psychological Review, 80,* 252-283.

MISCHEL, W. (1974). Processes in delay of gratification. In L. Berkowitz (Ed.), *Advances in experimental social psychology* (Vol. 7). New York: Academic Press.

MISCHEL, W. (1981). Metacognition and the rules of delay. In J. H. Flavell & L. Ross (Eds.), *Social cognitive development: Frontiers and possible futures.* New York: Cambridge University Press.

MISCHEL, W., EBBESEN, E. G., & ZEISS, A. R. (1972). Cognitive and attentional mechanisms in delay of gratification. *Journal of Personality and Social Psychology, 21,* 204-218.

MISCHEL, W., & METZNER, R. (1962). Preference for delayed reward as a function of age, intelligence, and length of delay interval. *Journal of Abnormal and Social Psychology, 64,* 1425-1431.

MISCHEL, W., & MISCHEL, H. N. (1979, March). *The development of children's knowledge of self-control.* Paper presented at the meeting of the Society for Research in Child Development, San Francisco.

MISCHEL, W., & PEAKE, P. K. (1982). Beyond *deja vu* in the search for cross-situational consistency. *Psychological Review, 89,* 730-755.

MITCHELL, D. E. (1981). Sensitive periods in visual development. In R. N. Aslin, J. R. Alberts, & M. R. Peterson (Eds.), *Development of perception: Psychobiological perspectives.* Vol. 2. *The visual system.* New York: Academic Press.

MOELY, B. E., OLSON, F. A., HALWES, T. G., & FLAVELL, J. H. (1969). Production deficiency in young children's clustered recall. *Developmental Psychology, 1,* 26-34.

MOORE, M. K., BORTON, R., & DARBY, B. L. (1978). Visual tracking in young infants: Evidence for object identity or object permanence? *Journal of Experimental Child Psychology, 25,* 183-198.

MORGAN, J. L., & NEWPORT, E. L. (1981). The role of constituent structure in the induction of an artificial language. *Journal of Verbal Learning and Verbal Behavior, 20,* 67-85.

MORISON, P., & GARDNER, H. (1978). Dragons and dinosaurs: The child's capacity to differentiate fantasy from reality. *Child Development, 49,* 642-648.

MOSCOVITCH, M. (Ed.). (1984). *Infant memory.* New York: Plenum Press.

MOSSLER, D. G., MARVIN, R. S., & GREENBERG, M. T. (1976). Conceptual perspective taking in 2- to 6-year-old children. *Developmental Psychology, 12,* 85-86.

MOYNAHAN, E. D. (1973). The development of knowledge concerning the effect of categorization upon free recall. *Child Development, 44,* 238-246.

MULLENER, N., & LAIRD, J. D. (1971). Some developmental changes in the organization of self-evaluations. *Developmental Psychology, 5,* 233–236.

MURRAY, F. B. (1983). Equilibration as cognitive conflict. *Developmental Review, 3,* 54–61.

MYERS, M., & PARIS, S. G. (1978). Children's metacognitive knowledge about reading. *Journal of Educational Psychology, 70,* 680–690.

MYERS, N. A., & PERLMUTTER, M. (1978). Memory in the years from two to five. In P. A. Ornstein (Ed.), *Memory development in children.* Hillsdale, N.J.: Lawrence Erlbaum Associates.

NAUS, M. J., & ORNSTEIN, P. A. (1983). Development of memory strategies: Analysis, questions, and issues. In M. T. C. Chi (Ed.), *Trends in memory development research.* Basel, Switzerland: Karger.

NEIMARK, E. D. (1975). Intellectual development during adolescence. In F. D. Horowitz (Ed.), *Review of child development research* (Vol. 4). Chicago: University of Chicago Press.

NEIMARK, E. D., SLOTNICK, N. S., & ULRICH, T. (1971). Development of memorization strategies. *Developmental Psychology, 5,* 427–432.

NEISSER, U. (Ed.). (1982). *Memory observed: Remembering in natural contexts.* San Francisco: W. H. Freeman.

NELSON, K. (1973). Some evidence for the cognitive primacy of categorization and its functional basis. *Merrill-Palmer Quarterly, 19,* 21–39.

NELSON, K. (1984). The transition from infant to child memory. In M. Moscovitch (Ed.), *Infant memory.* New York: Plenum Press.

NELSON, K. E. (1971). Accommodation of visual tracking patterns in human infants to object movement patterns. *Journal of Experimental Child Psychology, 12,* 182–196.

NELSON, K., & BROWN, A. L. (1978). The semantic-episodic distinction in memory development. In P. A. Ornstein (Ed.), *Memory development in children.* Hillsdale, N.J.: Lawrence Erlbaum Associates.

NELSON, K., FIVUSH, R., HUDSON, J., & LUCARIELLO, J. (1983). Scripts and the development of memory. In M. T. C. Chi (Ed.), *Trends in memory development research.* Basel, Switzerland: Karger.

NELSON, K., & GRUENDEL, J. (1981). Generalized event representations: Basic building blocks of cognitive development. In M. E. Lamb & A. L. Brown (Eds.), *Advances in developmental psychology* (Vol. 1). Hillsdale, N.J.: Lawrence Erlbaum Associates.

NEWPORT, E. L. (1981). Constraints on structure: Evidence from American Sign Language and language learning. In W. A. Collins (Ed.), *Minnesota symposia on child psychology* (Vol. 14). Hillsdale, N.J.: Lawrence Erlbaum Associates.

NISBETT, R., & ROSS, L. (1980). *Human inference: Strategies and shortcomings of social judgment.* Englewood Cliffs, N.J.: Prentice-Hall.

O'BRYAN, K. G., & BOERSMA, F. J. (1971). Eye movements, perceptual activity, and conservation development. *Journal of Experimental Child Psychology, 12,* 157–169.

ODEN, S., & ASHER, S. R. (1977). Coaching children in social skills for friendship making. *Child Development, 48,* 495–506.

ODOM, R. D. (1982). Lane and Pearson's inattention to relevant information: A need for the theoretical specification of task information in developmental research. *Merrill-Palmer Quarterly, 28,* 339–345.

ODOM, R. D., & GUZMAN, R. D. (1972). Development of hierarchies of dimensional salience. *Developmental Psychology, 6,* 271–287.

OLLER, D. K., WIEMAN, L. A., DOYLE, W. J., & ROSS, C. (1976). Infant babbling and speech. *Journal of Child Language, 3,* 1–11.

OLSON, D. R. (1972). Language use for communicating, instructing, and thinking. In R. O. Freedle & J. B. Carroll (Eds.), *Language comprehension and the acquisition of knowledge.* Washington, D.C.: Winston.

OLSON, G. M. (1976). An information processing analysis of visual memory and habituation in infants. In T. J. Tighe & R. N. Leaton (Eds.), *Habituation: Perspectives from child development, animal behavior, and neurophysiology.* Hillsdale, N.J.: Lawrence Erlbaum Associates.

OLSON, G. M. (1981). The recognition of specific persons. In M. E. Lamb & L. R. Sherrod (Eds.), *Infant social cognition: Empirical and theoretical considerations.* Hillsdale, N.J.: Lawrence Erlbaum Associates.

OLSON, G. M., & SHERMAN, T. (1983). Attention, learning, and memory. In M. M. Haith & J. J. Campos (Eds.), *Handbook of child psychology: Infancy and developmental psychobiology* (Vol. 2). New York: Wiley. (P. H. Mussen, General Editor)

OLSON, G. M., & STRAUSS, M. S. (1984). The development of infant memory. In M. Moscovitch (Ed.), *Infant memory*. New York: Plenum Press.

OPALUCH, R., & RADER, N. (1980). *Measurement sequences in Piagetian object permanence tasks.* Unpublished study, University of California at Los Angeles.

ORNSTEIN, P. A. (Ed.). (1978). *Memory development in children.* Hillsdale, N.J.: Lawrence Erlbaum Associates.

ORNSTEIN, P. A., & NAUS, M. J. (in press). Effects of the knowledge base on children's memory processing. In J. B. Sidowski (Ed.), *Conditioning, cognition, and methodology: Contemporary issues in experimental psychology.* Hillsdale, N.J.: Lawrence Erlbaum Associates.

ORNSTEIN, P. A., NAUS, M. J., & LIBERTY, C. (1975). Rehearsal and organizational processes in children's memory. *Child Development, 46,* 818–830.

OSHERSON, D. N. (1974). *Logical abilities in children* (Vols. 1 & 2). Hillsdale, N.J.: Lawrence Erlbaum Associates.

OSHERSON, D. N., & MARKMAN, E. M. (1975). Language and the ability to evaluate contradictions and tautologies. *Cognition, 2,* 213–226.

OSTER, H. (1981). "Recognition" of emotional expression in infancy. In M. E. Lamb & L. R. Sherrod (Eds.), *Infant social cognition: Empirical and theoretical considerations.* Hillsdale, N.J.: Lawrence Erlbaum Associates.

OVERTON, W. F., & JACKSON, J. P. (1973). The representation of imagined objects in action sequences: A developmental study. *Child Development, 44,* 309–314.

PARIS, S. G. (1975a, April). *Developmental changes in constructive memory abilities.* Paper presented at the meeting of the Society for Research in Child Development, Denver.

PARIS, S. G. (1975b). Integration and inference in children's comprehension and memory. In F. Restle, R. Shiffrin, J. Castellan, H. Lindman, & D. Pisoni (Eds.), *Cognitive theory* (Vol. 1). Hillsdale, N.J.: Lawrence Erlbaum Associates.

PARIS, S. G. (1978a). Coordination of means and goals in the development of mnemonic skills. In P. A. Ornstein (Ed.), *Memory development in children.* Hillsdale, N.J.: Lawrence Erlbaum Associates.

PARIS, S. G. (1978b, May). *Metacognitive development: Children's regulation of problem-solving skills.* Paper presented at the meeting of the Midwestern Psychological Association, Chicago.

PARIS, S. G., & LINDAUER, B. K. (1977). Constructive processes in children's comprehension and memory. In R. V. Kail & J. W. Hagen (Eds.), *Perspectives on the development of memory and cognition.* Hillsdale, N.J.: Lawrence Erlbaum Associates.

PARIS, S. G. & LINDAUER, B. K. (1982). The development of cognitive skills during childhood. In B. Wolman (Ed.), *Handbook of developmental psychology.* Englewood Cliffs, N.J.: Prentice-Hall.

PARIS, S. G., LIPSON, M. Y., JACOBS, J., OKA, E., DeBRITTO, A. M., & CROSS, D. (1982, April). *Metacognition and reading comprehension.* Papers presented at the meeting of the International Reading Association, Chicago.

PARIS, S. G., & MAHONEY, G. J. (1974). Cognitive integration in children's memory for sentences and pictures. *Child Development, 45,* 633–642.

PASCUAL-LEONE, J. (1970). A mathematical model for the transition rule in Piaget's developmental stages. *Acta Psychologica, 32,* 301–345.

PATTERSON, C. J., & KISTER, M. C. (1981). The development of listener skills for referential communication. In W. P. Dickson (Ed.), *Children's oral communication skills.* New York: Academic Press.

PATTERSON, F. C. P. (1979). *Linguistic capabilities of a lowland gorilla.* Unpublished dissertation, Stanford University.

PEEVERS, B. H., & SECORD, P. F. (1973). Developmental changes in attribution of descriptive concepts to persons. *Journal of Personality and Social Psychology, 27,* 120–128.

PERLMUTTER, M. (Ed.). (1980). *New directions for child development: Children's memory* (No. 10). San Francisco: Jossey-Bass.

PIAGET, J. (1932). *The moral judgment of the child.* New York: Harcourt, Brace.

PIAGET, J. (1952). *The child's conception of number.* New York: Humanities Press.

PIAGET, J. (1954). *The construction of reality in the child.* New York: Basic Books.

PIAGET, J. (1962). *Play, dreams and imitation in childhood.* New York: Norton.

PIAGET, J. (1968). *On the development of memory and identity.* Barre, Mass.: Clark University Press and Barre Publishers.

PIAGET, J. (1970a). Piaget's theory. In P. H. Mussen (Ed.), *Carmichael's manual of child psychology* (Vol. 1). New York: Wiley.

PIAGET, J. (1970b). *Genetic epistemology.* New York: Columbia University Press.

PIAGET, J. (1977). *The development of thought: Equilibration of cognitive structures.* New York: Viking.

PIAGET, J., & INHELDER, B. (1969). *The psychology of the child.* New York: Basic Books.

PIAGET, J., & INHELDER, B. (1973). *Memory and intelligence.* New York: Basic Books.

PICK, A. D., CHRISTY, M. D., & FRANKEL, G. W. (1972). A developmental study of visual selective attention. *Journal of Experimental Child Psychology, 14,* 165–175.

PICK, A. D., & FRANKEL, G. W. (1974). A developmental study of strategies of visual selectivity. *Child Development, 45,* 1162–1165.

PICK, A. D., FRANKEL, D. G., & HESS, V. L. (1975). Children's attention: The development of selectivity. In E. M. Hetherington (Ed.), *Review of child development research* (Vol. 5). Chicago: University of Chicago Press.

PICK, H. L., & PICK, A. D. (1970). Sensory and perceptual development. In P. H. Mussen (Ed.), *Carmichael's manual of child psychology* (Vol. 1). New York: Wiley.

PINARD, A., & LAURENDEAU, M. (1969). "Stage" in Piaget's cognitive-developmental theory: Exegesis of a concept. In D. Elkind & J. H. Flavell (Eds.), *Studies in cognitive growth: Essays in honor of Jean Piaget.* New York: Oxford University Press.

PINKER, S. (1982). A theory of the acquisition of lexical-interpretive grammars. In J. Bresnan (Ed.), *The mental representation of grammatical relations.* Cambridge, Mass.: MIT Press.

PREMACK, D. (1976). *Intelligence in ape and man.* Hillsdale, N.J.: Lawrence Erlbaum Associates.

PREMACK, D., & WOODRUFF, G., II. (1978). Does the chimpanzee have a theory of mind? *The Behavioral and Brain Sciences, 1,* 515–526.

PRESSLEY, M. (1982). Elaboration and memory development. *Child Development, 53,* 296–309.

PRESSLEY, M., BORKOWSKI, J. G., & O'SULLIVAN, J. T. (in press). Metamemory and the teaching of learning strategies. In D. L. Forrest-Pressley, E. MacKinnon & T. G. Waller (Eds.), *Metacognition, cognition, and human performance.* New York: Academic Press.

PRESSLEY, M., LEVIN, J. R., & BRYANT, S. L. (1983). Memory strategy instruction during adolescence: When is explicit instruction needed. In M. Pressley & J. R. Levin (Eds.), *Cognitive strategy research: Psychological foundations.* New York: Springer-Verlag.

RADER, N., & ASHLEY, S. (1983, April). *Avoidance behavior on an "actual cliff."* Paper presented at the meeting of the Society for Research in Child Development, Detroit.

RADER, N., BAUSANO, M., & RICHARDS, J. E. (1980). On the nature of the visual-cliff-avoidance response in human infants. *Child Development, 51,* 61–68.

RAMSAY, D. S., & CAMPOS, J. J. (1975). Memory by the infant in an object notion task. *Developmental Psychology, 11,* 411–412.

RAMSAY, D. S., & CAMPOS, J. J. (1978). The onset of representation and entry into Stage 6 of object permanence development. *Developmental Psychology, 14,* 79–86.

RATNER, H. H., & MYERS, N. A. (1981). Long-term memory and retrieval at ages 2, 3, 4. *Journal of Experimental Child Psychology, 31,* 365–386.

RESNICK, L. B. (1970, March). *Issues in the study of learning hierarchies.* Paper presented at the meeting of the American Educational Research Association, Minneapolis.

REST, J. R. (1979). *Development in judging moral issues.* Minneapolis: University of Minnesota Press.

REST, J. R. (1983). Morality. In J. H. Flavell & E. M. Markman (Eds.), *Handbook of child psychology: Cognitive development* (Vol. 3). New York: Wiley. (P. H. Mussen, General Editor)

RICCIUTI, H. N. (1965). Object grouping and selective ordering in infants 12–24 months old. *Merrill-Palmer Quarterly, 11,* 129–148.

RICHARDS, J. E., & RADER, N. (1981). Crawling-onset age predicts visual cliff avoidance in infants. *Journal of Experimental Psychology: Human Perception and Performance, 7,* 382–387.

RICHARDS, J. E., & RADER, N. (1983). Affective, behavioral, and avoidance responses on the visual cliff: Effect of crawling onset age, crawling experience, and testing age. *Psychophysiology, 20*, 633–642.

RICHARDS, M. M. (1979). Sorting out what's in a word from what's not: Evaluating Clark's semantic features acquisition theory. *Journal of Experimental Child Psychology, 27*, 1–47.

RINGEL, B. A., & SPRINGER, C. J. (1980). On knowing how well one is remembering: The persistence of strategy use during transfer. *Journal of Experimental Child Psychology, 29*, 322–333.

RITTER, K. (1978). The development of knowledge of an external retrieval cue strategy. *Child Development, 49*, 1227–1230.

ROBINSON, E. J. (1981a). The child's understanding of inadequate messages and communication failure: A problem of ignorance or egocentrism? In W. P. Dickson (Ed.), *Children's oral communication skills*. New York: Academic Press.

ROBINSON, E. J. (1981b). Conversational tactics and the advancement of the child's understanding about referential communication. In W. P. Robinson (Ed.), *Communication in development*. London: Academic Press.

ROBINSON, E. J., & ROBINSON, W. P. (1981). Egocentrism in verbal referential communication. In M. Cox (Ed.), *Is the young child egocentric?* London: Concord Books.

ROGOFF, B. (1981). Schooling and the development of cognitive skills. In H. C. Triandis & A. Heron (Eds.), *Handbook of cross-cultural psychology: Developmental psychology* (Vol. 4). Boston: Allyn & Bacon.

ROHWER, W. D. (1973). Elaboration and learning in childhood and adolescence. In H. W. Reese (Ed.), *Advances in child development and behavior* (Vol. 8). New York: Academic Press.

ROSCH, E., & MERVIS, C. G. (1975). Family resemblances: Studies in the internal structure of categories. *Cognitive Psychology, 7*, 573–605.

ROSCH, E., MERVIS, C. B., GRAY, W. D., JOHNSON, D. M., & BOYES-BRAEM, P. (1976). Basic objects in natural categories. *Cognitive Psychology, 8*, 382–439.

ROSENBACH, D., CROCKETT, W. H., & WAPNER, S. (1973). Developmental level, emotional involvement, and the resolution of inconsistency in impression formation. *Developmental Psychology, 8*, 120–130.

ROSINSKI, R. R. (1977). *The development of visual perception*. Santa Monica: Goodyear.

ROSS, G. S. (1977, March). *Concept categorization in 1 to 2 year olds*. Paper presented at the meeting of the Society for Research in Child Development, New Orleans.

ROSS, G. S. (1980). Categorization in 1- to 2-year-olds. *Developmental Psychology, 16*, 391–396.

ROSS, L. (1981). The "intuitive scientist" formulation and its developmental implications. In J. H. Flavell & L. Ross (Eds.), *Social cognitive development: Frontiers and possible futures*. New York: Cambridge University Press.

ROTENBERG, K. J. (1982). Development of character constancy of self and other. *Child Development, 53*, 505–515.

ROTHENBERG, B. B. (1970). Children's social sensitivity and the relationship to interpersonal competence, intrapersonal comfort, and intellectual level. *Developmental Psychology, 3*, 335–350.

ROVEE-COLLIER, C. K., & SULLIVAN, M. W. (1980). Organization of infant memory. *Journal of Experimental Psychology: Human Learning and Memory, 6*, 798–807.

SAARNI, C. (1979). Children's understanding of display rules for expressive behavior. *Developmental Psychology, 15*, 424–429.

SALAPATEK, P. (1977). Stimulus determinants of attention in infants. In B. B. Wolman (Ed.), *International encyclopedia of psychiatry, psychology, psychoanalysis, and neurology* (Vol. 10). New York: Van Nostrand Rheinhold.

SALATAS, H., & FLAVELL, J. H. (1976). Retrieval of recently learned information: Development of strategies and control skills. *Child Development, 47*, 941–948.

SAVITSKY, J. C., & IZARD, C. E. (1970). Development changes in the use of emotion cues in a concept-formation task. *Developmental Psychology, 3*, 350–357.

SCARDAMALIA, M. (1977). Information processing capacity and the problem of horizontal decalage: A demonstration using combinatorial reasoning tasks. *Child Development, 48*, 28–37.

SCARR-SALAPATEK, S. (1976). An evolutionary perspective on infant intelligence: Species patterns and individual variations. In M. Lewis (Ed.), *The origins of intelligence: Infancy and early childhood*. New York: Plenum.

SCHAEFFER, B., EGGLESTON, V. H., & SCOTT, J. L. (1974). Number development in young children. *Cognitive Psychology, 6,* 357–379.

SCHAFFER, H. R. (1971). Cognitive structure and early social behavior. In H. R. Schaffer (Ed.), *The origin of human social relations.* New York: Academic Press.

SCHAFFER, H. R., GREENWOOD, A., & PARRY, M. H. (1972). The onset of wariness. *Child Development, 43,* 165–175.

SCHIFF, W. (1965). The perception of impending collision: A study of visually directed avoidant behavior. *Psychological Monographs, 79* (11, Whole No. 604).

SCHNEIDER, D. J., HASTORF, A. H., & ELLSWORTH, P. C. (1979). *Person perception* (2nd ed.). Reading, Mass.: Addison-Wesley.

SCHNEIDER, W. (in press). Developmental trends in the metamemory-memory behavior relationship: An integrative review. In D. L. Forrest-Pressley, G. E. MacKinnon, & T. G. Waller (Eds.), *Cognition, metacognition, and performance.* New York: Academic Press.

SELMAN, R. L. (1976). Social-cognitive understanding: A guide to educational and clinical practice. In T. Lickona (Ed.), *Moral development and behavior: Theory, research, and social issues.* New York: Holt, Rinehart & Winston.

SELMAN, R. L. (1980). *The growth of interpersonal understanding.* New York: Academic Press.

SELMAN, R. L. (1981). The child as friendship philosopher. In S. R. Asher & J. M. Gottman (Eds.), *The development of children's friendships.* New York: Cambridge University Press.

SELMAN, R. L., & BYRNE, D. F. (1974). A structural-developmental analysis of levels of role taking in middle childhood. *Child Development, 45,* 803–806.

SELMAN, R., DAMON, W., & GORDON, A. (1973, May). *The relation between levels of social role taking and stages of justice conception in children ages four to ten.* Paper presented at the meeting of the Eastern Psychological Association.

SERAFICA, F. C. (Ed.). (1982). *Social-cognitive development in context.* New York: Guilford Press.

SHAKLEE, H. (1979). Bounded rationality and cognitive development: Upper limits on growth? *Cognitive Psychology, 11,* 327–345.

SHANTZ, C. U. (1975). The development of social cognition. In E. M. Hetherington (Ed.), *Review of child development research* (Vol. 5). Chicago: University of Chicago Press.

SHANTZ, C. U. (1983). Social cognition. In J. H. Flavell & E. M. Markman (Eds.), *Handbook of child psychology: Cognitive development* (Vol. 3). New York: Wiley. (P. H. Mussen, General Editor)

SHATZ, M. (1983). Communication. In J. H. Flavell & E. M. Markman (Eds.), *Handbook of child psychology: Cognitive development* (Vol. 3). New York: Wiley. (P. H. Mussen, General Editor)

SHATZ, M., & GELMAN, R. (1973). The development of communication skills: Modifications in the speech of young children as a function of listener. *Monographs of the Society for Research in Child Development, 38* (5, Serial No. 152).

SHATZ, M., WELLMAN, H. M., & SILBER, S. (1983). The acquisition of mental verbs: A systematic investigation of the first reference to mental state. *Cognition, 14,* 301–321.

SHERROD, L. R. (1981). Issues in cognitive-perceptual development: The special case of social stimuli. In M. E. Lamb & L. R. Sherrod (Eds.), *Infant and social cognition: Empirical and theoretical considerations.* Hillsdale, N.J.: Lawrence Erlbaum Associates.

SHIFFRIN, R. M., & SCHNEIDER, W. (1977). Controlled and automatic human information processing: II. Perceptual learning, automatic attending, and a general theory. *Psychological Review, 84,* 127–190.

SHULTZ, T. R. (1980). Development of the concept of intention. In W. A. Collins (Ed.), *Minnesota symposia on child psychology* (Vol. 13). Hillsdale, N.J.: Lawrence Erlbaum Associates.

SHULTZ, T. R. (1982). Review of Selman's *The growth of interpersonal understanding: Developmental and clinical analyses. Contemporary Psychology, 27,* 559–560.

SHURE, M. B., & SPIVAK, G. (1978). *Problem solving techniques in childrearing.* San Francisco: Jossey-Bass.

SHWEDER, R. A. (1980). Scientific thought and social cognition. In W. A. Collins (Ed.), *Minnesota symposia on child psychology* (Vol. 15). Hillsdale, N.J.: Lawrence Erlbaum Associates.

SIEGLER, R. S. (1976). Three aspects of cognitive development. *Cognitive Psychology, 8,* 481–520.

SIEGLER, R. S. (1978). The origins of scientific reasoning. In R. S. Siegler (Ed.), *Children's thinking: What develops?* Hillsdale, N.J.: Lawrence Erlbaum Associates.

SIEGLER, R. S. (1979a). Children's thinking: The search for limits. In G. J. Whitehurst & B. J. Zimmerman (Eds.), *The functions of language and cognition*. New York: Academic Press.

SIEGLER, R. S. (1979b). What young children do know (Review of Gelman and Gallistel's *The child's understanding of number*). *Contemporary Psychology, 24*, 613–615.

SIEGLER, R. S. (1981). Developmental sequences within and between concepts. *Monographs of the Society for Research in Child Development, 46* (2, Serial No. 189).

SIEGLER, R. S. (1983a). Five generalizations about cognitive development. *American Psychologist, 38,* 263–277.

SIEGLER, R. S. (1983b). Information processing approaches to cognitive development. In W. Kessen (Ed.), *Handbook of child psychology: History, theory, and methods* (Vol. 1). New York: Wiley. (P. H. Mussen, General Editor)

SIEGLER, R. S., & LIEBERT, R. M. (1975). Acquisition of formal scientific reasoning by 10- and 13-year-olds: Designing a factorial experiment. *Developmental Psychology, 11,* 401–402.

SIEGLER, R. S., & ROBINSON, M. (1982). The development of numerical understandings. In H. W. Reese & L. P. Lipsitt (Eds.), *Advances in child development and behavior* (Vol. 14). New York: Academic Press.

SILVERMAN, I. W., & ROSE, A. P. (1982). Compensation and conservation. *Psychological Bulletin, 91,* 80–101.

SIMON, D. P., & SIMON, H. A. (1978). Individual differences in solving physics problems. In R. S. Siegler (Ed.), *Children's thinking: What develops?* Hillsdale, N.J.: Lawrence Erlbaum Associates.

SINGER, J. B., & FLAVELL, J. H. (1981). Development of knowledge about communication: Children's evaluations of explicitly ambiguous messages. *Child Development, 52,* 1211–1215.

SLOBIN, D. I. (1966). The acquisition of Russian as a native language. In F. Smith & G. A. Miller (Eds.), *The genesis of grammar: A psycholinguistic approach*. Cambridge, Mass.: MIT Press.

SLOBIN, D. I. (1970). Universals of grammatical development in children. In G. B. Flores d'Arcais & W. J. M. Levelt (Eds.), *Advances in psycholinguistics*. Amsterdam: North-Holland Publishing.

SLOBIN, D. I. (1979). *Psycholinguistics* (2nd ed.). Glenview, Ill.: Scott, Foresman.

SMEDSLUND, J. (1964). Concrete reasoning: A study of intellectual development. *Monographs of the Society for Research in Child Development, 29* (2, Serial No. 93).

SMEDSLUND, J. (1969). Psychological diagnostics. *Psychological Bulletin, 71,* 237–248.

SMIRNOV, A. A., & ZINCHENKO, P. I. (1969). Problems in the psychology of memory. In M. Cole & L. Maltzman (Eds.), *A handbook of contemporary Soviet psychology*. New York: Basic Books.

SMITH, C. L. (1979). Children's understanding of natural language hierarchies. *Journal of Experimental Child Psychology, 27,* 437–458.

SMITH, L. B. (1981). Importance of the overall similarity of objects for adults' and children's classifications. *Journal of Experimental Psychology: Human perception and performance, 7,* 811–824.

SMITH, M. C. (1978). Cognizing the behavior stream. *Child Development, 48,* 736–743.

SNYDER, M. (1974). The self-monitoring of expressive behavior. *Journal of Personality and Social Psychology, 30,* 526–537.

SOPHIAN, C. (1980). Habituation is not enough: Novelty preferences, search, and memory in infancy. *Merrill-Palmer Quarterly, 26,* 239–257.

SPEER, J. R., & FLAVELL, J. H. (1979). Young children's knowledge of the relative difficulty of recognition and recall memory tasks. *Developmental Psychology, 15,* 214–217.

SPELKE, E. S. (1979). Perceiving bimodally specified events in infancy. *Developmental Psychology, 15,* 626–636.

SPELKE, E. S. (1982). Perceptual knowledge of objects in infancy. In J. Mehler, E. C. T. Walker, & M. Garrett (Eds.), *Perspectives on mental representation*. Hillsdale, N.J.: Lawrence Erlbaum Associates.

SPELKE, E. S. (in press). The development of intermodal perception. In L. B. Cohen & P. Salapatek (Eds.), *Handbook of infant perception*. New York: Academic Press.

SPELKE, E. S., BORN, W. S., & CHU, F. (in press). Perception of moving, sounding objects in infancy. *Perception*.

SPELKE, E. S., & CORTELYOU, A. (1981). Perceptual aspects of social knowing: Looking and listening in infancy. In M. E. Lamb & L. R. Sherrod (Eds.), *Infant social cognition: Empirical and theoretical considerations.* Hillsdale, N.J.: Lawrence Erlbaum Associates.

SPELKE, E. S., & OWSLEY, C. J. (1979). Intermodal exploration and knowledge in infancy. *Infant Behavior and Development, 2,* 13-24.

STARKEY, P., SPELKE, E., & GELMAN, R. (1980, April). *Number competence in infants: Sensitivity to numeric invariance and numeric change.* Paper presented at the meeting of the International Conference on Infant Studies, New Haven, Connecticut.

STARKEY, P., SPELKE, E., & GELMAN, R. (1981). *Detection of intermodal numerical correspondences by human infants.* Unpublished manuscript, University of Pennsylvania.

STERNBERG, R. J. (Ed.). (1984). *Mechanisms of cognitive development.* New York: W. H. Freeman.

STERNBERG, R. J., & NIGRO, G. (1980). Developmental patterns in the solution of verbal analogies. *Child Development, 51,* 27-38.

STERNBERG, R. J., & POWELL, J. S. (1983). The development of intelligence. In J. H. Flavell & E. M. Markman (Eds.), *Handbook of child psychology: Cognitive development* (Vol. 3). New York: Wiley. (P. H. Mussen, General Editor)

STEVENSON, H. W. (1972). *Children's learning.* New York: Appleton-Century-Crofts.

STEVENSON, R. (1980, September). *Does pre-linguistic communication explain language acquisition?* Paper presented at the meeting of the British Psychological Society, Developmental Psychology Section, Edinburgh.

STRAUSS, M. S. (1981, April). *Infant memory of prototypical information.* Paper presented at the meeting of the Society for Research in Child Development, Boston.

STRAUSS, M. S., & CARTER, P. N. (1984). Infant memory: Limitations and future directions. In R. Kail & N. E. Spear (Eds.), *Comparative perspectives on the development of memory.* Hillsdale, N.J.: Lawrence Erlbaum Associates.

STRAUSS, M. S., & CURTIS, L. E. (1981). Infant perception of numerosity. *Child Development, 52,* 1146-1152.

STRAUSS, S., & LEVIN, I. (1981). Commentary on Siegler's "Developmental sequences within and between concepts." *Monographs of the Society for Research in Child Development, 46* (2, Serial No. 189).

SULLIVAN, M. W., ROVEE-COLLIER, C. K., & TYNES, D. M. (1979). A conditioning analysis of infant long-term memory. *Child Development, 50,* 152-162.

SVEDJA, M., & SCHMID, D. (1979, March). *The role of self-produced locomotion on the onset of fear of heights on the visual cliff.* Paper presented at the meeting of the Society for Research in Child Development, San Francisco.

TAGIURI, R. (1969). Person perception. In G. Lindzey & E. Aronson (Eds.), *The handbook of social psychology* (Vol. 3). Reading, Mass.: Addison-Wesley.

TELLER, D. Y. (1981). Color vision in infants. In R. N. Aslin, J. R. Alberts, & M. R. Peterson (Eds.), *Development of perception: Psychobiological perspectives.* Vol. 2. *The visual system.* New York: Academic Press.

TENNEY, Y. J. (1975). The child's conception of organization and recall. *Journal of Experimental Child Psychology, 19,* 100-114.

THAYER, E. S., & COLLYER, C. E. (1978). The development of transitive inference: A review of recent approaches. *Psychological Bulletin, 85,* 1327-1343.

TODD, C. M., & PERLMUTTER, M. (1980). Reality recalled by preschool children. In M. Perlmutter (Ed.), *New directions for child development: Children's memory* (No. 10). San Francisco: Jossey-Bass.

TOLBERT, K. (1980). The contextual relativity of the grammatical morpheme. In C. M. Super & S. Harkness (Eds.), *Anthropological perspectives on child development (New directions for child development,* Vol. 8). San Francisco: Jossey-Bass.

TOUSSAINT, N. A. (1974). An analysis of synchrony between concrete-operational tasks in terms of structural and performance demands. *Child Development, 45,* 992-1001.

TRABASSO, T. (1975). Representation, memory and reasoning: How do we make transitive inferences? In A. D. Pick (Ed.), *Minnesota symposia on child psychology* (Vol. 9). Minneapolis: University of Minnesota Press.

TRABASSO, T. (1977). The role of memory as a system in making transitive inferences. In R. V. Kail & J. W. Hagen (Eds.), *Perspectives on the development of memory and cognition.* Hillsdale, N.J.: Lawrence Erlbaum Associates.

Trabasso, T., & Foellinger, D. G. (1978). The growth of information processing capacity in children: A critical test of Pascual-Leone's model. *Journal of Experimental Child Psychology, 26,* 1–17.

Trabasso, T., Isen, A. M., Dolecki, P., McLanahan, A. G., Riley, C. A., & Tucker, T. (1978). How do children solve class-inclusion problems? In R. S. Siegler (Ed.), *Children's thinking: What develops?* Hillsdale, N.J.: Lawrence Erlbaum Associates.

Trehub, S. E. (1976). The discrimination of foreign speech contrasts by infants and adults. *Child Development, 47,* 466–472.

Tulving, E. Episodic and semantic memory. In E. Tulving & W. Donaldson (Eds.), *Organization of memory.* New York: Academic Press.

Turiel, E. (1983). Domains and categories in social-cognitive development. In W. F. Overton (Ed.), *The relationship between social and cognitive development.* Hillsdale, N.J.: Lawrence Erlbaum Associates.

Tversky, A., & Kahneman, D. (1973). Availability: A heuristic for judging frequency and probability. *Cognitive Psychology, 5,* 207–232.

Ungerer, J. A., Zelazo, P. R., Kearsley, R. B., & O'Leary, K. (1981). Developmental changes in the representation of objects in symbolic play from 18 to 34 months of age. *Child Development, 52,* 186–195.

Uzgiris, I. C. (1976). Organization of sensorimotor intelligence. In M. Lewis (Ed.), *The origins of intelligence.* New York: Plenum Press.

Uzgiris, I. C. (1981). Two functions of imitation during infancy. *International Journal of Behavioral Development, 4,* 1–12.

Uzgiris, I. C., & Hunt, J. M. V. (1975). *Assessment in infancy: Ordinal scales of psychological development.* Urbana: University of Illinois Press.

Van den Daele, L. D. (1969). Qualitative models in developmental analysis. *Developmental Psychology, 1,* 303–310.

Vaughn, B. E., & Kopp, C. B. (1981). *The consolidation of self-control and the emergence of self-regulation from 18 to 30 months of age: Normative trends, individual differences and external correlates.* Paper presented at the meeting of the Society for Research in Child Development, Boston.

Vaughter, R. M., Smotherman, W., & Ordy, J. M. (1972). Development of object permanence in the infant squirrel monkey. *Developmental Psychology, 7,* 34–38.

Vurpillot, E. (1968). The development of scanning strategies and their relation to visual differentiation. *Journal of Experimental Child Psychology, 6,* 632–650.

Vygotsky, L. S. (1967). Play and its role in the mental development of the child. *Soviet Psychology, 5,* 6–18.

Wagner, D. A. (1981). Culture and memory development. In H. C. Triandis & A. Heron (Eds.), *Handbook of cross-cultural psychology: Developmental psychology* (Vol. 4). Boston: Allyn & Bacon.

Wagner, S., Winner, E., Cicchetti, D., & Gardner, H. (1981). "Metaphorical" mapping in human infants. *Child Development, 52,* 728–731.

Walk, R. D. (1966). The development of depth perception in animals and human infants. *Monographs of the Society for Research in Child Development, 31* (5, Serial No. 107).

Walk, R. D., & Gibson, E. J. (1961). A comparative and analytical study of visual depth perception. *Psychological Monographs, 75* (15, Whole No. 519).

Walker, A. S. (1982). Intermodal perception of expressive behaviors by human infants. *Journal of Experimental Child Psychology, 33,* 514–535.

Wang, M. C., Resnick, L. B., & Boozer, R. F. (1971). The sequence of development of some early mathematics behaviors. *Child Development, 42,* 1767–1778.

Waters, E., & Deane, K. E. (1982). Infant-mother attachment: Theories, models, recent data, and some tasks for comparative developmental analysis. In L. W. Hoffman, R. Gandelman, & H. R. Schiffman (Eds.), *Parenting: Its causes and consequences.* Hillsdale, N.J.: Lawrence Erlbaum Associates.

Waters, H. S., & Andreassen, C. (1983). Children's use of memory strategies under instruction. In M. Pressley & J. R. Levin (Eds.), *Cognitive strategies: Developmental, educational, and treatment-related issues.* New York: Springer-Verlag.

Watson, J. (1972). Smiling, cooing and "the game." *Merrill-Palmer Quarterly, 4,* 323–339.

Watson, M. W., & Fischer, K. W. (1977). A developmental sequence of agent use in late infancy. *Child Development, 48,* 828–836.

WATSON, M. W., & FISCHER, K. W. (1980). Development of social roles in elicited and spontaneous behavior during the preschool years. *Developmental Psychology, 16,* 483–494.

WEBB, R. A., MASSAR, B., & NADOLNY, T. (1972). Information and strategy in the young child's search for hidden objects. *Child Development, 43,* 91–104.

WEGNER, D. M., & VALLACHER, R. R. (1977). *Implicit psychology: An introduction to social cognition.* New York: Oxford University Press.

WEINREB, N., & BRAINERD, C. J. (1975). A developmental study of Piaget's groupement model of the emergence of speed and time concepts. *Child Development, 46,* 476–485.

WELMANN, H. M. (1977). Preschoolers' understanding of memory-relevant variables. *Child Development, 48,* 1720–1723.

WELLMAN, H. M. (1978). Knowledge of the interaction of memory variables: A developmental study of metamemory. *Developmental Psychology, 14,* 24–29.

WELLMAN, H. M. (1982). The study of preschoolers' cognition. *Newsletter of the American Psychological Association Division of Developmental Psychology..*

WELLMAN, H. M. (1983). Metamemory revisited. In M. T. H. Chi (Ed.), *Trends in memory development.* Basel, Switzerland: Karger.

WELLMAN, H. M. (in press). A child's theory of mind: The development of conceptions of cognition. In S. R. Yussen (Ed.), *The growth of reflection.* New York: Academic Press.

WELLMAN, H., COLLINS, J., & GLIEBERMAN, J. (1981). Understanding the combination of memory variables. Developing conceptions of memory limitations. *Child Development, 52,* 1313–1317.

WELLMAN, H. M., & LEMPERS, J. D. (1977). The naturalistic communicative abilities of two-year-olds. *Child Development, 48,* 1052–1057.

WELLMAN, H. M., RITTER, K., & FLAVELL, J. H. (1975). Deliberate memory behavior in the delayed reactions of very young children. *Developmental Psychology, 11,* 780–787.

WELLMAN, H. M., & SOMERVILLE, S. C. (1982). The development of human search ability. In M. E. Lamb & A. L. Brown (Ed.), *Advances in developmental psychology* (Vol. 2). Hillsdale, N.J.: Lawrence Erlbaum Associates.

WERNER, H. (1948). *Comparative psychology of mental development.* Chicago: Follett.

WERNER, H. (1957). The conception of development from a comparative and organismic point of view. In D. Harris (Ed.), *The concept of development.* Minneapolis: University of Minnesota Press.

WERNER, H., & KAPLAN, B. (1963). *Symbol formation: An organismic developmental approach to language and the expression of thought.* New York: Wiley.

WHITEHURST, G. J., & SONNENSCHEIN, S. (1981). The development of informative messages in referential communication: Knowing when vs. knowing how. In W. P. Dickson (Ed.), *Children's oral communication skills.* New York: Academic Press.

WILKENING, F., & ANDERSON, N. H. (1980). *Comparisons of two rule assessment methodologies for studying cognitive development.* Unpublished paper, University of California at San Diego.

WILKINSON, A. C. (1984). Children's partial knowledge of the cognitive skill of counting. *Cognitive Psychology, 16,* 28–64.

WILLIAMS, M. D., & HOLLAN, J. D. (1981). The process of retrieval from very long-term memory. *Cognitive Science, 5,* 87–119.

WINER, G. A. (1980). Class-inclusion reasoning in children: A review of the empirical literature. *Child Development, 51,* 309–328.

WINNER, E., McCARTHY, M., KLEINMAN, S., & GARDNER, H. (1979). First metaphors. In D. Wolf (Ed.), *Early symbolization (New directions for child development,* Vol. 3). San Francisco: Jossey-Bass.

WISE, K. L., WISE, L. A., & ZIMMERMAN, R. R. (1974). Piagetian object permanence in the infant rhesus monkey. *Developmental Psychology, 10,* 429–437.

WOHLWILL, J. F. (1973a). The concept of experience: S or R? *Human Development, 16,* 90–107.

WOHLWILL, J. F. (1973b). *The study of behavioral development.* New York: Academic Press.

WOODRUFF, G., PREMACK, D., & KENNEL, K. (1978) Conservation of liquid and solid quantity by the chimpanzee. *Science, 202,* 991–994.

YARROW, L. J., & PEDERSON, F. A. (1972). Attachment: Its origins and course. In W. W. Hartup (Ed.), *The young child: Reviews of research* (Vol. 2). Washington, D.C.: National Association for the Education of Young Children.

YONAS, A. (1981). Infants' responses to optical information for collision. In R. N. Aslin, J. R. Alberts, & M. R. Peterson (Eds.), *Development of perception: Psychobiological perspectives.* Vol. 2: *The visual system.* New York: Academic Press.

YOUNISS, J., & VOLPE, J. (1978). A relational analysis of children's friendship. In W. Damon (Ed.), *New directions for child development: Social cognition.* San Francisco: Jossey-Bass.

YUSSEN, S. R. (Ed.). (in press). *The growth of reflection.* New York: Academic Press.

YUSSEN, S. R., & BIRD, J. E. (1979). The development of metacognitive awareness in memory, communication, and attention. *Journal of Experimental Child Psychology, 28,* 300–313.

ZECHMEISTER, E. B., & NYBERG, S. E. (1982). *Human memory: An introduction to research and theory.* Monterey, Calif.: Brooks/Cole.

ZIMILES, H. (1971, July 4–8). *An analysis of methodological barriers to cognitive assessment of preschool children.* Paper presented at the International Society for Study of Behavioral Development, Nijmegen, Netherlands.

ZIMMERMAN, B. J., & BLOM, D. E. (1983a). On resolving conflicting views of cognitive conflict. *Developmental Review, 3,* 62–72.

ZIMMERMAN, B. J., & BLOM, D. E. (1983b). Toward an empirical test of the role of cognitive conflict in learning. *Developmental Review, 3,* 18–38.

ZIVIN, G. (Ed.). (1979). *The development of self-regulation through private speech.* New York: Wiley.

Name Index

Subject Index

John Flavell is Professor of Psychology at Stanford University. He received his B.A. from Northeastern University and his M.A. and Ph.D. degrees from Clark University. Before coming to Stanford University he taught at the University of Rochester and the University of Minnesota. He has done research on developmental aspects of memory, communication, social cognition, and other processes. He has written or co-edited six books, including *The Developmental Psychology of Jean Piaget*. He is past president of the Society for Research in Child Development and the Developmental Division (Division 7) of the American Psychological Association and is the recipient of the American Psychological Association Distinguished Scientific Contribution Award.